COUNSELING IN AN ORGANIZATION
A Sequel to the Hawthorne Researches

Counseling in an Organization
A Sequel to the Hawthorne Researches

WILLIAM J. DICKSON
Western Electric Company

F. J. ROETHLISBERGER
Harvard University

DIVISION OF RESEARCH
GRADUATE SCHOOL OF BUSINESS ADMINISTRATION
HARVARD UNIVERSITY
Boston · 1966

Foreword

IT IS a common observation that man's progress in understanding man has lagged far behind advances in science and technology. Certainly some of the most perplexing and urgent problems of our time are not technological, but personal, social, and spiritual. One way to advance man's understanding of these problems is through a wider sharing of the knowledge gained from meaningful experience or fruitful research.

It is in this spirit of sharing the meaning of a comprehensive experiment that the Western Electric Company joined the Harvard Business School in sponsoring the authorship of this book.

"Personnel Counseling," the subject of this book, was an early attempt to apply some of the findings of the original "Hawthorne studies" as outlined in *Management and the Worker* to the complex industrial situations from which they were derived. More specifically, it attempted to implement, to make viable and creative, the so-called "Hawthorne effect," which the authors describe in some detail. Counseling was not the only way the Company sought to approach this task, but it was one concrete way which, because of its structure, consistency, and duration, lends itself more readily to thorough analysis, especially in relation to social science.

To prepare this manuscript W. J. Dickson, a consultant in the Company's Personnel Division who was in charge of the program at the Hawthorne Works, was detached from his regular duties in order to work at Harvard with his former colleague, Professor F. J. Roethlisberger. Thus we are fortunate to have two well-qualified authors collaborating again after some thirty years on the analysis of a program they had helped to launch in 1936. They were provided complete freedom and responsibility for the design of the work, the selection of data, and the conclusions drawn.

It is our hope that the analyses these authors have prepared and their thorough and frank discussion will contribute in some measure to the field of knowledge about human behavior in an industrial environment.

Western Electric is grateful to Professor Roethlisberger for participating in this project and for his zeal in helping it through to completion. We are also grateful to Professor George P. Baker, Dean of the Harvard Business School, for making the resources of the school available for the project, and to Professors George F. F. Lombard, Associate Dean, and Bertrand Fox, Director of Research, for their support and helpful counsel.

P. A. GORMAN, *President*
Western Electric Company

New York, New York
August 1966

It is a privilege to be able to express for the School its appreciation to the Western Electric Company and its officers for making this study possible. The Company released Bill Dickson from other duties to take up residence at Harvard to carry out this project with his earlier collaborator, Fritz Roethlisberger; it made available for analysis the files and records relating to the counseling program so that others could learn from its experience; its officers were generous in giving time for interviews and for reacting to manuscript drafts; and, finally, the Company provided the bulk of the financial support for the study. I am confident that both the Company and the School will be amply rewarded if this sequel to *Management and the Worker* proves to be as illustrious as its predecessor.

BERTRAND FOX
Director of Research

Soldiers Field
Boston, Massachusetts
September 1966

Preface

IN A very real sense this book is a joint product. Neither of us could have written it without the other. One of the authors (W.J.D.) was one of the major architects of the counseling program. During the major portion of its existence, he was in charge of the program at the Hawthorne Plant of the Western Electric Company in Chicago, Illinois. In terms of intuitive familiarity and intimate acquaintance, no one was more qualified to write about it. The other (F.J.R.) had been instrumental in developing the ideas the counseling program sought to implement and had provided assistance to the counseling staff when the program was launched and for several years thereafter. To him these ideas and what happened to them was a matter of first importance.

So we were both involved in the counseling program but in different ways. One was focused more on the operations and outcomes of the program itself; the other was focused more on the ideas being implemented in a particular form by the program and what had happened to them. Obviously both foci were relevant. How we tried to integrate them, the reader will have ample opportunity to judge.

This book did not start with a joint authorship. The original assignment of responsibility for writing an account of the counseling program was given by the Company to W.J.D. and it was he who later sought the participation of F.J.R. when the possibility of writing the counseling story as a sequel to the original Hawthorne researches was envisaged. Under this broader framework we both had now a common personal stake in having an authentic story told. Neither author had the responsibility of pulling his co-author's chestnuts out of the fire. They could be toasted and roasted evenly on each side.

The division of labor between the two authors developed from this integrating framework. The co-author (W.J.D.) provided all the descriptive and illustrative case material about the program.

He processed all the data that were needed for the tables and diagrams. There is no chapter, except for Chapters I, II, XV, and XVI, in which he did not write the first preliminary draft. Chapters V through IX are his entirely. The co-author (F.J.R.) provided the analytical framework for each part of the book. Where clarification or restatement of the preliminary draft was needed, he supplied it. The role analysis in Part IV and the evaluations made from it in the conclusions are entirely his. In short, one author provided the source materials, the other the tools by which the material was analyzed, and occasionally for good measure his own personal brand of humor.

A preliminary draft of the book was sent to a number of former counselors who were still on the Company's roll and to other selected individuals for their comments and suggestions. Their comments were most helpful and to each of them our thanks. Our thanks also to the counselors whose interview and observational material we used but whose identity in most cases remained anonymous. To them we can say that we have tried to make the best use we could of their materials and have protected its confidential nature by using fictitious names and disguising work settings which might be identified by people within the Company.

The final prepublication draft of the book was circulated among interested and responsible members of the Western Electric Company for comments and suggestions which, when they involved matters of interpretation and not of fact, the authors could accept or reject. This was the arrangement that was made by the Western Electric Company and the Division of Research of the Harvard Business School under whose auspices the co-author (F.J.R.) worked and under whose research budget his services were charged when he entered into this collaborative venture. It was understood that as corporate entities neither the Western Electric Company nor the Harvard Business School does research; only individual persons do. So in no sense is this an official document; it represents officially the views of neither institution; it represents solely the views of the two authors. Hence the final responsibility, credit or discredit for these views, belongs solely to them.

For those who record and reconstruct the history of the persons who made it, the question of acknowledgments is indeed difficult.

To acknowledge all the persons who contributed to the counseling program—as employees, supervisors, counselors, and management—would constitute an exceedingly long list. As this is not feasible to do, we will mention only the names of a few persons whose very special contributions to the writing of this book we would like to acknowledge.

We would mention first Mr. Jonathan L. Thiesmeyer of the Company's Headquarters personnel staff who had the key role of administratively seeing the project through to completion. He strongly supported the project from its inception, made the arrangements with the Harvard Business School for carrying it out, periodically discussed the project with the authors, and contributed many helpful suggestions. To him, and to Mr. Robert G. Lawrence of the Western Electric Company with whom we also had many fruitful discussions, we feel a special debt of gratitude.

Among those who critically reviewed the manuscript in its preliminary form we are indebted to two behavioral scientists on the staff of the Bell Telephone Laboratories, Dr. Ian C. Ross and Dr. Bruce F. Gordon, both of whom contributed clarifying concepts and germinal ideas which were incorporated in the final draft. To Ian Ross we owe a special debt because it was he who first called the Company's attention to the urgency of undertaking the project while there was still time and before the main actors had passed from the scene.

Finally, within the Company, we wish to acknowledge the valuable assistance of Mr. E. C. Tessman of the Hawthorne Works who spent considerable time with us at critical turning points in the project. No one we know is more familiar with the subtleties and nuances of implementing such a program in an industrial structure, of practicing it, training others in it, and holding the world steady for those engaged in it. He helped us in many ways, in providing us with material from the counseling files, with historical data, and by his suggestions as the work progressed. For release of his time for this project and his personal support we wish to thank Mr. D. A. Moore, Industrial and Labor Relations Manager at Hawthorne.

At the Harvard Business School we are indebted in a very special way to Professor Bertrand Fox, Director of the Division of Research, Professor George F. F. Lombard, Associate Dean of the

Faculty, and Miss Ruth Norton, Editor and Executive Secretary of the Division of Research. Bert Fox and George Lombard participated in the project from the beginning, in sponsoring it, in making the facilities of the School available, in helping us chart our course, and by their helpful suggestions based upon their review of earlier drafts of the manuscript in the light of their extensive knowledge of the subject matter, especially George Lombard whose personal acquaintance with and interest in the counseling program goes back to its very beginning. To them our thanks for their generous help and cooperation. Miss Norton edited the manuscript, contributed many helpful suggestions, and steered it through the intricacies of publication.

On a note of historical continuity of the work reported here and our own pasts we were delighted that Mr. M. L. Putnam, who in the early stages of his career was in general charge of the Hawthorne researches and of the counseling program when it started, expressed a keen interest in reviewing the preliminary manuscript. This he did with vigor and refreshing candor. His reassuring comments were most helpful, particularly at a time when the outcomes of our labors seemed uncertain.

WILLIAM J. DICKSON
F. J. ROETHLISBERGER

September 1966

Contents

In-the-Interviewing Room Activities; Interviewing Facilities . . . The Counseling Organization: *Assignment of Counseling Territories; Officially Required Records for External Purposes; Records Required by the Counseling Organization for Internal Purposes; Intradepartmental Studies and Written Reports; Reports to Management* . . . Summary

PART II.   EMPLOYEE CONCERNS AT WORK

PART IV.   THE AMBIGUITY OF THE COUNSELOR'S ROLE

List of Tables

List of Figures

PART I

Introduction

CHAPTER I

An Overview of the Counseling Program and the Problems of Evaluating It

In 1936, following its Hawthorne studies, the Western Electric Company instituted at its Hawthorne plant a program called "personnel counseling" as a way of applying its research findings to the personnel problems that then confronted them. This program continued for twenty years, that is, until 1956, when it was discontinued.

Although its aims, methods, and rationale with some illustrations of its outcomes have been presented in articles and talks to professional groups and in reports to the Company management, a more complete evaluation of the program was never made. For many interested persons both inside and outside of the Company this was unfortunate. Here was an activity which had attempted to apply research ideas and findings to personnel practice. It had received considerable attention from persons interested in both the theory and the practice of personnel work. Because of its research origins and wide publicity, a more fitting closure—something more than an internal document to the Company—seemed to be indicated. Its results, many persons felt, should be shared with the wider management community.

This will be the aim of this book—to present an account of the counseling program which will allow a more total evaluation of it to be made. Obviously, the program could be evaluated from a number of different points of view. They could run the gamut from a narrow economic evaluation, such as, for example, did its benefits for the Company (expressed in terms of improved worker productivity) exceed its operating costs (expressed in monetary terms) to more general evaluations, such as, for example: To what extent had the program achieved its aims? In the process, what problems had it encountered? Had its unintended consequences in terms of organizational problems (costs in this broader sense) exceeded or been less than its intended favorable consequences for employees (benefits in a broader human-social sense)? Were there more or just as efficient alternative ways of achieving the benefits of counseling?

Because of this wide range of evaluations, the problem of how the counseling story should be told took up initially a great deal of the authors' time. It involved the questions of what kinds of data were needed as well as available and obtainable in order to tell what kind of story, from whose point of view, and to what kind of audience. As these were crucial questions, they deserve some discussion.

AVAILABLE DATA

The first thing the authors did was to survey the data that were available in the files at Hawthorne as well as at the other Company work locations to which the counseling program had been extended. These data consisted of:

(a) interviews with workers and supervisors
(b) special studies by counselors of individual and group problems in their territories
(c) studies by counselors of employees wanting, needing, and being helped by counseling
(d) records of weekly meetings of counselors with their counseling supervisors
(e) departmental reports and correspondence
(f) reports to management of employee attitudes
(g) minutes of Company conferences in which the counseling activity had been reviewed

Although some of these data had been destroyed, there were enough left to provide an over-all historical account of the program.

THREE CRITICAL PHASES OF THE COUNSELING PROGRAM

Thoughout its twenty years of existence, the counseling program had gone through roughly three critical periods demarcated by changes which are summarized in terms of six criteria:

Period One: 1936–1941

1. *Scope of Program:* a developmental period, that is, when counseling was a relatively small local activity operating principally in the shops at Hawthorne;

2. *Economic Conditions:* when the Company was moving out of the depression and trying to restore and improve its previous standards of efficiency;

3. *Management Orientation:* when the program had strong support from top management who viewed it as a long-range program, the benefits of which might not be evident for many years and so were not putting any pressure to evaluate the activity in terms of dollar costs;

4. *Counselors' Orientation:* which allowed the counselors to forge and crystallize their tools of counseling (observation and interviewing) addressed primarily to employees at the work level;

5. *Outside Interest in Program:* with the help and interest of the members of the Harvard Business School who had been originally involved in the Hawthorne Experiments (Mayo, Roethlisberger, Whitehead, Warner, etc.) while also considerable interest was being displayed in the program by other units of the Western Electric Company, by some operating telephone companies, and by the American Telephone & Telegraph Company's staff;

6. *Morale of Counselors:* when there was a high morale in the counseling organization who felt that they were innovating a new and promising personnel function.

TABLE 1.1

SCOPE OF THE PROGRAM AT HAWTHORNE PLANT: 1936–1941

	1936	1937	1938	1939	1940	1941
Counselors on roll	5	12	16	20	20	31
Employees covered	600	2,000	3,700	5,300	6,200	10,400
Employees per counselor	120	170	230	270	310	340
% total employees covered	4.0	12.0	35.0	47.0	44.0	58.0

Period Two: 1942–1948

1. *Scope of Program:* a period of expansion when counseling not only became a full fledged and accepted personnel activity at Hawthorne but also was packaged and transplanted to other work locations of the Company (Kearny, New Jersey, in 1942; Baltimore, Maryland, in 1942; Lincoln, Nebraska, in 1944; St. Paul, Minnesota, in 1945; Duluth, Minnesota, in 1947; and New York Headquarters, in 1947);

2. *Economic Conditions:* during a period when the Company primarily was concerned first with converting to the war effort and then with reconverting to peacetime manufacture;

3. *Management Orientation:* when for a time jobs were plentiful and when workers were hard to get and to keep, and when the adjustment problems of new workers unfamiliar with factory work and conditions (e.g., married women) and later of returning veterans provided an easy rationale for the counseling activity;

4. *Counselors' Orientation:* so that there was little need for the counseling organization to justify their activity as they were more than fully occupied with their daily jobs and attending to all the problems resulting from their rapid expansion, such as, for example, training new counselors and helping new organizations to staff counseling programs, and as a result had little time for research;

5. *Outside Interest in Program:* with less and less outside help but with a sustained interest from outside groups and the commencement of counseling programs at the Bell Telephone Company of Canada (1942) and the Ohio Bell Telephone Company (1945);

6. *Morale of Counselors:* when the morale of the counseling organization was high because they felt they were doing a meaningful job which was visible and spoke for itself and required little further conceptual and theoretical development or research.

TABLE 1.2

SCOPE OF THE PROGRAM AT HAWTHORNE PLANT: 1942–1948

	1942	1943	1944	1945	1946	1947	1948
Counselors on roll	30	32	36	42	40	52	55
Employees covered	10,700	12,800	16,200	15,500	17,800	21,000	21,000
Employees per counselor	360	400	450	370	440	400	380
% total employees covered	58.0	60.0	62.0	69.0	66.0	59.0	66.0

Period Three: 1949–1955

1. *Scope of Program:* a period of reappraisal, that is, when counseling became more and more the object of a critical re-evaluation by management and began to be cut back;

2. *Economic Conditions:* during an economic period of increased labor disturbances and of rapidly rising costs of manufacture when the Company adopted a policy of holding the line on prices to its customers and absorbing the rising costs by cost reduction all along the line;

3. *Management Orientation:* which resulted: (a) in increased plant decentralization (by 1961, for example, the manufacturing division's activities were being carried out in fifteen different locations as contrasted with the three when the counseling program first started), (b) in new directions in personnel policy, e.g., increased emphasis on supervisory and executive accountability for all phases of their jobs, including human and labor relations, and more management development programs devoted to human and labor relations training, while (c) many managerial changes were being made and a new management was taking over the reins of the Company, (d) who were raising more and more the question, "What were the benefits of the program in relation to its costs and were there not alternative and more efficient ways of realizing these benefits?";

4. *Counselors' Orientation:* so that more and more time was spent by the counseling organization in explaining, justifying, and defending their extended program to a new management, i.e., a management which was not too familiar with the rationale of the program as it had developed from the original research;

5. *Outside Interest in Program:* as also the interest in industrial counseling programs stimulated by the war emergency began to taper off;

6. *Morale of Counselors:* when there was an ever-increasing lower morale on the part of the counseling organization who felt that the importance, significance, and uniqueness of their activity was misunderstood and being confused with the industrial counseling programs which had sprung up during the war and whose origins, aims, methods, and rationale had been quite different and not so carefully thought through as their program had been.

TABLE 1.3

SCOPE OF THE PROGRAM AT HAWTHORNE PLANT: 1949–1955

	1949	1950	1951	1952	1953	1954	1955
Counselors on roll	41	38	34	34	14	14	8
Employees covered	14,800	12,400	14,100	14,300	16,400	14,800	7,300
Employees per counselor	360	330	410	420	1,170	1,060	910
% total employees covered	64.0	64.0	71.0	64.0	77.0	77.0	28.0

How Was the Counseling Story to Be Told?

A Historical Approach?

But was a detailed historical account of these many factors contributing to the rise and fall of counseling the essential story to be told? Did it need detailed documentation, and if so, just what was the point? In our above short version we felt that we had said all that we could say and wanted to say at this level. Any further refinement would involve us in a search for the heroes or villains of the counseling story. Who or what was primarily to be blamed or praised for its discontinuance? As we did not wish to engage in these futile polemics, we gave up a strict historical account as our major organizing principle, realizing, of course, that this dimension could not be completely ignored and at times would have to be considered.

A Pseudo-Factual Approach?

Even though we had the data to write a fairly detailed factual account of how the counseling program worked, we decided against this approach too. In many of our initial drafts we tried to do just this, but the outcomes were always unsatisfactory. Not only were they dull but also, no matter how factual and informative we tried to be, the question of why such a detailed description was worth making still remained latent. We could not just say what was done and how it was done without providing also the reasons for why things were done in the way they were. Such a blow-by-blow account of how it worked not only was ennervating but also could degenerate easily into an account of how it was supposed to work or how it should work, which in turn could become equated with how it had to work in the industrial setting. To confuse these different levels of *working* would be serious indeed and might tend to present an account of counseling defensive and justificatory in character, and this we wished to avoid.

New Data?

Still another problem perplexed us. Many questions that could be asked about the counseling program could not be answered very specifically, if at all, by the data we had. Should we try now to obtain new data? In many cases at this late date they would have been difficult to obtain. But also, the extra information that such investigations would provide often did not seem to us worth the cost of obtaining them.

So finally, we decided to postpone all matters of further research until after we had utilized and tried to make sense first of the data we had. We felt that further research at this time would not affect substantially the broad overall evaluation that our present data would allow us to make now. Only after this had been done would we be in a position to specify more clearly the salient questions for further research.

Coverage?

Although the counseling activity originated at Hawthorne, it was extended in time to other plants of the Western Electric Company. Should we try to cover the results of all these different experiences? We finally decided to confine our account primarily to counseling experiences with production workers at the Hawthorne plant. First, about them we had a great deal more firsthand intuitive familiarity. Second, the records in the Hawthorne files were more voluminous, detailed, and informatory, particularly with regard to the critical problems of implementation where their records were by far the best. In implementing the program some plants had introduced procedural changes, the results of which we could not evaluate because we had only hearsay and no recorded evidence to go on. For these reasons we gave up the attempt to try to cover all experiences with counseling at the various work locations.

Audience?

But to whom and for whom was this story about counseling being written? This problem also concerned us. There were aspects of the program that would be of interest to a number of different groups, from (1) industrial counselors to (2) personnel persons to (3) supervisors to (4) managers to (5) clinical psychologists to (6) industrial sociologists, and so forth. Either to narrow our story to just one of these groups or to broaden it in order to try to capture the special concerns of all of them would be hopeless.

So we posited an ideal reader with the following characteristics: a person in any one of the above categories who had broad interests in *both* worker and management behavior as well as in *both* the theory and practice of *both* counseling and administration.

For example, as we looked at our data, it was clear that we had none that would throw any new light on the counseling process *per se* or on counseling and psychotherapy *per se*. These matters had been studied by clinical psychologists in other contexts to a greater degree of depth than the counseling program had ever realized. So it seemed to us redundant to concentrate our account too much on these specialist concerns.

But we did have data—and we think new data—about counseling in an industrial setting, that is, about counseling in relation to the pervasive concerns of workers and management, and about the role of counseling in relation to the roles of supervision and management, in short, about the processes of counseling in relation to the processes of administration. To us it seemed evident that we should capitalize on these data and weave our essential story around them. *Counseling in an Organization,* therefore, became our major organizing theme and accounts for the title of the book.

The Four Organizing Ideas of the Book

In the many discussions we had about the counseling program, four ideas came up again and again which elicited our interest and excitement. About them we felt we had ample data to make the first preliminary and basic evaluation of the counseling program.

(1) The rationale of the program in terms of its research origins.
(2) The major concerns of the employees who had been counseled.
(3) The contribution of counseling to the resolution of these concerns.
(4) The ambiguity of the counselor's role in the industrial structure and the attempts to resolve it.

In terms of these four ideas we thought that not only a good part of the counseling story could be told but also the major lessons that could be learned from the counseling experience would be given. In such a version enough details about the practical operation of the counseling activity would be provided so as to satisfy those readers who were interested in these aspects of industrial counseling. But these details would be subordinated to the development of these four ideas which interested us and which we thought provided the major lessons that had been learned and could be learned from the counseling experience. So let us now turn to these four ideas which will constitute the organizing principle of this book.

The Rationale of the Program in Terms of Its Research Origins

In the next chapter (Chapter II) we will re-explore the research origins of the counseling activity which are related at considerable length in *Management and the Worker*.[1] In this re-examination we will proceed at a level of generality which will presuppose that the reader has looked at *Management and the Worker* and is also somewhat literate about the ever expanding body of literature on the subject. In short, because much water had gone under the bridge since 1939, we wanted to talk about these researches in the language of today and at a higher level of generality than we did in 1939.

We wished to do this because one important referent for the counseling program was its rationale. It had not just sprung from someone's bright ideas or from some edict from higher up saying, "Let there be a counseling program." Behind it resided some research findings, concepts, and abstractions—in short, a way of thinking about the behavior of people in organizations. Without some statement of this rationale the problems of implementing these ideas and findings would be deprived of one of their important sources of meaning.

Moreover, we felt that it was important to distinguish the ideas underlying the counseling program from the particular form in which they had been implemented. To confuse these two levels we felt would tend to foster defenses, justifications, and rationalizations and prevent new learning. It would tend to reinforce the notion that we were trying to make a case for the counseling program as the one and only way of implementing these ideas. To keep them

[1] F. J. Roethlisberger and William J. Dickson, *Management and the Worker* (Cambridge, Harvard University Press, 1939).

clear would allow us to proceed without making any such claim. It would allow us to scrutinize these ideas for any unwarranted assumptions, to consider alternative ways of implementing them, but, more important still, to see the particular problems that arose from trying to implement them in a particular form under a set of particular organizational conditions.

We felt that we could do this by examining how the set of descriptive propositions emerging from the original researches had become translated into a set of prescriptive propositions, i.e., into what we shall call a *role model* of how the counselor *should behave* in order to secure the aims of the program.

In Chapter III we will look at how this role model was formally "structured into" the Company organization. At this stage of the book, the aim of this chapter can be thought of as being primarily informative. It will provide the reader with the gross picture of how the program was formally organized from an operating point of view. How the counselors implemented their role model in their day-to-day activities with the different categories of persons with whom they had to be involved, we shall postpone until later (Part IV of this book) when we will want to make a more systematic and intensive analysis of the counselor's role. At that time we will want to refer back to both Chapters II and III as they were written in part with this future analysis in mind. But for the time being the reader can treat them as providing him with just enough information so that he can read the next section of the book (Part II) intelligently.

The Major Concerns of Employees

In Part II of this book we will attempt to analyze the major concerns of employees as revealed by the counseling program. The body of data we will use will come from the many interviews that counselors had with employees. Although hundreds of thousands of such interviews took place over a period of twenty years, they were never all completely recorded. Although an attempt was made to do this in the beginning, as time went on interviews were only recorded if they presented an unusually interesting situation or to help the counselor—particularly a new counselor—to improve his counseling skills and perceptions.

It may be well to remind the reader here that in time the counseling program became essentially a service organization. It was never primarily in the business of doing research. So in a research sense, these data we shall be using are not "hard" and moreover they are incomplete. However, they could be supplemented by many recorded studies made by counselors of problems existing in their territories, i.e., problems of technological change, wage incentives, absenteeism, long and short service employees, married women, etc. Also, for a while the counselors had attempted to evaluate the utilization of counseling by employees. Records had been kept of the benefits the employees had expressed from being counseled as well as the benefits the counselors thought the employees had obtained from this activity.

From such data we felt that we could say something about the major concerns of employees. We could analyze the total situations—the interplay between the individual and the organization—from which these concerns had emerged. This we will do in Chapters IV through IX. We will start with the many topical analyses that the counselors had made of employee concerns and proceed to a more situational analysis of them.

As this situational analysis was never made *systematically* by the counseling organization, it is in this sense new. That is, the categories of concerns generated by this method of analysis were never reported before as such by them. But as this situational orientation was implicit in the counselor's role, as we shall show later in Chapter II, we did not feel that this kind of analysis did any serious violation to the data we had. Instead, it provided a sound basis for showing how the counseling process worked in the industrial setting.

Just as we thought that the counselors' role model as derived from research would provide one important benchmark for the evaluation of the counseling program, so did we think that a situational analysis of employee concerns would provide another important one. What needed clarification was not only the counseling process as such but also the situations of employees to which it was addressed. Without such an analysis there would be remedial action before and apart from diagnosis—an all-purpose tool called counseling addressed to everything but nothing in particular.

The Contributions of Counseling to the Personal Resolutions of Work Concerns

Part III we hope will remedy this misunderstanding. In this part of the book we will treat the worker not merely as reacting passively to his situation but as more actively trying to cope with it. So we will restate his concerns in a more dynamic form. They all involved for him implicitly—and sometimes quite explicitly—a highly charged emotional decision and choice. Should I stay or quit? And if I stay, how much will I give (produce)? To what extent will I cooperate? Will I just try to get by? Keep my nose clean? Resist change? Or will I make suggestions? Try to improve my skill? My competence? My relations to my boss? My fellow workers? etc.

By restating them in this form we hope to show that the way these personal decisions were resolved by workers had outcomes not only for the employees themselves (in terms of their own personal satisfaction and growth) but also for the organization itself (in terms of the willingness of the employees to contribute their services to the purposes of the organization). This we will try to show in Chapter X.

But by this restatement we also hope to show the unique contribution counseling made and can make to the work concerns we considered in Part II of the book. In that part it was quite evident that other parties besides counseling (e.g., supervision, personnel, and management) had something to say and do about them. They were far from being the exclusive province of counseling. The question, therefore, arises, "What difference, if any, can counseling make?" Chapter XI will address itself to this question.

The Ambiguity of the Counselor's Role in the Industrial Structure

In Part IV we will examine the problems that arose from trying to implement counseling in the industrial setting. Continuing from the formal aspects of the counseling activity that we considered in Chapter III, we will look at how the counselors in terms of their role model (Chapter II) structured their relationships to the different categories of persons with whom they had to be involved. How did they seek to gain their understanding, acceptance, and cooperation? What problems did they encounter? We will do this in relation to (1) employees in Chapter XII, (2) supervision and other personnel services in Chapter XIII, and (3) management, the union, and the logics of organization in Chapter XIV.

From these data we will make a role analysis of the counselors' total job which included more than just the counseling of employees who wished their services. Although from the point of view of chronology one might have thought that we should have treated these problems of implementation prior to our analysis of employee concerns, there were more important considerations that dictated otherwise.

1. The problem of trying to introduce a new personnel role in the structure of the company was a broader organizational problem than the narrower and more circumscribed activity of counseling employees themselves. The story of this latter activity could be told without distortion quite apart from the broader organizational issues that the counseling activity raised; the reverse did not follow. For this reason we wanted to concentrate first on the positive outcomes of counseling employees themselves before we considered the wider organizational problems that the counseling activity generated.

2. Moreover, preceded by our analysis of employee concerns, this analysis of the counselor's role would allow us to make more understandable not only why the counseling program continued for twenty years but also why it was discontinued. Both facts needed to be explained. We thought that our role analysis would help to do this and that it would be better to do this at the end rather than at the beginning of the book.

Obviously, this part of the book will be the most controversial. It will be here where the different parties who were involved in the counseling program may not see eye to eye. So let us now try to say briefly what we were up to here and why we thought it was worth trying to do in spite of the risks involved.

1. It seemed to us that the counseling program provided an unusual opportunity not only to understand the activity of counseling itself but also to see how counseling, as an innovative role, fused and collided with the other more well established roles of industrial organization. Such an analysis could make a useful contribution to management.

2. In these daily problems of implementation we had some of our best

data. The files were full of accounts about the counselors' daily problems of implementing their prescribed role—problems of gaining acceptance of it, justifying it, defending it, accepting it, becoming more congruent and skillful with regard to it, and fitting it in the industrial structure. Much of the counselors' shop talk was about these problems.

3. Although these data had not been collected systematically by the counseling organization for the purposes of making a role analysis of their job, they could be employed for this purpose without misusing them or having the results of this analysis misunderstood provided that we could do two things: (a) demonstrate the utility of this role analysis for the understanding of the problem that we felt needed to be understood by all the parties concerned, while at the same time (b) admit freely that this analysis would tend to leave out many other aspects of counseling of importance to its practitioners.

4. The dangers of misinterpretation, as we saw them, were fourfold: By this method of analysis (a) because we would be leaving out many aspects of counseling of importance to those who were involved in the counseling program, and (b) because we would be reducing all the little bugs which plagued the implementation of counseling throughout its twenty years to one big bug which we will call "the ambiguity of the counselors' role in the industrial structure," (c) we would tend to make a caricature of the counseling program, and (d) we would be guilty of reducing the counseling story to an organizational story, that is, of using the counseling program to highlight an organizational problem.

5. Because of all these possible misinterpretations, we spent much time, as the reader will see when he gets to Part IV, in constructing the tool of analysis and in trying to show both its utility and its limitations. Because we felt that there is a limit to what can be said parsimoniously by the language of common sense, we felt that we needed this tool of analysis (a more technical language we borrowed from social science) in order to state succinctly the problem we saw; this is the only reason we used it.

6. This tool of analysis will reveal a problem that was never completely resolved by the counseling program and why this was so. This unresolved problem brings no discredit to the Company nor the counseling program. From our point of view it makes neither the company nor the counseling organization villains or fools. It remains still with us as the "no. 1 problem" in all endeavors today to apply knowledge about human behavior derived from research

to practice. It is the age-old problem of the relation of theory to practice—a problem that no matter how hard we try we can never disregard. Hence whatever little light the counseling experience could shed on this problem, it seemed to us would be a contribution, not only to industrial counseling, but also to management, personnel, and social science.

KINDS OF CONCLUSIONS REACHED

In Part V of the book we will state our conclusions from our four separate evaluations of the counseling program: (1) in terms of its rationale, (2) in terms of its relation to the major concerns of employees and (3) in terms of what difference counseling can make to them, and (4) in terms of the ambiguity of the counselor's role.

Interestingly enough, these separate evaluations will be converging on the same central problem. The analysis of employee concerns will allow us to see more clearly what counselors could do about them. It will show the counselor's unique role and contributions to these concerns; that is, it will show on the one hand how little he could do about them, while on the other hand the great difference this little difference could make, or the disproportionate consequences it could have in particular cases. At the same time this analysis will show that these employee concerns were not the exclusive province of counseling. It will raise the question of what management, other personnel services, and supervision could do and could not do about them as well.

Likewise, the analysis of the counselor's role will show how and why the counselor had been able to differentiate his role from the other members of his *role set* better than he had been able to integrate it with theirs. It will raise the question of how the counseling activity might have developed more in relation to and not apart from the other activities of the Company which were also involved with these major concerns of employees.

We will consider these questions in the concluding chapters of the book. We shall not give any answers but rather attempt to restate the employee problems to which counseling was originally addressed, as well as the organizational problems that the counselors had in addressing them. This restatement will allow us to consider more than one way of dealing with these problems of which the counseling program was one.

We will not attempt to make a case for restoring the counseling program as it was originally conceived and organized. This would mean that nothing has been learned by the counseling organization from their experiences. Rather from the different pieces which our separate analyses of the program generated, we would hope that new combinations could be envisaged. In short, our conclusions will be looking toward the future—not the past. The counseling program will always remain for us what it was—a very real and genuine attempt to address a very real and genuine problem. No one can take this achievement away. But that it also provided all the answers is too much to ask, and no such claims will be made.

As we now reflect upon our labors, it is our opinion that if this account has helped to give management a better understanding of the problems to which counseling was addressed and the problems counseling had in implementing its ideas, the company's experience with counseling will have paid its way a hundredfold. This, to us, is what is important and why the book was written in the way it was. If, by this account, we have also revived the spirit of inquiry with which the counseling program originated, we will have been amply repaid for our labors.

CHAPTER II

The Rationale of the Counseling Program

IN THIS CHAPTER we will be concerned with the research findings of the Hawthorne studies and how they led to the prescribed role of the counselors in the counseling program. In this journey from theory to practice we will be traveling along a road of ideas at a fairly high level of abstraction and generality. We will be concentrating particularly upon those points in the journey when a fork in the road appeared and the researchers decided to go down one path instead of another.

THE "HAWTHORNE EFFECT"

For many social scientists the major finding of the Hawthorne studies was what has come to be called the "Hawthorne Effect." Who coined this phrase first we do not know; it was not used by any of the original investigators but now it has become a generally accepted term in the literature. References are made to it in studies conducted not only in industry but also in many other areas, where the object of inquiry is to test for the effect of changes in a single variable upon the performances of people.[1]

Sometimes it is used to point to and explain the inconclusive results of such inquiries. It accounts for the unwarranted conclusions drawn by methodologically unsophisticated researchers. In this usage it becomes a sort of stealthy phenomenon whose effects should be minimized. But also it is sometimes used to point to and explain an often recurring positive finding of such inquiries; a uniformity which under certain conditions reveals itself again and

[1] See Desmond L. Cook, "The Hawthorne Effect in Educational Research," *Phi Delta Kappan,* December 1962, pp. 116–122.

again. In this usage it becomes an incipient healthy phenomenon of interacting human beings; something to be cultivated instead of minimized; something which if understood better might be made, to pay off.

A label which can do and explain so much deserves exploration, so we will consider first its stealthy aspect and then later its healthy aspect. We will start our search with the illumination experiments and the Relay Assembly Test Room study of the original Hawthorne studies. As we explained in Chapter I we shall not report these studies in detail again, as they were reported at great length in *Management and the Worker*. But for the reader unacquainted with them we will footnote passages in the book to which he can refer.

The Illumination Experiments—Inconclusive Results

From the results of the original illumination experiments reported first by C. E. Snow [2] and then later in *Management and the Worker*,[3] it was difficult to conclude just what the effect of illumination on productivity was. Some of the results of these experiments seemed to say that it was positive, some that it was zero, and some that it was screwy. For example, sometimes an improvement in illumination was accompanied by an improvement in output and then again, sometimes a positive increase in one did not produce an appreciable increase in the other. And then—this is the screwy part—quite often when the illumination intensity was decreased, output did not go down but remained the same and in some cases increased. In the face of these ambiguous results, all the experimenters drew one firm conclusion and some became curious.

The firm conclusion was to the effect that in the complex industrial setting it is difficult to test for the effect of a single variable, such as, for example, the effect of illumination on productivity. To do this it is necessary to control or eliminate all the factors influencing the dependent variable other than the one being studied. In

[2] "Research on Industrial Illumination: A Discussion of the Relation of Illumination Intensity to Productive Efficiency," *The Tech Engineering News*, November 1927.

[3] *Management and the Worker*, pp. 14–18.

most cases outside of a laboratory—and even sometimes there—this is often very difficult to do. But of all these factors, the greatest and most difficult to eliminate is the effect of the experiments or the experimenters themselves on the subjects being studied—what was then referred to as the "psychology of the human individual."

After having said this, however, some experimenters became curious as to why they should have had the effect they did upon those with whom they experimented. What was this effect that inadvertently they had wrought such that even when the illumination changes went in a negative direction, i.e., to lower and lower levels of illumination intensity, productivity changes remained the same and even in some cases increased? (Two girls, it will be remembered, continued producing at their former high level even after the intensity of illumination had decreased to "moonlight.") [4] Being good experimenters, however, they did not feel qualified to speak outside of the framework of their experiment, so little was said; just a few eyebrows were raised.

Here then we have the early observations and statements made about the Hawthorne effect before "it" was named. From them it can be seen that on the one hand a factor called "the psychology of the individual" was making for trouble, that is, ambiguity in drawing conclusive results from what at that time was considered to be good experimental design (i.e., approved by all accredited industrial psychologists in the twenties) while, on the other hand, it was making for the birth of a new curiosity about and interest in this factor which one might have thought the industrial psychologists in the first place would be trying to understand rather than to eliminate.

The Relay Assembly Test Room—The Beginnings of a Search

But the Hawthorne effect might never have been born, i.e., named, had it not been reinforced by another study called the Relay Assembly Test Room. As this experiment has been reported by many persons in many books, we can afford to be brief.

In this study [5] five girls, who were assembling telephone relays, agreed to be placed in a separate room and to be submitted to dif-

4 Ibid., p. 17.   5 Ibid., pp. 19–127.

ferent conditions of work, e.g., to the introduction of rest pauses of varying frequency and duration and to changes in the length of the working day and week. Thirteen experimental periods of different working conditions of the above kind were introduced in the first two years. Output was carefully measured; the time it took each girl to assembly a telephone relay of about forty parts (roughly a minute) being automatically recorded. The purpose of the experiment was to see what effect these different working conditions had on output.

During the first eleven experimental periods, as conditions of work improved, output rose steadily. Here was strong confirmation of the hypothesis that fatigue was the major factor limiting output. But in Period XII (about one and a half years later) when the experimenters went back to the original conditions of work (a forty-eight-hour week with *no* rest pauses) average hourly output did not drop appreciably. And in Period XIII, when the morning rest period was reinstituted, both output and the morale of the girls reached a new high.

In short, there was no simple correlation between variation in the output of these girls and variation in their physical circumstances. This was confirmed by many other studies made of these girls about whom a great deal of data besides their output and the different experimental working conditions had been collected.[6]

Here again we had an experiment with positive results (i.e., improved output) which could not be attributed to single changes in the physical circumstances of the subjects. This finding caused some consternation in both academic and industrial circles. It meant that all experiments in which a single change had been introduced with promising results now became suspect. It meant, for example, that all experiments in which improvements in lighting, heating, sound, noise, rest periods, methods, etc., had been made which had been accompanied for a while by an improvement in output were now in jeopardy. Their results were inconclusive because they could have been contaminated by the Hawthorne effect. The workers might not have been responding to the better working conditions *per se;* they might have been responding to an

[6] T. N. Whitehead, *The Industrial Worker* (Cambridge, Harvard University Press, two volumes, 1938).

awareness of the special treatment created by the artificial experimental condition.

As one commentator put it, "This awareness becomes confounded with the independent variable under study, with a subsequent facilitating effect on the dependent variable, thus leading to ambiguous results." [7] Any factor which can affect both the independent and dependent variables, that is, confounding one while facilitating the other, bears watching. This is enough to set any good researcher's teeth on edge.

Let us review briefly what our preliminary explorations have revealed so far about the Hawthorne effect.

1. It refers in the first instance to certain results of certain experiments conducted at the Hawthorne plant of the Western Electric Company. It (the name) did not create these results; these results and the phenomena underlying them existed before the name was given to them. So we cannot deduce the results from the name. But we can ask what were the characteristics of the results that called forth this name.

2. Stated simply, it was found that the output of workers did not respond to single changes in their external environment in a simple linear fashion. Sometimes they did for a while, but then when the independent variable was changed in a negative direction, the dependent variable did not go down too. For example, as illumination intensities went up, output sometimes for a while went up too; but then when they went down, output did not also go down. This is the Hawthorne effect at the phenomenological level. At this level with no preconceptions about how things ought to be, it is not newsworthy and hardly deserves to be given a name. This is the way the ball bounces.

3. But if someone thinks that the output of workers should respond positively to single external changes when the changes are going in a positive direction and negatively when the changes are going in a negative direction, a state of dissonance is set up. This means that for someone something needs to be explained. But what was to be explained?

4. One group of researchers saw in this phenomenon chiefly a methodological issue. They saw that if workers did not respond in the manner as stated in point three above, some other more powerful

[7] Cook, op. cit., p. 118.

factors influencing the dependent variable must be at work. But what were these powerful factors? Possibly the experimenters themselves, because they had ignored their effects on the workers being researched, but also possibly the workers themselves because what had been ignored was their "psychology." These factors together contributed to the ambiguity and inconclusiveness of the experimental results. For these researchers the inconclusive results were their chief concern. They were not so much interested in why the artificial experimental conditions, i.e., why the special treatment by the experimenters, had produced positive instead of negative results. This for them was *obvious*.

5. Another group of researchers saw in the phenomena described above primarily a uniformity in the exchanges going on between persons—difficult to state but which at a very general level went something like this. Most people tend to respond positively to people who show an interest in them and concern for them. Once this kind of concern is established, other things in the external environment may not make so much difference. So what seems strange at a manifest level does not become so strange at a more latent level. Under conditions where this kind of relationship has developed, what is the significance of one or more electric light bulbs or rest periods? Not very great. Note that this explanation is trying to account for the "positive" aspect of the Hawthorne effect. That it also accounted for the inconclusive results was interesting but not so exciting. The challenging question was why the experimenters had had in these particular experiments the particular effect that they did upon the workers' output.

For the Hawthorne investigators this was the aspect of the Hawthorne effect that was worth watching and that needed more investigation before making any premature explanations. So at this juncture this is the road they took. Instead of improving their experimental designs, they took another tack in their search for the positive Hawthorne effect.

As it is the search for this understanding of the positive Hawthorne effect that contributed so much to the later development of the counselor's role, we will need to follow it carefully. From the tentative explanation made above of the possible effect of the experimenters on the output of the workers, one can see that this phenomenon is an elusive one and hard to pin down in clear propositional form.

The Interviewing Program—Experimenting With a New Role

In 1928, after Period XII in the Relay Assembly Test Room, some Hawthorne researchers decided to take a new approach to their problem. They had become, so to speak, fed up with the independent variable that was being confounded by the workers' awareness of the special treatment being given them and the curious subsequent facilitating effect of this awareness on the dependent variable of producing a result which in the first place the independent variable was supposed to be getting. So they decided to confront the dependent variable with the independent variable and see what would happen. And this is how what came to be called the interviewing program started.[8]

But perhaps we should speak a little less loosely. They did not confront the workers' outputs (the old dependent variables) with electric bulbs of certain wattages (the old independent variables). They confronted the workers (persons) whose outputs were in question with persons, now to be called interviewers. As this shift from an experimental to a clinical role on the part of the investigators was a very radical one, it bears close scrutiny.

It will be remembered that everyone—no matter which version of the Hawthorne effect was his particular interest—had agreed that the curious, interesting, or troublesome results of the Hawthorne studies to date had been due to (1) *the lack of awareness* of the psychology of the worker by the experimenters who had been manipulating the old independent variables (electric light bulbs) and (2) *the awareness* of the experimenter's interest in their outputs by the workers whose outputs had been the old dependent variables. If this absence or presence of *awareness* seemed to be the problem, then it was good research strategy on the part of the investigators at Hawthorne "to place their ships alongside the enemy," a strategy by which, according to Lord Nelson, a great English admiral, "no ship captain can do very wrong."

So this is what we mean by the great confrontation between the two parties. In this confrontation the new independent variables were called interviewers; they were supposed to ask the new dependent variables—the workers—questions. They asked them, for

[8] *Management and the Worker,* pp. 189–205.

example, "How do you feel about this, that, and the other?"; the "this, that, and the other" being about matters that the interviewers thought were important to the workers, so let us see how the workers responded to these questions.[9]

"Just fine, sir," said the new dependent variables, "Ma Bell, Daddy Rice, and Charlie Western [10] are just fine and dandy, sir. We're just like one big happy family here, sir; what else would you like to ask me, sir." Shades of the old stealthy Hawthorne effect again—that facilitating phenomenon by the worker of pleasing the experimenters and thus producing inconclusive results.

It looked as if the switch in roles from experimenters to interviewers was not going to be so easy. Now confronted face to face with the new dependent variables, the interviewers were having a "sticky time." The great confrontation did not seem to be coming off. It looked as if the new dependent variables felt that they knew what the new independent variables wanted to hear and the new independent variables felt that they knew what was important to the new dependent variables, so that they were locked into what sociologists call a set of conflicting role expectations that were making for trouble.

But were these new independent variables behaving like free and easy phenomenological variables or being just their old stuffy selves and behaving like no variables at all? This question was discussed by a group of new independent variables and they agreed that as they were now interviewers and not experimenters, the words "independent" and "dependent" no longer had the same old precious meanings that they had had in the good old days when they were screwing electric light bulbs on and off. They were now new self-aware interdependent variables and so should start acting like ones. They agreed that asking people questions that they already knew the answers to was acting like the old stuffy manipulators of the old independent variables and not staying loose, and

[9] Ibid., pp. 201–203.

[10] By the employees of the Western Electric Company, the American Telephone & Telegraph Company—the parent company—was frequently referred to as "Ma Bell" (a supportive-maternal-nurturant figure?); the works manager of the Hawthorne plant at that time was referred to as "Daddy Rice" (a friendly-paternal-assertive figure?); and the Western Electric Company was referred to as "Charlie Western" (a friendly-uncle-permissive figure?).

this was no way for a new proactive interdependent variable to behave. And so a new role model was in the process of becoming born but the delivery pains lasted a long, long time because the old built-in habits of the manipulators of the old independent variables were deeply ingrained.

The empirical questions which the interviewers faced were these. "If we don't know what is important to the workers and this is what we want to find out, how do we behave in order to find out? If we are A's and the workers are B's, how does A behave in order to find out what is important to B?" As these questions are quite a shift in orientation, let us examine them.

It will be remembered that because of the effect of A on B, the Hawthorne studies had produced two results: (1) a set of ambiguous and inconclusive results about the effect of the old independent variables and (2) a sustained increased output on the part of the B's. The first results—although in one sense ambiguous—in terms of the framework of the original experiment were quite clear, namely, that nothing clearly could be concluded about the effect of the old independent variables on output. The second result lay outside of the framework of the original experiments so nothing in terms of it could be firmly concluded. Only unconfirmed speculations about how A had affected B in order to produce it could be made.

So when the interviewers began to ask the question of how their behavior was affecting the behavior of the workers, they were getting close to the question which the Hawthorne studies up to this point had raised but not answered. Their speculations went something like this: "If we keep acting as the manipulators of the old independent variables, we just keep producing inconclusive results. Can't we change our behavior so as to produce some other kinds of results? No matter how inconclusive in time they may turn out to be, anyway, let's get out of our old rut. Let's stay loose and curious and see what results we get by behaving another way. Perhaps it might help if we stopped calling ourselves experimenters, independent variables, or manipulators of independent variables, and also stopped calling workers subjects, dependent variables, and facilitators of the dependent variable. All these words just seem to be getting us into a role bind, i.e., reinforcing a certain kind of behavior that just keeps producing inconclusive results."

So in order to get themselves out of this bind they began to focus more and more of their attention on their behavior and their skills of interviewing. In this avenue of development they began to look upon themselves and their behavior as the instruments of research. By this route they found that not any kind of interest of the A's in the B's produced "positive effects"; some kinds of behavior of the A's produced "negative results"—what might be called a negative Hawthorne effect. If, for example, we equate positive results with workers talking freely about matters of importance to them and negative results with the opposite kind of behavior, then what the interviewers learned can be summarized as follows in Table 2.1.[11]

TABLE 2.1

CONSEQUENCES OF INTERVIEWER'S BEHAVIOR

Negative Results	*Positive Results*
If A behaves this way, B is less likely to talk about matters of importance to him.	If A behaves this way, B is more likely to talk about matters of importance to him.

1. Talks more than he listens	1. Listens more than he talks
2. Gives advice	2. Does not give advice
3. Approves or disapproves	3. Does not approve or disapprove
4. Listens only to what B says	4. Listens to why B is saying what he says
5. Listens only to what B says	5. Listens to what B doesn't want to say
6. Listens only to what B says	6. Listens to what B can't say without help
7. Ignores B's feelings	7. Listens to B's feelings
8. Approves of B's positive feelings	8. Accepts B's positive feelings
9. Disapproves of B's negative feelings	9. Accepts B's negative feelings
10. Evaluates what B says from his (A's) point of view	10. Evaluates what B says from B's point of view

[11] *Management and the Worker,* pp. 270–291.

In these findings [12] many of the interviewers felt they were getting closer to an understanding of the mysteries of the positive Hawthorne effect. For, if we remember, although one of the official activities of the manipulators of the old independent variables had been to screw electric light bulbs in and out, this did not describe quite accurately all of their activities as experimenters. As experimenters their role had been quite different from that of a supervisor. As experimenters they were not responsible for getting out output or seeing that output standards were met. They were curious about what was determining output. Obviously they could not suggest to the workers that they should work harder for if they had, they would not have been disinterested experimenters. Nevertheless, they had to try to get the workers to cooperate fully with the different experimental conditions imposed. For if they had not, a factor which they wished to keep constant would have been varying. But how did they keep this factor constant? Look at the right hand column of Table 2.1. Were they not behaving implicitly at least in terms of most of these rules? [13]

The Bank Wiring Observation Room—The Social Structure of Industry

This above observation played an important part in the next study called the Bank Wiring Observation Room. The methods of this study differed from those of the Relay Assembly Test Room in two important respects. In this study (1) no planned experimental changes were introduced and (2) the investigators' role shifted from that of experimenters or interviewers to more that of field workers. They were observing the activities and interactions of the workers as well as listening to their feelings and sentiments.

In this new role the investigators did not try to improve or alter anything either externally (electric light bulbs) or internally (workers' attitudes). They did not try to cultivate the Hawthorne effect,

[12] Many of these findings were confirmed by a completely independent set of studies reported by Carl R. Rogers in *Counseling and Psychotherapy* (Boston, Houghton Mifflin Company, 1942). These newer concepts in practice were read avidly by the Hawthorne counselors. See also his later book, *Client-Centered Therapy* (Boston, Houghton Mifflin Company, 1951). Both these books influenced the later development of the counseling program.

[13] *Management and the Worker,* pp. 179–183.

but being aware of it, they tried to take care of it by "skill" rather than by any improved experimental design and in this fashion to get as close to an "objective description" of the work situation—things as they actually were—as they could.[14]

This time not only did they not want to introduce any planned changes, but also they did not want to alter inadvertently the customary supervision of the workers in the room. It will be remembered that in order to set up the proper conditions for the experiment in the Relay Assembly Test Room, the experimenters had taken over the supervision of the room, so to speak, but had not behaved as supervisors, or putting it in terms of the categories in Table 2.1, they had supervised the room more in terms of the behavior described in the right-hand column than in terms of the behavior described in the left-hand column. This had been done not because of any planned decision on their part; it had just been accepted as a matter of course that they did not have the authority to act in the manner described in the left-hand column; this was a prerogative of management. So they had to get the cooperation of the workers to the experimental conditions imposed in a nonauthoritarian way. Anyway, as there were no imposed experimental changes in the Bank Wiring Room Study, the investigators in this study had no reason to interfere in any way with its customary supervision. In every way they tried not to alter the customary pattern of relationships that existed there.

This study opened up a great many new insights, but by far the greatest—and speaking at a high level of generality—was that the investigators at Hawthorne began to see the importance of trying to understand worker behavior in terms of the "social structure of industry." This new way of looking at organizations and worker behavior was predicated on the following assumptions:

(1) Organizations have purposes.
(2) In order to secure these purposes, formal structures are required; that is, certain activities have to be performed, certain roles have to be assigned and prescribed, certain standards of performance have to be set, etc.
(3) But also organizations are people, and
(4) People have needs which they are trying to satisfy.

[14] Ibid., pp. 379–408.

(5) In order to satisfy these needs, new social structures (informal organizations) also emerge.

It was these major dimensions of an organization—or boundary conditions—that set up all the human problems. If organizations had no purposes which set up certain organizational requirements, if organizations had no people, and if people had no needs, there would be no human problems. Or if all these factors meshed together so perfectly so that people obtained complete satisfaction from doing what was expected of them, so that what they ought to want to do and what they wanted to do coincided perfectly, there would be no human problems. Or if workers did not have needs to belong so that they did not need to interact with their fellow workers so that norms of behavior would not develop among them which might be at odds with what management expected of them, and so that, instead, the technical standards management set up for worker behavior coincided 100% with the social standards (norms) the workers set up for their own behavior, there would be no human problems. Or if by doing what was expected of them, relay assemblers or bankwiremen, for example, could fulfill all their needs for security, safety, belonging, status, self-esteem, self-actualization, etc., there would be no human problems.

But this Utopia did not exist. There were conflicts all along the line. The investigators began to suspect this in the Interviewing Program; it was clinched in the Bank Wiring Observation Room Study.

The Positive Hawthorne Effects—Different Explanations

So far we have tried to follow the developing research strategies of the Hawthorne studies; that is, the road the investigators took in their search for the understanding of the positive Hawthorne effect. Let it be noted that no premature explanations were made. At no stage did any Hawthorne researcher say finally and definitely, "This is it." Each study cast only new lights, shades, and depths of meaning and significance. As this dynamic openness—this refusal to make a premature closure to an interesting and important observation—is, in our opinion, by far the most important and least understood feature of the Hawthorne studies, we should like to comment further.

A number of different explanations can be given of the positive Hawthorne effects. Let us mention some in connection with the Relay Assembly Test Room where we have more data:

a. the "special" attention and treatment received by the workers from the experimenters, inadvertently produced by

b. the artificial conditions set up for measurement in a controlled experiment, which can be stated as

c. changes in the methods of supervision, the significance of which might be seen better as

d. changes in the methods of customary supervision which can be stated more operationally as

e. changes in the behavior of the experimenters in order to secure the cooperation and participation of the workers to the experimental conditions imposed, the significance of which might be better seen as

f. more "openness" of relationship of a more permissive, participatory, and transactional kind between experimenters and workers than customarily obtained between supervisors and workers, all of which (a, b, c, d, e, and f) might have been perceived by the workers as

g. "special" social treatment (social rewards), that is, in terms of the language of the workers

h. being treated as "human beings," as "persons" and as "members of the human race," that is, speaking more psychologically,

i. having their feelings, needs, and ideas recognized, particularly their needs to belong, to be wanted, to be heard, and to be respected, which resulted in

j. a "special" social position which they reciprocated by

k. changes in their personal attitudes, which also might have affected

l. changes in their relations to each other (a change in their informal social organization) which might be seen more clearly as

m. changes in the norms of behavior of the group, particularly their norms about output, which might have facilitated

n. changes in their relations to supervision and management; these changes—k, l, m, and n—being in the direction of

o. more cooperative relationships with each other at work (more team work),

p. an identification of themselves with the aims of the experimenters, i.e., as cooperative subjects in the experiment performing in accord with what they saw as the requirements of this role, which they might have perceived as

q. an identification with the aims of management, resulting in sustained high output.

We have kept these different explanations purposely interrelated in order to make a point. To select one or the other as *the* explanation, as many commentators of the Hawthorne studies have done, is often a misleading oversimplification. What does it mean to say that the positive Hawthorne effect resulted from the *special attention or treatment* the workers received? For many this statement becomes a premature closure, that is a kind of final buttoning up to the effect, "Well, we see now how silly the experimenters were in not seeing clearly what they were up to; they were, of course, giving the workers the special treatment; *ergo,* output went up. Now that we have settled this, let's think about something else." But what made this special treatment so special? In what way was it special? To whom and for whom was it special? Was it special to everyone? etc.

Note that each of the Hawthorne studies in turn was throwing more light on these questions. No premature closures were made. In the early illumination experiments, as no data other than illumination intensities and outputs of workers had been collected, nothing could be said about the positive result obtained. Only speculations about the psychology of the individual could be made and these were even less illuminating than the electric light bulbs.

In the Relay Assembly Test Room, by good fortune, the data collected had not been confined to just the different experimental conditions imposed and the output of the workers; a great deal of data had been collected—although not too systematically—about the workers themselves and their relations to each other and to the experimenters—sufficient to see in general how the customary conditions of a workshop had been altered by the artificial conditions of the experiment. But the full significance of this was not seen until much later and until after the subsequent studies had been made, and it was not until then that these data were scrutinized more carefully for what additional information they could provide for what in particular had been altered in the situation.

In the Interviewing Program where the investigators began to experiment with new ways of behaving in order to help the workers to speak more freely about matters of importance to them, they found themselves developing a role relationship that had no counterpart in the industrial structure and that even on many points seemed to be in opposition to the way a supervisor should behave (see Table 2.1). They thought that in this new role some of the mysteries of the positive effect might be understood. Not only had it provided better information about what was on the workers' minds, but also many workers expressed their appreciation of this new role relationship as something that they had not experienced before in their industrial lives.

In order to explore this further, the investigators looked at what an ordinary shop situation was like. They wished to understand better what the special attention and treatment the Relay Assembly operators had received had been about. In this study—the Bank Wiring Observation Room—not only did they find a conspicuous absence on the part of supervision of any mediating functions between the demands of workers on one hand and the requirements of production on the other; but also they found this function being performed among the workers' informal leaders. Also among the workers they found differentiation. Some workers were well accepted members of the small work groups in which they worked and some were not. This acceptance or rejection was in terms of the norms of acceptable behavior that had been developed by the workers themselves. Some of these norms of acceptable worker behavior regarding output were at odds with the aims of management, so for some workers there was a conflict between conforming to the standards of management on the one hand and the norms of acceptable worker output behavior by the group on the other. The way these conflicts were resolved by different workers led to many different kinds of behavior.

These findings raised new questions for the positive Hawthorne effect. For example, what had been changed by the special treatment in the Relay Assembly Test Room: (a) the personal attitudes of the individual operators in the room or (b) their norms of behavior with regard to acceptable output or (c) both; i.e., were these phenomena interrelated? Moreover, had the Relay Assembly Test Room been composed originally of highly deviant or isolated members, would the special treatment have produced the same positive effect?

These findings also gave a new depth of meaning to the positive Hawthorne effect. They illuminated more concretely what had made the treatment of the investigators in their earlier studies so special and in what particular ways it had been special, and hence why it had produced such special results, as we tried to show in the interrelated explanations of the phenomena we cited before. The positive Hawthorne effect was the result of a number of interrelated elements; it had resulted from a shift in a whole pattern of relationships. It was not a single effect produced by a single cause. To talk about it this way was a misleading oversimplification. It implied a closure to a question which at that time still needed more investigation than it needed a "quickie" interpretation or even, as yet, a reconstructed logic of explanation.

As can be seen, this search for a better understanding of the curious positive results of their early studies had forced the Hawthorne investigators step by step into a closer and closer examination of the interactions between persons and the sentiments associated with these interactions, for example: (a) the *interactions* between the experimenters and the workers in the early illumination experiments and the Relay Assembly Test Room; (b) the *interactions* between the interviewers and workers in the Interviewing Program; and (c) the *interactions* between supervisors and workers as well as the *interactions* among the workers themselves in the Bank Wiring Observation Room. This, too, was a common thread which ran through all the Hawthorne studies. This was the common and important element that could not be conveniently disregarded if their findings were to be understood. It was from this element—*interaction*—that their greatest insights into the positive Hawthorne effect had come.

First as *experimenters,* second as *interviewers,* and third as *field workers* they had scrutinized the effects of their behavior upon workers in terms of the *kinds of interactions* involved. They had looked at the exchanges going on between A and B, when B was a worker and A was not only an experimenter, interviewer, or field worker but also a supervisor or another worker. The intriguing question was, "What in the nature of A's behavior made these exchanges more or less rewarding to B and, yes, to A too?" Had the Hawthorne researches continued, it would be interesting to speculate now upon what their next study should have been. But other matters intervened to which we will now turn.

A New Approach to Personnel Practice

In late 1935 the management at Hawthorne posed the following question to those who had been involved in the Hawthorne studies, "In light of these research experiences, are there any changes or additions which should be made to the Company's personnel program to make it more effective?" The Hawthorne researchers were not unprepared for this question; they had speculated about it quite often among themselves. They too felt that the time had come to begin to apply what they had learned, and they had some ideas about how this might be done. So let us listen to them as they speculated about this question in 1935.

From their study of the Bank Wiring Observation Room, they came to the conclusion that many human problems could be conceived more fruitfully as manifestations of the underlying processes by means of which the requirements of individuals and organizations were kept in balance. These processes from which human problems arose they saw as being brought about by two general sets of forces: those imposed upon the industrial organization by the people in it and those imposed upon the human organization by the requirements of technical production. The relation between these forces they conceived as being at any one point of time in a state of dynamic equilibrium. Thus, human problems could be regarded as indicating disturbances in this equilibrium, whether brought about by changes in the requirements for technical production or changes in the requirements for effective collaboration arising from changing individual and social expectations.

If the human problems of industry arising from these underlying processes could be better understood and diagnosed, they felt that personnel practices could be improved. They felt that personnel problems, as customarily dealt with, resulted too often in symptoms being treated as causes, with the consequence that the underlying human problem, while perhaps temporarily alleviated, manifested itself again in time in the same or in a different form. The human problems with which management was traditionally concerned—complaints or grievances, labor turnover, absenteeism, lowered productivity, and morale—and the way they were organizationally dealt with too often did not get to an understanding or treatment of these underlying processes. The basic problem for improved practice was that of devising an approach which would get behind the symptoms of problems to these underlying processes.

The ideas emerging from the interviewing program suggested how this might be done. They suggested that instead of looking at complaints and grievances, labor turnover, absenteeism, lowered productivity, and morale in general, it might be more fruitful to look at them in the particular. It might be more to the point, for example, to look at the particular complaining and aggrieved individual worker—the particular worker who was trying to make up his mind whether to stay or quit, or who was often out sick, producing low, apathetic, and disaffected. By confronting these problems at the point of interaction with a skillful interviewer, the processes underlying them could be explored, clarified, and understood. Moreover, the clarification of these processes at the point of concrete interaction in the interview seemed to produce positive effects.

Here then were the two major insights in terms of which the early counseling program was designed. The one stemming primarily from the methods of observation developed in the Bank Wiring Observation Room said, "Can we make a better diagnostic appraisal of the actual human situation—both individual and group —within the Company?" The one stemming more from the interviewing program said, "Through the interviewing approach can we facilitate the processes of communication between employees, supervisors, and management?" By fusing the research and diagnostic techniques of observation from the former with the technique of fruitful listening from the latter, could not a new role for personnel work be developed which would facilitate the processes of social change? This new role would be performed by a person, now to be called a counselor.

The Emerging Prescribed Role for the Counselor

Let us look now at these ideas at a higher level of abstraction and generality than they were stated in 1935. How were these ideas derived from research to be applied for the improvement of practice? What new factor was to be introduced which would improve personnel practice? What did this new scheme for application reduced to its simplest term look like? Did it not imply something like this?

1. The Hawthorne researchers first reduced the positive Hawthorne effect to its most general terms. In each case it had resulted in general from a change in the properties of A's behavior, that is, from a *new kind* of behavior on the part of the A's toward the B's. From this they reasoned,
2. Were this new kind of behavior to be introduced into the industrial setting, certain beneficial effects—what might be called a generalized positive Hawthorne effect—would follow. But how was this to be done?
3. This new behavior needed to be embodied concretely in a person —a counselor—who viewed his own behavior and the behavior of others and their effects on each other in a new way and therefore would behave in this new way.

If we call this new behavior "the prescribed role of the counselor," or his new role model, the conceptual scheme for application looked diagrammatically something like Figure 2.1.

This scheme for application has some unusual features. If we think of the introduction of this new role model as the input and the beneficial consequences that were supposed to follow from its introduction as the outputs, then both the input and outputs were of a rather unusual sort. The input was a bit vague; it was not like an electric light bulb, a new method or management system; it was a *new kind of behavior*. Also, the outputs were of a rather general vague sort and difficult to make concrete in management terms.

In both cases, for example, they were quite different from the usual inputs and outputs of industrial efficiency which go something like this. "The introduction of changes (inputs) which allow some things to be done by workers in less space and time bring about the desirable outcomes (outputs) of lowered costs." The input in this new scheme for application was more like a seed which, when sown, would grow into a plant with roots and branches (the more generalized positive Hawthorne effect) from which in time

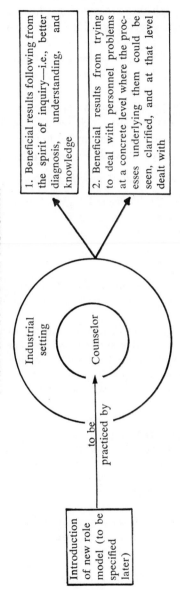

FIGURE 2.1

CONCEPTUAL SCHEME FOR APPLICATION

such things as high output, low costs, high satisfaction, and high morale (the more specific positive Hawthorne effect) might flourish.

As this hoped for—admittedly quite flowery—development depended a great deal upon this new role model, let us try to specify more concretely some of the ingredients that it was supposed to contain. As abstracted from the Hawthorne studies it was composed of two components which we shall call (a) the observer-researcher-diagnostic component and (b) the listening-helping-communication component. Let us look at each briefly.

The observer-researcher-diagnostic component

The counselor's role was defined in part as that of a researcher. He was trying to understand how things were and why they were the way they were; i.e., what factors were determining, here and now, what was going on. The role prescriptions for this orientation were:

1. *Don't try to change things.* You are not a reformer. You are not evaluating things as good or bad. You should just try to assess, "What is going on here."
2. *Be situationally oriented,* i.e., be oriented to the concrete and the particular. From this point of view you are not interested in the average, normal, or ideal worker, supervisor, manager, or group. Keep your eyes and ears on the concrete particular worker, supervisor, manager, or group with whom you here and now are being confronted.
3. *Act responsibly.* Your data are being collected under the burden of responsibility. Never forget that. You are no carefree researcher, manipulating independent variables promiscuously. Keep your data confidential.
4. *Diagnose and clarify the total situation.* Plot out tentatively and for subsequent correction the pattern of relationships that is being set before you. Keep clarifying and testing this pattern. Do not add or twist. You are clarifying a situation—not treating it. (For an example of a pattern, see the way we previously described the interrelated behaviors that were going on in the Relay Assembly Test Room.)
5. *Diagnose and clarify the total situation at a microscopic level in this way.* The major elements of the pattern that you are seeking will be composed at a microscopic level of the (a) *activities,* (b) *inter-*

actions, and (c) *sentiments and norms of behavior* of the person or persons you are observing.[15] Never treat these elements independently, always think of them interdependently. For example, never look at an activity apart from the system of interactions in which it is imbedded. Because interactions between persons always involve sentiments, clarify the latter too, but in a sense *interactions* are the most important elements for you to pay attention to. You can define your subject matter as being concerned with and "limited to phenomena in which interactions between persons seem to be important and cannot be conveniently disregarded." [16] As much as many have tried, remember that this was the one factor which could not be conveniently disregarded if one was to understand what was going on in the Illumination experiments, the Relay Assembly Test Room, the Interviewing Program, and the Bank Wiring Observation Room.

6. *Diagnose and clarify the total situation at a macroscopic level in this way.* The major elements of the pattern that you are seeking will be composed at a macroscopic level of (a) what needs people are bringing to the situation, (b) what management in terms of policies, standards, rules, and regulations is putting into the situation, and (c) the new values and norms of behavior that emerge under conditions (a) and (b). Treat these factors interdependently. Note that each of the above a, b, and c, if made operational, will always break down into the a, b, and c's enumerated in point five above. The latter may be roughly conceived as the atoms making up in different combinations the molecules in 6.

7. *Think in terms of a natural, organic, open-ended social system. Do not think in terms of a rational, inorganic, closed, or mechanical system,* no matter if the system around which for convenience you have drawn your boundary lines be an individual, a two-person relationship, a small group, a department, a division, the Western Electric Company, the Bell System, the U.S.A., the Common Market, or the United Nations. But in the beginning practice this way of thinking at the lower end of the continuum and remember every system by definition has an environment in which it is trying to survive, and with which it is trying to cope.

---

[15] These elements are treated more systematically in a book by George C. Homans, *The Human Group* (New York, Harcourt Brace & Company, 1950). See pp. 48–155 where he applies them to the Bank Wiring Observation Room.

[16] L. J. Henderson's definition of " concrete sociology " referred to in his *Three Lectures on Concrete Sociology,* unfortunately unpublished but read by the counselors.

8. *So think functionally.* Of any well-established pattern of behavior in any system ask what function it performs for (a) the maintenance of the system and (b) the system's capacity to cope with its environment.

The listening-helping-communication component

But the role of the counselor was not just that of a disinterested observer; he was also trying to improve his skill in the direction of opening up avenues of communication between persons and helping persons to help themselves. He was not just a researcher seeking knowledge; he was also a practitioner trying to improve his understanding, skills, and sensitivities about others and himself and by this improved practice trying to make helpful interventions. He was trying to clarify situations for others as well as for himself. The role prescriptions for this orientation were:

1. *Listen—don't talk.*
2. *Never argue; never give advice.*
3. *Listen to*
   a. *What the person wants to say.*
   b. *What he does not want to say.*
   c. *What he cannot say without help.*
4. *Become sensitive to the expression of feelings.* Learn to recognize and reflect them.
5. *Help the person to clarify and accept his own feelings.* Do this by summarizing from time to time what has been said (e.g., "Is this the way you are feeling?"). Always do this with great caution, that is, clarify but do not add or twist.
6. *Help the person to make his own decisions; do not make them for him.*
7. *Try to understand the person from his point of view; do not put yourself in his shoes.* Put him in his own shoes.
8. *Never forget that you are involved in the situations you are observing.* Learn to recognize and accept your own feelings. Don't try to escape from them—learn to accept them and deal with them through skill and understanding.
   a. *Take it easy.*
   b. *Stay loose.*
   c. *Be flexible.*
   d. *Internalize these role prescriptions so that they become congruent with yourself.* Don't be a copy cat. Be true to yourself.
   e. *Be natural.*

Remember: This Role Model Is an Abstraction

Let us pause for a moment to make some cautionary comments about this role model for the counselor that we have abstracted from the Hawthorne studies.

1. In translating the descriptive propositions derived from research into prescriptive propositions for the counselor's behavior, we have indulged in considerable oversimplification. So long as this is kept in mind, no harm will have been done. In abstracting the counselor's role model, our purpose has been to provide a convenient and fruitful focus for looking later at the problems of implementing the counseling program.

2. Obviously these role prescriptions should not be identified with the counselor's actual behavior. They constitute one important dimension of his behavior; they are not the behavior itself. We shall look at that later. In this chapter, we have been at the level of ideas—ideas derived from research. We have been looking at the counselor's role in relation to these ideas before they become contaminated, which always will happen, when they are applied to a concrete situation where other forces are brought into play.

3. What are some of these other forces? One set is the forces of industrial organization in which role models for the behavior of persons in other organizational positions exist. By abstracting the counselor's role model, therefore, we hope it will help us later to see how this role model will fuse or conflict with these other role models.

4. Another source of contamination derives from the persons who will have to practice these role prescriptions. Even a slight perusal of them will reveal that they are going to be a little difficult to live up to, live with, practice, train for, and administer in the counseling program. These abstractions therefore will help us to focus fruitfully on these problems later.

5. But also we want to look at these ideas before they become packaged in a particular form, called the counseling program at Hawthorne. These same ideas have been packaged in many different forms. By keeping these ideas separate and clear from their concrete embodiment, we can consider later other forms of implementation.

6. Obviously these ideas were not as clearly recognized or as explicitly stated in 1936 when the counseling program was designed as we have stated them now in this chapter. All of them are implicit in *Management and the Worker;* many of them are quite explicit but some are not. But more than this, even though verbalized, their significance and implications took a long time to be seen. This could only occur by practice. We do not think this more explicit statement, however, is a distortion. Even though more latent in 1936, these ideas were the underlying rationale of the counseling program.

7. Whenever someone asked of the counseling organization, "What are you up to and why are you doing what you are doing in the way that you are doing it?" up would pop one of these role prescriptions and its derivation from the Hawthorne studies. We will see these ideas cropping up at every stage of the program's development from its early design, to the way it was formally organized within the company structure, to its early implementation, and to its later modifications. To keep repeating them again and again as we tell the counseling story would be ennervating indeed. So we have wrapped them all up in one place for the reader to see and so that we can refer to them conveniently in a shorthand manner.

8. But now for the most difficult question—the problem of the beneficial effects of these role prescriptions. In the counseling program, these were always rationalized in one of two forms:

(a) The benefits that would follow from the spirit of inquiry itself, or to put it in our shorthand way: by the practice of that component of the counselor's role we have called observer-researcher-diagnostic, and

(b) The benefits that would follow in improved communication, coping, adaptation, and equilibrium by and between individuals and groups from the practice of that component of the counselor's role we have called listening-helping-communication.

9. We have kept these two sets of role prescriptions separate because, if it has not been evident to the reader already, they do not fuse automatically at all points into one congruent and unambiguous set of role prescriptions. The first set contains more of the pre-

scriptions for the improvement of research and knowledge; the second set more of those for the improvement of skill and practice. Although they reinforce each other at some points, they conflict at others. Around them choice points for either development can be made. One can go more in one direction than another; one can emphasize one more than the other; one can assess the values of one higher or lower than the other; one can feel more comfortable in one than the other. By keeping this in mind we will be able to see more clearly the development the counseling program took.

SUMMARY

In this chapter we have tried to follow through the developing research strategies of the Hawthorne studies up to their beginning application strategies and commitments. In this development whenever a fork in the road appeared where one could go this way or that way, we pointed it out and said which path the investigators took. Let us look at some of these forks and the path taken.

1. When the Hawthorne effect produced both (a) inconclusive experimental results and (b) a peculiar positive result, the Hawthorne investigators could have gone down path (a) and tried to improve their experimental designs. Instead they chose to go down path (b) on a chase for the positive effect. This involved them in a more clinical and situational approach.
2. When they started interviewing workers and saw that they could get their data from both (a) answers by workers to their direct questions or (b) behaving in a way which would help the workers to say what was important to them, they could have gone down path (a) and tried to improve their questionnaire designs and sampling techniques. Instead they went down (b) and tried to develop clinically their interviewing skills.
3. When they could have researched the Hawthorne effect from both (a) the point of view of the kinds of workers who would be apt to facilitate such an effect or (b) from the point of view of the kinds of behavior on their part which would facilitate such an effect, they could have gone down path (a) and researched the former. Instead they went down path (b) and developed the counselor's role.
4. When they saw that the interviewing method could be used to produce both (a) positive effects for the persons interviewed and

(b) research data, they took path (b) in the Bank Wiring Observation Room, but here they chose to develop both in the counselor's role.

In each instance we tried to make the best case we could for the path they took. We tried to avoid saying that one path was better than another in terms of some absolute logic or that they had to choose one path or the other. Given ample time, money, and resources they could have developed both. But we did try to show that the choices they made were not just arbitrary; underlying them was a reasonable research strategy in terms of the questions that interested them.[17]

This departure carried with it many assumptions which we will have to examine later in our conclusions at the end of the book. However—and this is the point we want to make now—this departure provided the counseling program with a sense of purpose and direction, particularly in its early days. With it a group of dedicated and committed persons—called counselors—developed. For many of them the opportunity for new careers emerged. They felt they were participating in something of importance and significance. They were participating in the adventure of science and at the same time were able to be of help to their fellow men.

[17] Perhaps we can state this in another way that will be more meaningful to some readers. The Hawthorne researches started out as "hypothesis testing" and in time became more "hypothesis generating" studies. As in terms of conventional procedures this progression looks like going backwards, we have tried to provide a logic for why it went this way. In our opinion, this did not happen because the experimental method cannot be applied to the study of human behavior. This is not the lesson to be learned from the Hawthorne researches; we are not anti-experimental. Rather it is our opinion that the hypotheses submitted for experimental testing in the early studies were not very precise and clear. Until they could be clarified it does not seem strange to see that they could not be easily verified.

CHAPTER III

The Formal Organization
of the Counseling Program

IN THIS CHAPTER we will examine how the counseling program was formally organized. We will consider such questions as, for example, to whom did it report? how were its services obtained? and how was it formally introduced in a department? In short, we will consider all those questions pertaining to how the counseling program was "structured into" the Company. We shall not consider in this chapter how the counselors themselves in terms of their own behavior and role model structured their relationships to the workers whom they counseled or to the other categories of persons with whom, in order to implement the program, they had to become involved. As we said in Chapter I, we will do this in Part IV of the book.

THE PLACE OF COUNSELING IN THE SUPERVISORY STRUCTURE

Figure 3.1 is a very simplified organization chart of the Hawthorne plant. It has been pared to its barest skeleton bones because in twenty years organization charts have a way of changing. As time goes on, boxes with new names become occupied by new incumbents with new titles, even though the activities performed within them sometimes remain somewhat the same. This is most fortunate for our purposes here, because all the reader needs to know is the general organizational pattern under which counseling operated during the twenty years of its existence.

Looking at Figure 3.1 the following points should be noted:

1. The counseling activity reported to Industrial Relations, a staff activity.

FIGURE 3.1

THE PLACE OF COUNSELING IN THE SUPERVISORY
STRUCTURE AT THE HAWTHORNE PLANT

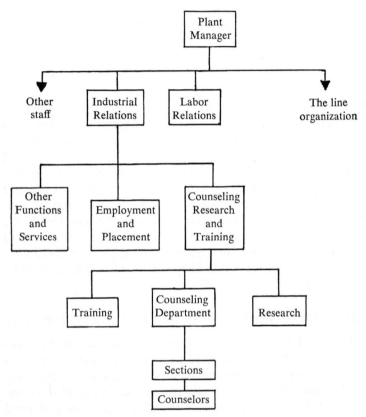

2. The person in charge of Industrial Relations was on a coordinate basis with the top person in charge of line operations; that is, they both reported to the plant manager at Hawthorne, whose superior had his offices in New York.

3. The counseling activity was on a coordinate basis with other personnel functions such as, for example, employment and placement

(placed on the chart for illustrative purposes only and which do not include by any means all of the personnel services provided by the Company).

4. The subbranch of which the counseling activity was a part normally carried on training and personnel research functions as well as counseling.

5. The counseling department was further subdivided into sections each of which was supervised by a section chief or first line supervisor.

6. These sections were made up of counselors who were assigned to a specific shop or organizational unit.

From this brief description, it can be seen that the counseling activity was on the same basis as any other personnel activity in terms of its place in the supervisory structure. It was a part of the industrial relations organization and bore a staff relation to the line organizations it served. The counselor was an "individual" (not a supervisor), he did not have any line authority. In these respects his organization role did not differ from that of most of the individuals in Industrial Relations.

How the Counseling Service Was Secured and Installed

The counseling service was voluntary; it was secured only upon the request of the organizations wishing to participate. The request was transmitted by the head of the organization wishing to have it installed to the head of Industrial Relations. His approval was mostly nominal; however, he did need this information in order to see that the additional counselors required to provide the requested service were available.

If and when this was so, the program was introduced through a series of informational meetings with supervisors. The first of these was held usually by the line superintendent with his assistant superintendents. In these meetings the superintendent conducted the meeting but he had members of the counseling staff present in order to explain the program and to answer questions. Following these meetings, the assistant superintendents held meetings with their lower level supervisors and again they had the counseling staff present to answer questions. The counselors who were to be initially assigned were included ordinarily in these meetings and were introduced to everyone present. Following these meetings the counselors visited each supervisor at his work place to get acquainted and to answer any questions the supervisor had.

The procedure followed in explaining the program to the union representatives varied somewhat. Usually the line assistant superintendent told them that counseling was to be introduced and explained its purposes. If more information was required, this was provided sometimes by the coordinator of labor relations and sometimes by the counseling organization staff. If the union wished to protest the program, it could do so to the director of labor relations. In many cases the assistant superintendent included the shop stewards in the supervisory discussions. In all cases the counselor, usually with his supervisor, contacted each shop steward at the time he started working in the organization in order to become acquainted and answer questions.

The procedure usually followed in informing nonsupervisory employees about the program was to have it announced to them by their immediate supervisor. He was asked to announce it as another personnel service, to give it his personal support, and to state that the counselor would go into more detail about the activity when he came around to meet them. When the counselor was ready to start in a group or section, the immediate supervisor was supposed to introduce him personally to each employee under his supervision.

In some locations where counseling was introduced, employees were sent an announcement signed by the organization head explaining its purposes. In other instances the program was announced in the plant paper accompanied by pictures of the counseling staff. Explanatory memoranda were also sometimes prepared and distributed to the entire supervisory staff requesting that they circulate it among their employees.

Introductory Meetings

In the informational meetings held with supervisors when introducing the program, the following points were covered:

1. The program was to be made available to every worker in the organization to be covered.
2. The counselor was to have the right of free access to the organizational unit that comprised his territory in order to observe activities there and to familiarize himself generally with the organization's problems.
3. He would be privileged to circulate among the employees while they were working for the purpose of keeping up contacts with employees whom he had already interviewed, meeting new employees, and keeping in touch with events in the work group. This on-the-floor activity, however, would be conducted so as not to interfere with the work of the group.
4. The selection of individuals to be interviewed, the order, if any, in which they would be interviewed, and the time the interview would be held was to be worked out between the counselor and the supervisor, with the right of final decision resting with the supervisor. The frequency of interviews with any one individual and the length of the interview were to be left to the judgment of the counselor.
5. The counselor was to have the right to take employees out of the department for interviews after obtaining approval first from the supervisor.
6. All interviews and talks with the counselor were to be confidential. The supervisor was not to inquire of the counselor or the employee what transpired in these discussions. Responsibility for maintaining these confidences rested with the counselor. In line with this, no reports on the counselor's work with individuals would be issued to supervisors.
7. General reports on employee attitudes and conditions affecting morale would be issued from time to time to higher levels of management but these would not identify any individual or any specific organization.
8. The counselors were not to give advice, suggestions, or information to the employees or initiate any action on their behalf. These were to be regarded as normal supervisory responsibilities, not to be disturbed by the counselor in any way.
9. In order that employees would suffer no loss in earnings, they were to be paid average earnings for the time spent in the interview. The counselor was authorized to approve time tickets for the time thus spent. At the termination of the interview he was supposed to fill in and approve a time ticket showing when the interview started, when it terminated, and the elapsed time together with necessary

identifying information. The employee was to present the time ticket to his supervisor when he returned to his department. A copy of the ticket was to be retained by the counselor for the counseling organization files.

10. The counseling activity would continue in effect unless terminated at the request of the line organization or at the initiative of the industrial relations organization.

Let us pause to comment upon the above points. Most of them pertained to the formal work arrangements which would have to prevail if the counselors were to be able to behave in a way that would not interfere with the formal responsibilities of supervision and also maintain the confidences of the employees. They were the organizational requirements for the practice of his role model. But these requirements to which the organization to be served by counseling agreed were also somewhat unusual. They agreed to the free and unrestricted access of a representative of an outside staff agency to its internal affairs in return for which no tangible benefits were promised other than those which were expected to accrue from the counselor's activities with employees.

How Requests for Interviews Were Initiated and Approved

There were three main ways in which requests for interviews could be initiated: (a) by the counselor, (b) by the supervisor, or (c) by the employee himself.

(a) The counselor was free to request (but not formally demand) an interview with anyone in his department but these requests needed to be approved by the employee's supervisor and were to be arranged at a convenient time from the standpoint of work.

(b) The supervisor could ask (but not formally demand) an employee to talk with his counselor or he could ask (but again not formally demand) the counselor to talk with an employee.

(c) An employee could request an interview with the counselor through his supervisor or directly of the counselor, but in either case the approval of the supervisor was necessary.

It should be noted that although all three parties—counselors, supervisors, or employees—could initiate an interview, requests for interviews that were initiated either by counselors or by employees needed the approval of the supervisor. These again were organization requirements in order to insure that the supervisor would be informed with regard to what the counselor was up to and would have a say if and when the counseling activity might interfere with the work that needed to be done. Obviously they did not make the counselor's job any easier or the employee's request for an interview any less threatening. But they were requirements for the practice of the counselor's role in a context that would not do violence to the role of supervision. As in time counselors became more accepted as persons by supervisors, the practice of these regulations became less rigid. In actual practice most supervisors granted counselors blanket approval to interview anyone they wished in a department without first obtaining specific approval. They expected, however, to be informed of any formal interviews which took place.

WHERE DID COUNSELING TAKE PLACE?

The activities of counselors could be put into two general classes. As these two classes of activities will keep coming up again and again and are essential for the understanding of the counselor's job, as well as for what we wish to say in a moment about the interviewing facilities, we will state them briefly now and save for later the elaboration of their significance. These two major activities were (1) what we shall call on-the-floor contacts or interactions and (2) in-the-interviewing-room contacts or interactions.

On-the-Floor Activities

A good portion of the counselor's time was on the floor in the department talking with and observing the behavior of workers. It was in this context that a great deal of small talk took place; it was here where counselors' or employees' requests for initial or follow-up interviews took place. It was here where often the counselor explained his purposes; it was here that his role model was most on public display and visible; and where his behavior was the least organizationally prescribed in the sense that he did not have to go to the supervisor and say, "Can I have a chitchat with Joe or Mary?" The one organizational rule applying to it was, "Behave in such a way so as to interfere least with the work to be done."

Obviously the point at which an interview became officially an interview was arbitrary. A counselor could listen to an employee on the floor in the same way that he listened to him in the interviewing room. From the point of view of the counselor's role prescriptions, as stated in Chapter II, the way he behaved on the floor was supposed to be of a piece with the way he behaved in the interviewing room; that is, his basic orientation remained the same. But obviously a worker at a bench, machine conveyor, or assembly line presented an increasing number of physical (and also sometimes social) constraints to free and easy communication. So for this reason, counselors invited workers to a place where this might be more possible. In the early days of the program the employee was taken to the Company restaurant or conference room, but later on special interviewing rooms were provided.

In-the-Interviewing-Room Activities

In the interviewing room the counselor could give full and complete attention to what the individual employee wished to say without having to worry about the effects of his behavior on others. At that time in this context the "system" with which he was concerned was "a two-person relationship." In this system he had to be concerned only with the effect of his behavior on the employee. In his on-the-floor activities, however, he defined his system as "the department" (see prescriptive rule 7, page 41). In this system his behavior with regard to B (a particular worker) could be perceived by C, D, or E (i.e., other workers) as preferential or discriminating. For example, C, D, or E could feel, "He (the counselor) likes me less or thinks I am less important than B," the worker to whom at that time the counselor was trying to give his attention.

We shall consider this distinction later but for our purposes now we wish to mention only the facilities provided for the in-the-interviewing-room activities of the counselor.

Interviewing Facilities

In time, to assure privacy during the interview, specially designed and equipped counseling rooms were provided for the exclusive use of the counseling staff. Typically, these were small compartments built within a larger enclosure having a main entrance and exit with locked doors to which each counselor had a key. The compartments were arranged within this larger enclosure so that people occupying the compartment could not be seen by someone entering a compartment in another part of the room. This arrangement was economical, it permitted several (as many as six) interviews to be held at one time, and it helped to overcome the reluctance that some persons might have had of being alone with another person in a locked room.

The interviewing rooms were centrally located in order to minimize traveling time to and from the counseling territories. They were provided with floor lamps, an end table, and two cushioned chairs. These chairs were built with sloping seats and backs so that a person sitting in them naturally could lean back and relax if he wished. There were no desks or standard office-type furniture in the room. Draperies were provided for the windows; there was sound proofing for the ceilings and a floor covering to deaden sound. Smoking was permitted. (At that time smoking was permitted only in the cafeterias, conference rooms, private offices, and on the grounds.) The location, design, and furnishings of the counseling rooms were intended to facilitate the process of talking not only in terms of social and organizational expectations but also in terms of what the worker as a person wanted to be and become, i.e., what was important to him as well as to the Company.

THE COUNSELING ORGANIZATION

As we saw in Figure 3.1 from the Company's table of organization, counseling was an administrative unit, called a department of the Industrial Relations branch. Let us look now and see how this department was organized for administrative purposes.

As the counseling activity expanded, its internal formal organization also proliferated. As can be seen in Figure 3.1, counselors reported to counseling supervisors, called section chiefs, who in turn reported to the head of counseling—a department chief. As supervisors, they were officially part of management. But also they were the guardians of the counselor's role model. Most of their activities were concerned with providing a favorable organizational environment for the practice of counseling. In time they became the mediators between the counselor's organizational role and his counseling role. But let us confine ourselves now to their official duties.

Assignment of Counseling Territories

Each counselor was assigned a territory comprising the employees in one or more departments, preferably within a shop or branch. The assignment of territories within an organization for which the program had been approved was the responsibility of the counseling organization.

The size of a counseling territory, measured in terms of numbers of employees, varied depending upon a number of factors such as type of work and proximity of work groups, but the desired ratio was about one counselor to 300 employees. There were both men and women counselors; men counselors interviewed men, women counselors interviewed women. The rationale for this was to be found in the mores of Hawthorne and the surrounding community. As we shall refer to all counselors by a masculine pronoun, the reader should keep in mind that "he or she" and "his or her" would be more accurate.

Officially Required Records for External Purposes

No official Company records about the employees counseled were kept, such as were generally required from other personnel activities as, for example, employment records and personnel records. This exemption from formal record keeping was unusual but necessary if the confidences of employees were to be protected.

For administrative purposes the counseling organization was required to prepare a budget for each fiscal year showing a forecast of the number of employees required for the year, salary costs, and other expenses. These forecasts were reviewed quarterly in relation to performance and required revisions were approved at that time. These budget estimates were combined with those of other organizations in the Industrial Relations branch and were formally issued as a branch budget.

The counseling organization was required to have data available about the scope of the counseling activity and to report upon them as needed. The data required were those showing: organizations requesting the activity, the extent of counseling coverage for those organizations, and the size of counseling territories.

Records Required by the Counseling Organization for Internal Purposes

The records required by the counseling organization for internal purposes consisted of two kinds: (a) control records to be maintained by the counseling supervisor and (b) records to be kept by the counselor.

The counseling supervisor was to maintain for each shop or branch to which the counselors were assigned a record of the number, size, and location of the departments for which counseling service had been approved. Against this picture he maintained data on progress in providing adequate counseling coverage and service. These data showed the counseling territories assigned and unassigned, and progress in providing coverage and service in assigned territories. To achieve the latter objective, the counseling supervisor maintained a record of the number of employees in the territory who had been contacted and of those contacted the number interviewed. From this he was able to judge the counselor's progress in providing counseling service to all the people in the territory.

The records required of the counselor were of two kinds: (a) records of the interviews and (b) records of his on-the-floor observations. The interview record was to be dictated in full detail and as accurately as the counselor could reconstruct it in verbatim form. Notes were ordinarily not to be taken during the interview so this reconstruction was to be done from memory. As in time this record came to be used primarily for the counselor's training and development, the requirement that the interview be dictated verbatim was relaxed as the counselor gained in proficiency. He was then permitted to prepare only a summary. The record was coded by the counselor to protect the employee's identity and the recorded interview was maintained in the counselor's file. The counselor was the only person who could identify the interview record and he was solely responsible for its safekeeping.

The record of observations made from their on-the-floor activities were descriptive statements pertaining to an individual or group and generally concerned an activity or event which the counselor thought was significant. These records were filed with interview records or as part of a log referring to a work group, depending upon the counselor's judgment of their significance. But again these data were the property of the counselor and not of the Company.

Intradepartmental Studies and Written Reports

From these two basic records various written documents, such as memoranda, studies, and reports, were prepared. Over the twenty-year span of counseling these written documents varied considerably in kind, quality, and amount. From them from time to time reports to management were issued about which we will talk in a moment. But besides serving this organization purpose, they also served very strongly felt needs on the part of the individual counselors and the counseling organization.

One set of documents arose from the need on the part of the counselors to conceptualize what they were listening to and observing. Just to record uninterpreted interviews and observations was not enough. Let us remember that one of their role prescriptions was to seek for the patterns of behavior that were being presented before them. So some counselors felt the need to prepare reports from their interviews and observations of a more general and systematic nature. Some of these were case studies of interesting individual and group situations and some were organized around problems, such as, for example, absenteeism, married women, minority groups, long-service employees, and the introduction of technological change.

Another set of documents arose not so much as above from the counselor's concern with "living up" to his role model but rather from his concern of "how do we live with it," particularly on the floor. It will be remembered that none of the role prescriptions, specified in Chapter II, had said, for example, just how many people in one day a counselor can be expected to listen to with sympathy and intelligence; it had just said, listen. They had not specified (a) to whom should a counselor listen? (b) who deserves to be listened to? and (c) what is a fair day's work of listening? In organized human activities, these questions cannot remain unspecified; they are of the essence in organizational life.

So many of the counselors' reports went in the direction of correcting for this deficiency. They were concerned with such problems as (1) gaining acceptance of counseling not only from employees but also from supervision and other personnel services, (2) managing efficiently the time they spent in their (a) on-the-floor activities, (b) in-the-interviewing-room activities, and (c) in-their-offices activities keeping up their basic records, and (3) problems in maintaining a proper balance between the quantity (coverage) as well as the quality (helping someone who wants and needs to be helped) of their service.

So from the counselors themselves and particularly as the counseling program expanded, there was considerable pressure in the direction of standardizing and formalizing the role model of the counselor with organizational procedures such as: "How do we explain the program?" "How do we answer these sorts of questions?" "How do we deal with employees who do not want to be counseled?" "How much time should we spend in on-the-floor activities?" and so on and on. These became the topics for many discussions, formal and informal, and from them the internal organization of the counseling organization developed. We shall have a great deal more to say about this later in Part IV of the book. Just now all we wish to point out is that the internal formal organization of counseling was an emergent phenomenon. It developed over a course of time. Once counseling was approved by management, the way in which it organized and administered itself in order to achieve its aims was left to them. The individual counselors as well as the counseling supervisors participated together in this development.

Reports to Management

As we said before, the counseling organization issued from time to time reports to management about employee attitudes on problems of general interest and concern to both employees and management. Some reports prepared by the counseling organization, however, originated more directly from management itself. The counseling organization was frequently asked to contribute items to quarterly meetings of the Manufacturing Department staff and to semiannual Company-wide staff conferences in each of which a section was allocated to employee relations. The material prepared by the counseling organization for these meetings generally included a statement of prevailing employee attitudes with some interpretation of contributing factors as well as suggestions for improvement. In addition to providing this sort of information about timely topics, comments were often invited by the management on the possible consequences in terms of employee situations or proposals or programs under consideration in the field of industrial and labor relations.

Obviously communication between management and the counseling organization about the purposes and results of their activities were not confined to these periodic reports. But this development of counseling in relation to top management we shall consider later. Here we are concerned only with its formal aspects.

SUMMARY

As we have presented the reader with so many details of organizational arrangements and procedures in which he can get easily lost, let us summarize briefly some of the major points we should like him to keep in mind. We have wanted him to see:

1. Many of these formal arrangements, particularly those between the counseling department and the line organizations they served, were made in order to facilitate the practice of the counselor's role, particularly in his relations to employees. He was placed in an organizational spot where he had no line authority and could maintain the confidence of employees. In these respects his organization role and counseling role were congruent.

2. In setting up these conditions, however, the line organizations did agree to having a member from an outside staff agency observe their internal affairs. As a consequence the counselor would be privy to many of their secrets which they might rather keep to themselves. No formal rules could prevent the irresponsible use and

misuse of such information. But here the role model prescriptions were very clear.

3. To protect the supervisor, work arrangements were stipulated so that the counselor could not interfere with his line authority and undermine the duties, responsibilities, and privileges of his position. Some of these arrangements did not make the counselor's job any easier. But perhaps, also interesting to observe, was the fact that the organizational prescriptions to the counselor in relation to the supervisor were stated in proscriptive terms, e.g., "Do not interfere," "Keep out of his hair." Likewise the relations of the supervisor to the counselor were stated proscriptively, e.g., "Don't ask for information from the counselor that he cannot divulge." But what their role relations to each other should be in more complementary and cooperative terms remained organizationally undefined. This was something that would have to be worked out later.

4. What the relations of counseling to other personnel services should be was not considered at all. This too was something that would have to be worked out later.

5. The counseling activity depended upon the active cooperation and support of employees, the line organization and other staff services, as well as, of course, management. This cooperation and support was not automatically guaranteed; it could not be secured by any formal rules. In the last analysis it had to be gained by the behavior of the counselors themselves in their territories and the results that they were able to obtain there. In these respects in many ways counseling did not differ from many other personnel and staff activities. But it had some unusual features.

6. The counseling activity, as envisaged, was far from being something to be practiced in a pure clinical, pure research, or pure service setting. It combined elements of each. The counselors were engaged in activities in three quite different organizational-spatial settings: (a) on the floor, (b) in the interviewing room, and (c) in their offices, involving quite different roles.

   (a) In their activities on the floor, they were not just in the role of observers. While there, they were supposed (1) to become acquainted and pave the way for the development of a counseling relationship with everyone in the territory (i.e., secure coverage) and (2) to identify those employees who wanted and needed counseling help. And still in addition (3) to gain the acceptance of themselves by both workers and supervisors as persons worthy of trust to whom confidences could be given and (4) to further the understanding of the counseling activity itself as something which would be useful to them. This involved quite a mix of roles, as we shall see later.

(b) In their activities in the interviewing room, the counselors often had to continue their activities of explaining counseling and gaining its acceptance, but here they were able to remain more in the role of counselors and provide the intrinsic services for which their role was designed.

(c) In their activities in the office, they kept up their basic records, tried to make sense to themselves of what they had seen and heard, developed their own procedural rules for their activities on the floor, and prepared their reports for management.

PART II

Employee Concerns at Work

CHAPTER IV

Situational Sources of Concerns at Work

PART II of the book will be concerned with identifying and illustrating the general concerns of employees. In this chapter we shall be working toward a schema for the analysis of employee concerns which we shall be using in the next five chapters that follow (Chapters V through IX). We will start with certain content analyses made by the counselors of employee concerns and see what information they provide. We will then discuss why the distinction between personal and work concerns was not too useful for our purposes and why we finally decided to make a more situational analysis of them.

THE MANIFEST CONTENT OF EMPLOYEE CONCERNS

During the counseling program the counselors made a number of studies of the manifest content of employee concerns. In one of them they tried to evaluate the percentage of employees in the plant population who had concerns about their situations both at work and outside of the company.

Percentage of Employees Expressing Concerns

The data for this study were collected over a period of fifteen consecutive three-month intervals, from January 1, 1948, to October 1, 1951, and are summarized in Figure 4.1. Let us examine first how this figure was constructed.

1. At the end of each three-month interval, each counselor, aided by a research assistant, appraised the uses made of counseling in his own territory during that period. These quarterly appraisals were made fifteen consecutive times, that is, over a period of about three and a half years. The number of employees covered in each period

FIGURE 4.1

PERCENTAGE OF EMPLOYEES EXPRESSING CONCERNS ABOUT
PERSONAL AND WORK SITUATIONS

(Average for 15 Consecutive Three-Month Intervals,
January 1948—October 1951: Hawthorne Plant)

N = 10,000 employees

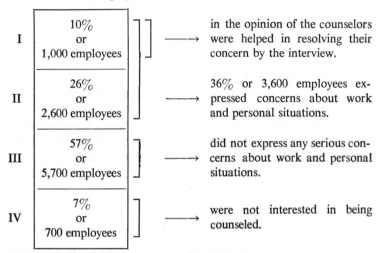

I	10% or 1,000 employees	in the opinion of the counselors were helped in resolving their concern by the interview.
II	26% or 2,600 employees	36% or 3,600 employees expressed concerns about work and personal situations.
III	57% or 5,700 employees	did not express any serious concerns about work and personal situations.
IV	7% or 700 employees	were not interested in being counseled.

for all the counseling territories ranged from 6,000 to 10,500. The number of counselors making these appraisals ranged from 35 to 50. For each period these appraisals for each territory were totaled for the plant population covered by counseling.

2. In Figure 4.1 we averaged these total quarterly assessments of employees "not interested," expressing "no concern," "concern," and "being helped" for the fifteen periods in which these appraisals were made, and we stated the resulting percentages also in terms of 10,000 employees merely for graphic purposes. The variation in percentages for each category from quarter to quarter was too small to be significant. Category I was remarkably constant; Categories II and IV showed a slight trend downward while Category III showed a slight trend upward.

3. The counselors used the following criteria for assigning employees to one of the four categories.

(a) In any one quarter all employees who had been contacted at least once and given an opportunity to talk and declined for any reason were classified as "not interested in being counseled."

(b) All employees who had been contacted at least once, who were quite willing to talk, and who in many cases were interviewed but who, in the opinion of the counselor, did not seem to be seriously bothered about anything in particular were placed in the "not seriously concerned" category, while

(c) All employees who dwelt for some time and with some feeling about some situation or circumstance, and particularly those who assumed the initiative in seeking an interview with the counselor as well as those who took the initiative in the interview itself, were placed in the "concern" category. Taking the initiative in the conversation was considered important in revealing urgency or centrality of importance. To illustrate, if an employee said, "I didn't get the raise I expected," but did not go on to elaborate its significance to him, he would be placed in the no concern category. If, however, he went on to develop the topic by expressing how he felt about not getting an increase in his pay or dwelt upon other felt injustices, he would be placed in the concern category.

(d) Two criteria were used to place employees in the "helped" category.

(1) One test was whether the employee acknowledged a benefit to the counselor. This had to be more than a polite acknowledgment of the counselor's interest and needed to have corroborative evidence in the interview. If an employee had been considerably disturbed by a problem during the interview and then had said to the counselor that he felt better after having "gotten it off his chest," this would be taken as indicative of a benefit. Or if the employee had talked at length about a misunderstanding with a member of his family, had determined upon a course of action during the interview, and had indicated subsequently that he had carried it out with evident satisfaction to himself, this too would be construed as indicating a benefit.

(2) The second criterion pertained to evident changes in the employee's attitudes and behavior following an interview, even though the employee had not openly expressed a

benefit to the counselor. Examples of this would be changes observed by the counselor in the way in which the employee approached his job, in the way in which he related himself to others, or in his subsequent expressions about the problem of his original concern which indicated that for him the problem had been resolved. Comments from supervisors such as, "I don't know what you did to Joe, but he acts like a new person since you talked to him," were also taken as indicative of a benefit to the employee.

These ground rules obviously left much room for differences of opinion among counselors in determining whether an individual should be classed as being concerned or unconcerned or helped or not helped by the interview. In order to reduce these variations in individual judgments, the compiling of the reports was assigned to the counseling research section. This unit developed descriptions and examples of the kinds of evaluations to be made, reviewed them with each counselor and counseling supervisor, made refinements in them from time to time, reviewed with each counselor how he evaluated his material at the quarterly appraisal period, and tried to iron out differences in the counselor's concepts and evaluations. This type of central coordination brought about more uniformity in procedures but it could not be said to have eliminated entirely the subjective element.

While the subjectivity of the data warns against easy generalizations based upon them, to dismiss the evidence as of no moment would be equally unwarranted. Perhaps most impressive are the large numbers involved. The population included ranged in numbers between 6,000 and 10,500 employees, representing all shop and most office clerical occupations in the Hawthorne plant. Included were hourly rated men and women in all age, service, pay, labor grade, and occupational categories. In short, it represented all the shop and office occupations of a large, complex, modern factory. The uses made of counseling by this large population were periodically assessed by a large counseling staff, ranging from 35 to 50 in number, using the ground rules and point of view we have tried to specify. At any one time this could be considered a snapshot picture, but it was taken fifteen consecutive times at three-month intervals, and showed remarkable consistency period after period.

So from these data the finding that for the Hawthorne plant population during 1948 to 1951 approximately 60% of the employees could be considered to be in general equilibrium with their environment while roughly about 40% had concerns that might be affecting their work cannot be lightly dismissed. This is also true for the finding that about 30% of the employees with serious concerns or roughly 10% of the total population in any one quarterly interval seemed to be helped by counseling. They do provide one rough gross benchmark for evaluating the counseling program. With a few assumptions about the possible improved efficiency of this group, an estimated dollar result could be figured which could be compared against the counseling program's operating costs. But we will not attempt any such computation. These data contained too many unsettled questions about which we could only speculate.

Probably one of the most interesting questions is, "Who were the individual workers that constituted the concern and no concern categories for each period and which ones shifted from one of these categories to another from one period to another?" Figure 4.1 does not answer these questions and the counselors gathered no data which would allow us to try to answer them.

It is our impression that had this been studied, the concern category might have shown a split between two quite different groups of employees: (1) a group of workers that would have appeared in all or most of the fifteen periods and (2) another group that would have appeared in only one or few of the periods. Moreover, as the population for each territory was constantly changing through turnover and replacements and by transfers in and out of the territories, it would have been interesting to know if the workers affected by these changes appeared more often in the concern category than those who had not.

It is also interesting to note that for each period a rough 40% to 60% split occurred between the concern and no concern categories for the total plant population. The variation that existed in these percentages for the separate counseling territories seemed to iron out when totaled for the plant population so that for fifteen consecutive times about three-fifths of the employees expressed no serious concerns while about two-fifths did. Why this is so we do not know, but that the majority of the workers were fairly well satisfied one might expect, for short of this there would have been little basis for stability in the company.

Likewise the constancy of the percentages of employees helped by counseling from period to period aroused our curiosity. Among other things it suggested a possible output norm among the counselors. But about this we had no data.

Topics of Expressed Concern

We have selected one fairly typical study from among many that were made from time to time to show the topics which employees said were of concern to them. This study is based upon the reasons given by 736 employees for wishing to talk to the counselors during the period September 1953 through December 1954. The reasons given were broken down by the counselors in terms of nine general groupings and the results of this analysis are shown in Table 4.1.

To some extent the concerns expressed in this particular study reflected the local business conditions at the time. As can be seen from Table 4.1, concerns about demotions and downgradings ranked third. The greatest discrepancy between men and women occurred in topics 4, 6, and 1. Men were more disturbed about their progress in the company than women. Women were more concerned with their relation to fellow workers as well as their familial relations than men.

By combining certain of the headings shown in Table 4.1 we can group them as shown in Table 4.2 under the headings of personal, work relations, and other job factors. The latter cannot be broken down further because of the ambiguity of the subject headings in the table.

From this table we can see that far more (63%) [1] of these em-

---

[1] In further corroboration of this figure, it can be said that an analysis of the reports on which Figure 4.1 was based, for eight consecutive quarters, January 1948–December 1949, in each of which the concerns of an average of 3,753 employees were examined, showed that 39% were concerned about personal problems and circumstances and 61% about work-related matters.

(*continued on facing page*)

TABLE 4.1

TOPICS OF CONCERN
EXPRESSED BY 736 EMPLOYEES WHO
REQUESTED INTERVIEWS WITH COUNSELORS
SEPTEMBER 1953–DECEMBER 1954

	Total			Men			Women		
Reasons	*No.*	*%*	*Rank*	*No.*	*%*	*Rank*	*No.*	*%*	*Rank*
1. Disturbance in outside relationships (fiancé, wife, husband, in-laws, neighbors, etc.)	182	24.7	1	54	16.3	3	128	31.6	1
2. Dissatisfaction with present job or salary	135	18.3	2	61	18.4	2	74	18.3	2
3. Demotion and downgrading (loss in status, reduction in pay, etc.)	84	11.4	3	46	13.9	4	38	9.4	4
4. Disappointed or frustrated over lack of progress in the company	83	11.3	4	62	18.7	1	21	5.2	7
5. Illness or concern over health	81	11.0	5	46	13.9	4	35	8.6	5
6. Disturbance or breakdown in relations with fellow employees	80	10.9	6	20	6.0	7	60	14.8	3
7. Disturbance or breakdown in relations with supervision	57	7.7	7	27	8.2	6	30	7.4	6
8. Employee not measuring up to company requirements (attendance, efficiency, etc.)	21	2.9	8	2	0.6	9	19	4.7	8
9. General personality disturbance (moody, alcoholism, irresponsible attitude, etc.)	13	1.7	9	13	3.9	8	—	—	9
Totals	736	100		331	100		405	100	

There were slightly over 30,000 separate appraisals made during this period, thus providing considerable weight of evidence in support of this figure. We did not include these data in Table 4.1 because they were broken down only as between work and personal categories and did not show a breakdown by sex and the subheadings shown in Table 4.2.

TABLE 4.2

GENERAL AREAS OF CONCERN REFLECTED
IN 736 EMPLOYEE-REQUESTED INTERVIEWS
SEPTEMBER 1953–DECEMBER 1954

Areas of Concern	Total		Men		Women	
Personal *	37%		34%		40%	
Work relations †	19%	⎫ 63%	14%	⎫ 66%	22%	⎫ 60%
Other job factors ‡	44%	⎭	52%	⎭	38%	⎭

* Combines "disturbances in outside relations," "illness or concern over health," and "general personality disturbances."

† Combines "disturbances or breakdown in relations with fellow workers" and the same with supervisors.

‡ All remaining headings in Table 4.1.

ployees were concerned about work-related problems than about personal problems, and that men outnumbered women in this respect—66% contrasted with 60%. More women than men were concerned about personal problems and interpersonal relations at work, and more men than women were concerned about other job factors. These findings support what are generally held beliefs about these matters. The dominance of work-related concerns among both men and women, however, should serve to dispel any assumption that employee concerns were primarily about matters unrelated to their work situations.

Summary of the Two Studies

If we combine the results of Figure 4.1 and Tables 4.1 and 4.2, it can be said that about one in three of the employees in counseling territories at any one time expressed concerns about their situations at work and outside the company. Of these, some two-thirds or two out of three concerned employees were disturbed by factors in their work situations. The remaining third were bothered by personal situations and circumstances outside the Company, women more so than men. Within the work setting, interpersonal relations loomed large as an area of concern, accounting for nearly a fifth of all work-related concerns. The data available do not permit further distinctions among other work-related factors.

Toward a More Situational Analysis of Employee Concerns

While the data presented thus far tell us some things about employee concerns in terms of their manifest content, they tell us little about the situations giving rise to them. This is the task to which we now want to turn.

Let us start by reflecting upon the kind of analysis which might be more useful for our purposes. Many of these content analyses made by counselors, while useful to management in indicating the broad scope and gross magnitude of employee concerns, seemed to us to fall short of what was needed. Also the attempt to separate out those concerns arising primarily from circumstances outside of the Company did not seem too relevant. Such analyses did not help to show the situational sources of these concerns or the nature of the contribution that counseling could make to them. The specific contribution of counseling was to assist the employee in clarifying for himself the total situation giving rise to his concerns, and thereby better preparing himself for achieving a more workable and therefore a more satisfying resolution of them.

The Difficulty in Distinguishing Between Personal and Work Concerns

Let us examine first the distinction between personal and work concerns. Actually no hard and fast line can be drawn between them. They merge and influence one another and only in a few instances can they be called with some degree of confidence clearly one or the other. Obviously all concerns have both an inner (personal) as well as an outer reference. So it can be said that in one sense all concerns are personal (it would be hard to conceive of an impersonal concern) while in another sense all concerns are never purely personal, that is, unrelated to any outside object.

Again and again the counselors had difficulty in applying this distinction. In the interview itself it was for them an irrelevant and extraneous way of thinking, and after the interview it was a difficult judgment to make. For them a worker who sits and broods over a domestic problem is distracted from his work quite as much as one who is disgruntled over his rate of pay. Likewise a worker concerned about his failure to meet a standard can react by self incrimination as well as by attacking the standard. Is the former a personal and the latter a work concern? Or is a worker who is having arguments with his wife over a change in his shift arrangements and is reluctant to go to his boss about going back to his old shift to be classified as having a personal family problem or a work problem or both?

A False Dichotomy?

But this dichotomy between work and personal concerns was not only difficult to apply; it had serious overtones for the whole counseling program. In the minds of many persons, both inside and outside of the Company, work concerns became associated with matters that management did something about while personal concerns became matters that counseling did something about. So for many persons, personal concerns came to be regarded as the special province of counseling and because work and personal were treated as mutually exclusive and collectively exhaustive subsets of the total set of employee concerns, it followed that counseling had little to do with work concerns. This is a very serious distortion of the counseling program.

Let us examine first how this distinction between work and personal concerns developed. One of the referents for this distinction was the concern of management which ran something like this: If we can establish more clearly or even roughly those concerns which arise from circumstances outside the plant from those which arise from circumstances inside of the plant, we will be better able to settle what and what not we are responsible for. A second referent for the distinction was the concern of the counselors and ran something like this: Many interferences from preoccupations about matters outside of work prevent the worker from attending to his job. If these preoccupations can be diminished, better attention to the job at hand will follow. But a third referent for the distinction arises from the concerns of the social scientist about what is "psychological" and what is "sociological"; that is, what is "personality" and a "personality problem" and what is "social structure" and a "human or social relations problem."

In writing this book we did not wish to get entangled with these powerful concerns, which, as we saw them, were not too closely related to the concerns of employees, and to become engaged in trying to settle between work and personal concerns: which one comes first, which one is more important, and for which one is whom responsible? Could we not accept a condition of mutual interdependence between them and stay as closely as we could to our data, no matter how soft they were? We thought we could.

In line with this reasoning we felt that what was needed was an analysis of employee concerns that kept them in their organizational context. This context, as stated in Chapter II, when discussing the research component of the counselor's role, contained three major elements: (1) the needs the employee brought with him to his work situation, (2) the requirements of the Company for efficient production, and (3) the values and norms of behavior which developed under these conditions. Such an analysis would be situational in character in that it would take into account these major factors as mutually interacting elements. Stated in other terms, it would not abstract one dimension for separate analysis but would keep psychological, technico-economic, and sociological elements in relation to one another as they occur in a specific work situation at a given time. Such an approach, it was reasoned, would provide a useful context for evaluating the relative significance of employee concerns in individual as well as in organizational terms and also for considering what might be done to alleviate them.

Concerning the Wealth of Experience We Had and the Kinds of Data We Needed to Objectify It

But could we make such an analysis with the data available to us? Had the counselors been able to make such an analysis while the program was in effect, aided by the advances in techniques which have taken place in the intervening years, our task would have been simpler, but such analyses were not available. What we had was an abundance of data collected for other purposes and a wealth of experience unanalyzed for the purposes we now wished to use them.

The counselors had had hundreds of thousands of interviews with workers (1) in a large-scale manufacturing concern at different locations with a representative spectrum of jobs, technologies, and skills, (2) during a period of twenty years, a period marked by a recovery from a severe depression, two major wars, and a postwar period of rapid growth in the national economy. Many of these interviews had not been recorded, however, and among those which were many had been destroyed. But from this wealth of experience and the recorded data available, could we make a rough analysis of the kind we have stated? Admittedly, it would be gross and not as refined as we would like, but would it have the merit of being rooted in extensive experience and substantial enough to serve the purposes we would make of it? This is the problem we faced.

But where did this wealth of experience exist? Alas, it did not exist in the files of the Company; it existed in the minds of the counselors and those who had been responsible for the counseling program. But where were these persons? Some were dispersed in all parts of the Company and some even in different companies in all parts of the country. Could we interview them? Yes. Did we want to interview them? No. Why? We discussed this in the first chapter of the book and stated the decision we reached.

Whose wealth of experience could be most easily and least costly tapped? Here the authors will have to divest themselves of some of their modesty. In our combined experience we had had considerable experience with counseling not only at Western but also in other institutions. As researchers, field workers, superiors, and subordinates we had listened with interest, sympathy, and some curiosity to persons who as our clients, subjects, subordinates, or superiors wanted to tell us about matters that concerned them. Our lives—it might be said—had been dedicated to this—sometimes rewarding and sometimes frustrating—experience. Should we now in the name of neutrality and objectivity not use it? Our answer was "No." We decided to utilize without shame or guilt our intuitive familiarity with the phenomena with which this book is concerned. As sensible persons and not as pseudo objectivists we decided to make use of all the resources available to us, including ourselves.

Why We Chose Not to Treat Personal Concerns Separately

But still another consideration clinched our decision to treat employee concerns in their organizational context. In the world today "personality" is not only a serious subject; it is also a very popular subject. Bookstores are filled with books on sex, Freud, the id, the ego, and the superego. Novels are teeming with persons suffering from all sorts of perversions, complexes, and personality disorders. These are the persons to whom the label personal concerns rather than work concerns most often apply. Such situations are filled with human interest.

As we said in Chapter I, the counseling program had little new light to throw on the serious side of these personality disorders, and the popular side of these problems we did not want to write about. Obviously the counselors met occasionally among the workers the alcoholic, the pervert, the neurotic, the psychopath, the psychotic, the person contemplating suicide, homicide, incest, larceny, desertion, and so on and on. In some cases the counselors were able to help. But were these cases the major objective of the counseling program? And about them did we have anything new to say? We did not think so.

The counselor also met workers who were contemplating whether they should get engaged, married, or divorced, have children, live with their in-laws, move to another neighborhood, take night courses, etc. How much space should we give to discussing these personal concerns? We did not think much. Not that the counselor did not meet many such situations and in many cases was helpful. But again it stressed these problems about which much more research had been done by marriage counselors, family counselors, career counselors, etc., than by the counselors in the counseling program at Hawthorne.

Then there were personal problems of a more pervasive sort. These are the problems which most of us face in the transition from (a) the child-parent relation to (b) the husband-wife relation to (c) the father-mother-child relation in which first as sons or daughters and second as husbands or wives and third as fathers or mothers, we try to grow up. This transition of role relationships from the family of orientation to the family of procreation we did not think was the unique experience of persons with personality disorders; they were the common experience of most of us.

Again the counselor met many such personal problems and also again in many instances was most helpful. But again did the counseling program have something to say that had not been said before by many sociologists? Again we did not think so except in Chapter IX where we will discuss briefly individual development in relation to job development.

So what experiences and data did we have that other disciplines had not researched before? In our opinion the counseling program at Hawthorne provided an unusual opportunity to see the constraints and opportunities in an industrial setting for the realization of the workers' needs. It was from this point of view that we wished to explore employee concerns. We felt that the most pervasive concerns of employees would center around their basic needs as human beings and reflect the constraints to their fulfillment in the organizational setting.

Three Sources of Employee Concerns

Figure 4.2 shows the model we shall be using for the understanding of the employee concerns we shall be considering in the next five chapters. It specifies the three previously mentioned interrelated components from which the concern arises. Two of them —company requirements and group values and norms—we shall treat as environmental constraints or opportunities for the realiza-

Figure 4.2

Major Sources of Employee Concerns

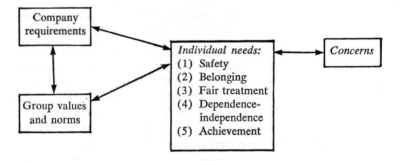

tion of the third component—employee needs. Let us begin by stating what we mean by each of these components.

Individual Needs

The first major source of employee concerns we thought would be found in what the individual himself brings to the work situation. He, of course, brings his own individual characteristics and personality traits as well as the competences and skills which he utilizes in performing his job and in meeting Company requirements. Here we wish to call special attention, however, to the needs which he seeks to fulfill at his place of work.

A. H. Maslow,[2] at Brandeis University, has provided us with a useful way of thinking about human needs which lends itself well to our purposes and we shall draw heavily from his work. He identifies in man's needs a hierarchy of prepotency such that until those lower down in the scale are satisfied, those higher up fail to emerge. Once man has satisfied his more basic needs—subsistence, safety, and social—they no longer motivate but instead allow higher orders of need to come into play. These higher needs, for self-esteem and self-fulfillment, when activated tend never to be satisfied. Unlike appetites which, when fed, become satisfied, needs for knowledge, creativity, and self-expression tend to feed on prior accomplishment. This theory is positive in the sense that it assumes that man, in striving to fulfill one order of need, is setting the stage for a higher one to emerge. He is thus oriented in the direction of growth as a person.

Maslow postulates five orders of needs: *physiological needs, safety needs, belonging and love needs, esteem needs,* and the *need for self-actualization.* The order of needs which we shall use, while generally following those of Maslow, has been modified for our purposes. For our purposes we shall speak largely of safety needs as most primary for the population studied but in doing so we do not deny the primacy of physiological needs, only that generally they were being met. We shall use safety needs and belonging needs exactly in the same sense as Maslow. But then we depart by stating the next order of needs in terms that made more sense with

[2] *Motivation and Personality* (New York, Harper & Brothers, 1954).

the data we had. Here then is the hierarchy of needs we postulated in our analysis:

(1) *Safety needs*—Securing, holding on to, protecting, and conserving the job as a source of a livelihood.

(2) *Friendship and belonging needs*—Satisfactory relations with fellow workers and supervision, commonly expressed as the need for belonging.

(3) *Needs for justice and fair treatment*—To be adequately rewarded for contributions in comparison with others.

(4) *Dependence—independence*—To be treated as a responsible adult in whom needs for both dependence and independence are recognized.

(5) *Needs for achievement*—Opportunity to develop in one's job, to become what one has the potentiality of becoming.

Company Requirements

The second source of concern we thought would be found in the demands made by the organization of the individual worker. These we expected would stem from the system of standards and the provisions made for rewarding workers who meet them and withholding or withdrawing rewards for those who did not. The more important of these are shown in Figure 4.3.

Every employee is expected by the Company to meet certain established standards with reference to output, quality of work, cost (utilization of manufacturing facilities and materials), and attendance. If he meets or excels in meeting these standards, the Company makes provisions for him to be rewarded. Failure to meet Company standards may be met by withholding rewards or by withdrawing them through actions ranging from reprimand to separation from the roll. Provisions for granting, withholding, or withdrawing rewards are commonly referred to as the formal incentive system.

Group Norms

We expected to find a third major source of employee concerns in the expectations of him by the work group of which he is a member. These would center around the work group's norms of behavior and the rewards to be obtained or withheld from con-

FIGURE 4.3

COMPANY STANDARDS AND REWARDS

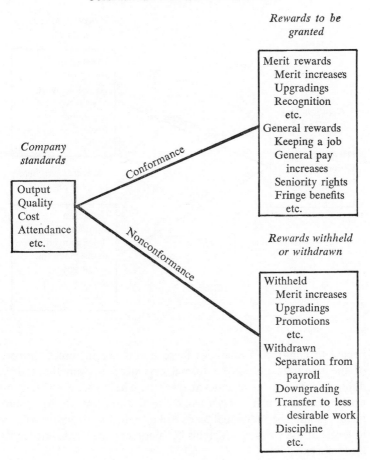

Rewards to be granted

> Merit rewards
>   Merit increases
>   Upgradings
>   Recognition
>   etc.
> General rewards
>   Keeping a job
>   General pay
>   increases
>   Seniority rights
>   Fringe benefits
>   etc.

Company standards

> Output
> Quality
> Cost
> Attendance
>   etc.

Conformance

Nonconformance

Rewards withheld or withdrawn

> Withheld
>   Merit increases
>   Upgradings
>   Promotions
>   etc.
> Withdrawn
>   Separation from
>   payroll
>   Downgrading
>   Transfer to less
>   desirable work
>   Discipline
>   etc.

forming or not conforming to them. The more important of these are shown in Figure 4.4.

Through daily interaction and association in a common situation, employees come to develop certain norms of behavior with reference to which the conduct of its individual members is ex-

FIGURE 4.4

GROUP NORMS AND REWARDS

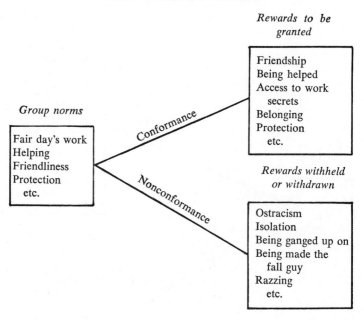

pected to conform. Sometimes these norms are in direct support of the requirements of the formal organization, sometimes they differ in one or more significant respects. These group norms generally pertain to a fair day's work and to requirements for group membership. The individual tends to be evaluated by his associates in terms of the ways in which his behavior signifies conformance to these norms.

Just as there are rewards available to the individual for meeting or excelling in Company standards, so there are rewards to him for conformance to group norms. The well-accepted person may have access to help from his co-workers if he seeks it and assistance in learning his job. These kinds of help may be very necessary to him in meeting the Company's requirements for continued employment. He can find in the work group a source of help, friendship (both inside and outside the plant), and protection—in short, a source of personal support and stability.

Forms of group discipline for nonconformance to their norms tend to be more immediately implemented and more personally expressed than those of the formal organization. They arise spontaneously in the system of interpersonal relations and are expressed in face-to-face daily interaction. Among the more common forms of group discipline are refusal of help and instruction, denial of friendship and group support, and expressions of hostility, such as casting blame, criticism, ganging up on the offender, making the offender the fall guy or the target of humor, sarcasm, ridicule, and subtle forms of hazing.

FIVE SYNDROMES OF CONCERN

In the next five chapters the above framework of analysis will be applied to five basic concerns of employees. In settling upon these five concerns the authors drew upon their intuitive familiarity with the phenomena as well as upon the recorded interviews available to them. The concerns identified are those pertaining to:

(1) Keeping a job
(2) Friendship and belonging
(3) Felt injustices
(4) Authority
(5) Job and individual development

It is important that one does not read into these five concerns something that is not implied by them. For example, it would be incorrect to treat them as being mutually exclusive and collectively exhaustive subclasses of employee concerns. This is why we called them "syndromes" rather than "categories" of concerns. In time there may be a way of classifying employee concerns more logically but this is *not* what we are doing here.

Also, it would be incorrect to expect that there should be any simple one-to-one correspondence between the manifest content of employee concerns and the above five syndromes of concern. Topics such as standards, supervision, and seniority, can appear and will appear in every one of our syndromes. Seniority, for example, has significance in relation to keeping a job. But it can also appear as a symbol or topic in relation to authority, fair treatment, etc.

Although each of these concerns is the outcome of the interaction among the three situational sources of concern we previously described, it will be well to remember that each of these three sources can vary in degree and kind. For example, employees can vary in their needs for affiliation and achievement. Likewise the requirements of the organization can be implemented by different leadership and interpersonal styles. Under these different conditions work groups can emerge with different values and norms of different intensities. This is why these concern syndromes may vary in importance for different individuals and groups and for the whole organization at different times.

What we will do, however, as we consider each of these syndromes, is to treat two of the sources (1) company requirements and (2) group norms as having certain pervasive characteristics while we explore the employee's hierarchy of needs one at a time in relation to them. So in one way each of our syndromes can be regarded as being a convenient way of talking about a very complex matter one step, that is, *one need* at a time. Using Maslow's hierarchy of needs concept, we will proceed from the employee's lower order needs for safety to his higher order needs for becoming a competent worker and person.

In following this procedure of treating the worker at one level of abstraction (need) at a time, there exists the danger of implying, "This is all he is and nothing more": for example, of implying that he is *just* a security-seeker (as in the case of syndrome 1), or that he is *just* a good Joe (as in the case of syndrome 2), or that he is *just* concerned about being treated unfairly (as in the case of syndrome 3), or that he is *just* counter-dependent (as in the case of syndrome 4), or that he *just* yearns for autonomy and self realization (as in the case of syndrome 5). So it will be well to reserve any of these conclusions until after the next five chapters are read. To us these syndromes are saying that collectively he is a bit of all these things, and at times and under different conditions he is one more so than the other, and that one will understand why this is so if one looks at the organizational environment in which he tries to realize his hierarchy of needs.

But these syndromes are more than just a way of allowing us to talk about one thing at a time. Each is a cluster of things that hang together in our modern technologically organized world of work. Each makes sense not logically but phenomenologically. This is why too we called them syndromes. At times one of them may loom large and like a "disease entity" seem to encompass the whole situation. But then, too, like a disease entity it may subside and not seem so dominant.

In settling upon these five concern syndromes there was one factor to which we gave great weight. Each syndrome had behavioral manifestations in actions as well as in words. The counselor saw them manifested while on the floor as well as while in the interviewing room. Each of these concerns can develop into semi-institutional forms of behavior, such as, for example, into accepted ways of not sticking your neck out and of how to keep your nose clean (see syndrome 1), to ways of getting along while also trying to get ahead (see syndrome 2), to routines and procedures for insuring fair and just treatment and for seeing that merit as well as seniority counts or vice versa (see syndrome 3), to ways of ingratiating yourself with the boss (see syndrome 4), and to ways of maintaining a social climate that rewards initiative, openness, and self development (see syndrome 5).

But now we hope we have said enough, not only to whet the appetite of the reader while he peruses the next five chapters but also to keep him from drawing any conclusion until he has completed reading all of them.

SUMMARY

In the next five chapters we will illustrate with examples the five major concern-syndromes of employees at work which we have identified. As we have shown, these syndromes were constructed in part from our intuitive familiarity with the phenomena and in part with the aid of the analytical scheme we brought to bear upon them. However, it should be added that in reviewing the existing recorded interviews at Hawthorne, these five syndromes manifested themselves with a degree of frequency which left little doubt in our own minds about their reality. We had no question that they were "there" (i.e., in the preoccupation of the workers as well as in their recorded interviews) but "how much" or "how often" we made no attempt to determine, except by the process of inspection we just mentioned.

Nor did we attempt to find out if these five concerns exhausted completely the repertoire of concerns at work the employees had. No statistical content analysis of the available recorded interviews was made. In no sense were these syndromes derived from any rigorous, analytical, systematic, statistical examination of the available written interviews.

We wish to emphasize the essentially clinical nature of these categories of concerns, because in the development of knowledge such categories and the generalizations we will make in terms of them later belong to its earlier stages and so have a limited status. But they can be useful so long as they do not masquerade for what they are not and they remain just what they are—no more, no less —as something one can *point to*. This is the way we will use them in the next five chapters, and by that means try to convince the reader, as we have convinced ourselves, of their reality. But in the realm of science this is not the highest form of persuasion; it is only one of its earlier rudimentary forms.

CHAPTER V

Keeping a Job

IN THIS CHAPTER we will be looking at the industrial environment in relation to the worker's needs for the safety and security of his job. We shall proceed by (1) identifying the major elements in this concern syndrome, (2) illustrating the various ways in which the concern is expressed, and (3) showing the more general ways in which employees tend to resolve these concerns and the significance of these forms of resolution to the organization and to the individual.

We will be addressing ourselves, not to the problems of unemployment, the problems confronting the man who has lost his job, but to the concerns aroused in the person remaining employed that this eventually might occur to him. By focusing upon the ways in which the employee seeks to ward off or avert the loss of his job we can better see the personal and institutional consequences of the syndrome when it is aroused.

ELEMENTS IN THE JOB SECURITY SYNDROME

The major elements we wish to consider in the job security syndrome are shown in Figure 5.1. The concern about keeping a job is seen as arising from the interplay of (1) the need for safety or job security, (2) the job which the employee must hold to meet his minimum safety needs, and (3) the company's requirements for its own economic survival.

The Need for Safety

As Maslow uses this term, and as we shall also use it, safety is a need which when aroused can be as all pervasive as hunger. In

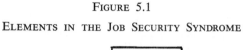

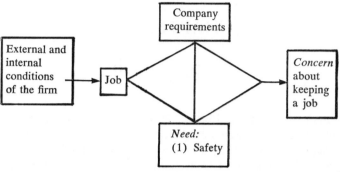

industrial organizations it is expressed in terms of holding on to and protecting what one has, in stabilizing one's work routines, in resisting change, and in all sorts of defenses against real or fancied threats to one's security.[1]

The Job in Relation to Safety Needs

In this syndrome we are abstracting the most elemental aspect of a job. We are conceiving the job as something the worker must keep and protect in order to meet his elemental subsistence needs. From this point of view the job becomes simply a task to be performed and the worker is, in effect, a pair of hands; we will not be considering whether the job is the one best suited to the worker's interests and training; the job becomes equated to man's daily bread.

Company Requirements in Relation to Safety Needs

Company requirements for its effective functioning and survival are related to the worker's safety needs (1) through changes which he can interpret as a threat to his job, and (2) through the stand-

---

[1] The industrial reader will note that as used here the term safety is not to be confused with the needs to which safety practices are addressed.

ards, rules, and evaluational processes in terms of which he feels his job performance is being evaluated.

Forces making for changes in jobs

There are powerful forces at work within and without the organization which may threaten a man's job regardless of how well he does it or however much he tries to hold on to it. These are shown in Figure 5.2.

FIGURE 5.2

FORCES LEADING TO CHANGES IN JOBS

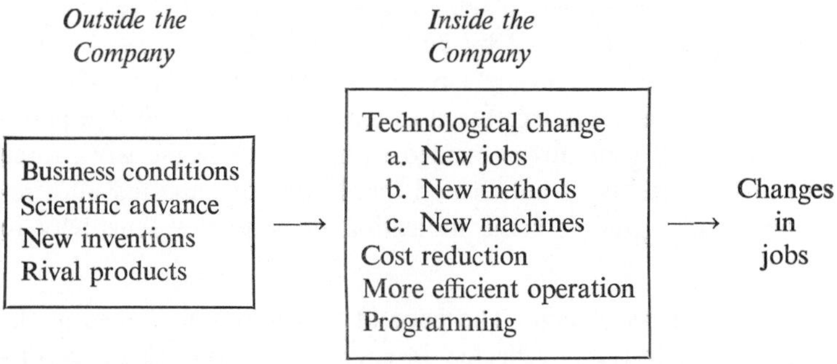

Outside the Company	*Inside the Company*	

Business conditions
Scientific advance
New inventions
Rival products
	Technological change
	  a. New jobs
	  b. New methods
	  c. New machines
	Cost reduction
	More efficient operation
	Programming
		Changes in jobs

⟶   ⟶

The influences within the company making for changes in jobs are those of technological change, cost reduction, improvements in operating efficiency, and better programming. These internal changes are influenced by forces arising outside the company itself which are often beyond its control. Among these are general business conditions, scientific advance, new inventions, and competition from rival products. The response of the industrial organization to these external forces and to those originating internally creates new jobs and changes or cancellations in existing jobs. The most dominant factors are business conditions, technological change, and cost reduction.

Business conditions. Business conditions affect employment opportunities directly through changes in work schedules. As work schedules increase, jobs are created and employees are added. As schedules decline, jobs are cancelled and employees are let go.

During the years of the counseling program, 1936 to 1956, there were ten years during which concerns about layoffs were quite widely expressed by employees at Hawthorne.[2] These are marked on Figure 5.3 which shows changes in the year end population of the Hawthorne Works during the twenty-year span covered by the program. The years 1936 and 1937 were years of recovery from the great depression. In 1938 there was a sharp recession shared by the economy generally. From 1938 to 1947 there was a steady rise interrupted by the change from war to peacetime manufacture following V–J Day in 1945. From 1947 to 1950 there was a steady decline partly due to the 1948 recession but largely due to the transfer of work to new plants. There was substantial recovery in 1951 and 1952 followed by cutbacks in 1953 and 1954, again chiefly because of a business recession. The years in which considerable concern was expressed to the counselors about the possibility of layoff generally coincided with declines in the work force but in some instances anticipated the decline or persisted after recovery. This gives us some indication of employee sensitivity to this threat.

Technological change. The pace of technological change in the telephone industry is reflected in such innovations as direct distance dialing, automatic message accounting, telstar, and picturephone. These are but surface manifestations of vast changes in the underlying technology. These changes extend to all phases of telephone communications manufacture.

At Hawthorne almost the entire product line has changed within the past twenty years with the consequence that scarcely a job has remained untouched. Jobs such as relay assembly and bank wiring around which much of the Hawthorne research of the late 1920's

[2] During the years included in the analysis shown in Figure 4.1, which gave us the figure of 36% of the work force expressing concern, three of the four years were periods of sharp cutback in the work force. These years were, therefore, atypical in this respect and the percentage of employees expressing concern for this reason was probably higher than any time since the 1938 recession when fear of unemployment was widespread. This does not necessarily mean that the percentage of the work force expressing concern for all reasons was higher during these years than at other times. One need only recall the problems and anxieties of the war years under conditions of full employment for confirmation of this.

Figure 5.3

Number of Employees on Hawthorne Roll: 1936–1956
(showing years in which fears of layoff
were a major expressed concern)

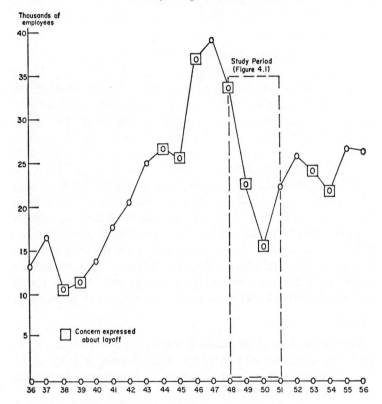

and early 1930's centered no longer exist except as small local operations to meet special needs. Both have been replaced by new designs and automated processes. Even such an established trade as tool making is undergoing rapid changes by the development of new processes of tool manufacture.

What this means to us here is that the task, the one thing more than any other that helps the worker establish himself, cannot be taken by him for granted. It is subject to change, and when it does change the man who holds it must acquire new skills or change to a different kind of work. If we visualize the worker as desperately trying to protect his job, we can easily understand his apprehension of its loss through the processes of technological development and change. We have here, consequently, another significant source of concern. It is all pervasive, ever present, and impersonal in origin and application.

Cost reduction. One of the desired effects of technological change is to reduce costs of manufacture. In addition there are a host of other activities which go under the heading of cost reduction: reductions in direct labor cost through improved methods, machines, and materials; reduction of indirect costs in relation to direct costs; improved procurement, material handling, and shipping; reductions in inventory—in short, careful scrutiny of every element of cost. The magnitude of these operations can be judged from the fact that in 1964 the Company's prices to the Bell System were 14% lower than in 1950 even though labor costs had risen 86% and raw materials 29% since that time. Some of these changes affect the worker's job by eliminating it, combining it, or changing it. While some aspects of cost reduction may not change jobs or job assignments, its total effect is that cost reduction becomes another major factor alongside technological change and business conditions which, through changes in jobs, poses a threat to job security.

Company standards

The standards in terms of which the worker is evaluated are extensive in scope and often complex. The following is a list of the chief standards applicable to workers at Hawthorne during the years of the counseling program:

(1) *Output Standards*
   (a) *Expected hourly output.* Based on time standards, compiled from time studies, specifying the time required to complete an operation by an average experienced operator.
   (b) *Bogies.* An expected level of output established by line supervision for the purpose of bringing output up to standard. Usually the equivalent of expected hourly output.

(c) *Learning time.* Specified time allowed to learn a job performed under a wage incentive plan, that is, to achieve expected hourly output. The individual does not participate fully in the earnings of the payment group during the specified learning period.

(2) *Quality Standards.* Established by engineering studies of technical requirements for effective functioning and durability.

(3) *Earnings Standards.* What an average experienced operator should produce to meet minimum guaranteed piece work earnings—usually 15% over day rate or 100% efficiency. (Output required corresponds to expected hourly output.)

(4) *Attendance Standards.* The hours of work required and their arrangement into tours of duty. Observance of routines for registering in and out on time clocks, passes for admission to and exit from the plant or special buildings or organizations such as medical, personnel, etc., related to the implementation of attendance standards.

(5) *Safety Standards.* Prescribed by a hazards engineering group to protect the worker from injury due to accidents, exposure to dust, acids, fumes, radiation, noise, etc.

(6) *Behavioral Standards.* Factory rules relating to such matters as noninterference with the work of others, talking, unauthorized smoking, obscenity, cheating, stealing, gambling on company property, and destruction of company property.

This list of standards suggests their nature and scope. We should note that they are not of the same order of importance in determining whether an employee will be separated from the roll for failure to meet them. If he meets standards of output and quality, he will by that fact normally have met standards relating to payment, learning time, and use of materials. On the other hand, he can meet performance standards and still be terminated for failure to meet attendance, safety, or disciplinary standards.

In summary, our brief examination of the industrial environment at Hawthorne shows that there were present in varying degrees at all times many forces which might activate an individual's elemental concerns about keeping his job. Let us next illustrate some of the various ways in which the concerns thus aroused were expressed.

How Concerns About Keeping a Job Were Expressed

Concerns About Being Laid Off

The primacy and urgency of safety needs makes any threat to them appear to be dangerous. As illustrative of the ease with which concerns about losing a job can be touched off, the following incident may be cited.

Three months after the new supervisor was transferred to this work group, efficiency improved and it was possible to combine several jobs, thus creating a problem of surplus help. Three operators were selected for transfer, two of whom were outstanding in performance. They were notified two weeks before their transfer was to take place. Rumors grew out of this and immediately there was considerable apprehension expressed among most of the operators. "Was the combining of jobs eliminating operators?" "Had there been a decrease in schedules?" "Who would be next to go?" "Would a layoff follow?" These questions persisted even though the supervisor tried to explain to them that there was plenty of work in the plant and that none of them would be laid off.

Once a layoff starts, speculation often shifts to who will be affected, how deep it will be, and how long it will last. Employees watch closely to see if, by observing those who are selected for layoff, they can determine the severity of the decline by the policy being followed. If the policy is to weed out some undesirable longer service employees through discharge before cutting very deeply into shorter service ranks through layoff, one is likely to hear immediately that the company is laying off people with eight or nine years of service and employees who thought they were safe may begin to worry. If married men are let go while single or married women are kept on, feelings of injustice may arise among the men. If shop people are laid off and salaried people are kept on, one may hear, "Why doesn't the Company get rid of those free-riders; they don't do anything anyway," and so on and on.

If a period of layoff continues and becomes general, pessimism seems to grow and fill the air. The subject is then on everyone's tongue—"I wonder when it will end," "So-and-so lost his house," "Jim's boy had to quit school and go to work," "I wonder what

they will do about it," "What's that government good for anyway," etc. To anyone who lived through the depression of the
1930's the all pervasive atmosphere of pessimism, gloom, and de-
feat will be remembered. A sense of impending disaster filled the
land which seemingly escaped no one.

Concerns About Job Transfers

The forces making for changes in jobs, shown in Figure 5.2, may
lead to the loss of employment but they also may make for frequent transfers of workers to other jobs. Many of the resistances
to being transferred to other work, while sometimes expressed as
a dislike for the work itself, may be rooted in a feeling of job in-
security. To change from a known job situation to an unknown one
may carry risks of failure on the new job or increased vulnerability to bumping or layoff. This fear is readily apparent in such statements as the following:

"About the time I start getting up my efficiency I'm moved to another job. Then I have to start all over again. They tell me it is good
to be versatile but I would like to stay with one job until I can make
a showing on it. Otherwise how can they tell how I compare with
others?"

*　　*　　*　　*　　*

"I wonder whether I did the right thing in refusing to accept that
transfer with a down-grading. Maybe it would have been better to take
it and protect my years of service. The way I sit now I might get
knocked off."

*　　*　　*　　*　　*

"When I was transferred to this job the boss told me that I should
take it because I wouldn't have to take a cut in earnings. But it is new
to me and I haven't been on it long enough to compare as favorably
with the rest of the gang as I did in the old department. And here my
seven years of service don't seem to cut so much ice. In fact, there are
only three with less than that. So I sort of feel vulnerable over here."

*　　*　　*　　*　　*

"When you get pushed around from job to job like I've been, without any improvement, you begin to wonder whether it's because someone wants you or because everyone wants to get rid of you."

*　　*　　*　　*　　*

"When I got into relay adjusting I felt I had something real good and I really went at it hard. I learned how to adjust every relay that came in and there were only a few fellows who could do better. Then the work slacked off and I was transferred over here. Since then I've been on three jobs that anyone could do. They could just about hire someone off the street to do this work."

These comments illustrate some of the variety of ways in which job transfers tend to activate the job security syndrome. The worker often feels that he has lost his anchor, that there is nothing that he can hold on to so he can dig his toes in. He has a job but feels he has lost his security.

Concerns About Standards

The following comments illustrate some of the variety of ways in which concerns about standards were expressed.

"They came in here and timed this job when we had a long running job and not many things going wrong. They took that as the standard but ever since we've had short runs of many different types. We complain about it but they tell us that these changes shouldn't make any difference if you're onto your job." (This employee brought out in the interview that he was afraid of failure on his job.)

*   *   *   *   *

"The girls told me that if I turned out more than 1,100 parts a day, I would kill the job."

*   *   *   *   *

"If you turn out more than 800 units a day, you're just going to make it tough for yourself and everybody else. If you turn out more, they'll just raise the rate and ask you to do more for the same money. And then there are those slower guys in there, they would just be that much worse off, they might lose their jobs."

*   *   *   *   *

"She told us no matter what happens we have to look busy. . . ."

*   *   *   *   *

"The Group Chief tells us we're not supposed to talk, he got after me yesterday, but I just can't help it. . . . I've got to watch my step after this though."

*   *   *   *   *

"I was lucky to get a job here in the first place and if I asked the department chief for a transfer so soon he'd probably think I was ungrateful. . . ."

* * * * *

"I was going to go up and talk this over with the boss and then we started hearing about layoffs and so I decided to keep my mouth shut."

* * * * *

"I just don't see how I can change to that later shift. I thought of asking the supervisor to let me stay on the day shift but I'm pretty new here and I have to keep my job."

We can see from these comments that concerns about standards tend to become an ever-present dimension of the job security syndrome. The worker is never wholly freed from the concern that what he does is being evaluated and may count in determining his job security. His concern may be directed toward the standard, toward the way it is implemented, or toward those responsible for developing it. The underlying concern is fear of punishment, the most extreme form of which is dismissal. In this perspective the standard and anything that in the employee's view is related to it assume significance.

How These Concerns Become Institutionalized

We have illustrated some of the various ways in which concerns about keeping a job are verbally expressed. Here we will examine some of the ways in which they are reflected in the worker's behavior. This will enable us to see more clearly how these concerns tend to become institutionalized, that is, how they lead to forms of behavior which tend to be commonly accepted and form a persistent, enduring aspect of the industrial culture.

A Case of Keeping a "Bank"

The following is an excerpt from a counselor's record:

"Since I have gained the confidence of the employees and supervisors in this section they seem to welcome my presence, and I have been spending a good deal of time on the floor going from one work position to another and chatting with each of them while he works.

This has enabled me to keep in daily touch with the employees and also to learn a great deal about the various jobs and the employees' work habits.

"One of the more interesting practices is that of concealing pans of completed parts. They call this their bank. The supervisors are aware of and condone this practice. The operators regard their bank as security against emergencies. In case one of them isn't feeling well or for some other reason fails to meet his quota, he draws on the bank and then replenishes it when things are running smoothly. The supervisors look upon the bank in much the same way. If there is a machine breakdown or a shortage of help because of absences, they have a ready reserve for meeting their schedules.

"Considering the function of the bank in this instance we can see that it works (1) to stabilize the relations of the employees to the supervisor—their output holds up to the accepted level day after day so no questions are asked, (2) to stabilize the supervisor's relations with the operators—shortages of parts for which he is responsible are not as disruptive, and (3) to stabilize the supervisor's relations with his superiors. He gets recognition for keeping the group's output up week in and week out and has no ups and down to explain. The bank thus serves to help stabilize the entire work unit."

Here we see one of the ways in which concerns about job security are expressed in work behavior. Through tacit consent of all those involved an accepted way of dealing with work emergencies has developed which provides them with an increased feeling of security.

A Case of a "Club House"

This is another experience related by a counselor.

"I was coming back from the main restaurant with a man I had interviewed there. It was about half an hour before quitting time and he said, 'Say, have you seen our club house?' I said, 'You mean over at the gymnasium?' 'No,' he said, 'I'll show you.' He then led me into an out-of-the-way passage and we finally came to a little used storage area. There a little space had been cleared away and a few tables and chairs had been set up. Several of the chairs were occupied by men the employee knew very well and he introduced me to them. They were all in the same line of work. He said they usually ate lunch there and played cards. We stayed there and chatted a little while and then one of them looked at his watch and said, 'Well it's about time to go,' whereupon they all got up and left. The fellow I was with said, 'This comes in handy if you have a little time to kill before getting back.' I asked him what determined that and he said, 'Well, you got to kind of regulate things. There's no point in getting a new project started this late in the day.' "

The usual expression for this behavior is "spinning out the work." In this instance it seemed to be an accepted practice by the work group.

A Case of a Warning Whistle

One of the counselors recorded the following experience in his daily log.

"I walked into my territory about nine o'clock this morning. The men all had their heads down and were working at top speed. Suddenly I heard a shrill whistle coming from a far corner of the room. Everyone looked up and they seemed to slack up in their work pace. Then one of them let out a big laugh and said, 'I guess Tony doesn't know you, he must have thought you were a rate setter.' "

Here we see another protective norm built up around output. There is a widely held belief that if a piece-rate setter catches an operator working at top speed he may cut the piece rate on the assumption that the operator was holding back when his timings were made. This also relates to spinning out the work and in some instances to protecting work secrets.

A Case of an Intercepted Suggestion

A counselor had spent an entire interview listening to a worker trying to clarify a suggestion he had been working on for speeding up the work process. If adopted, the employee thought, it would result in substantial savings and earn him a sizable reward through the Company's suggestion system. When he had spelled out all the details of the suggestion to his satisfaction, the employee thanked the counselor for his assistance and the interview terminated.

A few weeks later the counselor visited the employee at his place of work and asked him how he had made out with his suggestion. This is what he said.

"I guess it was all a waste of time. I had it all set to go but thought I'd try it out first on one of the fellows I know. That's where I made my mistake. When he saw it he hit the ceiling and accused me of trying to capitalize on something they all knew about. He said if I sent it in I'd live to regret it because we would have our rates cut and we would just have to turn out more work for the same money. The way he talked I thought they would all be down on me so I decided to skip it."

Here again there appears to have been a protective norm built up around output. In this case it clearly relates to protecting work secrets and comes in as a barrier to upward communication.

A Case of Withholding Short Cuts

Charlie was an inspector who had recently been transferred to a different job and was concerned about meeting the inspection standards required in his work:

"Downstairs I didn't have anyone particularly to compete with as I was the only one. Up here we got a variety of people, including some old timers who know all the short cuts, know how much you have to do to get the job done and know how you can make the thing look tough and really not be, in other words know how to get by with the least amount of effort and the most amount of recognition. Well, that's okay except it's a little tough on the newcomer because they're not at all willing to show you anything because they figure you'll come out there and take it away from them."

Here we see a work group refusing to share their work secrets with one of their members. Charlie is a newcomer and they apparently don't know whether they can trust him not to divulge them to others outside the group. So they play it safe by keeping him at arm's length.

A Case of an Unused Conveyor

In a specially designed shop for the fabrication and finishing of a telephone component a conveyor was constructed for transporting the component from one work station to another. After a number of trials the workmen demonstrated to their supervisors' satisfaction that it wouldn't work. As a consequence they reverted to their old work habits and the conveyor remained idle for several months even though engineering studies showed that it would speed up the work and reduce costs of manufacture.

Here we have an instance to resistance to a technological innovation which disturbed the customary work habits of a group. Resistance to change is one of the more general manifestations of the job security syndrome.

Summary

In the above illustrations we have been looking at some of the more significant ways in which concerns about job security are reflected in work behavior. These forms of behavior center around and give expression to group norms which spontaneously develop as ways of coping with safety needs under the constraints encountered in the industrial environment. These norms specify how the members of a work group should behave to protect their collective security. In the next section we will look at how these norms pose a problem to the individual in choosing a course to follow in resolving his own safety needs.

Forms of Individual Response to Protective Norms

Within a work group whose concerns about job security are reflected in protective norms such as we have indicated, every individual is confronted with the alternative of conforming or not conforming to them. By conforming he obtains the rewards of membership, to be developed in the next chapter, but he does so at a certain cost, namely, by sacrificing the rewards an outstanding performance record might bring. Nonconformance, on the other hand, may bring the rewards accruing from an outstanding performance record but at the cost of the rewards to be obtained from group membership. These alternate types of accommodation are both protective; the difference is in the route chosen to achieve protection. The one tends to do only that which is expected of him. His behavior is restrictive, restraining, circumscribing in nature. The other chooses a different route and seeks security by establishing an outstanding performance record. These alternate types of response are reflected in the following two cases. The first is that of a woman worker who was producing all she could to protect her job.

The Case of Big May

The case of Big May illustrates one type of response to restrictive output norms.

Big May was foreign born and could neither read nor write English. She was 40 years old, had three years' service, and was employed as a machine operator. She had two children, a boy aged 18 and a girl 16, whom she had supported since infancy, her husband having deserted her shortly after the girl was born. She took great pride in her children, they were musically inclined, the boy was very bright and wanted to go to college, and she provided a good home for them. Her life revolved around her children and her work.

The counselor had been told by the supervisor and several operators that they didn't think much of Big May, that she was a rate buster and continually tried to show them up in output and this they resented. The supervisor suggested that the counselor interview Big May and some of the others.

Big May was glad to go with the counselor. On the way to the counseling room the counselor asked her if she would like a cup of coffee.

"Oh, I don't drink coffee except at breakfast and lunch. Then in the evening I have a glass of warm milk before I go to bed. That keeps me nice and strong. Look at the muscles I got here. They're just as big as a man's. That's from doing a lot of hard work and eating the way I should."

Big May then went on to talk about her children, her husband and how he had left her, and the difficult time she had making ends meet while on relief. She talked at some length about a previous job where every time she started to make good piece work earnings the boss transferred her so she quit and came to Western.

"I knew I'd have to start at the bottom again but that didn't make any difference. I came anyway. I'm making more money now than some of the girls who have been here five years. I know they don't like it because I turn out away over my rate. I turn out three or four hundred a day over my rate and those girls all come around and tell me I shouldn't work that way. They make fun of me and tell me to relax and take a cup of coffee once in a while. They don't like to have me show them up.

"You know I'm working for the bosses, not the girls. I put out just as much work a day as I can. I don't care what those girls say. They come around and say a lot of nasty things that don't agree with me at all, but I just don't care. I told them that I bet when the layoff came I wouldn't get laid off if I was a good worker and did all the work I was supposed to.

"There's Rose in our department. She won't speak to me at all. She's working on that job she is on now, and I walked over to her and I said, 'You know, I know how to do that job a lot easier, so that you can put out a lot more work.' She told me to shut up and mind my own business, not to pay any attention to her job, do my own the way I wanted to. Well, that made me plenty mad, I didn't say any more to her and just decided to leave her alone. . . .

"The only way we can work is to go our own ways. I wouldn't want her to tell me how to run my job because I know I can put out more work than she can and that's why I am here, because I just have to have that job and I'm hoping that when the layoff comes again they'll think twice before they let me go. I stayed on the last time when they let girls with six months' more service go. The bosses must have known how much I needed the job and what a good worker I am."

Big May's central concern is the route she has chosen to keep her job. In pursuit of this objective she strives for excellence in output even at the cost of incurring group enmity. Her comments about her healthy diet and keeping strong suggest her desire to keep physically fit for her job. She puts out all the work she can in order to build up a good record so that "when the layoff comes," which she regards as inevitable, she will win out over longer service women by keeping her job.

The Case of Art Tray

This case concerns a young man who came to the Company because he thought it offered more opportunity than his previous place of employment and he was desirous of getting ahead. The counselor held six off-the-job interviews with him during his first year of employment. The first interview was initiated by the counselor at the request of the employee's supervisor who said the employee was failing on his job as a relay adjuster and that he might have to dismiss him. We have abstracted from the voluminous record of interviews only those portions which illustrate how group norms may influence the course an individual takes in a significantly different way from that chosen by Big May. In doing so we shall follow the chronology in which the interviews were taken, beginning with the young man on his first assignment.

First Interview (February 9)

In this interview the employee spoke at length of his feelings of frustration in learning the job, his fear that he might be dismissed, and his job aspirations.

"I know that my efficiency is down and my defects are up, but as hard as I try I don't seem to get anywhere. I feel like there was a 500 pound weight on the floor and I try to lift it up but can't . . . I went up to see my supervisor and told him how I felt about the job and he said I fooled around too much and if I didn't catch on pretty soon there wasn't anything else they could do but let me out. But, gosh, I don't want to be let out of here, I quit another job to come here . . . I'd like to get a job where I could be more active, maybe something around machines . . . The way I feel about a job is that I'd rather be on a job that I can do well, and possibly become the boss, than work on a job where I could never get anywhere. I would rather be a ditch digger and know I could do ditch digging and possibly become the boss of all the ditch diggers even though that job wouldn't pay as much as relay adjusting."

The remainder of this interview was taken up in his reviewing his plans for getting more education (he had only finished the eighth grade) and his plans to marry a girl who had a high school education and whose two brothers had graduated from the university. The picture was that of a young man who spoke of high aspirations and was trying to find himself on a job he found tedious and unrewarding.

Second Interview (February 12)

In his second interview he said he had been moved under a different instructor and was doing much better.

"Here it is only 2:15 and I've got 320 springs to my credit. That's about twice as many as I ever did before in a whole day. Of course, I don't think I'll turn all of those in because they will make my efficiency jump too quick. I'll hold some of those until Monday and that way make my increase in efficiency more gradual. I think it's a lot better when a fellow does it that way, than to one day be doing very little and the next day to jump up all of a sudden. They're liable to wonder about that, and I don't want any question about my production."

Why, when he has achieved a good record, doesn't he record it for the supervisor to see? Is he trying to play it safe? It appears so. But not safe enough to satisfy the supervisor as develops in his fourth interview. His third interview was largely personal.

Fourth Interview (April 21)

The employee began this interview by stating that he had seen the Personnel Department about getting a transfer to machine work or some other job he might be interested in. But when he spoke to his supervisor about it he found that the supervisor had apparently got the same idea and had already arranged for him to be transferred to a punch press job. This gave him some qualms about his standing.

"When I asked him why he was transferring me he said he had to get rid of some of his people. That doesn't sound quite right because they're bringing in men from cable forming and wiring and they're going to teach them relay adjusting. That doesn't quite add up. . . . I didn't say anything because I didn't want to cross anybody. That would only get me into a jam. . . . If I stay on relay adjusting and I refuse transfers, I figure that eventually they'll let me out and I don't want that because, after all, I need a job. Honestly, I felt I was doing O.K. but apparently they don't think I'm going along so hot. But I'm not sure whether I want to go on a punch press or not. I ought to have a choice . . . I guess I've got to buckle down here and get my job down pat because otherwise it's my tail and, as I said, I can't afford to lose my job."

After some further discussion the employee decided to accept the transfer. The fifth interview was concerned largely with his plans for attending night school provided he could get a transfer to a different shift. This request, the counselor later learned, could be granted only if the employee could find someone to change places with him, and this he could not arrange. The sixth interview finds him quite happy with his punch press job and apparently doing well at it.

Sixth Interview (September 17)

"The job is really going a lot better here . . . you know I'm getting so that the fellows—some of them, the new ones—are coming to see me and ask questions about the presses and things like that, and that makes me feel pretty good . . . You know when they come up to you it means that they're sort of giving you a little authority of some kind. Then there's an old man over there—he can't read or write English.

He comes up to me every night and asks me to make out his bogey sheet. Well, I like that too. You know, all these things help—you're not just another pea in the pod when they act like that. I feel like I'm getting to be somebody over here."

Then there come the following statements which seem incongruous with all he has said about his desire to get ahead.

"You know, meeting the output on those presses is really simple. . . . To tell you the truth most of those bogeys are set too low. Any of the fellows can make them if they want to, but we just meet the bogey and let it go at that because if that's all the bosses want, why that's all we're going to give them."

The counselor asked him whether some of the fellows didn't exceed the bogey.

"No, they don't—We get together pretty much on that and talk things over. There's only one fellow that ever went over the bogey and he's an outcast now. Nobody talks to him and he has to eat lunch by himself. They just don't bother with him because they figure if he don't want to play ball with them, why heck, what do they care about him?

· · · · ·

"Say, I just thought. They're bringing some punch press men over from the other side of the plant. Their bogeys are pretty darn high and they can beat ours without half trying. Maybe that's why they are bringing them in, to show us up. That's not going to be so good for us. The supervisors will begin to wonder what we've been doing all the time but then, what the heck, there's no sense in doing more than you're supposed to."

We can readily see the contrast in the ways in which Big May and Art Tray responded to protective norms built up around job security. Big May repudiated them by achieving an outstanding performance record. Art Tray at times talked as though he aspired to the same goals as Big May but the route he chose was distinctly different. He seemed oriented toward meeting minimum standards and little more. By so doing his behavior was in accordance with group norms around output and he apparently found safety there rather than in outstanding task performance.

GENERAL SUMMARY

We can summarize this chapter with reference to Figure 5.4 which shows the major outcomes of the job security syndrome (p. 108).

We have been examining the most elemental need postulated for the work population considered, the need to keep and not lose a job. We examined the constraints to the fulfillment of this need commonly encountered in the industrial setting and found that they were of two general kinds, those arising from technico-economic forces and those implicit in the system of standards. Whatever the source, we found that the concerns they gave rise to were the same and these concerns centered around keeping and holding a job.

We next looked at the ways in which this general concern was reflected in employee comments and attitudes and found that they were not confined to the job sector as such but tended to become generalized and to be projected upon the entire constellation of forces impinging upon the worker and his job.

We then looked at the ways in which these attitudes were expressed in the overt behavior of employees in relation to one another in the work group and found that they gave rise, in part, to all kinds of restrictive norms expressed in such phenomena as resistance to change, protection of trade secrets, restriction of output, and resistance to authority.

Finally we examined the ways in which individuals in their actual work behavior responded to group norms around job security and identified two alternate courses which were chosen. One of these courses was that in which the worker sought to achieve job security by an outstanding performance record. The other was that in which the worker sought to protect his job by playing it safe and by conformance to group norms. Taken together these manifestations form a syndrome which when activated tend to dominate all other work concerns.

SOME FURTHER REMARKS

In this chapter we have refrained from introducing qualifications which might detract from our main theme. Now we are in a better

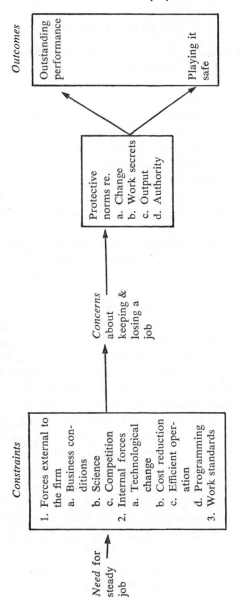

FIGURE 5.4

OUTCOMES OF THE JOB SECURITY SYNDROME

position to do this. It will have occurred to the reader that some of the evidence available may belie the elemental significance we have attributed to keeping a job. If it is so vital, why, it may be asked, do some workers quit their jobs or seemingly welcome a layoff? The fact that they do act this way seems to suggest that the need we speak of may no longer be as vital in our society as we have assumed it to be.

To this we would answer that there are instances in which holding a job does not appear to be too vital, for example, the housewife who is working to augment her husband's savings, or the young man working to earn pocket money for his school term, or the girl working until she gets married. While these come readily to mind as exceptions, at the level we are considering the need, they are not. What we are in effect saying is that in our society the main breadwinner can ordinarily take care of the basic needs of those dependent upon him and, if needed, the government or the union may, under certain conditions, make other resources available to him. But without bread man goes hungry and when he is hungry that need dominates. This is the point we are making.

The other apparent exception is the long service employee whose job is protected by the presence of shorter service employees, who would be laid off first. Given enough service and a sufficiently large number of shorter service employees, there was little or no likelihood that a person at Hawthorne would be laid off. For these people, would not the threat we speak of be such a remote possibility as not to be a matter of concern at all? To this we would reply yes, there were thousands of employees at Hawthorne whose employment would not be threatened by even a big depression and for them the threat of unemployment was of no concern. The threat of losing a specific job due to downgrading, bumping, and transfers was very real, however, as was the ever present system of standards. The factors that tend to evoke a defensive response were still present although not in the same degree perhaps as among shorter service employees.

In summary, we can say that under certain conditions there were large groups of employees whose safety needs were being satisfied. At times, as, for example, during periods of stable or rising employment, there were possibly as many as 95% of the work force for whom this was not the dominant concern expressed in their interviews. This is one of the paradoxes of this concern. It may not be uppermost in the worker's thinking during good times, but when we look at his actual behavior we find it is being manifested on all sides. The point is that the concern becomes institutionalized and influences his behavior in the same sense that all our other social codes do—automatically and without much conscious intent. The very latency of this concern syndrome even under good conditions attests to its primacy.

CHAPTER VI

Friendship and Belonging

IN EXAMINING concerns related to keeping and losing a job, we considered the worker in relation to his safety needs. The job was thus conceived in elemental terms as providing three square meals a day and nothing more. Of course, man does not live by bread alone except in the special circumstances we have assumed. He wants more reward from a job than a meal ticket, and he wants the job itself to be something more than sheer drudgery. Having satisfied his safety needs, other orders of needs begin to be felt and these increase the demands he makes of his job.

The need we are to consider is the need for friendship and belonging or congenial work relations. The importance of this need is evident in the family, the church, the school, and in the proliferation of lodges, clubs, and other forms of association. That these same needs manifest themselves at work and become a dimension of work concerns has been well documented in many research studies as well as in the counselors' experiences.

In this chapter we will proceed as in the preceding chapter, first, by identifying the major elements in the belonging syndrome, second, by illustrating the ways in which concerns about friendship and belonging are expressed, and, finally, by showing the ways in which these concerns are resolved and the significance of these forms of resolution for the organization and the individual.

ELEMENTS IN THE BELONGING SYNDROME

The general elements we shall be using in looking at these concerns are shown in Figure 6.1.

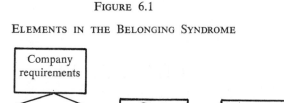

FIGURE 6.1

ELEMENTS IN THE BELONGING SYNDROME

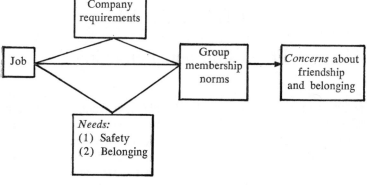

The Need for Friendship and Belonging

We use the terms friendship and belonging to express man's need for association with others. In industrial situations the fulfillment of the need to belong is expressed in such terms as feeling a part of, included in, or being a member of, a work group. To achieve this condition the individual must be acceptable to the work group and their values and norms of behavior must be acceptable to him. The needs involved are viewed as being less primal than needs for job security, yet they are brought into play in every work situation simply because work situations are peopled and supervised. Coping with these relations is to be regarded as an inevitable consequence of holding a job.

The Job in Relation to Belonging Needs

The job the worker holds is related to his needs for friendship and belonging in that it determines the group with which he will be associated in direct face-to-face work relations. He does not select the employees or the supervisors with whom he will be associated; the company does. The status of the job, its relation to other jobs in the flow of work, its requirements for initiating action on others or accepting action initiated by others are all determined by the job the worker holds, and all these factors have a bearing upon the position he will occupy in the group. For example, whether he is a trucker or an inspector will make a difference in his position in the work group. The job is thus, in this context, not just something to hold on to; it is also something that determines his associates and serves to give him a place among them. We are here speaking at a rather elementary level; we are not implying that the position he may ultimately hold or the esteem in which he comes to be held by others is determined only by the job he holds—far from it. His status is also influenced by such factors as his skill and competence, his personality make-up, and his observance in his conduct of the sentiments and accepted norms of the group. But the job sets the stage for him, influences others' expectations of him and his of them, and determines in some degree the acceptability to him of the position he occupies among them.

The Work Group in Relation to Belonging Needs

The need for friendship and belonging is fulfilled in association with others both inside and outside the plant. Within the plant the immediate work group provides the richest source of gratification for this need. Here the individual is brought into daily interaction with others and in that setting friendships are formed which frequently last a lifetime.

Observers of employee behavior at work are often impressed by the spontaneous friendliness with which they are received and the generous treatment accorded them. They are also often impressed by the great variety of activities in which the need for association is expressed. At Hawthorne, for example, many of these activities were organized under the aegis of an employee club which sponsored a wide range of educational, athletic, helping, and purely social activities. The need was also expressed in many less formal ways such as coffee breaks, card games at lunch or rest period time, collections for gifts to the needy or those out sick, kidding and friendly banter.

The norms governing participation in and being rewarded by

group membership were similar to those encountered in life outside the plant. Generally, they could be stated as:

—Be friendly, helpful, and generous.
—Don't act too superior or too subservient.
—Show you can both give and take in verbal repartee.
—Don't be a bore or chronic complainer.
—Be good natured, don't lose your temper, show you want to be one of us, etc.

As we progress in this chapter we will be principally interested in seeing how these membership norms sometimes take on a protective character in response to what the work group construes to be threats to their safety needs arising in the external environment. Under these conditions membership norms tend to develop around and reinforce restrictive output norms as a way of regulating the internal group life. These situations are of particular interest because in them the individual experiences the most conflict in choosing a course to follow—whether to conform and achieve the rewards of membership at the possible cost of increased rewards from management or vice versa.

Company Requirements in Relation to Belonging Needs

Company requirements for effective functioning seem to be related to membership and belonging needs through (1) the employees it hires, (2) work arrangements, (3) job changes and movement of personnel, and (4) rules and standards.

1. The composition of the work force is determined by the people who are hired. Those hired are determined by employment policy and this in turn is governed largely by the needs of the business for efficient manning of the jobs to be performed and social policy considerations. As a consequence, especially in large metropolitan centers, the work force is heterogeneous, varying widely in age, education, nationality, race, religion, family, and social background. These personal characteristics and their relation to group acceptance are not a focus of this chapter but we mention them because they enter into the picture in varying degrees.

2. Work arrangements and the positioning of jobs are made with reference to technical considerations and requirements for efficient

operation. Whether workers are clustered closely together or situated widely apart, for example, is determined not by their needs for sociability but by the needs of the technology.

3. Job changes and the movement of personnel may result in constant change in the composition of the work group, in an individual being shifted from group to group so that he is continually confronted with the problem of relating himself to new groups, or, as in the case of work transferred to another plant location, in the complete breaking up of groups which may have been established for years. Here we see job change, which we identified as a major factor making for concerns about job security, also coming in as a major disturbance to needs for belonging.

4. Standards and work rules, which as we saw play an important part in arousing concerns about job security, come into this syndrome in a somewhat similar fashion. Industry is not intended as a place to make friends; it is a place to produce goods and services. Work standards are established on the assumption that the worker will concentrate on his task for the full working day, if he fools around or engages in social conversation, this is to be construed as prima facie evidence either that the work standard is too low or that he is not putting forth his best effort. Thus, work standards tend to rule out needs for belonging as having no logical place in the work setting. The talking problem in industry is universal; any form of association above that required by work routines runs counter to the logics of efficiency and is to be engaged in at the risk of punishment.

Summary

From this brief consideration of the major elements in the belonging syndrome we can see how the worker, in seeking to satisfy his needs for friendship and belonging, is faced with a dilemma. The alternatives open to him are to live up in every respect to what the company expects of him or to conform to group norms. By pursuing the former course he may more fully achieve the benefits of an outstanding performance record but at the possible penalty of ostracism by the group. The second course, while bestowing the satisfactions of membership, may lead to fewer rewards from the Company. He is caught between two conflicting sets of expectations which he must resolve in seeking how best to satisfy his own needs. This is a conflict he cannot well avoid. It gives rise to many concerns and its resolution may take forms of the utmost importance to the individual and the organization.

How Concerns About Friendship and Belonging Were Expressed

In taking up these concerns we shall proceed by first discussing and illustrating this need as it is manifested at fairly simple levels. We shall then go on to show how, under the constraints to its fulfillment in the industrial setting, it can become a major intervening variable affecting productivity and organizational effectiveness.

Simple Friendship and Belonging

"I remember arriving at Hawthorne in the summer of 1929 and being impressed with the size of the place. . . . It took a great deal of doing just to find my way around through the maze of buildings . . . but the thing I remember most was the friendliness of the people. At noon (the supervisor) invited me to go along with him and the others in the department to the cafeteria. . . . I still recall how everyone went out of his way to make the new fellow from out of town feel at home."

To be warmly received, to be shown around, to be taken to lunch, to be made to feel at home—these seemingly small things loom large in everyone's recollection of his first days at work. They leave an indelible imprint and often have a significant bearing on whether a person will stay with an organization or leave.

In the studies made by the counselors, loneliness was a constantly recurring theme. Among new employees this tended to be a dominant concern until they became established. Sometimes these feelings of loneliness reflected not only newness to the work situation but strangeness to the city as well. The following is one of many examples of this.

"Every place you go around the city is a strange place where you've never been before. You feel lost most of the time. I don't know if I'll ever feel at home here. . . . Another thing that makes it hard is that the people are so different from what they were back home. They pass you on the street without even noticing you are there. I've never been one to push myself but I'll have to learn to talk to those people even though they don't seem to be interested in me. . . . I don't know whether I'll ever like it here in Chicago. I'll try it a little longer and if I still don't like it I'm going back home."

Here is an instance in which loneliness is expressed as having no one to talk to:

"If I had only known about your job a year ago. I was so depressed and I had no one to talk to. I sat and thought all day, I didn't make any friends, I wasn't inclined to. It worked out, but it could have worked out a lot sooner if I could have talked to someone."

Work as a Social Occasion

Elton Mayo, in an article entitled "What Every Village Knows," [1] speaks of the time when as "a little-pitcher-with-long-ears" he was taken one day by a Victorian aunt to her weekly sewing circle. Chatter was incessant, sometimes general, sometimes broken among small groups. The topics were almost always persons and events, the work was seldom mentioned. Events of the week were reviewed and appraised, people were discussed and given their place. The topics of conversation, he says, clearly had woven themselves into the fabric and became a part of a general mosaic. The work, if done in isolation, would have been monotonous, but when accompanied by the society of others, it gained dignity and interest as an essential part of a social function. He concludes that in any situation where people work together "the organization of the situation as relationship between persons will inevitably take priority over technical logic and over the immediate material interests of the individual."

The Case of Angelina, Comfortable Relations

While in an entirely different context from Mayo's illustration, and far removed in time, space, and social distance, the following comments by a woman worker at Hawthorne, whom we shall call Angelina, nevertheless provide a striking confirmation of his point. Angelina was married, her husband was also working, and in her talk with the counselor she was weighing the pros and cons of a transfer to an outlying plant much nearer her home. As she talked

[1] *Survey Graphic,* December 1937, pp. 695–698.

about leaving her present location, she began to develop second thoughts on the matter.

EMPLOYEE: I don't know if I'd take the transfer over there if they put me on assembling or something different from what I am doing. I like this wiring and soldering. It's very interesting, you get to read blueprints and the work is different all the time. And the girls are nice, I kind of hate to leave them. We have our section parties, you know, and the girls have showers for one another when they're getting married. They're really nice and sociable.

I talked to several girls from the other plant and asked them how they liked it over there. Of course, some say it's very nice and others don't like it at all. The ones who say it's very nice say that, "Well, they're more friendly over there and they have a lot of fun all the time." Then the ones that don't like it say that it's too cold in the wintertime, the heating isn't very good, and the locker rooms aren't as clean. I guess there's a lot to both sides of it. Some of the girls tell me that there aren't too many jobs like I'm doing now and I like the job so much.

The girls here are nice and the supervisors are, too. They give you the breaks, well, whenever they can give them to you. They let you go out to the hospital and don't ask you any questions when you come back. They let me come out and talk to you without any questions at all.

The girls tell me that over at the other plant it's a very friendly place to work and all that but at the same time they sort of crab about the seating being too hard, the heating far too cold, and the locker rooms aren't kept as clean, and sometimes the supervisors don't seem to be quite as nice as the ones we've got here. . . .

But I just don't like this transportation every morning. In the summertime it really isn't so bad, the air is so fresh. Just today I walked five blocks and it was real nice after these hot, sticky days. You get on the train and there's a cool breeze blowing but in the winter I just don't like it. This plant is really nice enough in the wintertime, though, warm enough.

Gee, I don't know what it would really be like to be over at the other plant. It may not be so good after all. I'd have to meet a whole lot of new people and make new friends. The other girls in the department here seem to like me pretty much. I get along with them. You know what I think I'll do?

COUNSELOR: What would you like to do, Angelina?

EMPLOYEE: I think I'll ask my group chief to have my bench moved closer to the window or something. It would help a lot if I could get a breath of fresh air once in a while. Being by the window ought to do it. They'd let me do it because I've been here a long time and they seem to like me and they've never turned me down yet and there's no harm in asking. Then maybe they wouldn't have to go through all that trouble of getting me a transfer. Then I could stay here with all the girls I like and the supervisors and I wouldn't be as cold in the winter if it's so cold in the winter at the other plant as they say. Yeah, I guess that's what I'll do.

In this interview the social situation at work seems to be all important to Angelina. She is obviously a well accepted group member. One wonders whether the warmth of which she speaks isn't quite as much the warmth of personal relations as the room temperature. Also, whether what lends interest to her work isn't quite as much its social overtones as anything intrinsic to the task. The importance of congenial relations to her outweighs the cost and inconvenience of thirty minutes' additional traveling time each way and, as she indicates, in the heat of summer and cold of winter on crowded trains this can be quite a hardship.

The Case of Jim Branch, a Returned Veteran

The following excerpts from an interview with Jim Branch, a returned veteran, illustrate the loneliness he feels from no longer being an accepted member of his work group.

"The Company's been really fine to me in every way. I got my old job back and I've gone up two grades. The only thing is that the people seem different. Even my friends, at least I thought they were my friends, aren't my friends any more." (Here he talks at length about the good times he used to have with his fellow employees and other friends, but now their interests are no longer the same and they don't invite him to their parties any more.)

"I feel left out. They don't seem to think the same way I do any more. Something must be wrong. It's always that they are going to some tavern or doing things like that whereas before we all liked sports and hunting and fishing. . . . They seem to be so different from the way they used to be. . . . I feel like an animal in a strange world. People don't seem to want me but I want them. I want them to like me, to be my friends. Instead it goes the other way. . . . There must be something wrong with me. . . .

"On this job I feel just like a bird in a cage. It's a good job but hard for me to do. I can't relax like I could in the army. I'm losing weight and can't get my appetite back. I wish I could move around on the job and talk to the fellows in there like I could in the army. That would make me feel better, I might even forget some of the things I don't like about this job."

Here we have an instance in which an employee wants desperately to be accepted by his old group but something stands in his way. They won't take him in. This affects his appetite, his health, and his interest in his work. Apparently the group's membership norms changed while Jim was away in the army and their interests and values are no longer the same as his. But to be accepted by a group one must accede in some measure to the group's values. Jim seemed to feel that theirs were wrong and his were right which may account for his being left outside and feeling constricted like a bird in a cage.

The Case of Bill Beach, Recently Transferred

A transfer to a different work group can give rise to feelings of being left out similar to those expressed by Jim Branch. This is well illustrated in the following interview with Bill Beach.

"I have only got four years of service. Most of that time I worked in the Cable Plant. I've only been transferred here a little while now. I liked it a lot better over in the Cable Plant. The fellows were a lot more friendly there. They sure in heck aren't friendly here. I don't know, you just can't get acquainted with the guys. They stay all by themselves and don't talk to you or crack any jokes. You even get into trouble when you try and get snuff from a guy. I had trouble like that when I first came over here. I asked one of the fellows to give me a chew of snuff and he said, 'Oh, what are you, a cadger?' I tried to tell him that I was new in the organization and that I couldn't go down to the store then but that I would give him a whole can back. No, he wouldn't give me any. He said, 'The hell, we don't like those cadgers around here.' I told him right then and there that I never wanted to talk to him again, and I won't either. Why should I bother with a guy like that? Is that any way to talk to a man? Couldn't he understand the position I was in then? I don't chew snuff very often but I always used to have a can around anyhow. I only chew when I'm on the job. One of the other fellows came around, though, and I got a chew from him.

He's a pretty nice fellow—that was the inspector. He said, sure, he'd give me a chew any time. I told him I'd buy him a can the first chance I got and he said, 'Oh, you don't have to bother.' I like a guy like that. But some of the other guys, you try to ask them questions about the job or something and they don't seem to want to talk to you. I don't know what's the matter with them.

"In my old organization it seemed to be so different. I knew everybody down there and we used to get along very well. A bunch of us used to have a pinochle game every Friday night. We'd get our little beer and have a good time. Oh, we'd maybe get feeling good but we wouldn't get drunk and if a guy did get drunk at my house, I wouldn't let him drive his car home. If he insisted on it, I would take the rotor arm out of the distributor, and then he couldn't drive it. I don't ever let a guy drive his car when he's drunk. I don't think you'll ever get a gang of these guys down here to get a pinochle game going though. They just don't seem like the type. I'm sorry I got transferred out of there, but the work dropped off and I had to take this transfer."

Bill Beach appears to have been well accepted in his former group and their activities carried over to their social life outside the plant. He wants to be friendly and have friends in his new situation but, as with Jim Branch, something stands in his way. In his new situation he seems to have made the social error of asking for a chew of snuff before the group had fully sized him up and was willing to accept him. The man he tried to bum the snuff from, possibly having had little indication of the kind of a person he was, construes this as a signal and says, "So that's the type you are." The inspector favors him with snuff and he says he likes a guy like that. But what were the relations of the others in the work group to the inspector—friendly? antagonistic? We do not know but this could have made a difference in their opinion of Bill Beach. Significantly, they will not share with him their snuff or their job knowledge. As in the case of Jim Branch, there are membership norms operating here and their consequences for the individual's acceptance and feelings about his work appear to be much the same in both instances.

The Case of the Girl Who Talked Too Much

One day a high ranking executive was to make a tour through a portion of the plant. As was frequently the case, word of his visit came down the line well in advance, thus allowing local supervision time to make the necessary preparations for a good showing—seeing that the aisles were cleared, pans of parts neatly stacked, and everything in its place.

On the appointed day, the executive, accompanied by the shop superintendent, came through one particular department in which an earnings problem had existed for some time. As they passed one of the conveyors he looked inquiringly at one of the operators who, while working steadily, was busily talking to an operator seated beside her at the conveyor. He commented to the shop superintendent, "I see your girls talk to each other a good deal."

Upon returning to his office the shop superintendent called the department chief and told him that he was embarrassed by the high ranking official's comment and instructed him to see that such open violation of the rules, especially while the organization was in trouble on output, be stopped. Thus started a chain reaction which almost ended up in one of the most efficient operators being fired.

The shop in question had recently been changed from day work to piece work. Under the day work system output was considered high by the line management and a generally relaxed environment prevailed in which the operators talked and often sang at their work. In fact, on the particular conveyor involved in the talking problem, the girls had developed a song in rhythm to the work pace on the conveyor. They had pushed the conveyor to its limit and had asked the engineers to adjust the controls so they could speed it up.

Under the piece rates introduced, the old day work levels of performance no longer sufficed and the organization lagged behind its expected increase in output. The reasons for the lag had been debated at higher levels with the result that more and more attention was directed toward cutting out all interferences to production. The higher level official had been a party to these discussions and this was why his comment had such pointed significance to the shop superintendent.

The person on whom criticism fell was the lead-off operator. There had been changes in the supervision on the floor with the result that the department chief who cautioned her was unaware of her good record. She agreed to talk less but seemingly did not take it too seriously because she soon was talking and regaling the group with her comments as much as ever. The department chief took this as a personal affront and cautioned her more strongly. There ensued a long series of incidents in which the lead-off operator was moved about or others were moved beside her in an effort to diminish the amount of talking. Finally the department chief transferred her to a heavy, demanding job usually performed by men. He said he would like to fire her but this was the next best punishment he could think of. After a period of talking to the counselor, who had followed all these events, and with the prompting of her immediate supervisor, she talked to the department chief, apologized for her conduct, and was restored to her old job.

The above incident, presented here in condensed form, serves to highlight the way in which the enforcement of a rule can have far-reaching repercussions. Here there was no problem of gaining acceptance by the group; the person disciplined was well accepted and an informal group leader. The problem arose in the relation of company requirements, expressed in the no-talking rule, to the individual's needs for sociability and her position in the work group. The no-talking rule threatened to deprive her of the satisfaction of her friendship needs and the special talents she exercised in maintaining her informal leadership.

The Case of the Conflicted Secretaries

The illustrations we have given cover some of the more significan aspects of belonging as manifested in face-to-face interactions. We now want to show some of the more far-reaching ramifications of this need as reflected in, for example, questions of identification with the Company or the union. We realize that in extending the concept of belonging beyond the boundaries of a primary group we may be doing some violence to the concept. However, we have not postulated identity with a reference group or collectivity as a separate need for the population considered.

The secretarial staff at Hawthorne formed a well-defined social structure in which rank varied with that of the people to whom they were assigned. Normally a beginner started at the bottom and rose in rank with service and demonstrated proficiency. Many secretaries spent their entire careers in this system, the pinnacle of which was secretary to the plant manager. Needless to say, many status symbols and rules of protocol built up around this system.

In 1953 the union petitioned the NLRB to represent certain salaried clerical workers at Hawthorne. In the hearings which were held to determine the appropriate bargaining unit it became necessary to distinguish between management and nonmanagement employees. This discrimination hinged on whether the secretary had access to and was required to use or keep confidential management information. A typist in the counseling organization, for example, would be considered management since she typed confidential interviews. A typist in a shop clerical unit would be nonmanagement and thus eligible to membership in the union.

As a result of the various discriminations made to determine union membership eligibility, some of the secretarial staff, which as a whole had always identified themselves with management, now found that they were in the bargaining unit. This made them feel that management had deserted them and that in reality perhaps had always regarded them only as workers. When the election was held, the petitioning union local was certified as the bargaining agent and thus a jagged fault line developed in the secretarial hierarchy. This fault line did not extend higher than the assistant superintendent secretary level. From there on down two substructures developed—one associated largely with shop operations, the other with staff functions.

The impact of this change was most acutely felt among the secretaries assigned to the assistant superintendent level. This was a high-ranking secretarial position. To achieve it normally required long years of hard work and the occupants were generally regarded by everyone in the unit under the assistant superintendent as a dependable and indispensable source of help and information on forms, routines, procedures, and protocol. They were the ones who made things tick and even their bosses depended on them to see that there was no slip up in routines, some of which were of critical importance—payroll routines, for example.

As a result of this Labor Board ruling, secretaries who had sat side by side for years now found themselves being treated differently. They were assigned different grade designations, one series for union and another series for management. This was only a symbolic change; the grades remained the same as they had always been. The secretaries with the grades designating membership in the bargaining unit felt they had been lowered in social standing and penalized for no act of their own. Then as a result of the bargaining which took place shortly thereafter, the unionized secretaries were granted a negotiated increase in salary whereas the management secretaries were not. The management secretaries had to rely for salary advances on merit increases in pay. As a result some secretaries in the union who would not have earned a merit raise got an increase in pay, thus putting them ahead of their management colleagues. The latter now began to wonder whether being classed as management was worthwhile after all. The resulting inequities were, of course, corrected at the next rate review period but the split between union and nonunion remained.

In this illustration, a group which in their own and management's thinking had been closely identified as management now found themselves cut off or rejected. They could no longer belong in the same sense nor could they be repatriated except by a change in the bargaining unit. As members of the bargaining unit they were supposed to think and act as union members. Under this mantle they could refuse to perform any former function which could be shown to be a management function. This could have been an issue because the line between the two was indistinct and came into being largely by virtue of the decisions which had to be made in determining the appropriate bargaining unit. Management's expectations of them, however, as reflected in the demands of those they served, were unchanged. As far as those to whom the secretaries reported were concerned, the change was a technicality which the secretaries should ignore. Hence the conflict. This instance of conflict was structural and could not be corrected short of a structural change agreed to by the agencies responsible for bringing it about.

The Case of the Apprentice Instructors

The case to be described involves a conflict in loyalties among a group of apprentice instructors precipitated by a strike called by the union representing tool and model makers, machinists, and apprentices at Hawthorne. The instructors, themselves all graduate apprentices, were on the roll of the training organization and were classed as management employees, whereas those in the trades they served and with whom they had strong craft affiliation were out on strike. In this situation their conflict of loyalties became acute. To refuse to go out on strike would make them out to be "scabs," yet to do so might subject them to penalties for being disloyal to management. The strike, which was over the terms of the contract undergoing negotiation, lasted about one month when it broke up because the employees involved began to return to work of their own accord.

The apprentice training program at Hawthorne was a long-established function of the Industrial Relations branch when the strike occurred. There were at the time some 125 apprentices in training. They were under the direction of a staff of full-time instructors on the training department's roll. Most of these instructors were graduates of the course and were regarded as the cream of the crop, both technically and for their teaching and leadership skills. A tour of duty as an instructor normally was a prelude to advancement in supervision. The paths open to them were many, in the school itself, in their chosen trades, or in shop operations. They thus had a heavy stake in making good on their training school assignments.

When the strike occurred most of the apprentices, who were carried on the rolls of the organizations for which they were being trained, went out with the craftsmen. Some few chose to work but under threat of physical injury by the strikers soon joined their colleagues. This left the instructor staff with nothing to do and they too were under pressure and harassment to join the others.

Most of them felt strongly that their success as instructors would be jeopardized if they stayed on because they needed the active cooperation of the older heads in the tool rooms in placing apprentices for practice assignments. The trainees alternated between the school and the tool rooms, taking first classroom training and practice on one phase and then acquiring proficiency on it in the tool rooms. The seasoned tool makers were expected to cooperate with the instructors in working out these assignments and in following through on them. This collaboration needed to be voluntary and something the senior craftsmen wanted to do if it were to be effective, and it was this element of spontaneity which the instructors thought they would lose.

They were also concerned about how crossing picket lines would affect their future careers in the tool rooms. Some of the craftsmen had always belonged to the union, most of them identified themselves with their craft quite as much as with the company, and sentiments against "scabbing" were very strong. One instructor, an old timer who had served his apprenticeship in Germany and who had worked in numerous places as a journeyman and was a member in good standing in his union, became ill worrying about what his colleagues would think of him for not joining them.

In this situation feelings ran high and the problem of which way to turn mounted to a crisis stage. The Training Department supervisors arranged a series of meetings with all the instructors to discuss the situation. The first question asked by them was why the instructors couldn't just stay at home. It was pointed out to them that as instructors on the Industrial Relations branch roll they were a part of management and were expected to attend unless threatened by bodily injury.

The discussion then turned to work assignments. All but one or two said the one thing they wanted to avoid was doing productive work in the tool rooms because this would make them out to be strike breakers. Various kinds of assignments were worked out and they were given a choice of which one they would like to accept. On this basis the problem was eventually worked out.

In this instance a latent conflict in loyalties was thrown into bold relief when the group with which the instructors most closely identified themselves went out on strike. This raised the issue of where their loyalties really lay in a form which called for an open declaration. One need not have witnessed the incident to sense the acute agonies which accompanied it.

How the Resolutions of These Concerns Are Manifested in Organizational Behavior

There are logically three resolutions to the individual's needs for belonging under the organizational constraints discussed in the first part of this chapter. The individual can conform, remain conflicted, or protest. The following cases illustrate each of these alternatives.

The Case of Axel, the Conformist

Axel was of Scandinavian descent; he had finished two years of high school, was 29 years old, and had seven years of service. He was one of a group of fifteen wiremen who had worked together for about three years. He was well liked by everyone, worked steadily all day long, and was considered a good producer.

Axel said that when he first started with the company he had resolved to do everything he could to get ahead and in a short time was exceeding in output those with several years of service. Instead of gaining the recognition he thought his performance record warranted, he said it only resulted in trouble. The supervisor, he said, used it as a club to beat the others in the group over the head. He said this made him unpopular with the men and he didn't like to feel that he was responsible for their punishment.

When he was transferred to his present job, he said he decided that he would do a good day's work but not try to be a race horse. "It's not worth it," he said, "You don't get any rewards for being at the top and you just disturb things. You have to work all your life and it's better to have it pleasant."

The counselor noted that Axel commanded the respect of the other wiremen and that he had an attitude of amused tolerance toward their horseplay and jostling one another. When he returned after being loaned out for a period of three weeks, he said it was nice to be back because he'd never found a better bunch of fellows to work with.

Here we see a man who, when he was a newcomer, had aspirations to achieve an outstanding record. One of the unanticipated consequences of this was that it resulted in criticism of his co-workers and their criticism of him. We now see him conforming to the group's expectations and finding pleasure in doing so.

In the next case the employee felt that he was being pulled in different directions by his need to produce at a high level and his need to conform to group expectations. He articulates his conflict very well. Portions of this interview were quoted in the preceding chapter.

The Case of Charlie, the Conflicted Inspector

Charlie was a young man with five years of service who had recently been transferred to a new process inspection job.

EMPLOYEE: It won't be long before I start having the quality checker (the person who checks on the inspector's work) looking at my work and I can't learn the job quite that fast. You see, here's the hooker. You're given six months to learn that job. Well, the job isn't really too tough, but I'm expected to learn it slowly. If I learn it too fast they will figure the job is too easy and how come the rest of the boys aren't doing it. So, I'd have trouble with them. If I go too slowly then, of course, it's my own neck. So I got to watch my step pretty carefully and not get my boss mad at me or the boys mad at me because either way I'll need both of them at one time or another.

COUNSELOR: You want to stick to the middle of the road.

EMPLOYEE: Yeah, I suppose you could call it that. It's really trying to satisfy two things that overlap a little bit. . . .

Charlie could learn his job faster and thus be more assured of making a good showing when his work was inspected by the quality checker. But he is aware of the group's expectations toward him so he compromises at some risk of incurring demerits for poor work. The conflict, the hooker, is readily apparent and of some concern to him.

The Case of Jim Gray, the Rate Buster

Jim Gray was a returned veteran who had been released from active duty after four years in the army. The war was still going on and he was glad to come back to the company so that he could continue to help out in the war effort. "I knew exactly what the needs were of the boys out in the field," he said, "I knew they really needed materials and they weren't getting them in sufficient quantities."

In the short time since his return he had found much to complain about but what bothered him most was his conviction that the workers around him "didn't seem to know there is a war on" and were insensitive to the emergency. Let us hear what he had to say.

"When I walked into this plant I saw that the people were laying down on the job, and I mean really laying down. I can tell you specific examples on that and that's right in my own type of work. When I came in here they were working on a casting job and they told me they were turning out about eight castings a day and that's what the supervisor told them to do. Well, I tried to go along with the boys. They asked me not to put out too many so one day the boss came over to me and he said, 'Say, Jim, what are you laying down on the job for? You're the only fellow around here that isn't making twelve castings a day.'

"Well, I'm telling you, that really burned me up. Here they had asked me to go along with them—that that was the rate and we had to take it easy because the job was tough and had to be very accurately made. Well, I didn't want to start any trouble so I went along with them for a while and then I ran into this. So the next day I made up my mind that I didn't give a damn what the fellows would say any more—I would make as many as I could. I felt kind of bad about only making eight or nine a day anyway, but I was told that that was what the supervision wanted us to make. So, after I got that bawling out by the boss I really started working and within a short time I had the rate up to 31 a day and then you should have heard the rest of the fellows. They really let out on me then and I've cracked every rate that's been set so far. There isn't one that they've been able to set that I haven't been able to crack wide open.

"I think it was damn rotten of the fellows to try to get me off to a bad start just because they wanted to show the supervisors that they could make more parts than I could. Well, they're getting their medicine this time. They're working like hell and they're not making half as many parts as I am. The other night I turned out 31 parts and every one was passed by inspection the same night. I'm telling you, even the supervisors have to say that that is quite an accomplishment."

We can readily see what has happened in Jim Gray's case. The men must have sensed his hostility toward them when he returned from the service and contrived to maneuver him into producing at a rate so low they knew he would be criticized by the supervisor. Jim must have wanted their acceptance because he went along with them in holding down his output. What infuriated him was the revelation that he was being made the goat and that they were secretly against him. The interesting aspect of the case is in how Jim tried to correct the score. He hit them where it hurt the most by consistently showing them up in their output rate. He struck back by trying to destroy their membership norms, thus hitting at the system of values in terms of which he was made an outsider.

General Summary

We can summarize the points we have been developing about the need for friendship and belonging with reference to Figure 6.2.

The fulfillment of the need to belong is contingent upon two principal dimensions of the work situation—company requirements and expectations and group norms. Where group norms are in support of company expectations, teamwork develops and there is no conflict for the individual. Where, however, group norms are at variances with company requirements, the individual is faced with the problem of deciding where his allegiance lies. This gives rise to the concern characterized as role conflict.

The behavioral manifestations of this conflict take many forms but the alternate types found in industry are the isolate, the conflicted, and the socializer. The isolate becomes the rate buster, the conflicted becomes uncertain of his reference group, and the socializer becomes the restricter. Thus we see how membership norms themselves and the forms of behavior resulting from the individual's attempts to resolve his needs for belonging in relation to them result in forms of behavior which have a significant bearing upon worker satisfaction and productivity.

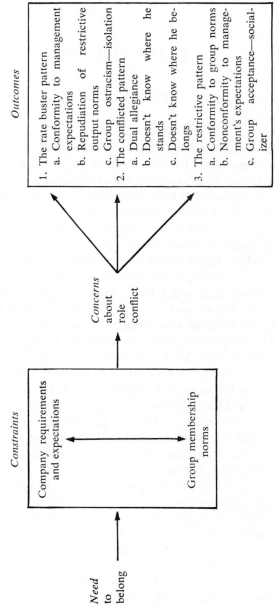

FIGURE 6.2

OUTCOMES OF THE BELONGING SYNDROME

Constraints

Company requirements and expectations

Group membership norms

Need to belong

Concerns about role conflict

Outcomes

1. The rate buster pattern
   a. Conformity to management expectations
   b. Repudiation of restrictive output norms
   c. Group ostracism—isolation
2. The conflicted pattern
   a. Dual allegiance
   b. Doesn't know where he stands
   c. Doesn't know where he belongs
3. The restrictive pattern
   a. Conformity to group norms
   b. Nonconformity to management's expectations
   c. Group acceptance—socializer

CHAPTER VII

Felt Injustices

WE NOW HAVE our worker about halfway up the hierarchy of needs we postulated for him. He is no longer concerned just with the job or just with belonging; he has advanced to the stage where he now is beginning to look at his job and himself from a different point of view. Instead of looking at the job as something to hold onto for dear life and himself only as a pair of hands, he is now becoming concerned about his job as a social exchange or transaction in which higher orders of need come into play. In this exchange he is looking at his rewards from the job not merely as three square meals a day but in terms of higher values such as its intrinsic interest and status, and he is looking at himself not merely as a hewer of wood or carrier of stone but as a human being with a bigger stake in the job and in the Company than a bare livelihood. In short, he is now standing more on his own two feet with more of a sense of his own worth and with courage enough to say, "I now am no longer going to accept just a meal ticket; I am Bill Jones and I am going to be a judge of this transaction in terms of what is proper, fair, and just to me." So we will be considering him not just as a grateful acceptor of rewards but as an evaluator of them, and we will be looking at the concerns of felt injustice which arise from this process.

The concerns we will be considering were the most general and often the most vehemently expressed of any the counselors listened to. Concerns about wage differentials were probably the most common, but the interviews were strewn with many others expressed with reference to such changes as upgradings, downgradings, and transfers into which wage treatment enters.

These concerns are well known to every supervisor and wage administrator. Probably no topic is so familiar or worked over more continually in management circles as the appropriate basis upon which to distribute rewards. Whether to recognize only merit in adjusting rates of pay or to include other factors such as length of service, and if so, in what degree, is a perennial topic of discussion. Equitable distribution of rewards is one of the thorniest problems an administrator has to face.

ELEMENTS IN THE FELT INJUSTICE SYNDROME

The elements we wish to consider in examining these concerns are shown in Figure 7.1.

Fair Treatment

Fair treatment, as we use it, will refer to the worker's evaluation of the relation between what he puts into his job and what he gets out of it. The yardstick that occurs to him in making these evaluations is usually his perception of the treatment accorded to others with whom he compares himself or of what he might obtain from alternate forms of employment. Principally involved is the company's reward system in relation to individual and group values.

Group Norms

Group norms develop around what is considered fair treatment just as they do around output and membership. One of the most common of these is, "A fair day's work for a fair day's pay." Others develop around commonly shared sentiments as to how older people should be treated compared to the young, how people with long service should fare compared to those with short service, how men should be treated compared to women, how married people with families to support should be rewarded compared to single people with no one to support, and so on. These are sentiments which are shared in common with the wider society and they constitute an important referent in terms of which the fairness of the distribution of rewards is gauged.

Investments and Rewards

For the most part, concerns about fair treatment were expressed in some such terms as, "I don't feel that I have been fairly treated."

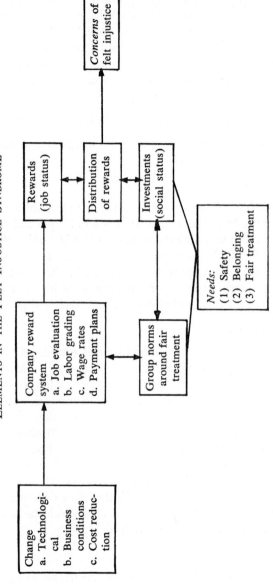

FIGURE 7.1

ELEMENTS IN THE FELT INJUSTICE SYNDROME

The reasons given were usually stated in comparative terms such as, "I am working harder and turning out more work than B but he makes as much money as I do," "Service doesn't count," "Ability isn't rewarded," "The youngsters get all the breaks," "The boss shows too much partiality," or, in the case of some women, "This is a man's world, a woman doesn't stand a chance around here." They were saying that their treatment, as they saw it, was not in line with their ability, service, age, sex, or some other factor in terms of which they felt they should fare as well as or better than someone else. These complaints of distributive justice could all be seen as efforts on the part of the individual to rectify a felt imbalance in the treatment accorded him compared to others.

In examining concerns of this kind and the conditions under which they occur or do not occur, George C. Homans [1] distinguishes between two kinds of status factors: (1) those which an individual member of a work group brings with him from his past or puts into his work and (2) those which he expects to derive from his job. The first he calls investments, the second, rewards.

Investments (social status)

An employee's investments in his job are usually considered to be the skill, experience, and effort he puts into his job to accomplish the task for which he is paid. But to restrict our view to these factors fails to account for why the basis for the concern is so frequently expressed with reference to differences in age, seniority, sex, and the other factors we have mentioned. In accounting for this Homans points out that the worker tends always to relate his rewards to the factors which determine his position or social status in the group and so do those around him. In short, the context in terms of which he views his rewards is not the logics of the payment plan but the nonlogics or social logics underlying the group structure and his position in it.

In terms of this enlarged concept of how rewards are evaluated

---

[1] "Status Among Clerical Workers," *Human Organization,* Spring 1953, pp. 5–10, and his books, *The Human Group* and *Social Behavior: Its Elementary Forms.* See also A. Zaleznik, C. R. Christensen, and F. J. Roethlisberger, *The Motivation, Productivity, and Satisfaction of Workers* (Boston, Division of Research, Harvard Business School, 1958), pp. 48–56.

by the recipient of them we can see that any factor of significance in determining his social status in the group must be counted as an investment to be rewarded in ways appropriate to the status the individual holds in the group. Among the factors entering into an individual's social status which he invests or puts into his job, then, Homans includes not only his education, experience, skill, and effort but also his service, age, sex, marital status, race, religion, nationality, and any other factor which becomes a dimension used by the group in assigning an individual a place among them.

We might note here that some of these status factors, such as age, sex, and family background, cannot be changed; others, notably effort, can be increased or withheld. For our purposes we shall be considering principally such investments as age, service, and sex because these seem to crop up in the interviews more than the other factors listed.

Rewards (*job status*)

The rewards from a job are what the worker gets in exchange for his investments. These also enter into and affect his standing in the group but they come from and are determined by the company rather than by the group.

The rewards to be derived from a job include the status of the job itself and its intrinsic possibilities for the exercise of skill and ingenuity, its relation to other jobs, the possibilities it offers for growth and advancement, the monetary rewards that go with it, the recognition accorded the holder of the job by supervision, its assurance of job security, and other factors such as the symbols of status surrounding it. All these are rewards from the job and make up what the worker gets in return for his investments. These we will sometimes alternately refer to as his job status.

According to Homans, when the investments of an individual are higher than those of another with whom he compares himself, distributive justice requires that his rewards be higher too. Under these conditions of status congruence a balance is achieved and the situation is believed as being proper and just by both the individual and the other group members. For example, it may be felt proper by a young man with short service, little experience, and two years of high school that he should get lower pay than a man with higher age, education, and service and the latter may feel that this is proper too. In each instance rewards are seen as being proportional to investments.

Concerns of felt injustice arise when the worker sees his investments as being greater than other members of the work group with whom he compares himself but regards his rewards as being proportionately less. The greater he perceives this discrepancy to be, the greater his discomfiture and the more he is likely to seek some correction. In seeking a correction he can attempt to increase his rewards by demanding more pay, for example, or, failing that, he can reduce his investments. If, on the other hand, the individual sees his rewards as being greater than his investments, he may feel that he owes the company something and this may lead to his increasing his investments by working harder, doing more than is expected of him, or by trying to assume informal leadership.

The Company Reward System

In taking up the company reward system and how it enters into this syndrome we need to distinguish between rewards which are directly related to the task and those which are peripheral to it. The former includes all the rewards we have mentioned as entering into job status; the latter includes what are referred to as fringe benefits peripheral to it. We will be concerned largely with the former and, among them, largely with the system of direct payments for work performed. Fringe benefits do not enter directly into the problem we are considering because they uniformly accrue to everyone on the roll.

Since we will be looking at the company reward system in its relation to the reward-investment ratio, we need first to clarify some of the assumptions underlying it. Perhaps the most general assumption underlying the reward system is that the employee should be rewarded in proportion to the value of his contribution to the company. Among production workers this translates readily into quantity and quality of work. At this level it matters little to the company what his investments are so long as he does his job well.

A second assumption is that the employee will work harder, that is, increase his investments, provided the opportunity for increased rewards is open to him, for example, the prospect of more pay, a better job, or an upgrading. Toward this end incentive plans are designed to establish a 1:1 relationship between output and earnings, opportunities for merit increases are provided, and performance appraisal plans are introduced.

A third assumption is that the needs of the business should always govern in any situation in which company interests may be at stake. This means, for example, that if work falls off and the worker is downgraded, his pay should be brought in line with that of the workers in the lower grade even though he has worked many years to reach the higher grade. From a company point of view wages are a cost and if not kept in line with the worth of the job they can threaten the survival of the firm.

With these preliminary remarks let us next examine the company's reward system. This will require that we describe briefly: (1) the job structure, (2) the labor grade structure, (3) the wage structure, (4) payment plans, and (5) individual rates of pay.

The job structure—job evaluation

All hourly and most salaried jobs were arranged in a hierarchy through a process of job evaluation. Somewhat different plans were used in evaluating hourly and salaried jobs but they both used a point system of evaluation and the procedures involved were the same. We shall here refer only to the hourly rated plan.

In evaluating a shop job, eleven job factors were used with a scale of points for each factor. The scores for these eleven factors were totaled and this score determined the job's position in the total hierarchy of jobs. The factors used in evaluating a shop job were: education, experience, initiative or ingenuity, physical demand, mental or visual demand, responsibility for equipment or process, responsibility for material or product, responsibility for the safety of others, responsibility for the work of others, working conditions, and unavoidable hazards. It is important to note that some of these factors, such as education and experience, sound like our listing of investments but they are not to be confused. These are here viewed as job requirements; they have no necessary relation to the attributes of the person holding the job—for example, he could well have far more education or experience than the job requires or he could have less but make up for the deficiency through application and training as was widely done during the war.

The labor grade structure

The process of job evaluation resulted in a positioning of every job relative to others, some ranking higher, some lower, and some the same. To administer this complex structure the company grouped jobs according to their point score into ten labor grades numbering from grade 32 at the bottom to grade 41 at the top. The labor grades thus represented a range of point scores, and the score of any particular job determined in which grade it fell. Since, as we shall see, payment was directly tied in with labor grades and the grade was always used in designating an employee's job status, as, for example, a grade 32 assembler or a grade 38 machinist, an employee's labor grade became the chief determinant of his formal position in the company.

At this point it is well to emphasize that the job structure and the grade structure, although arranged in order by the same process, were two quite different entities. The job structure represented concrete tasks, the grade structure was only a convenient device for administering them. The labor grades could be increased or decreased in number by changing the range of point scores encompassed by each grade without any change in the job structure. But when a dollar value is attached to each labor grade, we have something else again for now every job within a labor grade is declared to be of the same value, and if a widely divergent assortment of tasks were included within a grade it would make quite a difference to the workers involved because they would then all have the same formal status.

The wage structure

The next step we need to consider is the way in which wage scales were developed for each of the labor grades.

Each job grade carried a starting and a job rate, the latter representing what an average experienced operator should be paid for his grade of work. Job rates were determined by comparison, through wage surveys, of company wage scales with those being paid for comparable work in the local labor market adjusted for consistency with other rates within the labor grade and policy considerations.

The payment structure resulting from these operations paralleled the grade structure but again the two should not be confused. The wage scales could be increased with no change in the grade structure as is demonstrated in negotiating general wage increases. In theory they could also be decreased but this never happened in negotiations at Hawthorne.

FIGURE 7.2

SIMPLIFIED CHART ILLUSTRATING RELATION OF JOB STRUCTURE, LABOR GRADE STRUCTURE, AND WAGE STRUCTURE

Job Structure	Labor Grade Structure	Wage Structure
Task 1		
Task 2	Grade 4	—($3.25) job rate
Task 3		—($2.75) start rate
Task 4		
Task 5	Grade 3	—($2.65) job rate
Task 6		—($2.20) start rate
Task 7		
Task 8	Grade 2	—($2.10) job rate
Task 9		—($1.80) start rate
Task 10		
Task 11	Grade 1	—($1.75) job rate
Task 12		—($1.50) start rate

We can best sum up the distinctions we have been trying to make so far by reference to Figure 7.2 which shows the three structures we have been identifying and how they are tied together. These structures did not spring full-blown out of somebody's head; they were developed over time in a sincere effort to stimulate worker productivity and to reimburse them fairly for their job contributions.

Payment plans—day work and piece work

We must next consider the ways in which payments were administered. This was accomplished through two methods of payment known locally as day work and piece work or incentive work.

A day worker was assigned a straight hourly rate corresponding to those provided in the rate ranges for his grade of work.
Day-work jobs included such assignments as new jobs under development, those in which output was difficult to measure, for example, a repairman, and those in which too much emphasis on
output might jeopardize quality of work as in the case of a skilled
die maker. The bulk of the jobs were on piece work.

A piece worker's earnings varied with output. The prevailing
form of piece-work payment was what is commonly known as a
group incentive; that is, the output of all the production workers
in a payment group, which could vary in size from a section with
twenty or thirty workers to a department with over a hundred,
was pooled and the amount in excess of the expected hourly outputs (arrived at from time standards) was expressed as a percentage of the latter. Each individual's hourly rate or base rate was
then increased by this percentage and this constituted his take-
home pay.

Piece workers were guaranteed 15% over their base rates which
were somewhat lower than day-work rates, but there was no assurance of a 1:1 relationship between output and earnings as there
would be under a straight or individual piece-work system. If, however, worker A had a higher base rate than worker B, A would
earn more than B and if the differential in their respective rates accurately reflected differences in performance, as in theory they
should, A's higher efficiency would be reflected in his earnings. A
1:1 ratio could only be maintained if hourly rates could be adjusted upward and downward at fairly short-time intervals, and
company policy as well as the union contract prevented reductions
in hourly rates unless the employee was downgraded or was so fla-
grant in his violation of rules and standards as to constitute a disciplinary case. Also, an outstanding employee's base rate could not
be indefinitely increased without doing violence to the labor grade
concept.

In theory, the group incentive system tended to mitigate problems arising from some piece rates being set too tight or too loose,
one of the main pitfalls encountered in a straight or individual piece-
work plan. Also pooling the efforts of a group was intended to encourage the development of a cooperative group spirit. Since the
earnings of each individual were influenced by the performance of

every other person, it was assumed that faster workers would concern themselves with inducing slower workers to speed up and that a self-disciplining group would emerge. That this does not always occur but indeed that restrictive norms often develop, we have already had occasion to point out in the preceding chapters.

Individual rates of pay

Ordinarily an inexperienced operator would be assigned the starting rate of his grade. As he gained in proficiency he was given automatic progression increases every three months until he reached the job rate. Merit increases could be awarded after reaching the job rate for better than expected output.

Employees normally started at one of the lower grades and worked their way upward in the grade structure as suitable openings for which they were qualified became available. When upgraded they were eligible to an hourly rate of pay within the grade to which they were upgraded. This could be the starting rate of the higher grade but it could be higher depending upon their experience and hourly rate in the lower grade.

Employees who were transferred within the same grade retained their hourly rate. Those downgraded might incur no reduction in rate of pay if their hourly rate was in line with those of other employees in the grade to which they were downgraded. Also they were not reduced below the highest rate they had earned in the lower grade before they were upgraded. If the downgrading of an employee was severe and a sizable differential existed between his rate and the highest rate paid in the lower grade, he would incur some reduction in hourly rate, but this was tempered by such considerations as his length of service, his work history, and his general worth. All these considerations applied to both day workers and piece workers.

The Impact of Change Upon the Reward-Investment Ratio

We have shown in Figure 7.1 changes brought about by technological advance, business conditions, and cost reduction activities as also being a major element in this concern syndrome.

The structures identified in Figure 7.2 will help us to see the impact of these changes upon these structures and the resulting consequences for the reward-investment ratio. As a general statement, it can be said that any change in the task structure, the grade structure, or the wage structure, as well as any change in the individual's position in these structures, will affect this ratio and result in some sort of social dislocation. We shall try to illustrate this without enumerating all the possibilities.

Consider first a technological change which affects the task structure. This can bring about the elimination of a task or its being combined with others with the consequent dislocation of the workers assigned to it, to a change of the task in the labor grading structure, either upward or downward, and again to the dislocation of the workers assigned, or, assuming no change in labor grade, the change in method may be so great as to call for new time standards with a consequent change in the piece rate calling for greater investments for the same reward.

Changes in business conditions directly affect the number of workers required for each task. Increases in the numbers required tend to increase opportunities for rewarding investments through upgradings and promotions. Decreases in the numbers required create surpluses which may mean that some workers may have to be transferred, some downgraded, and some laid off. Any movement of this kind may result in increased investments for the same rewards, as in the case of a person transferred laterally who has to accommodate to a new group and learn new methods of work, or it may lead to a reduction in rewards along with a loss of investments as in the case of a person downgraded or laid off. A person who is downgraded suffers a loss in social status (investment) even though his rate of pay is unchanged. Layoff results in the total cancellation of rewards and investments.

Changing business conditions or collective bargaining can lead to changes in the wage structure directly without affecting the task or the grade structure. An example of this would be a general wage increase. Let us see how this might affect the rewards-investment ratio.

Let us first take a flat, across-the-board increase in all rates of pay. This results in increased rewards for the same investments. Is there any social dislocation here? Yes, because the differential expressed as a percentage between lower rated and higher rated employees is reduced. The higher rated employees may feel that they are not given their just share. So let us assume that the general increase is apportioned as a percentage of each man's hourly rate with corresponding changes in starting and job rates. Here again rewards are increased relative to investments. Is there any social dislocation here? Yes, again, because the higher paid worker gets a larger increase per hour than the lower paid worker and the lower paid worker may feel that he should have the larger increase. Also, the faster worker sees the slower worker faring proportionately as well as he does.

Let us next consider a case in which there is no change in the job structure, labor grades, or wage scales, but there is a change in individual hourly rates; let us say merit increases are granted. These increase the rewards for some but not for others—the percentage of the work force considered eligible may vary: 10%, 25%, or some other percentage—but someone is always left out or it wouldn't be a merit increase. Is there any social dislocation here? Yes, because the slower worker's rewards relative to those increased are proportionately lowered. Or there may be a highly proficient worker whose rate is so high above the job rate that he must be left out—he may feel outraged that shorter service and less proficient workers than he are getting all the gravy—not to mention all the others who may feel that they are as deserving of an increase as those who get them.

Finally, we might consider what happens when the labor grade structure is changed, the job structure remaining the same. This has occurred only at rare intervals at Hawthorne so we shall here be speaking somewhat theoretically. Let us first assume that the number of labor grades is decreased, say from ten to eight. The effect of this is to compress a wider range of tasks within a grade, to reduce the number of rungs in the social ladder up which employees progress, and to increase the distance between the rungs, making it harder for some workers to make the next step. Job status differentials within a grade are reduced and those between grades are increased. The introduction of more grades for a given job structure increases the number of rungs in the social ladder and makes it possible for some workers to climb higher than they could with fewer grades and thus increase their job status relative to what it had been before. Adding more grades, let us say, at the top of the structure gives more scope for progress and increased job status for those at the top of the job hierarchy but lowers, relatively, the job status of those in the lower grades.

We have perhaps said enough now to substantiate the two major points we wanted to make about the impact of change on the reward-investment ratio. The first is that these forces are all-pervasive in their effects upon the reward system, a system which in its structure seems always to assume a static or stable state of affairs. The second point is that these changes come in as uncontrolled variables which continually affect the worker's rewards from the job independently of his investments. Thus the stage is set for concerns of felt injustice to arise.

How Concerns of Felt Injustice Were Expressed

We shall here proceed by presenting and commenting on various kinds of illustrations of the ways in which concerns of felt injustice were expressed. In doing this we shall again proceed from relatively simple to more complex situations. In each of them there is expressed some out-of-lineness between perceived rewards and perceived investments.

Why Shouldn't We Be Paid a Little Bit More?

Let us begin with the following illustration in which a woman with ten years of service feels that she is not sufficiently rewarded in comparison with girls with shorter service.

"I suppose that when the new operators are doing the same job as we are they should be paid the same. But it just seems funny for a girl who has been here only six months to be making almost as much as we are when we've been here 10 years. We're both doing the job about as well as it can be done—and both trying hard; so as long as there is no better job for us old timers to do—something that would need our experience—why shouldn't we be paid a little bit more?"

This experienced operator sees her social status in the group and the advantage she has gained by her ten years of service being gradually whittled away. The wage differential which gives expression to only one value—relative efficiency—logically decreases as the newer employee acquires proficiency. The value of seniority as a mark of relative status is thus steadily eroded. The most tangible way in which the older employee could maintain her social distance in the face of this encroachment was by moving up in the grade structure, a course not open to her, or by having her wage differential maintained by percentage wage increases comparable to those given to the newcomers, a course which would not make sense in terms of the logics of the payment system. So she feels she is blocked with no recourse other than that of seeing the status differential between herself and the newcomers steadily diminished. This she feels is not fair.

Woman's Place Is in the Home

"I don't see why they don't get rid of some of the women around here before they get rid of the men. A lot of these gals around here are just working for orchid money. They come down here wearing orchids, and here a guy with a wife and a couple of kids is the first one to be let out. They make more money, have better jobs, and the men have to do all the tough back-breaking work. Oh, I think if a woman is supporting a sick husband or something like that, or needs the money because she's a widow, that's okay, she should be able to work just as long as a man does. But for these gals that are working and their husbands are working too, and they're just salting it away, they ought to lay them off first. They don't need their jobs, they'd probably be better off if they weren't working anyway; they might stay home and raise their kids right. I don't see why the Company doesn't take that into consideration."

This is a common variation on the man-woman theme. Where both men and women are employed, a layoff policy based primarily upon seniority is likely to collide with sentiments held by men about working women, married men about single men, single career women about married women whose husbands are employed, etc.

The Informal Leader and the Bogey

An old timer had worked at his own speed over the years and felt that he was doing a good job. A system of keeping a bogey was introduced in the group. The group reacted unfavorably but finally accepted it, but the old timer flatly refused to keep the necessary records. The counselor found that the employee considered this record as a check on his honesty which reflected on his personal integrity. It was also a blow to his pride of position in the group.

This old timer was apparently looking at the bogey not just as a measuring device, as he might look at a thermometer, but as a check upon his honesty and personal integrity. This, he felt, was not in keeping with his long established position in the group. The innovation thus served to reduce his rewards relative to his investments and he reacted by refusing to accept the bogey plan.

The Case of the Checkers, Kate and Sue

In the next illustration we have a more complex situation in which a severe disciplinary problem arose because of a controversy between some long-term and short-term employees in a work group.

A counselor was asked by a supervisor to interview a group of women who were at loggerheads with one another and getting little work done. He said that the trouble seemed to center around a difference in age and service but that he was unable to get to the bottom of it.

The problem arose when a group of women were hired to handle an increase in the work load normally processed by a group of long service women. After an initially friendly period of about a week the relationship of older to the new employees suddenly cooled and became hostile. The newer employees struck back and soon there developed name calling and quarrelling to the extent that some of the newer women quit and others asked for transfers.

Initially the interviews centered around personalities, the employees citing instances in which they had been ridiculed or insulted, the older ones saying the newcomers were calling them old bags and the younger ones voicing similar complaints. The moment of insight came when Sue, one of the younger women, said:

"You know when I came in here I was assigned to work with Kate (an experienced, long service checker), and one day we were working away and she said, 'You know, you should average about 23,000 a day because I average 30,000. You are new on the job so you should do that much less than I do.' That sort of started me wondering about my output; I hadn't given it much thought before, so I decided to count it and I found I was doing 27,000. Then it dawned on me that she wanted me to do a lot less than she *because I was sort of new and she didn't want me to do so much.* She was sort of jealous of me and I think that's where the whole thing started."

This is what Kate said of Sue: "I know when I was new, I didn't try to push my way in on things and it was a long time after I worked here before I went to any parties or asked people to go out with me on my rest period or anything like that. I always waited for other people to ask me, but Sue doesn't seem to feel that way. She acts as if she can get right in with us, right after she first came she seemed to feel that way. . . . It just doesn't seem right somehow."

This case brings out as clearly as any we have the spontaneous way in which concerns about status factors are manifested. At issue was the senior position of the longer service women in the group, a position which they apparently felt they could defend only in terms of a differential in output rate compared to those with short service. There was obviously nothing intrinsic to the job to bolster their position, and if a young upstart, in a short time, could do it as well as they could, of what value was their ten years of service? Obviously not much in terms of their relations with the newcomers unless the newcomers took a good deal of time to bring their output rate up to theirs. This would make their skill look more difficult to achieve and this, in turn, would lend some more tangible support to the position of the more experienced women. A properly deferential beginner should, in this view, be modest in output as well as in deportment.

This can also illustrate how barren some work situations are in providing rewards for social investments. Here there was apparently nothing intrinsic in the job to justify a service differential so the employees created an artificial one which unfortunately, from a company point of view, tended to retard efficiency and arouse group dissension.

The Case of Merit Increases in a Group

The incident to be described occurred among a group of women inspectors following a semiannual merit rate review. As a result of the increases granted and withheld an already existing negative differential in the rate of the employee with the longest service was further accentuated with the repercussions described.

For convenience in following the narrative the following information will be helpful:

Inspector	Years of service	Rate of pay	Merit increase	Rate when laid off	Rate at recall	Difference in recall rate
A	8	$1.19	$.10	$.80	$.74	$.06
B	7	1.04	.08	.64	.64	.00
C	13	.99	.00	.85	.59	.26

On the day the merit increases were announced the counselor observed that C was crying and the others working in stony silence. She approached A who said:

"I suppose I should feel happy today but I don't—oh, Mary, I feel so bad. This morning when Joe (Group Chief) came up to me I just had my fingers crossed hoping I wouldn't get a raise but I did. You see, I like the money—that isn't the thing, but it's the other girls—you see, C didn't get a raise and she's got a lot more service than we have. Now, she's getting a lot less money. You see, mine was sort of a lucky break from the start. After I came back (recalled from layoff) I was made an instructress and I was the only one of the girls to get a raise that time and they gave me 10 cents. Well, that put me up above any of the rest of them and now it seems no matter how much we try, those other girls will never catch up—I just keep on going ahead of them. We've had it out before on occasions but this time, really, *I just prayed and prayed I wouldn't get a raise but I did. Is there any way I could give it back or anything?* You know, it seems to me that money isn't everything and I'd rather have C's friendship. It's made a difference already—I've noticed it. You know, that makes me feel awful bad because she's a friend of mine and I think she deserved a raise as much as I did probably—I don't know why she didn't get one. *I'd rather she'd had it than I did because she's got more service.* I wish you'd go over and talk to her and try to cheer her up—only don't say I said anything about it, for goodness sakes."

The counselor then went over to C, the girl who had not received a raise. She was blowing her nose and wiping her eyes when the counselor came up:

"I just had a terrible disappointment. You know, Mary, I counted on a raise—at least certainly if somebody else was getting one and I simply can't understand it. Here I am with 13 years' service with this Company—I started inspecting relays like this when this department first opened, but, of course, I was out during the layoff time, but I've had 13 years' service on these jobs and these other girls haven't had even ten years yet, and yet here's A getting $1.19 an hour since her 10-cent raise, B getting $1.04 an hour, that's what the figures are over here that I've been writing down. You see, I figured out that when A was called back she came back at 74 cents an hour and B came back at 64 cents an hour. That was the same as she had when she left. A had been making 80 cents an hour so she took a cut, of course, coming back—me, I'd been making 85 cents an hour but they brought me back at 59 cents an hour. Well, I always felt kind of bad about that because here I was taking too much less to start with. Well, then it seems like I've never been able to catch up with them. *They've got less service than I have but they've always had more pay and now, finally, this time they both get raises and I don't get anything at all.* That puts me way back. I'm only getting 99 cents an hour now and they're getting $1.19 and $1.04. I simply can't understand it. My work has been good."

The counselor asked if she thought that possibly her leave of absence could have accounted for it.

"No, I don't think that could be it because of my leave of absence counting on the next six months' raise instead of this one—we figured out that they must close in August in order to figure for December raises and I didn't take my leave of absence until September, so that was for the next six months; if I didn't get a raise this time I probably won't be eligible this next time. It certainly takes the heart right out of you. I asked Joe about it and he said my name wasn't on the list when it came up—that wasn't much of an explanation. Oh, well, there's no use crying over spilled milk, I guess, but as I say, it really does take the heart right out of you. Even if I would get a raise next time just think of all the money I'm missing in the meantime."

The next day the counselor went to the third inspector (B), the one who had received the 8-cent raise, who said:

"Well, I suppose you heard all about our little rumpus the other day—I saw C talking to you. You know, it's too bad but that's something we go through every time raise time around here—I'm just kind of hardened to it. I'm going to get my raise anyhow—I'm just putting it all in the credit union and saving it for my old age or something.

"You know, C is a very difficult girl to get along with—you can't work against her and you can't work with her—you see, we've worked together quite a long time now and I know for an awful long time I was taking the dirty end of the deal. She was making me cater to her every little whim and whenever there'd be any trouble it was always blamed on me. Finally, I just had it out with her. Then I made up with her and now I'm nice and polite and we talk and everything, but I'm not intimate with her any more as I was before. That taught me a lesson. But now A is taking it to heart.

"I remember—I guess it must have been last December, I was 11 cents underpaid and C was 2 cents overpaid (in relation to performance) and we got the same raise. She turned around to me and said, 'You lousy so and so, what do you mean by getting the same raise I did?' Just as though it was my fault the kind of raise I got—then she wasn't going to speak to me for a while. She takes everything like that personal. She seems to think that just because she's got more service she's entitled to more money—more consideration and everything. Of course, it was unfortunate that she ever found out how much we were getting. You see, when I came back in here they took me back at 64 cents—the same rate I got when I was leaving. Well, according to her it hurt because when she left she was getting 85 cents and they brought her back at 59 cents. However, I think there must have been a reason for that. I don't know, but she was laid off sooner than I was even though she had more service, and she was longer in coming back. You can't tell me the Company doesn't do that without a reason. But anyway she's always held it against us every time that we get more money than she does. She was just making it miserable for us all yesterday— she can be very, very mean and nasty about everything and A was taking it to heart—but she's like that—she holds a grudge for a long time. It will be quite a while before she gets over it. In the meantime, we'll have to make the best of it. One thing I'm lucky about—that I'm getting that much money—that I'm here at all."

Subsequently, the department chief was discussing the various employees who had received raises, why they deserved them and how happy they were to get them. The counselor commented that she noticed C had not received a raise and the other girls had. The department chief replied:

"Yes, I'm trying to get a rerate for her—she was out on a leave of absence at the time the revisions were being considered. Consequently, she got left out. The section chief brought it to my attention a little while ago and I'm trying to see what I can do for her."

The next day he told the counselor that he had managed to get C a rerate of 5 cents an hour, taking her up to $1.04 an hour, the same as B.

Here is an instance in which rates of pay were in line with efficiency but out of line with seniority. This out-of-lineness is keenly felt by C who feels her service has not been adequately rewarded in comparison with the others and that she can never catch up. It is also keenly felt by A who would rather not have her raise in pay than provoke ill feeling with C. B, having the least service, had apparently borne the brunt of C's ill temper and she seemed to feel all right about C's treatment.

It has often been said that differentials in rates of pay are the focus of more attention than the absolute level. This is brought out forcefully in the situation described. Note first of all that each operator knew not only the other's rate but also her rate history. Each knew what the others were earning before the layoff, their reinstatement rates, and subsequent adjustments in rates. They knew all of this to the penny. This information was not given out by the Company; they picked it up by themselves.

B says that there must have been some good reason why the Company rehired C at a much lower rate than she had when she was laid off. She also notes that in spite of her service C was laid off sooner and called back later than the others. This reinforces her conviction that some unstated reason was involved. This bothers C too although she doesn't say much about it. No doubt there was a good reason for this but the counselor's record doesn't bring it out. The likelihood is that she returned to a lower grade of work or to a job on which she was inexperienced and was assigned a rate in line with her contribution to the group's earnings. Actually she must have been a good worker because the absolute increase in her rate since being rehired, even before the correction made by the department chief, was equal to that of B (40 cents) and after the correction was equal to that of A (45 cents). Thus she was steadily closing the gap.

A Case of Incongruity in the Reward System

The counselors listened to many employees express concern about what seemed to them to be an incongruity between their movement in the labor grade structure and their resulting take-home pay. In some instances they said that they had been upgraded with no increase or a reduction in take-home pay or that they had been transferred laterally with a cut in take-home pay. This result usually came about because their piece-work earnings were higher than on the jobs to which they were upgraded or transferred. It appeared that in these instances the operation of the wage incentive system posed an internal contradiction to the logics of the labor grade structure which held basically that an upgrading should bring increased rewards, a downgrading reduced rewards, and a lateral transfer the same rewards.

In order to see what the actual relation might be between changes in grade and earnings we obtained the data for the Haw-thorne plant for the year 1964, which are summarized in Table 7.1. The data include all movement of personnel whether volun-tary or involuntary for the hourly rated force. The outcomes shown for 1964 are not unusual when compared to what has occurred in other recent years.

TABLE 7.1

CHANGES IN EARNINGS LEVELS WITH UPGRADINGS, DOWNGRADINGS, AND TRANSFERS AT HAWTHORNE PLANT: 1964

Changes in Earnings	Upgradings		Downgradings		Lateral Transfers		Total	
	No.	%	No.	%	No.	%	No.	%
Increase	876	92	168	62	448	53	1,492	72
Decrease	36	4	95	35	121	14	252	12
No change	38	4	7	3	283	33	328	16
Total change	950	46	270	13	852	41	2,072	100

This table shows that in 1964 there were 2,072 changes involv-ing upgradings, downgradings, and lateral transfers (without grade change). These took place among 9,400 employees and assuming that a different individual was affected each time, this would mean that about one in five was affected in some way.

Of those who experienced some change 950 were upgraded, 270 were downgraded, and 852 were moved laterally. The signifi-cant point the table is intended to bring out is that changes in grade bore no necessary relationship to changes in earnings. Those up-graded predominantly did get an increase in earnings; however, 62% of those downgraded and 53% of those moved laterally did too. The picture was similarly ambiguous with respect to losses and no change in earnings.

Numerous considerations enter into the end result shown in Table 7.1. Among those upgraded with a reduction in earnings, for example, there may have been some who changed from a piece-work to a day-work job and their increase in hourly rate was insufficient to compensate for their loss of piece-work earnings. Similarly, some may have changed from a shop job with high piece-work earnings to a salaried job, such as output tracer, where the salary was insufficient to make up for the loss in piece-work earnings. Such a reduction, however, might very likely be temporary and many employees willingly sacrifice an immediate reduction in earnings to get into a job they prefer and which normally offers them more opportunity for salary progress than the job previously held. Another situation which may result in an upgrading with lowered earnings is that in which the piece-work earnings in the higher grade are sufficiently lower than those earned in the lower grade to offset the increase in hourly rate accompanying the upgrading. Similar considerations account for upgradings with no change in earnings.

Among those downgraded and transferred with an increase in earnings, the chief factor accounting for the seeming anomaly would be variations in piece-work earnings between the old and the new payment groups. However, these categories might well include some who went from a day-work job to a piece-work job. These considerations could also account in major part for losses in earnings among those transferred with no change in grade.

Enough has been said to warn against making any value judgments of the outcomes shown in Table 7.1. In each instance the action taken resulted from the logics of the payment system and careful consideration of each case. Our purpose in presenting it is to show some of the apparent contradictions which arise in the reward-investment ratio from the administration of a complex payment system. The principal factor making for these imbalances would appear to be a wage incentive system which, while rewarding increased investments so long as an individual remains in his payment group may result in inequities when he is transferred out or moved to a higher or lower grade. Movement of personnel under these conditions is usually made with an eye toward earnings and the labor grade tends to become of secondary importance. We will come back to this point in considering job development. The feelings of injustice arising from the changes we have been considering are illustrated in the following cases.

The Case of Slim, the Wireman

Slim had been a grade 34 relay adjuster; when interviewed he was a grade 35 wireman. Both jobs were on piece work.

"Before I came into wiring I was on relay adjusting. I liked the work and was doing very well at it. The group was only earning about 35% at the time. Then I was offered this upgrading to a grade 35 wiring job. I didn't want to take it but was talked into it.

"There were eight of us who were offered this job. The Section Chief on wiring got us together as a group and he sure painted a beautiful picture of what we could expect. He said output was going up in the wiring group and with the higher grade we couldn't miss. Then he let us take five minutes extra on our rest period and told us to go to the cafeteria, have a smoke and a cup of coffee, and talk it over among ourselves. We were all enthusiastic about it and couldn't see how we could possibly go wrong in taking it.

"Since then four of those eight have been put back on adjusting, they just couldn't make the grade. We work harder and we just don't seem to be able to get our percentage up. In the meantime, though, the relay adjusters have pushed their output up to where they are making $60 a month more than I am on my grade. I wanted to go back but when I talked to my supervisor about it he said, 'Okay, but I will have to lay off one of the adjusters to make a place for you.' Well, I didn't want that to happen so I told him to forget it."

The Case of the Demoted Supervisor

Nine months before this interview took place the employee had been "busted from a section chief back to an individual." As a section chief he talked freely to the counselor about his job but never personally. Even after his demotion he had talked about it only superficially. He held himself in high esteem and felt that a person of his intellectual capacity should be able to handle anything that came up satisfactorily himself. Then one day he asked for an interview. The following are expressions of his feelings about his demotion:

"I just can't reconcile myself to what has happened to me as you very well know. I've been counseled by my section head, my department head, and my assistant superintendent on this matter, and have received no satisfaction whatsoever. Oh, I shouldn't say I haven't gotten any satisfaction. There has been some, but it has been very slight, and I have always sunk back each time to feeling as badly if not worse about this thing as I did in the beginning.

. . . . .

"For nine months now—ever since this thing happened—I've fought with myself and thought and talked to myself about this thing and I still can't make any sense out of it. I've tried talking to my supervisors, but I can't really get any permanent satisfaction out of it. (pause) I just feel that a wrong has been committed and I know that there is nothing that can be done about it, but I'm just not going to be satisfied until something is done about it.

. . . . .

"I'm physically fine—I'm performing my work satisfactorily, I'm sure, and efficiently—but I'm mentally sick. I have, well you might say, a cancer in my mind. I just can't accept, in the light of what I think about how I performed as a supervisor, what they have said about me and the treatment I have received.

. . . . .

"I'm interested in my work—I try to do a good job—I've always tried to do a good job, and I still want to do a good job, but this thing just eats away at me and it has me in a mental turmoil all the time.

. . . . .

"I certainly have suffered anguish from this thing. Oh, I've tried to maintain an outward, cheerful appearance, but there is that inward turmoil. Every once in a while I can't catch myself—and it will pop into my mind and I'll say to myself, 'Oh, damn it anyway, how could this have happened to me?' I don't know, maybe I'm crazy in a way—not crazy but you've heard of people having two personalities, haven't you? Well, sometimes I feel that way, sometimes I feel two people inside my head and I carry on conversations with myself, that is, in my head. I try to counsel myself as it were and it is all very confusing. Here I am an intelligent adult. But no one can explain this to me. Maybe I would feel better if someone tried, but there is just nothing that can be said.

. . . . .

"I keep thinking of things that I have to my credit and I can only think of a few instances that I might have done something that might have been to my discredit. Say, perhaps, the only criticism of me as a supervisor could be that I was over-zealous in my work and perhaps appeared a little brash at times; but that very activity was exactly the way my higher supervision acted and if that is what I did wrong, I was certainly never told about it. That's why it is so damned hard to understand—there are all these things spinning around in my head all the time—it's so hard to think about them clearly. One thing pops up after another. For instance, I'm thinking now—it's a little thing but it is something—I'm going into my eighth year now without an absence. I'm on the monthly roll and I'm getting on in years and I could take some time off and nobody would think anything about it, but it is just that my health has been good and I'm not the kind of a person who does that. I want to do my work, but I haven't yet received recognition for that, I feel good—I'm alert and I haven't slipped back at all, I am not an old codger. I have about six more years to go before I'll be sixty and I know I can handle my job and more, and yet here I sit. You see how puzzled this gets me? Do you understand what I mean?

. . . . .

"Maybe it would be better if I took all those books I have in my drawer that say all those good things—all the notes I've kept, maybe it would be better if I took them and just threw them away, and try to start all over again for my few remaining years.

. . . . .

"I know they have had to demote a lot of very good men, a lot of excellent men, and to do that they have had to make some pretty serious charges against them for one reason or another. I wish I could feel really sure that that's what happened to me. That my supervisor feels that I really did a good job, that they just said what they said to form an excuse and that it won't be held against me in the future. I don't know, I talk about this thing and talk about this thing. . . ."

This interview is illustrative of one of the more extreme forms of loss of investments. Downgradings in which a nonsupervisory employee is reduced in grade also represent loss of investments but they ordinarily are not as keenly felt as a demotion from supervisory rank back to nonsupervisory status.

This interview brings out clearly the shattering effect such action can have on the individual's morale. He feels a loss of social status, a loss of identity with the organization, and a deterioration in his concept of himself. The anguish and self-incrimination resulting from this type of action is less when one is caught up in a wholesale demotion due to declining business, but even when this occurs one is never sure that his rank will be restored. This uncertainty is reflected in the interview. He wonders why, if his demotion was due solely to declining business, his supervisor had to cast about for some other logic. This rankles in his memory; he thinks and thinks about it and begins to have doubts about himself. We see how his whole self-concept has been blasted, he has been shaken to the core, and this gives rise to all sorts of apprehensions, doubts, and inner searchings.

The Case of a Man Laid Off

The company reward system promises that if the employee works hard and does a good job, he will be rewarded; if not, his rewards will be reduced or withdrawn. It does not say that under certain conditions this may be reversed and that he may have his rewards completely withdrawn and his investments cancelled, even though he does a good job. Yet this is what can happen during a layoff; he can be the best worker in the whole department and still lose his job.

Losing a job through being laid off may, to the employee, represent an injustice of the highest order. It deprives him of his means of a livelihood but more than that it comes about for reasons which, try as he will, he cannot control. He can meet all the standards anyone can conceive of and still lose his job. Further he fares no better—worse if he has less service—than someone else who is doing just enough to get by. Such a worker can keep his job while the better worker loses his—what could be more unjust?

Any eventuality which can take away the employee's means of a livelihood while he is fulfilling the prescription for keeping it is likely to arouse concern and some bafflement. This is well expressed by a worker who was being laid off.

"Yeah, this is quite a joint. A guy has been in the service and he comes here looking for a job and they give him a big glad hand over in employment. So a guy gets to working here and he works as hard as he can, tries to do a pretty good day's work and doesn't fool around or get in trouble or anything, kind of keeps his nose clean. In the meantime he gets married and he has a kid or two. Now he's got about three or four years' service and the company says, 'Sorry, Bub, you've got to go.' And there's some guy over there came in during the war; he's nothing but dead wood anyway, always fooling around, but he's racked up six or seven years' service. So he stays and he stands there laughing up his sleeve at you. What's a guy supposed to think of something like that? I think it's a bum deal myself. There's no reward for doing a good job."

In cases such as these as well as in downgradings and demotions the employee's investments are reduced or wiped out. Perhaps all that one has invested in his career is leveled at a single stroke. Under these conditions we have a reversal of everything the organization has been trying to build up; under conditions of a severe reduction in force it goes by the board. This can serve to undermine the worker's confidence in the reward system and foster a get-by attitude.

How the Resolution of These Concerns Is Reflected in Organizational Behavior

The resolution of these concerns may be reflected in various forms of behavior at work. In the case of the person who feels that he is properly and fairly rewarded for his investments, for example, he may feel loyal to the company, act dependably, and feel a close identification with the organization. If he feels that his rewards are in excess of his investments, he may feel grateful and perhaps a little guilty. He may respond by increasing his investments; doing more than he needs to or helping out in various ways. If he feels that his rewards are less than his investments, he may complain and try to get increased rewards for his investments or he can slack off and reduce his investments or he can quit and withdraw them completely. All these forms of behavior can be looked upon as efforts to establish or maintain an equilibrium in the rewards-investments ratio. In some instances the worker's response is active, in others passive.

For our purposes we would identify as representing the two alternate extremes of behavior, (1) that in which the worker perceives his rewards as in excess of his investments and works harder to rectify the balance as is frequently evidenced, for example, among younger workers who are experiencing rapid advancement, and (2) that in which he sees his rewards as less than his investments and responds by slacking off. The following case illustrates this latter form of resolution.

The Case of the Slow Down on Conveyor #1

The slow down came spontaneously and without warning. One Monday morning the men on conveyor #1 instituted a slow down which reduced their efficiency from 127% to 107% and the night shift that followed them slowed down in exactly the same amount. Efforts of the supervisors and the union stewards to break the slow down failed and the stalemate continued for several months until broken up by a reduction in work schedules which necessitated the reallocation of personnel.

The conveyor group involved in the slow down was adjusting relays which, when completed, were wired by a group of women on an adjacent conveyor. Unless the second conveyor kept pace with the first conveyor, work would pile up and reduce the efficiency and the earnings of the men on conveyor #1. There were two other conveyors in the department which were similarly related and all four were operating on a two-shift basis. The employees were on a group piece-work incentive plan in which the entire department formed one pay group. Thus the output of each conveyor had an important bearing on the percentage earned.

Because of the introduction of a new type of switch and the conveyorizing of the work some six months before, earnings had been pegged at a level of 136% to permit the operators time to pick up efficiency under the new setup without loss of earnings. It was understood that unless actual earnings increased to this level within a reasonable time the percentage paid would be gradually reduced. This arrangement had been agreed to by the union. At the end of the fiscal month preceding the slow down the management had decided that a reasonable amount of time for bringing up the output rate had elapsed and that the scheduled reductions in allowances would be put in effect.

The men on conveyor #1 were the most efficient in the department and before the work was conveyorized had performed at 180% efficiency. However, under the new setup they found that their efficiency was being limited by the women's conveyor to the extent that they had never been able to exceed 127%. With the threatened reduction in their piece-work earnings unless they could bring their output up to 136% and the limitations on their doing so imposed by the speed of the adjacent conveyor, tension among the men steadily mounted and they vehemently expressed their dissatisfaction to supervision and to the union.

The last straw which precipitated the slow down occurred when the departmental supervisors, in an attempt to break the bottleneck, decided to schedule the women's conveyor group for Saturday work. The slow down occurred the Monday following the first Saturday the women worked. Efficiency dropped to 107% which according to the supervisor was an all-time low.

These are some of the men's comments on the situation:

"The responsibility of the supervision is to figure out a way to keep enough skilled help on conveyor #2 to complete all the units we turn out. Instead they don't do anything about it and don't seem to care."

*   *   *   *   *

"What got our cork out was rewarding those women for laying down on the job. They don't care whether school keeps or not. Look at the absentee rate among them. Some of them stay home under any pretext."

*   *   *   *   *

"Some of them take advantage of Saturday overtime to stay home other days. Some of them take off Monday and Tuesday and they only lose half a day's pay" (based on a five day week).

*   *   *   *   *

"If those supervisors knew anything they would pick girls for that (bottleneck) job who wanted to work and we could rely on."

The supervisors responded to the slow down by first trying to persuade them to drop the tactic. A meeting was held for this purpose in a higher supervisor's office to which all the men and the union representatives were invited. The union maintained that the supervision was wrong in threatening to reduce the percentage and that the group should continue to be paid 136%. The supervision would not agree to this but instead insisted that the arrangement of working the girls on Saturdays from time to time enabled them to handle all the work conveyor #1 could turn out. All that was needed to avert the reduction in earnings, they pointed out, quite logically, was for the men on conveyor #1 to turn out all they could. With the slack provided by the overtime arrangement the group could in fact increase their earnings if they would apply themselves.

These arguments failed to sway the men and the slow down continued. In retaliation the scheduled reduction was allowed to take effect and the men were admonished never to leave their work positions or talk to one another unless absolutely necessary. As a part of this disciplinary action the counselor was requested to suspend his activities temporarily so as not to provide a loophole for the no-talking rule. This was soon dropped when it was observed that the men were not obeying it anyway. Not only did they continue to talk but they also would occasionally go out on the bridge for a smoke or absent themselves for some other pretext.

As the supervisors increased their pressure on the men, some of them began to find ways to retaliate. One of the group chiefs was fairly new to the department and the men were aware that he didn't know much about the type of work they were assigned. Increasingly as time went on he became the target for ridicule and abuse. One of their maneuvers was to bait him in some way to cause him to display his ignorance of the job. As an example, one of the workmen when asked by the group chief to work on a certain type of relay refused to do so. He was actually working on that type of relay at the time but the group chief didn't know it. The group chief reported him to the department chief and when "called" by the department chief the employee denied that he had refused to do the work requested of him by the group chief. Later in the counselor's presence, the employee called the group chief over and asked him why he had lied about him to the department chief. An argument followed in which the group chief, still not aware of the employees' trump card, insisted he was right. At the most telling time in the argument, when all the others were listening, the employee revealed that he had been working on the relay in question all the time, thus making his point that the group chief had misrepresented him. At this point the others in the group, who were following the argument closely, broke into loud laughter.

The group chief later commented to the counselor: "Boy, I'm telling you this thing has got me crazy. I come in on a Monday morning in a frame of mind to overcome anything. Before I'm on this job an hour my disposition is spoiled. I'm ready for ulcers. I'll admit I'm having a lot of trouble and the infuriating thing is that I don't know what to do next."

Considering first the rewards-investments problem here, we see that a group of men, previously regarded as outstanding performers, suddenly found themselves through no fault of their own with some of their rewards wiped out. What had formerly been a satisfactory level of output was now, because of the conveyor setup, too low. The management recognized that a period of time would be necessary before they could bring their efficiency up, so in order to permit this they pegged the earnings at 136%, making up the difference between what the employees earned and what they were paid by an allowance. So right from the start we have a situation where the men were being told not only that their investment was too low to earn what they had been paid in the past but on top of that they were given a dole or charitable dispensation out of management's kindness. From the men's point of view this was not an equitable transaction. Their rewards were being reduced because they had to turn out more work just to stand still. A further aggravation was that their own efficiency was being held down by the women's conveyor. So not only were the men faced with the prospect of fewer and fewer rewards for their investment, but they could do nothing about it. They were boxed in; the whole situation was one of rank injustice.

To superimpose upon this a reversal in the roles traditionally assigned to men and women brought their feelings of injustice to a head and the men erupted in anger. By scheduling the women to work Saturdays, and this is the second point, there was not only a reversal of roles in the sense that the man is the principal breadwinner and therefore the more deserving of overtime but, in addition, the women were being rewarded for lying down on the job whereas the men were penalized for doing all they could. So there was a double penalty for the men, their rewards had been reduced by the management and their social status was ignored in the treatment accorded the women. This was literally adding insult to injury. The men responded by withholding their effort, thus reducing their investments.

SUMMARY

We can summarize this chapter with reference to Figure 7.3. The need we have been considering is one of being treated fairly

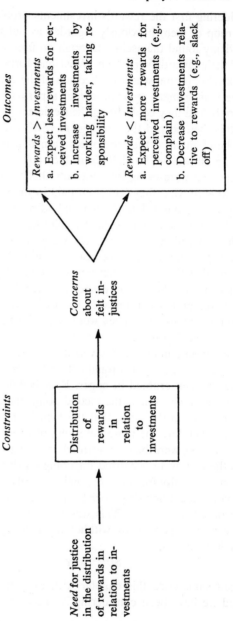

FIGURE 7.3

OUTCOMES OF THE FELT INJUSTICE SYNDROME

in relation to others. The constraints to the fulfillment of this need arise from the ways in which rewards are distributed in relation to investments. Any out-of-lineness gives rise to a concern of felt injustice. The behavioral outcomes depend upon whether rewards are seen as greater or less than investments. If greater, the employee may react by demanding less rewards for his perceived investments or he may try to increase his investments by improved performance, doing extra jobs, and generally making himself useful. If he sees his rewards as being less than his investments, he can protest or he can reduce his investments. Some of the common forms of the latter are slacking off in work, stalling, and, in extreme cases, walking off the job.

CHAPTER VIII

Authority

CONCERNS about authority are intrinsic to the human organization of industry and affect the behavior of every employee even though the majority may not be disturbed about it. Most employees seem to make a successful accommodation to authority if only at the level of pleasing the boss. Others, while outwardly complaisant, may harbor inner protests while still others go on to higher levels of accommodation in which needs for growth and independence are achieved. Whatever the forms of its resolution, the concern is general and coping with it becomes an ongoing process, stimulating some to high levels of achievement, some to low level accommodation, and still others to abject surrender or open rebellion.

In proceeding, we will first develop the framework in terms of which we will be looking at this syndrome. As a second step we will present four cases illustrative of extreme manifestations of dependency. We will then, as a third step, examine the role of the supervisor in relation to these concerns. This will center around a case study of three supervisory styles. Using this case study as a base, we will then, as a fourth step, try to show the relation of the supervisor's interpersonal style to the need for interdependence. This will show how supervisory behavior can promote balanced distance between the individual and the organization such that a healthy relationship of interdependence is maintained. From this there emerges the profile of the "fair" supervisor, skilled in maintaining a balance in the relation of rewards and investments.

ELEMENTS TO BE CONSIDERED IN THE AUTHORITY SYNDROME

The elements we wish to consider in discussing the authority syndrome are shown in Figure 8.1.

FIGURE 8.1

ELEMENTS IN THE AUTHORITY SYNDROME

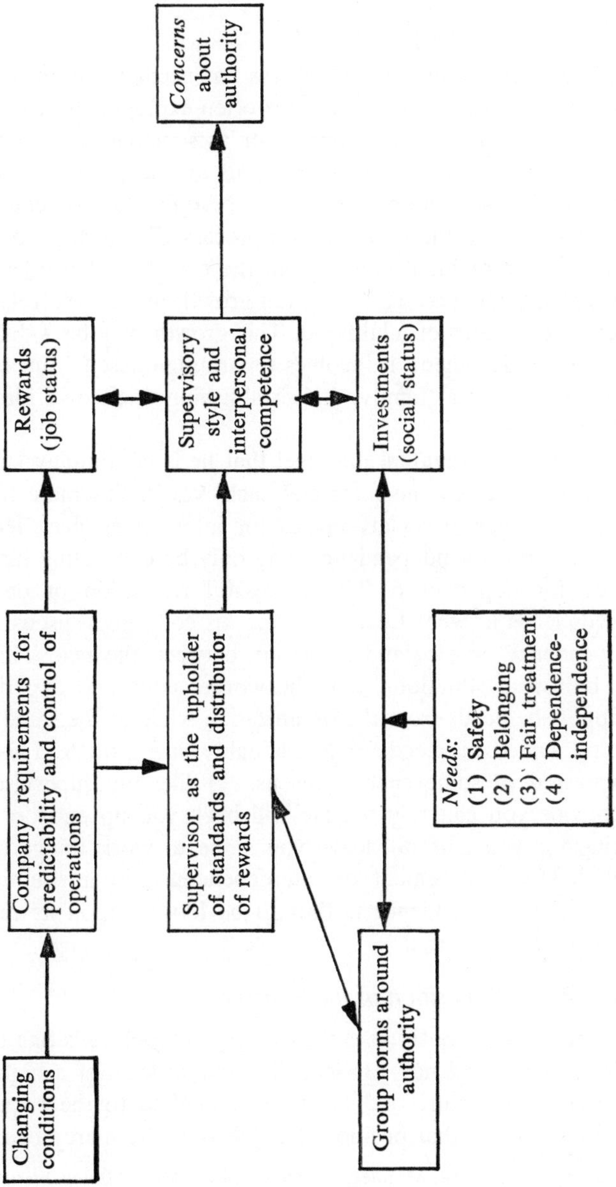

The Need for Interdependence

Every person in varying degrees has needs for both dependence and independence. Dependence is often expressed as a need for direction, sustenance, and support or as someone or something one can depend upon. Dependency needs are deeply imbedded in the personality, stemming from the embryonic state of complete dependence upon the mother. The process of growing up is one in which the individual moves from the complete dependency of infancy through successive stages of growth toward the relatively independent status of adulthood. This growth may be a difficult and painful achievement; it involves separating oneself from one's parents, the parental family, and establishing one's own identity and place in society.

While the individual may feel that he is continually striving for independence, no one completely achieves it. The mere fact of being a member of society makes for interdependence. The person who asserts his independence may only be concealing his extreme need for dependence. The successful resolution of dependency needs leads to what Levinson [1] and his colleagues discuss as interdependence or a balanced relation between the two. This means, in industrial situations, that the worker comes to experience the support he needs from the organization while at the same time not being denied his need for individuality and growth. This is often expressed in some such terms as, " I like my supervisor, he is someone you can rely on. He will back you up and do the right thing for you and still leave you alone to work things out yourself." The achievement of interdependence in a situation often making for dependence is thus to be looked upon as realizing a higher order of need.

The Worker's Position in the Structure

The worker's position in the Company structure is one of almost complete dependency. He is at the bottom level of a highly stratified social structure and must accommodate to the requirements and changes of that position. His job is at the mercy of economic

[1] Levinson, Price, Munden, Mandyl, Solley, *Men, Management and Mental Health* (Cambridge, Harvard University Press, 1962), Chapter IV.

forces over which he has no control and he must conform to the requirements of rules and standards to keep this job.

This position of subordination becomes a daily reality in his interactions with the supervisor. Here he is continually cast in the role of a subordinate, he is at another's beck and call and must continually accommodate to actions initiated on him by others. Being at the bottom of the structure, he cannot pass orders and directions along to someone else; he must accommodate to them or pay the penalty for failing to do so.

It is at once apparent that there is little room provided in the technology for accommodating the worker's needs for growth and independence. The whole thrust of the situation is toward dependency and conformance. The organization of work for efficient production requires that the worker be in attendance and perform the operations required of him to keep the job moving. The system of rewards and penalties reinforces this tendency and requires conformance if the individual is to be rewarded. In this view the work situation fosters dependency and rewards it, independency can be tolerated only in a limited degree and at the risk of sanctions. The work situation, then, does not look hospitable to the need for independence—one wonders how in fact any room can be made for it.

Group Norms

Group norms around authority can be seen as coming into being to provide some room for needs for independence. These norms arise from and give expression to the worker's position in the structure and are directed toward the control of the forces of subordination. Some of the more commonly expressed group norms around authority are:

—Don't squeal or tell tales out of school.
—Don't put the boss in a hole if he is a good guy.
—Don't be a brown-nose always sucking up to the boss.
—Don't be a fall guy and let them manipulate you to show up the group.
—Protect trade secrets.
—Watch out for spies.
—Play dumb.

One can see that implicit in these norms is the admonition to resist or subvert the formal authority, and they further imply that by doing so the individual can show that he is not a mere pawn of organizational forces but has a need for and should show some measure of independence. By acting in these ways the worker may feel that he is more of a man in his own right and will not be pushed around.

But when viewed in the light of the need we are considering, it seems clear that rigid adherence to these norms fosters not interdependence but counterdependence; that is, they serve to resist the formal authority rather than to foster a viable accommodation to it. Thus, while perhaps making the worker feel more of a man, they become counter-organizational forces and his needs for interdependence go unfulfilled. To achieve interdependence the group's norms would need to be restructured to permit and foster a higher order of accommodation.

The Role of the Supervisor

The supervisor comes into this picture in his role as an upholder of standards and distributor of rewards. A too rigid enforcement of rules and standards leads to the denial of needs for interdependence and to the strengthening of group norms making for counterdependence. Similarly, should he go to the other extreme and seek to identify himself with the group, the supervisor abnegates his position and himself becomes at odds with the system he is supposed to uphold. Either course fosters dependency at the cost of interdependence.

How then does the supervisor, in the conduct of his job, avoid this dilemma while helping to promote the growth of interdependence? One approach is through the supervisory style and interpersonal competence he displays in maintaining balance in the rewards-investment ratio. While he is limited in the formal rewards he can give and the investments these take into account, he can always enlarge upon them, for example, by granting recognition and appreciation for work well done, by seeing that the worker is not made to suffer from delays and interferences beyond his control, by being dependable and predictable in his behavior, by preparing the worker for change, by the training and help he gives, and by the care he exercises in making job assignments. These are all ways in which he can enlarge upon the reward side of the equation.

On the investment side of the ledger not only can he take into account the investments for which formal rewards are granted but he can also take into account the myriad of social status factors valued by the group. These encompass such things as finding ways to recognize age and seniority in his day-to-day relations, learning how to take into account the informal group structure and the positions of the individuals in it, and by the attention and understanding he displays in dealing with each individual. In short, by conceiving of his relations with subordinates as a series of psychological or social transactions in which investments are recognized and rewarded in kind and degree, the supervisors can build up a counteroffensive to the forces making for dependency and counterdependency and foster the development of growth and interdependence in man's relations to the organization. These processes, in turn, tend to feed back and influence group norms away from counterdependence toward interdependence.

We are not implying in the above that the supervisor is a free agent in making it possible for employees to work out these accommodations. If he is under strictures from those above him to enforce standards rigidly, he may not feel free to recognize and reward social status factors. If, however, he is delegated responsibility and given room to make his own decisions, he can enlarge upon both rewards and investments and keep them more in line than if he continually has to conform to rules and procedures imposed upon him from without. Such prescriptive rules are based upon a logic of rewards which tends to ignore social status factors. He needs sufficient flexibility to deal with the work situation in all its complexity if his leadership qualifications are to pay off.

ILLUSTRATIONS OF EXTREME MANIFESTATIONS OF DEPENDENCY

In this section we wish to look at some of the more extreme manifestations of dependency in the relation of subordinate to superior. We shall proceed by presenting four illustrations of commonly encountered situations centering around the dependency syndrome. All of these are illustrations of coping with dependency needs. The list is not exhaustive but only representative of certain types of response.

(1) The Case of Marie, Excessive Need for Approval
(2) The Case of Red, Baiting the Boss
(3) The Case of Steve, the Malingerer
(4) The Case of Joe, the Rebel

The Case of Marie, Excessive Need for Approval

Marie was young, single, engaged to be married, and had two years of service. She had worked in several other plants and had an excellent work record with all of them. The following is a brief synopsis of her career with the Company before and during the period of the study.

August 1950

Hired as a welding machine operator. Achieved spectacular success, breaking all output records. Liked her job but showed extreme sensitivity to any criticism of the quality of her work.

Spring 1951

Decline in schedules. Marie heard from one of the girls that she was to be transferred because of her short service. This upset her so that she could hardly work. When called to see the department chief about a transfer, she cried and asked to stay on. Permission granted for a time.

December 1951

Transferred to a bench job in another section of the plant. She made this adjustment quite easily but said she did not like bench work.

January 1952

Requested interview with counselor. Cried hysterically and was almost incoherent. Her complaint: The group with which she worked was criticized for poor quality. Marie took this criticism personally. She felt her work was perfect but because it was mixed in with that of the other operators she could not be given proper credit. She asked her supervisor for machine work but he refused her request because the work her group turned out was so poor.

She cried continually throughout the interview, reviewed her past work achievements as proof of her good workmanship, and spoke longingly for a machine job where she alone would be responsible for her output and where she would always know where she stood.

At the end of the interview she seemed to feel better and said she would keep her work in a separate box so it could be inspected separately. She expressed great fear of her supervisor and hoped for a transfer to machine work soon.

February 1952

A practice was introduced by Marie's department whereby the older girls would train new girls for the job and then move on to another job themselves. This was intended to increase their versatility and required fairly frequent job changes. These changes upset Marie because she thought her supervisors were pushing her around so that she couldn't make a good showing on any job and this would give them an excuse for laying her off.

March 1952

She was rotated onto the night shift. After two nights she reported sick and came in the following week with a doctor's certificate stating that she could not work nights at all. At this time she told the department chief all about her frustrations in getting onto a machine job. He promised to give her a spool winding job and if she did well on that to upgrade her to a coil winding job. Marie was "in seventh heaven" after her talk with the department chief.

April 1952

Marie worked hard and in four weeks' time had reached a level of output normally reached only after three months. Work slacked off and the instructress, knowing nothing about Marie's talk with the department chief, moved her to other work. Marie thought that because the instructress had moved her, she did not like her and had contrived a plot to criticize her. Again she broke down and cried.

Two weeks later the counselor found Marie in the rest room crying hysterically with the matron and a secretary to a higher ranking supervisor trying to comfort her. This was Marie's account of what had transpired:

1. The job had been put on piece work and the instructress had admonished all the girls to come to her immediately upon finishing a job so that she could assign them another one. Marie said this was a bawling out but it was for all of them and she didn't take it personally.

2. Marie ran out of work and immediately went to the instructress as directed. The instructress was busy so she told Marie to wait at her bench. After fifteen minutes had gone by, Marie thought the instructress had forgotten her and so she went to her again. The instructress, angry at the intrusion, ordered her back to her bench. At the end of the day

Marie had forty minutes' idle time to account for and she didn't know how to figure her bogey without having this idle time count against her. In addition she knew her department chief would be watching her efficiency to determine whether she merited an upgrading to coil winding and she felt that he would be critical of her low output record for the day.

The next day the instructress assigned her to a former job which neither she nor the twelve girls she had trained for it liked. The newer girls refused to go back on it but Marie while inwardly protesting accepted the change. "I don't know why I have to go back on it," she said, "when I am an old girl around here and none of the new girls have to stay on it."

On this occasion she decided not to acquiesce to this objectionable assignment so readily and protested to the instructress. "The instructress," she said, "got real nasty and told me to get back on that job and do as I was told. . . . I could just feel the tears coming."

Shortly after this encounter the section chief, who was fairly new in the department, came over to her and said that he had heard that she was complaining about the kind of work she got. She explained that she didn't mind the work so much as being changed from one job to another all the time. He said, "Well, it's good to know all sorts of different jobs. That makes you a versatile operator and then you are more useful."

At this Marie said she wanted to cry again because it seemed to her that no matter what she did or whom she talked to, she just got pushed around from one job to another and other girls with less service and less experience than she got promoted to machine jobs. She said she talked to everyone about it and nobody did her any good. She finally decided to see the higher ranking supervisor, found him not in and ended up in the women's rest room crying hysterically where the counselor found her.

The sequel to this story was that the new section chief had a long talk with her in which she poured out her tale of woe. When she finished he said he could not promise her a machine job but that he could place her on a wiring job if she thought she would like it. Since she had had some experience as a wireman in a radio factory she said she thought she might like it. He said he would, however, mention her interest in machine work to the department chief.

A few days later the counselor again found Marie in seventh heaven. She said that the department chief had stopped by her work place and had told her she was doing very good work and that the section chief had spoken very highly of her to him. A few days later she was given a coil winding job and from this point on Marie's talk with the counselor shifted to her plans for her approaching marriage.

In the case of Marie we see a young woman desperately struggling to achieve an outstanding performance record. In this she is continually frustrated by arbitrary job changes. Her frustration grows until finally, crying hysterically and in a fit of desperation, she bursts into a higher ranking supervisor's office only to find him not in. In the sequel a kindly section chief listens to her story and gives her the approval and support she is seeking.

Marie's overriding concern centered around the authority figures with whom she had to deal. Toward them she displayed an attitude of mild paranoia and feelings of persecution. In every incident reported she saw some hidden conspiracy intended to thwart her aspirations. With each repetition she became increasingly distraught until finally in desperation she in effect threw herself at the big boss's feet. This episode brought about the kind of attention she desired and once it was accorded her she calmed down and became quite serene.

Of special significance in this case is the role of the supervisor in relation to her dependency needs. All of her immediate supervisors except the last one seemed strangely insensitive to the needs she was seeking to express to them through her outstanding performance record. Not only did they fail to provide her with the support she needed, they continually thwarted her by too frequent job changes. When, finally, the friendly section chief understood her needs and took measures to assure them she, as she said, was in seventh heaven.

The Case of Red, Baiting the Boss

In the case of Marie we see one variant of dependence upon authority; there are others including the person who is so lacking in self-confidence that he continually fails to meet job requirements and the person who invites subordination by baiting the boss. The case of Red illustrates the latter.

This employee, whom his co-workers called Red, was a high-grade electronics inspector who had secured employment with the Company after the war. He claimed to have been a PT boat commander in the Pacific and to have worked at his trade in several other large concerns in the Chicago area before that. He was 40 years old, had five years of service, and was married with two children. Slight of build, he had a ruddy complexion, thinning red hair, and a volatile temper which flared up at the slightest provocation. His chip-on-the-shoulder attitude had got him into trouble with his officers in the Navy and with his supervisors wherever he had worked. He was an outstanding worker, however, and his supervisors were willing to put up with him for this reason.

In the short time he had been employed by the Company he had advanced to the top grade in the department and found himself with no place to go. He had repeatedly demanded that he be given a super-visory post or an ungraded position in which he could make more money. As it was, he was earning $145 a week with overtime which, with his wife's salary, brought their total income, as he said, to a very comfortable level. Speaking of his salary to the counselor he said:

"I know I make out pretty well; $145 a week isn't exactly chicken feed but it doesn't last long. I like to spend money, that's what it's for. I tell my wife to buy anything she wants and we like to splurge a lot. I don't worry about a thing, all I want is more money."

Red's need for more money was a recurring theme in his interviews and in pursuit of this objective he began baiting his group chief, a supervisor who was generally well regarded both by his superiors and by the men. Standing at his bench one day he said to the counselor, "I ask the boss for a raise every day—I mean it—*every* day. In fact every time I see him I ask him for a raise."

As if to prove his statement, later in the day in the counselor's pres-ence he turned to the group chief who was nearby and said, "How about a raise, boss? I've got to have more money. I'll be leaving for my vacation next week and it would be nice to have a raise when I return. Can't you do something for me?" The group chief shook his head and said it was too bad he'd be gone only two weeks. Soon another em-ployee walked up and Red said, "I'm having a hard time getting a raise out of this fellow." At this point the group chief walked away. As he walked down the aisle, Red shouted after him, "Don't forget that raise."

What made Red's persistent prodding especially annoying to the group chief was that it aggravated an unfavorable morale situation among his employees which the group chief thought could, if it got further out of hand, ruin his chances for a much desired promotion. The morale problem centered around the labor grades which the men thought were too low compared to those assigned other types of skilled work.

The group chief sympathized with the men's complaint and had repeatedly tried to obtain a higher grade for the work of two of his longest service men. He finally succeeded but only by building a shaky case. "The work," he said, "barely called for it but I made such a strong story I was able to push it through. Now it back fires in my face."

What he was referring to was that the men whose work was upgraded, instead of expressing gratitude, asserted that the action only proved that they had been cheated all along. But more alarming was the rising chorus of protest by the other men that their work should be upgraded too. The group chief's gambit had not paid off and he now found himself faced with the possibility that he might be censured for showing poor judgment, if not misrepresentation of facts, in pushing the upgrading through; thus he felt his career could be in jeopardy.

Confronted with this situation the group chief decided the best thing he could do was to silence Red who he felt was at the bottom of much of the unrest. "That guy, Red," he said, "is becoming downright annoying. He doesn't ask for a raise just once a day but two, three, and four times a day. I've decided to have it out with him, either he toes the mark or I'll transfer him." This confrontation occurred shortly after Red returned from vacation. Faced with these alternatives Red at first protested and then backed down. The group chief in relating this episode concluded with a smile he could not repress, "That was two weeks ago and I haven't heard a peep out of him since." As if in vindication of his action, the group chief was shortly thereafter promoted and transferred to another organization so for him it ended on a happy note.

One possible interpretation of Red's backing down is that when he was confronted by the alternatives offered him by the group chief he really got what he was unconsciously seeking—a more tightly structured situation. This interpretation assumes that the bully by inviting more intervention secures support for ungratified dependency needs, that while outwardly independent he is internally dependent. The fact that Red had had a long series of altercations with authority figures wherever he had been would seem to support this interpretation.

The Case of Steve, the Malingerer

One of the common forms of protest against authority is seen in cases of malingering. Here there is a latent hostility to authority but instead of rebelling the person attempts to subvert it. These characteristics are observable in the following illustration:

Steve operated a riveting machine on a conveyor line. He claimed that he was unjustly being held accountable for defects which were in the components before they reached him. This led to several altercations with his supervisor, with Steve insisting he was not responsible and the supervisor insisting that he was.

After one such incident Steve complained of soreness in his right arm and was sent to First Aid. After examining him the doctor placed him on a restriction with limited use of his right arm and upon his return to the department he was assigned a day-work job pending removal of the restriction.

After working on this job for approximately one-half day Steve contacted his section chief and requested that the transfer be made permanent. He explained to the section chief that he was too nervous to continue with his former job. The section chief notified him at that time that on removal of the restriction he would be put back on the conveyor job. The counselor contacted Steve shortly after the conversation with the section chief took place. The following is a summary of that interview.

Steve stated that the section chief had heard from someone in the group that he had made the boast that he would get off the conveyor job by some hook or crook. According to Steve this made the section chief more determined that he would return to the conveyor job; also it seemed to give the section chief the idea that Steve was using his injury as an alibi to keep from working on the conveyor. He also explained that the section chief apparently was dissatisfied with his work performance and had stated that Steve used to be the number one riveter in this section but lately had slipped to a position comparatively low.

Steve said that the replacement for his job had made the statement that he would rather do riveting than any other job in the section. Steve also said he had heard that production had gone up since he had left the conveyor. Using these points as a basis for his thinking, he was unable to see why the switch could not be made between him and his replacement. He informed the counselor that he had tried to discuss the situation with the section chief on this basis but to no avail.

On the following day the counselor again contacted Steve and an off-the-job interview was arranged. While talking on the job the employee informed the counselor he was still on restriction and hoped that he would remain on restriction for some time.

EMPLOYEE: My father had another laugh on me. I learned something in just the short while I've been here that he said took him ten years to learn.

COUNSELOR: What was that?

EMPLOYEE: The idea that if you go along and do a job it's okay and if you do more than you're supposed to, that's okay, too, but once you stop and just do the normal run-of-the-mill job they get p.o.'d down here. That's the way the situation is down here now. It was okay as long as I was working my head off taking over everybody else's responsibility but as soon as I stopped doing that, when I realized it wasn't getting me any place and I started doing just the job that's mine on the job operation sheets, then I'm no good anymore, not a good employee. I'm a bum as far as they're concerned. That's practically what the section chief told me when he talked to me yesterday morning. That guy's really a strange one. No matter how much I argue or discuss something with him he still is able to retain his point of view. I can present fact after fact and at the end of it all he'll still have the same idea that he did when we started, you just can't reason with a guy like that. You know, I don't see why as long as he feels I'm not doing a good job and he feels that my replacement is doing a better job than I was able to do, and as long as my replacement wants to remain on the job and I'd much rather get off, I don't see why he doesn't go ahead and get rid of me—transfer me permanently over to the job I have now.

I've been up on top as far as work in the group is concerned and there's nothing up there as far as rewarding me for all that work, so as far as I'm concerned I might as well go to the bottom again, you get as much thanks down there. I won't do any more than the required job, if they expect me to that's too bad. I've definitely made up my mind that I'm going to stand by my guns.

The case of Steve illustrates a way of undermining authority by getting around it. Faced with criticism for permitting excessive defects in his work to go through undetected (which, by the way, can be a subtle way of flouting authority) Steve seeks to avoid criticism by withdrawal. This can be looked upon as one way of repudiating authority or perhaps more accurately as inviting punishment by flouting authority.

The Case of Joe, the Rebel

For many employees there is a very fine line between tolerable and intolerable forms of authority. They have a low boiling point and flare up in anger when they feel subordinated. An illustration of this is seen in the case of Joe. (The following is a summary. The full interview is shown in Chapter XI, The Difference Counseling Can Make.)

Joe, a machine helper, had asked his department chief for a raise. The department chief told him he was at the top of his grade and couldn't be paid any more. At this Joe retorted that he knew some others in his grade who got raises and that anyway he should be a grade higher. This argument continued, growing more and more heated, until at last Joe told the department chief to make out his time and stalked away. He talked to the counselor shortly thereafter. The following quotations indicate his state of belligerency.

"These goddam bosses around here, they aren't worth a damn. They . . . you have a raise coming and they won't give it to you. They give other guys raises all around you and they won't give you a raise. This goddam place stinks. The sooner I get out of here the better I'll feel.

"Hell, he sure burned me up. He tells me that if I think I'm due for a raise, I'm in the wrong place. Well, that sure is a hell of a way to talk to a guy simply because I ask for a raise, he tells me I'm working in the wrong place. . . . When a guy talks to me like the department chief did, I can't work for him at all. I wouldn't work for the s.o.b. at all."

Here we see a man who feels so outraged by having his request denied that he decides to quit (a decision he later revoked) and gives vent to his feelings to the counselor. The reaction here is not to subvert or withdraw but to show the boss that he will stand by his guns even though he has to quit his job. The underlying mechanism here is similar to that expressed in submission or withdrawal except in such instances it is internalized whereas in aggression it is externalized. The supervisor's behavior in this instance tended to further aggravate rather than placate Joe's hostility.

A STUDY OF THE REACTIONS OF EMPLOYEES TO THREE SUPERVISORY INTERPERSONAL STYLES

In the cases presented we have illustrated some of the more extreme manifestations of dependence needs. In order to show some of the more common everyday manifestations of concerns about authority and the role of the supervisor in relation to them we want to use a case study of the reactions of employees to three supervisory interpersonal styles.

The study to be presented is a synopsis of an extensive observational study made by a man and woman counselor of supervisory roles in a shop department extending over a period of thirteen months, April 1951 to May 1952. The group selected for study comprised 25 men and 15 women who were engaged in miscellaneous telephone parts manufacture. During the period of the study three different supervisors were in charge of the same group of workers. Since their supervisory practices were quite different, we have an opportunity to observe varying employee reaction to three quite different supervisory styles which might be called distant, accommodative or transactional, and close. Supervisor A, the distant type, was observed for five weeks, April 16 to May 20, 1951, but the counselors had had extensive acquaintance with him before. Supervisor B, the accommodative type, who replaced A, was observed for 18 weeks, May 21 to September 23, 1951. Supervisor C, the close type, replaced B and his supervisory practices were studied for six months when the project ended.

The Case of Mr. Black, the "Distant" Supervisor

Mr. Black was middle aged, mildly ambitious, a family man and boy scout leader, with specialized training for his job. He had about five years of service, all in the same organization. We shall first describe his interpersonal style and then the employees' reactions to it.

A. Mr. Black's Interpersonal Style
  1. *Keep at a distance.*
       "They teach us in charm school (Human Relations Course) about how we should get to know our people. So what happens? We start talking to Joe or Mary and get to know them and then they hit us with their complaints which always end up in more money. So then you're stuck with something you can't do anything about anyhow."
  2. *Wages are all that count.*
       "You see surveys that rank money about seventh on a list of factors important in employee morale. They got it wrong end up. Unless money demands are met, nothing else counts much."

3. *There's not much you can do.*

"With the class of people we get nowadays there's no use getting excited about absenteeism and lack of interest in the job. You just have to take them the way you find them."

4. *Problems will work out if you give them time.*

"Most problems will wash out if you can keep people from talking to you about them. Just reassure them and wait and see."

5. *Avoid taking action unless you have to.*

Two girls complained that they were incorrectly graded. He said he would look into it but if he did he never told them what he had found out.

6. *If complaints stop after you take action, chances are you acted hastily.*

A woman had complained to him and the union for a year that her work was too heavy. He finally got a man to replace her. Later he commented "I'm kind of sorry now I got that fellow to replace her. She hasn't said anything for over a month now so she probably would have calmed down anyway."

7. *Just keep cutting and cutting.*

"The only way to find out if you are overstaffed is to wait and see how they do when someone is absent. If they can keep up chances are you can get along without them. Just keep cutting and cutting and that way you can keep your costs down."

B. Employee Reaction Toward Mr. Black

1. *They felt reluctant to bring even job problems to him.*

Example 1

Employee #1's machine broke down. He complained about it to employee #5 who said he would have to see the supervisor. Employee #1 said he was afraid to and he didn't think the supervisor would do anything anyway. (This, even though he knew the supervisor was the only one who could get anything done about it.)

Example 2

The supervisor observed some boxes scattered about on the floor. He told the nearest employee they shouldn't be that way and to straighten them up. The employee said nothing and did as he was told and then complained to a co-worker that he was not to blame, that another worker had left them that way. (Why didn't he say this to the supervisor?)

EXAMPLE 3

They felt they had too much supervision and would be better off with an extra worker or two. "He's no use to us. We could do better without him."

2. *They felt he did not understand their problems and only half listened to them.*

EXAMPLE 1

One day he came down the aisle and in a cheery voice said to employee #5, "Well, things are looking up. Everyone is in today." The employee said, "I don't see #13." Mr. Black replied, "Oh, he's loaned out, you have #6 to fill in." Employee #6 was spending only part time on #13's duties, thus placing a heavier burden on the work group. Employee #5 said to the counselor, "He just doesn't see the situation we are up against and no one can tell him otherwise."

EXAMPLE 2

They felt he showed no appreciation for the extra effort they were putting into their jobs. They carried the load when short handed but no one seemed to appreciate their efforts. "In most departments you get something to show for your extra effort but not around here. They don't pay us any more and no one seems to appreciate what you do. We break our backs to help them out and then they don't seem to care one way or the other."

3. *They didn't trust him.*

EXAMPLE 1

Employee #7 told the counselor that they had not filled in for an employee on sick leave. When he returned he stayed a short time and quit. Mr. Black said he would get a replacement. Two years went by and he never did.

EXAMPLE 2

Mr. Black promised an employee he could take an extra week's vacation if he could get a replacement. He did nothing about it so the employee went to enlist the aid of another supervisor for whom he had previously worked.

EXAMPLE 3

An employee talked to Mr. Black about getting the labor grading people to restudy his job. He thought it should be higher. Mr. Black said he thought the employee had a good point and would look into it. Weeks passed and nothing happened. The employee finally asked him what had happened and he said nothing had come of it. The employee thereupon went to see the department chief.

4. *They felt that he would not go out of his way to do anything for them.*

EXAMPLE

New employees were given a tour of the plant as a part of a recently inaugurated induction program. Some of the longer service employees had never been out of their immediate location. They asked him to arrange a tour. He said it was impossible to spare them. They commented to the counselor, "It's darn funny that he can always get along when one of us is out sick."

5. *They felt he had pets.*

EXAMPLE 1

One was a woman about to retire. They said he couldn't do enough for her, saw her often and was always telling her to take it easy. They thought this was okay but it only added to their work load.

EXAMPLE 2

The other was a person no one else liked because of his independent ways, overbearing manner, and ever-readiness to contradict what anyone said.

EXAMPLE 3

After meeting an unusually heavy end of the month schedule, Mr. Black called them into a meeting to give them a pep talk and congratulate them on their performance. The only one who talked favorably to the counselor about this episode was the one no one liked. The others felt it was "too little and too late" in view of their everyday contacts with him.

6. *They felt he had no sense of humor.*

"You can never kid around with him."

C. COMMENTS ON MR. BLACK

Summarizing, we can see that Mr. Black had many of the attitudes of what might be called the minimal supervisor. He preferred to remain distant from his people and displayed little interest in them. If we conceive of the interactions between supervisor and subordinate as a series of exchanges in which each is in some sense rewarded by the other, it is obvious that in this instance the ledger was heavily in favor of Mr. Black. He asked much of his people but gave a minimum in return. As a result they felt rebuffed and unrewarded. The work got done but they felt over-taxed and had little zest for it.

The Case of Jim Green, the "Accommodative" Supervisor

Jim Green (he was generally addressed by his first name) was in his middle thirties. He had five years of service in various occupations; he was married, a home owner, and had been an independent contractor before coming to the Western Electric Company.

A. JIM GREEN'S INTERPERSONAL STYLE

    1. *He got acquainted with each employee.*

    EXAMPLE

        On coming into the organization he planned his time so that he could meet each employee individually, find out about his work, and then keep in personal contact with him.

    2. *He gave immediate attention to problems brought to his attention even though they were complex and time consuming and tried to be helpful.*

    EXAMPLE 1

        Two operators became disgruntled when another employee with shorter service had been transferred in and given a higher grade of work. He had been on the higher grade in his former department but both the operators felt they had first claim to the opening. Mr. Black had told Jim Green to let it ride. Jim talked with the operators and told them he understood their complaint and while there were no openings at the time, he would do all he could to get them an upgrading when the opportunity arose. At the first opportunity he upgraded the one with the longer service, explained the basis for his selection to the others, and within a few months secured an upgrading for the other. He kept in touch and reported progress with the second during this period.

    EXAMPLE 2

        Two employees, Slim and Rusty, worked side by side. They had the same service and age but Rusty's work was two grades higher than Slim's. The work was quite different but Slim thought he was just as good as Rusty and deserved the better job as much as he did. Rusty was on a grade 38 job, the only one in the department, and Slim's rate of pay was over the top of grade 36. It was impossible to upgrade Slim to grade 38 without moving Rusty, and it was also impossible to increase his rate of pay unless there was a general increase in the payment structure. This would not, of course, alter the differential in pay between them.

Jim Green explained all this to Slim but still he complained and even suggested that they each be changed to grade 37, then they would be equal. Jim tried to explain that labor grades were not established this way but Slim was not convinced. Realizing that the grade situation could not be changed and that the complaint was unjustified, Jim nevertheless did the following:

1. He brought the labor grading organization in to restudy Slim's job. He did this to assure Slim that he was not taking an arbitrary stand and wanted to give him the benefit of a doubt. The grade was confirmed.
2. He then sat down with Slim and went over the job layout and checked it with what Slim was actually doing. He found he was performing a checking operation not called for in the layout and arranged for another man to do this.
3. He then arranged for Slim to work Saturdays in another organization on an overtime basis to give him a chance to increase his take-home pay. Slim remained dissatisfied with his grade.
4. He then called in the placement organization to see whether they could arrange a transfer to a higher grade of work for Slim. The placement organization was unable to find such a job for which he would qualify. Jim and the placement representative sat down with Slim and went over this.
5. When all this failed to placate Slim, the supervisor told him he had done all he could but would continue to keep his interests in mind. Slim continued in his resentment toward Rusty but seemingly resigned himself to the situation.

EXAMPLE 3

The operators complained of a shortage of pans. The utility operator said he had checked and all were in use. The supervisor then went on a search of the plant, found a stack of unused pans in storage which if altered could be used, arranged for the alteration, and thus assured an adequate supply.

EXAMPLE 4

He worked along with the employees to help them out of a jam. One day when it was particularly important to get the schedule out he went to them and said, "Now look—after all, the most important thing is to get these parts out. So I'll come back here and we'll work together. Let's see what we can do by three o'clock (quitting time) and if we're not through then, Rusty says he will stay and finish it up."

3. *He had no hesitation interceding in the employees' behalf.*
   EXAMPLE 1

   A jitney driver who moved materials in and out of the department and who reported to another organization was about to be relieved for poor performance.

   Jim went to the driver's supervisor, said he had observed him driving his truck, and thought his problem was lack of training. The driver's supervisor then arranged to send him to the school for jitney driver training.

   EXAMPLE 2

   A stockroom was being consolidated with another, thus leaving the stock selector, a man with ten years' service, without a job. The department chief arranged to have the employee tested to see whether he could be placed on an office job. The employee had no clear idea of why he was being tested; he was fearful of the tests and resented the idea that after ten years of service the department chief felt he had to have him tested to determine his capabilities.

   When Jim heard of this, he told the department chief he would like to have time to talk to the employee, explain why the tests might be helpful to him, and allay his fears. The tests were postponed to allow him time to do this.

4. *He didn't mind sticking his neck out if he thought the circumstances warranted it.*
   EXAMPLE

   Jim had had trouble getting a stack of empty cartons and skids moved from the loading platform where they were a hazard. His supervisor had criticized him for this. On the following Saturday he rounded up a trucker and had him move the materials to the warehouse. The warehouse had not been notified and had no one to unload the truck. They lodged a complaint with Jim's boss who again criticized him this time for taking things into his own hands. He grinned as he told the counselor, "I had to go a rough five minutes but at least I got that stuff out of there."

5. *He felt it necessary to maintain his supervisory role in dealing with employees.*

EXAMPLE 1

Slim called Rusty "that Pollack" in complaining about him to Jim. "I told him that attaching nationality labels was out as far as I was concerned. I told him my parents were immigrants and his were, too."

EXAMPLE 2

He told the counselor that while he agreed with some of the things Slim said about Rusty, he could not let Slim know this. "As long as Rusty holds his grade I will maintain his right to receive the support that goes with that grade."

EXAMPLE 3

One of the workers was forever trying to impress him by saying how he came in early to get the job going, took on responsibilities he didn't need to, etc. One day Jim came in at 6:00 A.M. to check up. The employees started at 7:00 A.M. By 7:00 the employee hadn't shown up. Jim found he had punched in a few minutes before 7:00 and then had gone out for a smoke. "He didn't come in until 7:15. I looked right at him and he looked at me, and you could tell that right then there was a perfect understanding between us. I didn't look at the clock or say a thing. He went right to his job and didn't look up all morning. Along about lunch period I decided there was no sense in keeping him in suspense so I dropped by and started chatting. We talked about the job a bit but I never said a word about his coming in late. We get along fine now."

6. *He tried to promote more congenial relations among the workers.*

EXAMPLE 1

The employees when in need of help were prone to ordering one another about. This created a good deal of friction and resentment. "I've been telling them that if instead of ordering someone, like 'Step over here and give me a hand,' it might help if they said, 'When you have a chance would you mind helping me with this' or even saying please or thank you once in a while." He added he thought getting them to act this way would be a long, slow process.

EXAMPLE 2

Before assigning another employee to work alongside Slim, he took him aside and explained that he might encounter some difficulties with Slim but not to take them seriously and try to make the best of it. Later the employee said to the counselor, "I get along okay with Slim but I have to give in to him a lot. With a lot of people you don't feel like letting them take advantage of you but with Slim I let it pass. After all, his wife died and he has a son in service. When you sympathize with a person you can overlook a lot."

EXAMPLE 3

Just before the standard vacation period shutdown, Jim brought in a huge cake on which was written, "Happy Vacation Time." They all shared it during rest period time and several commented they had never experienced anything like that before.

EXAMPLE 4

An employee dropped a pan of parts making everyone jump. With mock seriousness, Jim looked over and called out, "What's your clock number?" Everyone broke into a hearty laugh and several scurried around picking up the parts.

EXAMPLE 5

When Jim was congratulated in an organizational meeting by the assistant superintendent for the fine job he had done, he went around to each employee and told him the organization had been commended for its performance and he wanted to thank each employee for his contribution.

B. EMPLOYEE REACTION TOWARD JIM GREEN

1. They felt they could talk to him about their problems and that he would do something about them. "If you ask him to do something you always know it will be done right away."

2. When he could not get the answers they wanted to their problems, they felt that he had done everything anyone could and appreciated his efforts.

3. They liked the way he worked with them when they needed help.

4. Several employees commented that what they liked about him was that he "didn't hang over them" while they worked. "He tells you what he wants done and then leaves you alone."

5. They liked the way he let them know when he was pleased with their work and went out of his way to show his appreciation to them.

6. They appreciated his efforts to keep them informed about anything that might affect them.

7. Generally they felt he was "a good supervisor" and "a good guy to work for." The job setter said, "Jim is the only supervisor in the organization who is worth anything."

8. They enjoyed his sense of humor and felt he was "a guy who gets a kick out of things."

C. Comments on Jim Green

The counselor observed that Jim was casual, friendly, and informal in his approach but that he could be firm. He had a frank, straightforward manner which left no doubts as to his sincerity. He never acted hastily, preferring to weigh the matter, make a decision, and then follow through on it. When something angered him, however, the counselor said that he got it out of his system then and there. He told the counselor that he never took his problems home with him. He had a sense of fun and liked to joke and kid around occasionally, and he enjoyed this kind of behavior when addressed to him. He was bored by paperwork and spent his time on the floor. He came into the organization on a promotional basis and everyone was glad to see him get it.

We can see from the foregoing that Jim tended to reduce the social distance between himself and his employees. He accomplished this not by relinquishing his role or intruding on the privacy of his employees but by being open and human and objective in his approach. He in effect took his own and the personalities of others for granted and focused upon problems rather than personalities. He maintained this initial assumption of trust and mutual respect unless he had good reason not to as in the case of the man who said he came in early to get the job moving when actually he punched in early and then went out for a smoke. Even here Jim proceeded tactfully and in such a way as to strengthen his relationship with the man.

The response to this method of supervision was entirely positive, old issues were settled, irking conditions were corrected, and attention turned toward the task at hand.

The Case of Mr. White, the "Close" Supervisor

Mr. White was 50 years old, had 20 years of service, had taught school, and had worked on various other assignments. He had suffered a heart attack a year before and on his return to work had been given an office assignment. He did not like office work because "nothing ever got finished and I always took work home with me." He had previously held the position occupied by Jim and was glad to get back to his old operating job again.

A. Mr. White's Interpersonal Style

1. *He attached great importance to past practice and routine.*

EXAMPLE 1

When he took over the job, he immediately reintroduced practices he had followed before without examining improvements other supervisors had made.

EXAMPLE 2

He spent a great deal of time out on the floor checking up on what was going on and making sure that rules were being followed.

EXAMPLE 3

He was a stickler on detail and gave precedence to routine. All requisitions and reports were carefully scrutinized and filed promptly.

2. *He placed a strict interpretation upon policy and practice.*

EXAMPLE

Shortly after a man was hired he asked for a transfer, saying that the employment interviewer had promised him a transfer after a few weeks. Mr. White said he needed a permanent employee and rather than arrange a transfer permitted him to resign. There was a general shortage of help at the time.

3. *He felt that the more he knew about the personal lives of his employees the better the human relations job he was doing.*

EXAMPLE 1

He was an ardent disciple of what he called "the human relations school," which, as he saw it, stressed the importance of developing "a personal relationship with each employee." To him this meant finding out all he could about each person's private life even though it entailed direct questioning and prying.

EXAMPLE 2

Mr. White told the counselor that a newly hired young man's parents were divorced. Here he paused to say, "You see, I told you I usually find out a good deal about my employees even though they have only been with me a short time." He then went on to reveal the details about the family's financial difficulties.

EXAMPLE 3

He suggested that the woman counselor see a 62-year-old woman in his section on the grounds that she had recently remarried without telling anyone about it. He asked the counselor not to mention that he had said anything about the woman's marriage because he had found out about it second hand himself, and it was only when he confronted her with it that she confessed about it.

EXAMPLE 4

He would follow up on his "human relations responsibilities" by seizing every opportunity to question employees about new developments in their personal affairs. They told the counselor he was always "sticking his nose in where it didn't belong."

4. *He enjoyed airing his views and telling his employees what they should do.*

EXAMPLE

He held meetings about every three weeks with his employees because he thought they were desirable from an employee relations standpoint. He always dominated these meetings, spending most of the time orienting the employees to the way he wanted them to carry out the work and setting forth precepts of good conduct. When employees started to talk, he would interrupt them to defend his position without really knowing what they were trying to say.

B. EMPLOYEE REACTIONS TOWARD MR. WHITE

The employees' comments about Supervisor C were tempered by their sympathy for his poor health and their feeling that he was sincerely trying to do a good job. Nevertheless the following statements indicate the general tenor of their responses:

1. *They objected to his continually checking up on them.*

EXAMPLE 1

They were aware of the supervisor's constant surveillance of the way things were going and felt he was "checking" on them. "Seems like every time you look up he's breathing down the back of your neck."

EXAMPLE 2

They tended to ridicule his over-zealous attempt to supervise every detail. "There he goes again like a chicken with his head cut off."

EXAMPLE 3

They resented what they called his prying tactics. "You never know what he's driving at when he comes around like that." "Sometimes I feel like telling him it's none of his damned business but I guess he means well so I let it go."

2. *They felt that he was a little like an old maid school-marm.*

EXAMPLE 1

A jitney driver was bringing a load through the swinging

doors at one end of the room when Mr. White called to him, "Be sure and see that those doors are closed behind you." The driver retorted, "It's pretty hard to go through doors and close them at the same time." He later told the counselor that if Mr. White kept on treating him like a child, "We're going to have a real run-in some day." This feeling was expressed by several other men in the organization.

EXAMPLE 2

An employee stepped on a round piece part, fell, and hurt himself. Mr. White asked him whether he wasn't the guilty one. Before the employee could deny it, a co-worker spoke up and said he had dropped the parts but thought he had recovered all of them. Mr. White spoke up in a loud voice saying, "Let's all see that this doesn't happen again." The first employee felt Mr. White was "trying to get something on me or he wouldn't have singled me out in the first place."

3. *They felt his meetings were a bore and an annoyance because they took up too much time they had to catch up on.*

EXAMPLE 1

Red: "The supervisors are having a long meeting today (with pretended delight). Maybe that means we'll have another meeting."

Tracy: "Yeah, prayer meetings" (all laugh).

Counselor: "What are the meetings about?"

Tracy: (Laughing) "I don't know, I guess we're just from the old school." (Others express hearty agreement.)

Red: "I guess we're just too set in our ways to want to change after all these years" (again sounds of concurrence).

EXAMPLE 2

The counselor was sitting with several employees at rest period time. Smitty yawned, stretched, and said, "What a night." (Then brightly) "Say, why don't we have a meeting this afternoon? It's about time." They talked about the meetings a while and someone observed that other organizations didn't have them.

Stew: "Probably we're the only outfit that needs them."

Smitty: "Say, we can't have a meeting. I just remembered, Red is off today. (To the counselor) You know at the last meeting Red came in late and sat away over to one side. He then pretended to be smoking a cigar on a toothpick, alternately puffing and blowing rings—obviously not giving a damn. He looked so funny even old man White couldn't keep from laughing."

EXAMPLE 3

On the way back from a meeting in which the supervisor had talked about the importance of good relations, Stew, who was in the lead, turned and with a show of excessive politeness said, "Canst I assist thee o'er yon puddle?" amidst much bowing and scraping by the others.

4. *They felt that, while overconscientious, Mr. White was trying to do a good supervisory job.*

EXAMPLE 1

They felt that he acted on their complaints when he thought they were justified. They said he secured help when needed and at times helped out himself.

EXAMPLE 2

An operator complained that the parts supplied him were faulty, thus making it difficult to use them. Mr. White, accompanied by the operator, went to see the department chief who supplied the parts. This department chief insisted the parts were good enough. Mr. White then went over the quality specifications and showed him wherein the parts were out of limits. The department chief still insisted that they be used. At this Mr. White said he would personally take it up with the assistant superintendent. The department chief then backed down. When word of this got back to the operators, they voiced their approval with such expressions as, "He'll stick up for you when you're right" and "Whatever else you say about him, he'll back you up when the chips are down."

C. COMMENTS ON MR. WHITE

Mr. White may be said to be an instance of too much supervision. The phrase "acting like an old maid school marm" probably best epitomized his general attitude and demeanor. Implicit in this attitude was the assumption that his people had to be told what to do. This they sensed immediately and with one exception, called appropriately teacher's pet, they resented it. His belief that the Company's courses in human relations gave him sanction to probe into the personal lives of his employees is in keeping with his general practice and illustrates one of the common misconceptions of such programs. It is this "too close" type of supervision which is likely to touch off latent hostility toward authority and may erupt in open rebellion.

Summary

This view of three supervisors with three characteristically different styles of supervision clearly illustrates that attitudes toward authority vary with the type of supervision exercised. With Mr. Black, the distant supervisor, they felt neglected, whereas with Mr. White, the close supervisor, they felt he intruded in their private affairs. In the former dependency needs seemed to be insufficiently recognized, whereas in the latter the need for independence was continually frustrated. Jim Green, the accommodative supervisor, was closer to his employees in terms of social distance than was either of the other two. Mr. Black was both physically and socially distant. Mr. White was physically closer but socially distant. Jim Green tended to put himself on the employees' level yet maintained a relation of mutual respect. As a consequence the employees were not nearly as apprehensive of authority with him as they were with Mr. Black or Mr. White, their actions were more open and spontaneous, they talked to him freely and generally felt they were part of a team.

If we were to conclude from the three supervisory situations cited that the employees were concerned about authority under supervisors Black and White, but not under Jim Green, we would miss the nature of the syndrome we are considering. It would be more accurate to assume that such concerns were present in all three situations but that they were more allayed in the case of Jim Green. What gave his supervisory style its special luster was the fact that he was addressing these concerns, he was taking them into account, it wasn't as though they were not there.

Supervisory Interpersonal Styles in Relation to the Need for Interdependence

With these three supervisory styles and the reactions of the same employees toward them before us, let us see if we can relate them to the need for interdependence. We believe we can do this by making a comparative analysis of these three styles, using as our base the questions about supervision which seem to be implicit in the concerns of the employees with respect to them. By abstracting these questions we are provided with a convenient framework for specifying more clearly in what respects each of these styles tends to foster dependence, counterdependence, and interdependence. The questions employees have concerning the supervisor's role can be identified as follows:

(1) Is he someone who can be influenced?
(2) Is he someone who can be trusted to represent you and your concern?
(3) Is he someone who is willing to listen?
(4) Is he someone who is just production oriented?
(5) Is he someone who is accommodative?
(6) Is he someone who recognizes his dependence on you as well as your dependence upon him?
(7) Is he someone who is transactional?

Can He Be Influenced?

The role of the supervisor has been extensively studied as it re-lates to influencing the behavior of the worker. In the examples cited we can readily see the reciprocal aspect of the problem, namely, whether the supervisor is susceptible to influence by his subordinates. Used in this way the term may be misinterpreted as meaning political influence or as suborning the authority in the sit-uation. We use the term in the sense of influencing supervisory behavior in the direction of achieving goals—both those of pro-ductivity and those of worker satisfaction.

An example of what we have in mind here is to be seen in the contrasting behavior of Mr. Black and Jim Green in the matter of providing replacements when someone was out sick or had left the Company. Mr. Black ignored the problems created for the em-ployees by such understaffing, whereas Jim Green initiated imme-diate action to provide replacements. In this instance, Jim Green didn't need to be asked, he was influenced by his lively awareness of what action on his part the situation called for. Another illus-tration of the same sort of thing is seen in the contrasting treat-ment accorded the two long service men. Mr. Black ignored their demands for an upgrading whereas Jim Green did all he could to obtain upgradings and was ultimately successful. Influence, then, to be effective must be reciprocal, and when exerted in only a downward direction without any room provided for reciprocity it arouses feelings of neglect and subordination.

Can He Be Trusted to Represent You and Your Concern?

In the formal supervisory hierarchy the employee's immediate supervisor not only represents the management to the employee but also the employee to management. This two-way aspect of the supervisor's role is commonly designated as two-way communication. In industry considerable stress is placed upon the importance of both functions, the latter having come into prominence with the human relations movement. However, the pervasiveness of this manifestation of the authority syndrome is often missed by construing it to apply only to verbal communications and to them too literally.

A supervisor is considered trustworthy by the Company if he discharges his duties in accordance with the needs of the business. From this point of view all three of our supervisors were trustworthy. From the standpoint of meriting the trust of the employees, however, Jim Green was far ahead of the other two with Mr. Black a poor third. Mr. Black only half-listened to what his employees said and he made promises he did not keep as in the case of the man's vacation schedule. Clearly he could not be trusted by employees to represent their concerns. Jim Green, on the other hand, not only paid attention to what his employees said but he made his own investigation of the surrounding circumstances as a preliminary step in processing a complaint or suggestion. If he didn't think the circumstances merited the requested action, he said so and explained why, as in the case of the man who wanted an upgrading because a colleague with the same service was two grades higher than he. Once he decided an action was justified, however, he persisted until he achieved a satisfactory solution. In this respect he demonstrated that he had management's confidence in the reliability of his judgment. This is a very important aspect of trust in one's superior. There are many instances in which employees lose confidence in their superiors because they are unable to secure effective action on what they have agreed to be a just complaint.

Is He Willing to Listen?

In the performance of his two-way communications function the supervisor is generally inclined to give more weight to the downward than to the upward flow, little realizing that the effectiveness of the latter has a significant bearing on the former. Employees tend to listen to and attempt to understand communications from their supervisors better when their supervisors show an interest in understanding them. Many information programs have failed for this reason. A problem arises, management thinks something should be done about it, and an information program is launched in an endeavor to get employees to see it from management's point of view. If employees feel that management has shown little disposition to understand them in the past, they are likely to give scant heed to management's own plea to be understood. Similarly the supervisor who only half-listens, like Mr. Black, or who takes what is said out of context, like Mr. White, is not likely to encourage upward communications from employees.

One of the most frequently expressed concerns of employees at Hawthorne pertained to their apprehensions about taking their problems to their supervisors. These were expressed in a great variety of ways, the chief of which may be briefly illustrated:

1. If I ask him for help, will he think I am incompetent and not capable of holding down my job?
2. If I protest the action taken (such as transfer, downgrading, or failure to get an increase in pay) will it jeopardize my standing and chances of (a) remaining on the roll or (b) prospects for the future?
3. If I talk to him, will he be annoyed by my taking up his time?
4. Can I talk to him without his putting the wrong interpretation on what I say? Will he think I'm being critical of him or the Company when all I'm trying to do is give him the picture as I see it. Will he conclude from what I say that I'm a trouble maker and not a desirable employee?
5. How can I talk to him about my situation when he is partly responsible for bringing it about? He must have known how I'd feel when he took the action he did. I'd only run into an argument and I'd be beaten before I began.
6. How can I talk to him about my personal affairs?

a. He is a busy man and has no time for such matters.
b. Personal matters shouldn't be discussed on Company time anyway.
c. If he knew the trouble I'm in, he would change his opinion of me.
d. I don't want my personal life gossiped about up and down the line and become a part of the unwritten record.

7. He would probably think I'm looking for advice, and if I didn't follow through on it, he would conclude I didn't think much of it or of him.
8. He would probably feel compelled to take some action when all I want is for him to know the circumstances.
9. The fellows may think I'm toadying to the boss or maybe squealing on them.

Is He Just Production Oriented?

The supervisor who is only production oriented fails to understand and take into account the values residing in the social organization. He is exclusively oriented toward the technical organization and the logics in terms of which it is administered. This orientation results in a lack of understanding of what is taking place at the employee level, to misevaluations arising from taking items out of context, and to a species of double talk in which the communicants are using the same words while meaning quite different things.

Examples of this one-sided orientation are seen in the supervisory practices of both Mr. Black and Mr. White. Mr. Black's puzzling comment that he made a mistake in placing the woman who complained about heavy work on light work because she now no longer complained might be understood in this light. He is saying that he lost money by hiring a man to do her work and that her complaining was probably unrelated to her work anyway. Why he would have concluded this from the evidence to the contrary is difficult to understand except in the light that he was blind to people. This inference is borne out in many of his other statements as, for example, the less you talk to your people the fewer the complaints you have to deal with.

Mr. White, while professing to be human relations minded, is as blind to the facts of social organization and human motivation as

Mr. Black. Mr. White gets a feeling of smug self-satisfaction from ferreting out bits of information about the personal lives of his employees and justifies his indulgence under the guise of "getting to know his people." An example was his gloating over his discovery that the 62-year-old woman had secretly married.

Incidents such as these and others in the record suggest that supervisors Black and White had an atomistic view of their employees. They saw the employees as isolated adjuncts to the technological process. The idea that they were a part of a human organization with its values, sentiments, and needs seemed to be totally lacking. Jim Green, on the other hand, implicitly understood this and took it fully into account in everything he did. The concern about whether the supervisor is only production oriented, then, is the concern whether the worker will be seen and treated not just as a cog in the wheel but as a person in a social context.

Is He Accommodative?

The technical organization requires only that the employee accommodate himself to its requirements. The employee in wondering whether his supervisor is accommodative is in effect asking whether the technical organization will be made responsive to his needs. As with the question of influence there is a danger that this will be meant as condoning relaxation of standards. What is meant, rather, is that the supervisor extensionalize his thinking about human organization just as he does about technical organization and that he work out a viable accommodation, thus maintaining the integrity of each. Stated in another way, within the requirements of technological space he creates as much social space as he can consistent with the needs of the business. Scope for social needs is thus kept from contracting as it might unless the supervisor makes a real effort to find ways of extending it in all directions. Among other things this means making room for individual differences, individual needs, and personal circumstances.

In the cases cited Mr. Black reduced everything to one dead level and was interested only that the work be done. The accommodation made was largely in one direction, that of technology. Jim Green, in contrast, developed room for accommodating human needs and in doing so enhanced both the technical and the human aspects of the job. This was reflected in the trouble he went to in helping them out on the job, in seeking better placements for them, and in following through on their suggestions or complaints. One of the most interesting examples of what we have in mind here was his sharing in their jokes and evidencing spontaneous good humor. "This is no school room," he was saying, "You are not children and furthermore I am not a stuffed shirt."

Does He Recognize His Dependence upon You as Well as Your Dependence upon Him?

In the industrial structure there is a strong presupposition that the subordinate is dependent upon his superior but not vice versa. For a superior openly to recognize his dependency upon subordinates might be construed as weak-kneed of him indeed. Yet all organization is of this character and everyone intuitively knows it. It comes vividly to the fore, for example, when an organization fails to meet a schedule, when suddenly all attention from top to bottom swings into a downward focus.

The employee is dependent upon the Company for his job, upon his supervisor for help, encouragement, and support, and upon his colleagues for friendship and protection. Conversely, the Company depends upon him for production, the supervisor for his own and his organization's success, and his colleague for his friendship and protection. Each is dependent upon the other and the more explicitly this is recognized the greater the possibility of balanced relations being maintained.

Is He Someone Who Is Transactional?

The minimal supervisor, represented by Mr. Black, assumes that the rewards from a job are those which come from meeting Company standards and that these contributions are adequately rewarded by the daily wage. In this conception of the worker and his work, higher orders of need and the role of the supervisor in relation to them are not recognized.

The fair or transactional supervisor, represented by Jim Green, not only recognizes these higher orders of need but, more importantly, conceives of his role as providing scope for their development. In the examples cited we see that Jim Green conceived of his interactions with his subordinates, including those which they initiated, as a series of transactions each of which was to be evaluated, acted upon, and brought to a close as soon as possible. In prosecuting these transactions he was businesslike, that is, he regarded them each as worthy of careful examination and appraisal and as calling for some action. His examination and evaluation were made without prejudice and when there was any doubt he gave the benefit of it (the baker's dozen) to the employee. They felt in balance, rewarded in particular ways for particular contributions, as they went along from day to day. Their rewards were thus cumulative and when he praised them for a job well done they regarded it, not as too little and too late as they did with Mr. Black, but as a bonus, as something added to what they already had. In summary, what the supervisor and the employees had done for each other was done in response to the other's needs and it was so evaluated. As a consequence each felt rewarded by the contributions of the other, the transactions were fair, and the supervisor was just.

The transactional supervisor, accordingly, is one who looks upon the daily interactions of the individual and the organization as a series of exchanges in which each is rewarded by the contributions of the other. But these exchanges go beyond the economic and include social and psychological contributions as well. Generally, the nature of the needs to be recognized are set forth in the employee relations policy but these tend to be materialized in the form of concrete programs and removed from the area of daily interaction. The transactional supervisor in effect includes the recognition of these needs in his daily relations with employees, thus providing them with a broad spectrum of social, psychological, and economic rewards.

Summary

Implicit in employee comments about supervision is a concept of how they would like to see him conduct himself in relation to them. One can see from the questions in terms of which we have organized their concerns that many of these relate to his dependability. They want a supervisor on whom they can depend to mediate their relationships to the organization. But more than this,

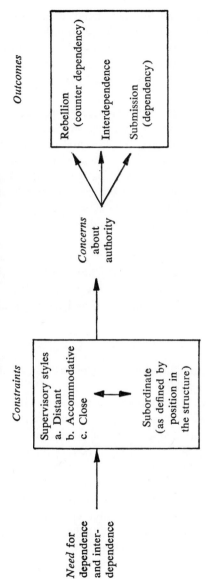

FIGURE 8.2

OUTCOMES OF THE AUTHORITY SYNDROME

they want these relationships handled in ways appropriate to the individual and the subordinate relationship in which he finds himself. From their point of view they want a supervisor who is close to them, one who is accessible and responsive to their needs but not too close; they want a space for themselves in which he does not intrude.

We have suggested that the ideal supervisor from the employee point of view intuitively takes dependency needs into account. He does this by adopting a transactional orientation toward all interchanges between himself and those reporting to him. He looks for the psychological and social as well as the physical investments the employee makes in his task and rewards each of them in kind and appropriate degree. In this way he extends the concept of a business transaction to the adjudication of psychological and social investments. Insofar as he is capable of doing this, employees tend to regard him as fair and just. The ledger is kept in balance, all debts are discharged, and the employee knows where he stands. In short, a condition of equilibrium will have been established in the relations between the individual and the organization.

GENERAL SUMMARY

We can summarize the main points of this chapter with reference to Figure 8.2.

Concerns about authority form one of the most significant and pervasive syndromes in industry. Involved are man's needs for dependence and independence and the constraints to their development in the industrial setting. These needs are projected upon the organization and focus upon the supervisor as a symbol of authority. The behavior of the supervisor can lead to feelings of neglect, foster submission, or provoke rebellion in the subordinate which leaves the basic problem of interdependence unresolved. Or, as we have seen in the case of the fair supervisor, his behavior can go far toward inducing interdependence through mediating the relations between the individual and the organization.

CHAPTER IX

Job and Individual Development

IN THIS CHAPTER we will consider the worker's need for the achievement of task competence in relation to the constraints to its realization arising from within the industrial structure and from his developmental history. The task structure provides the setting and conditions in terms of which the need for the achievement of task competence must be resolved, but the individual's need for achievement and his perseverance in overcoming the constraints he encounters to it stem in large part from his past development. Our main focus of attention will continue to be upon the individual in his industrial environment—in this instance, the task structure and his position in it—and while we will want to consider the relation between his personal development and his job development, we will not go deeply into the individual's personal history as that is beyond the scope of this chapter.

We have divided the chapter into two parts. The first section is concerned with identifying the elements entering into what, for brevity, we shall refer to as the development syndrome. In the first part we will be concerned with (1) examining the task structure from the standpoint of the scope it provides for task competence, and (2) identifying the forces operating upon the task structure which may tend to divert the achievement need away from task competence toward extrinsic rewards.

In the second section we will illustrate the forces in (2) above by looking at interviews with four workers who occupy three different designations—unskilled, semiskilled, and skilled—in the task structure. We will also comment as we go along upon the close connection we see between job development and personal development in these four situations.

Elements in the Development Syndrome

The elements we shall consider in examining this syndrome are shown in Figure 9.1.

Figure 9.1

Elements in the Development Syndrome

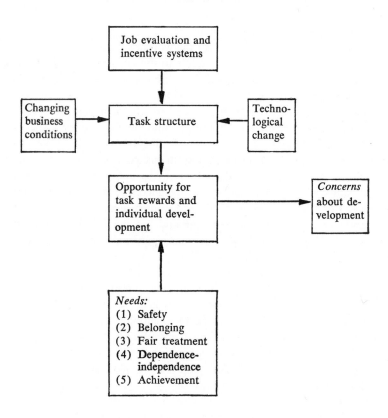

The Need for Achievement and Growth

The need we are considering is of the highest order we postulated for the population studied. We conceive of it as a general human need which emerges after the individual has satisfied his lower order needs and its direction is toward increased competence, self-direction, individuation, and independence. The worker whose achievement needs are activated is no longer passively accommodating to the pulls and pushes of the circumstances in which he finds himself but is actively seeking to cope with them in an endeavor to emerge as an autonomous individual with the capability of making his own decisions and assuming responsibility for them.

He is seeking to achieve his individuality in a situation in which, as we have seen, he must often contend with powerful organizational forces making for conformance and dependence, a situation in which individuality may easily be submerged or expressed only in deviant ways. He is in an area where personal decision making becomes of crucial importance in determining the outcome for by implication he is no longer content with accommodating to organizational decisions, he is committing himself to making his own decisions and choosing his own course. In making these decisions as to the course to follow, he must unavoidably take into account not only their possible outcomes for his career but for his entire personal and social situation as well, for now all these considerations come to a focus. It is at this level in the worker's development that counseling can play its most crucial role as an aid in personal decision making.

Intrinsic and Extrinsic Rewards

The rewards from a job are of two kinds, those which are intrinsic to the task and those which are extrinsic to it. Intrinsic rewards are found in the satisfactions of performing and achieving mastery and competence in a skill, in the recognition accorded the competent worker by the work group, the supervision, and management, and in the material rewards of salary, merit increases, upgradings, and promotions accorded by management for task competence. Extrinsic rewards are those which accrue from salary, general wage and salary increases (unrelated to merit), seniority, interpersonal relations, accommodative supervision, pleasant working conditions, and fringe benefits. We have included wages and salary under both headings because, as we will see, under certain conditions in which the task offers limited scope for intrinsic rewards, the worker tends to become oriented toward salary and social mobility as extrinsic rewards somewhat unrelated to task competence.

It will be noted that intrinsic rewards depend largely upon the skill components of the task whereas extrinsic rewards relate largely to the context in which the job is performed.[1] The work of a tool maker, for example, provides considerable opportunity for intrinsic rewards, that of a special machine operator or a relay adjuster less so, and that of an assembler even less. However, these possibilities are never absent, for even in the most humdrum occupations there is always room for a factor of competence. This is readily observed among, for example, elevator operators, janitors, and manual laborers.

Extrinsic rewards, on the other hand, are available to the worker who performs satisfactorily in his work however unskilled it may be. These rewards depend not upon the skill components of the task but upon the conditions which surround and support it. These become a focus of concern when there is little opportunity for intrinsic task rewards or when, as we have seen, inequities in their distribution arouse feelings of injustice.

Organizational Constraints to the Achievement of Task Competence

Before proceeding we should try to clarify the sense in which we will use the term "task competence." This is a relative concept which if used too loosely could readily be equated with the efficient performance of any job. At the other extreme, if used so strictly that it applied only to professional people or skilled artisans in their own employ, it would rule out everyone who has the status of employee. We must avoid either of these extremes if the concept is to serve any useful purpose. For hourly rated workers we feel we can rea-

---

[1] This distinction is analogous to that made by Herzberg and his colleagues between "motivators and satisfisers." Cf. Frederick Herzberg, Bernard Mausner, and Barbara Block Snyderman, *The Motivation to Work* (New York, John Wiley & Sons, Inc., 2d ed., 1959).

sonably say that the need for task competence is best gratified by a job which provides (1) interesting and challenging work, (2) opportunity to develop and practice a skill, and (3) a sense of identity with a craft or special group which is recognized beyond the boundaries of the firm. Competence, thus defined, means that the individual has achieved identity with a group or trade and that he has achieved some measure of independence; that is, he is not so dependent upon the organization and the threat of severance is not as catastrophic as it would otherwise be.

While the achievement need is perhaps best evidenced in the skilled crafts and trades, its presence, we assume, is found in workers at all levels in the job structure. We will therefore also want to consider its more general manifestations among lesser skilled employees if we are to see the alternate forms of behavior its resolution gives rise to.

The sources of organizational constraint to task competence were identified in Figure 9.1 as technological change, changing business conditions, and job evaluation and incentive systems. These forces operate in different ways to bring about constraint; technological change directly affects the task structure itself and its potentiality for providing intrinsic rewards; business conditions make for changes in work schedules, thus affecting the movement of employees in terms of the task structure—upgradings, downgradings, and transfers are of particular interest here—whereas evaluational procedures affect the incentives to task achievement. The possible impact of the first two upon the achievement need is generally understood. We would like to comment on the significance we see in the third, job evaluation and incentive systems. But first we should know more about the task structure itself.

The task structure

In examining the task structure to which the workers at Hawthorne were adapting we shall make use of recent data because they are readily available. In 1964 there were 174 hourly rated occupations in the manufacturing department of the Hawthorne plant. These ranged from common laborer (there were only 17 employees out of 8,830 listed as such—which is itself a commentary on the nature of a modern complex task structure) to the skilled crafts and trades in which there were some 1,200 or 20% of all hourly rated male employees. The most highly populated single occupation was that of bench hand (1,188), next, in order, wireman (765), assembler (655) and, close by, adjuster (620). A number of occupations had only one occupant: blacksmith, boring mill operator (trades), butcher (company restaurant), engraving machine operator, glazier, glue press operator, vacuum frame equipment operator, and wood working machine operator. All told there were 69 occupations which had ten or fewer occupants.

The training period ranged from a short period of orientation, at one extreme, to some four years for skilled crafts and trades trainees, at the other. For the bulk of the relatively unskilled work the training period (on-the-job training) extended from one to three weeks.

Distribution of occupations by labor grades. Through job evaluation procedures as outlined in Chapter VII, these 174 occupations were arranged into a labor grade structure of ten grades, each with a starting and a job rate, ranging from grade 32 at the bottom to grade 41 at the top. Figure 9.2 shows the distribution of occupa-

FIGURE 9.2

DISTRIBUTION OF 174 OCCUPATIONS BY LABOR GRADES,
HAWTHORNE PLANT: DECEMBER 1964

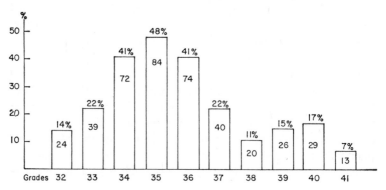

tions by labor grades. The total is in excess of 100% because many occupations extend over two or more grades.

This figure shows that the distribution of occupations by labor grades formed a normal frequency distribution if we omit the top three grades, 39, 40, and 41, which were populated by skilled crafts and trades. These form a secondary distribution at the top of the scale. The heaviest concentration of tasks occurred in grades 34, 35, and 36. These had from 72 to 84 separate occupations within each of them.

Distribution of employees by labor grades. In Figure 9.3 we have shown the percentage distribution of employees by labor grades and have contrasted this with the distribution of occupations shown in Figure 9.2. This chart shows (1) that there is little relation between the number of occupations in each labor grade and the number of employees in each grade, and (2) that the higher

FIGURE 9.3

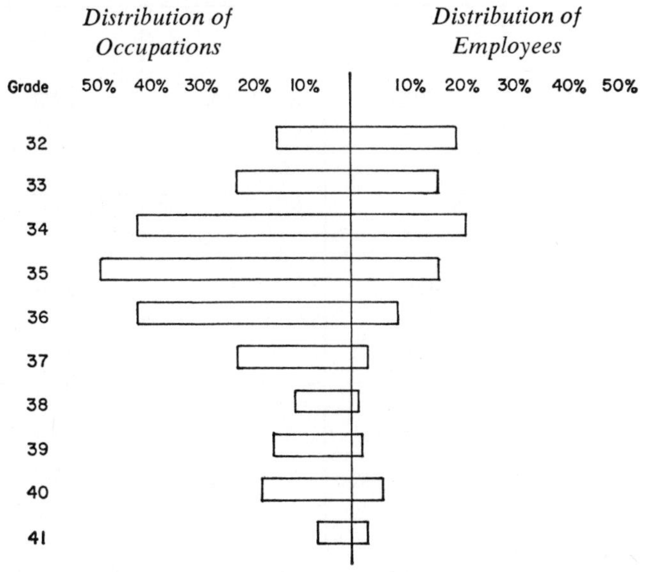

DISTRIBUTION OF OCCUPATIONS AND EMPLOYEES BY LABOR GRADES, HAWTHORNE PLANT: DECEMBER 1964

the grade the less populated it becomes. An exception is seen in certain jobs such as tool and machine construction which span the top three grades. The employees tended to be concentrated in the bottom four grades which account for 76% of the entire population.

Distribution of men and women by skill categories. A further question concerns the distribution of men and women in terms of skill categories. To answer this we have combined the three lowest grades, the next three higher grades, and those remaining to produce Figure 9.4. These groupings are those generally recognized in the Company as designating skill bands.

By combining the grades as shown in Figure 9.4 we see that

FIGURE 9.4

PERCENTAGE DISTRIBUTION OF HAWTHORNE
EMPLOYEES BY GENERAL SKILL CATEGORIES:
DECEMBER 1964

	Men	Women	Total
Skilled (Grades 38–41)	20%	0.0%	13%
Semiskilled (Grades 35–37)	47%	2%	32%
Unskilled (Grades 32–34)	33%	98%	55%

55% of all employees were in the unskilled category, 32% were in semiskilled work, and the remaining 13% were in crafts and trades. If we look only at the distribution of women workers, we see that all but a handful (2%) were on unskilled work. Among the men the situation was much more favorable with 20% on skilled work, 47% on semiskilled tasks, and 33% on jobs classed as unskilled. From this we can conclude that the type of work to which practically all the women were assigned offered relatively little opportunity for intrinsic task rewards. Compared to women, the situation among men was much more favorable in this respect with opportunity for skilled and semiskilled work provided for two-thirds of them. How this would compare with other large firms we do not know, but it would appear that the task structure offered considerable scope for the achievement of intrinsic rewards for men.

Labor grading and the task structure

In Chapter VII we discussed how labor grading through compressing a range of tasks within a grade and assigning them the same dollar value can give rise to feelings of injustice in the distribution of rewards among the workers assigned to the tasks so compressed. That this process also has significance for task competence is readily seen. The grade structure says to the occupants of such diverse tasks as assembler, adjuster, brake operator, buffer and polisher, cable former, cleaner, core maker, dispatcher, fireman, guard, oiler, packer, sawyer, etc., "We have looked at your jobs in terms of our job evaluation plan and you all come out in the same grade of work, grade 35. This expresses the relative position of your jobs in relation to all those in the structure." In short, whatever differences there might be in this range of tasks for the achievement of task competence are declared to be of no conseqence so far as monetary rewards are concerned. Here we see the first step in the diversion of the need for task competence away from intrinsic task rewards toward extrinsic rewards. Attention tends to swing away from task proficiency toward what it will pay, and the worker who wants to get ahead starts thinking in terms of getting more pay quite as much as the intrinsic rewards of the job itself. This process is accentuated by any system of wage progression which automatically increases every worker's rate of pay at stated intervals until the job rate is reached. With such a feature included in the wage plan the Company tells the worker that not only does it not value differences in tasks within a grade but neither does it value contribution above the minimum required to stay on the roll until after the job rate is reached.

The complication of wage incentives

When we bring in the wage incentive system, another step is taken in focusing the attention of employees and supervisors on extrinsic instead of intrinsic rewards. This is brought out vividly in the case (Table 7.1) showing that upgradings, downgradings, and transfers bore no necessary relation to earnings. It will be recalled that of the 2,072 employees who experienced some change in jobs in 1964, 950 were upgraded, 270 were downgraded, and 852 were moved laterally. Of those upgraded, 92% did get an increase in earnings; however, 62% of those downgraded and 53% of those moved laterally did too. The principal factor making for this ambiguous result was stated as being the variation in the piece-work percentages earned by the different payment groups to which the individual was moved. Among piece workers, consequently, take-home pay could override in importance the grade structure. As we pointed out, in such a situation movement of personnel comes to be made always with an eye toward earnings and thus the diversion from intrinsic to extrinsic rewards, which we first detected in the setting up of a grade structure, is furthered under the workings of the incentive system.

Summary

From this analysis of the elements in the development syndrome, we can see that the constraints to the achievement of task competence reside not only in the skill components of the task as such but also in the organizational forces impinging upon it. Technological change and division of labor do make for job simplification and the erosion of the skill factors upon which the achievement of task competence depends. But also important are the evaluational, control, and incentive systems which surround and dominate the task system. These do not alter the skill components of the task, but they do affect the meaning and significance these components have to the worker. By subordinating intrinsic task rewards to monetary rewards they help set the stage for the diversion of the achievement need away from task competence toward the extrinsic rewards of salary and social status. We will next examine some interviews to see how these constraints work out at different levels in the task structure.

HOW CONCERNS ABOUT JOB AND INDIVIDUAL DEVELOPMENT WERE EXPRESSED AND THEIR BEHAVIORAL OUTCOMES

This analysis will center around the interviews with four young men, all about the same age. The first is with a worker assigned to unskilled work whose job and individual development appears to be at a low level. The other three are with workers whose achievement needs have been activated in varying degrees. One of these is also on unskilled work, the second is on a semiskilled job, and the third is in the skilled category. We include the worker whose development seems to be retarded to provide a contrast between his orientation and that of the other three and also because it provides a good illustration of the relation of job and personal development. Some of the more significant passages in the interviews have been italicized for emphasis.

The Case of Mike, an Unskilled Worker

This is a condensation of an interview with a returned veteran who had been working as a production machine operator for two years since his release from the Army. The man had applied for admittance to the in-plant training course for precision machine operators and had been told that enrollments for the current class had closed and that he would be called in for tests at the next enrollment period.

EMPLOYEE: It sure is hot as hell out there in that damn shop, I'm telling you. I don't see why they couldn't get some fans up there or something like that because it certainly makes you hotter than hell out there, and you get all those steel shavings on your arms and everything else. It's pretty damn hard to take it all day long, then you have to keep putting out so many parts too, you know, so that makes it even tougher. I don't like it too well but what the heck are you going to do. You gotta make a living someway but then when you got a girl that wants to get married and everything but you don't know how you'll make ends meet in case you do. *It's all pretty much of a muddle just trying to live, I'll tell you that.*

COUNSELOR: You find things pretty well mixed up then.

EMPLOYEE: Oh, they're not mixed up. *It's just the way they all happened to come, I guess.* I think I mentioned to you that *I got shoved around again on the school business.*

COUNSELOR: Yeah, but I didn't get all the particulars on it.

EMPLOYEE: Well, just like I told you. The next day I went to see the boss and he gave me time off to go over and see the training people at Hawthorne (he was working at an outlying plant). So, I spend two and a half hours going over there and talking to him and everything. I found out that it wasn't all too hot anyway. He said I'd have to wait about six months to take the test and when I did take the test, why, if I passed and everything, I'd have to wait six more months at least before I could go to school. It did go a lot better than I thought though. I didn't have to go to see so many people about it but *I knew I was going to get turned down and that's just about all there is to it. I can just see myself sitting here though for years and never get anyplace unless I get some schooling.* You know, it's going to be pretty tough to get anywhere if you don't get some schooling nowadays. I've got to get a trade. If I get a trade then I'm going to be all right but if I don't get a trade why, it's going to be pretty rough I think.

As I said, the girl wants to get married and she wants everything all the time and she's always hollering at me about working nights so she can't go out and everything. It certainly makes life pretty damn miserable, I can tell you that. I don't know what to make of all of it. It gets to be pretty rough at times around here, I can tell you that. If I could only get this schooling—if I can only go to this turret lathe school—I'd be all right. I like machinery—I like to work around it and I don't want to do anything else. I've tried all these other jobs. Don't want to do anything else. This is the only work I really like.

I like the big machines—I like to do big things with them but I sure ain't getting nowhere now. But *I can't expect too much I guess because I gotta just kind of sit around here and pass the time until I can get along here to the point where I can get someplace.* I don't like it but I don't know what else I'm going to do. I'd rather work for

Western Electric than anybody else so I can tell you that. I've been at all of them and they didn't give a damn whether you existed or whether you just rot, so it makes it a pretty rough proposition to try to do anything and you get blocked everytime you try to do something. It's just like a football game. You get taken out all the time if you ain't careful. *Boy, they've thrown so many blocks into me that I don't know whether I'm going or coming. I hate to be pushed around.*

COUNSELOR: It's all kind of confusing.

EMPLOYEE: I guess it is, but it's been that way all my life so I'm kind of used to it. I just spout off, some days you're up and some days you're down. Today happens to be a day I'm down, I guess, but the trouble is that most of my days are that way. *It seems like everybody is always pushing me around all the time.* They don't help much by pushing me all the time. I wish I could get some education and then they wouldn't do it so much. But that's going to be hard to do, too. The only other thing I can do is to learn to be an operator on a turret lathe. That looks like that's out of the question now, too. I *don't know what the heck I'm going to do, but just sit back and work here.* I'm not particularly happy about the situation the way it is right now, but I think what I'll do is stick it out for a while and see what comes up. *Maybe something will really break here for me and I'll be able to get someplace here someday.* That's far off and I'm not sure whether I can do it or not.

I didn't tell my mother that I was going to go in and see about this job over here so I don't think she's going to be too unhappy and say, "I told you so." *I didn't tell her on purpose because I thought well, it won't go through and she'll say well, that's just another time that you fell down again, I guess.* My girl friend didn't say anything about it, but I think she was kind of disappointed that it didn't go through, but they don't tell the truth. *If I get ahead, okay; if I didn't, okay. As long as they can get what they want, that's all that's necessary.* She says she'll be very happy when I get off nights and we can go out and do something once in a while. My gosh, I can't do much more I think, because hell, I spend enough of my money as it is now. I don't know how in the world you can expect anybody to save any money anyway these days. She certainly asks an awful lot of a guy.

You know the other day when I went over to see about the job, why I got here at three o'clock and the boss called back about three-thirty and he told me to get right on the streetcar or the bus, and

see if I couldn't find out about this school. Well, by the time I got
over there and saw him and everything it was pretty doggone late.
It was almost five o'clock and so I got on the streetcar and came
back. Well, I killed half a day right there doing that. That suited
me all right because I didn't feel like working that day anyway. Then
I had to go down and see the nurse (about a cut finger) and then
I ate and came back up and it was too late then to get much done
so I just kind of fooled around and I don't think I even made my
20% but I just had a feeling that day that I didn't want to do anything. *I'm only making 20% and the rest of the guys are all down
on me around there, especially the supervisors, because I'm not doing what I should do.* So, I don't know what you think about it, but
I think I'll just hang on here for a little bit and see how things are.

I'd like to start up a shop of my own sometime. Boy, if I could get
a hold of two or three drill presses and a couple of lathes and a
couple screw machines, boy, I'd put out a lot of work. *I'd hire guys
and make them work. I'd make them put out a thousand parts an
hour.* I'd run the thing so I'd make some money on it. That'd be a
pretty nice deal, I think I could really make some dough. I wouldn't
fiddle around with a lot of these little things either. I'd make big
stuff. I'd make all kinds of things but I don't know where the hell
I'd get the money to get started. Then I wouldn't have to take the
back seat from any of these guys around here. I could do as I pleased.

Oh, I guess I'm just daydreaming again. You know, I do that so
damn much anyway. *I get all excited about something and find in
the long run it don't mean a damn thing anyhow.* I guess it just can't
be helped though. I'd sure like to do something like that though because it would help an awful lot when it comes to getting married.
But I'm not sure I could handle anything like that because I've got
to have more schooling. I couldn't keep books or nothing like that,
though. Maybe I wouldn't have to keep books, though. Maybe I
could just do it some way so I wouldn't have to. But as far as the
machines go, I could do that. But when you get to thinking about it,
there's an awful lot of stuff to contend with there and I don't know
whether it would be such a good idea or not. It's pretty hard to decide what to do sometimes. But I've got to get more schooling; I
know that. Maybe I better do that first. What do you think about
that?

COUNSELOR: To start a business like that does take a lot of consideration. There are a lot of things that you have to take into account.
Of course, it's your decision and you're the one that's going to carry

the thing out. I think it's pretty much how a man feels about it, whether he's capable or not.

EMPLOYEE: Well, that's about the way I feel about it, too, I guess, because I don't think I could really do anything like that. After you get to thinking about it, why it's pretty hard to figure out anyway that it's going to work out for you. First of all I ain't got no money, and second, I ain't got the education I should have. Third, I guess, I got some kind of an experience, but I don't know whether I could do anything like that or not. I guess that pretty well rules it out.

COUNSELOR: You brought up some important points that are worth considering, all right.

EMPLOYEE: Yeah . . . *I guess, I better just forget about that kind of thing because I could never make a go of it anyway.* But it doesn't hurt to dream. I'll just keep going here and maybe in a couple of years I'll get to go to school and maybe in that time I can get married and settle down a little bit—*stick here at Western Electric and get that service in. That's what counts. That old service you know. That's what everybody's always talking about and it's the only way you can get around anything here.* If you've got your service you're going to be able to get ahead. If you haven't got it, you just can't get anyplace around this joint. *Service means an awful lot and if you've got it you're going to get places.* You could even get to school, I betcha, if you had more service. I bet if I had, it'd have done more for me this time but I didn't have it so that's that. How you going to get around it when they turn you down and don't say anymore but that you can't take the test for six months. *Oh well, I'm not too anxious to try it again anyway. I'll just wait a while and see how things turn out and maybe it'll turn out all right,* and then I can go ahead and go to school. It gets so it's the same old thing day after day. You get down there and they expect you to make the rate. You can't do it and it gets on your nerves. I'm lucky if I make 20% but I just keep plugging and I still can't make any more. *So, they can take it or leave it. If they don't like it they know what they can do. They got all these rates set too high anyway around here.* You can't make them anyhow. Some days I feel like working real hard and I'll sit there and do it and get all of it done I can and go as hard as I can. I've never been much over 20% since I've been here. So, I don't know what they're thinking about.

The trouble is that there's just so many of these things that I'd like to do and I'm not able to do. *But I don't see any way out of it at all except just to sit back and do the best I can on this damn stuff.*

It's not going to do any good to keep belly aching about it—I can see that. I got all the supervisors out here down on me now because I keep asking for something all the time and keep raising hell for this and that, I just know I have. *But I'm not going to let anybody step on me* and if they want to do anything around here to shove me around, why, they're going to find here's one guy they can't do it too, that's all.

Well, I'm not going to worry my head over any of it. I'll get my 20% out or more if I can and if they like it, okay, if they don't like it, okay too. There's plenty other jobs that I can do and I'm not going to sit down here and take anything off of anybody. I'll get transferred into another department or I'll try to get to school or I'll just quit. *Life's too short to be worrying about things like that all the time. I'm going to show my mother and my girl friend though one of these days. I'm going to do something here that's going to make them feel a lot better about me.* I'm getting tired of them saying that I'm no good and all that stuff. I'm going to come up one of these days with something that will really surprise them.

Comments on the interview

There appear to be three major themes in this interview. One is a generalized feeling of failure which is expressed in terms of not being able to measure up to anyone's standards, the army's presumably, the Company's, his mother's or his girl friend's.

The second, arising from the first, is that he feels pushed around. He feels he is a victim of circumstances and is expected to conform to the wishes of others and to disregard his own feelings and preferences. He has developed an almost paranoid attitude toward those who implement the standards—his supervisors, the training director, and even his girl friend.

The third is his reluctance to take any responsibility for what happens to him. He does not try to meet the production standards expected of him largely on the grounds that he just doesn't want to put forth the effort. Not only does he not try to improve his performance at work, but also he does not consider, for example, going to night school in order to improve his education or learn a trade. Instead of doing any of these things, he chooses just to sit, build up seniority (in order to "get around things") and see what will happen. One finds few expressions of personal responsibility or self-reliance.

In this interview one gets the impression that Mike's personal development and job development are closely interrelated and in combination they serve to keep his total development at a low level. His orientation is toward the extrinsic reward of seniority; task competence is only something he daydreams about.

The Case of Henry, an Unskilled Worker

Henry was an assembler of telephone apparatus, age 25, with five years of service. Before coming to the Company he had worked in the shipping department of a large jewelry concern. The interview started with his reviewing that experience.

"Oh, it seems sort of as if I was in a rut down there—I didn't get a chance to get out—once you get in that rut why you're stuck. Oh, I don't want any more of that—it's just that, well, all you do is the same thing all the time—it was a pretty good job, though—it was inspecting, but still, I don't know—you see, that wasn't what I wanted either. *I wish I did know what I wanted.* I'd been taking this drafting for five years nights, and then I find out here that it might not work out so well because, as the fellow says, I'm in competition with college men and if it's that way I'll probably never get anywhere.

.   .   .   .   .

"You know, some people like to feel that they're all set—that the thing they've got is just what they want and they're willing to hang on to it for the rest of their lives—they don't care whether they get any better or any more money or anything like that. Well, I'm not that kind of a guy. I want to feel, see, that I can learn something—I want to feel that, well, whatever job I'm in I'm more than just an ordinary cog in the machine—I tell you, when you're just a cog in a machine you haven't got a chance. Boy, when I was laid off I found that out. They would be advertising in the help wanted ads for guys, you know, with trades—tool and die making—screw machine operators, welders, and things like that, but me, what the devil did I ever learn? I just learned something silly—something that anybody could do, see. Well, that's what I don't want—I don't want to be just another workman but the trouble is there's no sense in going a lot more to school if I can't learn something that's going to help me.

"I enjoyed night school, too. When you stop to think about it I gave up an awful lot of fun to take night school in those years—what have I got to show for it? Oh, sure, I like drawing—drafting—it's a good job—it would be something I really like but there's not much sense in taking up two or three more years if I can't see my way clear to something. You see, I can't say that I can here. I would think, though, that with all that training I had with blueprints and stuff I would be able to use it around here some day—on some job around here. I wasn't able to use any knowledge of drafting at all on all the crappy jobs I did when I was out. I tell you I did damn near anything. I was glad to get it, too. I'm glad to be called back here—don't get me wrong—the money's pretty steady but still, well, when I think about this Company, see, I think about a Company that will allow somebody to get ahead—to work up to somewhere—I'm glad to get back here even if I did take a cut from what I made before. When you get right down to it, though, this job isn't a big one—anybody can do it—the pay isn't very good, either—I mean comparing it to some of the other jobs, for instance. This job isn't very important, either, but I'm glad to be back, see, and I'm hoping that I can get located on something.

> .   .   .   .   .

"If I could settle down on relays or switches—maybe earn around $60 a week—that would be something. You know, that's really about what I want. Why I could begin to settle down on $60 a week, you know that? That's good pay and those guys out there get that. That's what I'm really shooting for, see. At the same time those would be jobs, you know, that would be sort of like a trade inside the Company. But that's what I think about. Well, if I could get on one of those jobs I'd really show them. Yeah, I'm not the fastest man in the world and I know it and I don't pick things up too fast, either, but, boy, once when I get it I've got it for keeps and, you know, you need a guy that's pretty thorough on that kind of work. When it comes to adjusting you've got to really know your stuff.

> .   .   .   .   .

*"I don't want to have to have things like my old man had them— or my brother, either—*you see, those guys they worked on a whole bunch of different jobs and they work a couple of weeks and they're off a week and then they maybe work a month and then they're off a week. It's not steady—they're not real tradesmen, see, and as a result, well, hell, we've always had to scratch around for dough and the old man can't count on anything and it's made my mother so she's always worried and I know it's made her older than she should be and, well,

maybe it sounds funny for me to talk this way but I'm the kind of a guy that wants to settle down—heck, I'm getting to be older now—I'm 25 and one of these days I want to get married and get started and have a home and a family and, gee, you can't even begin to hope to try to do any of that unless you've got a job that's going to hold you—you know that yourself and, well, *you see guys, some of the guys you went to school with passing you up there*—some of them got good jobs and they're located, and here I am the same age and I'm really not, well, I can't say that I even got my foot in the door—what's worse yet, I don't know what door I want. There's a lot of trades they've got in here, I know, that they could use—like they must have a welding school down here—steamfitting or something like that—anything like that— see, a real trade, that's what I want and if I can get into that, boy, I'd really hold that job and then once you get into those jobs you can start working yourself up—oh, you don't have to be a boss but you can get to be what's known to be a darn good man and that's what I want, but, see, it isn't any one thing—oh, I'd like drafting—I would really want that if I could get it.

"What I would really want is to get a job that would pay me, you know, give me these other things, you know, a car and that stuff. Then once you've got those things, well, it's the kind of a job that you can lose yourself in—that's really what I want to do—well, what's hap- pened as far as I see is that drafting was way in the back of my head and that was what I was going to end up as and I studied for it and worked like hell for it and, boy, I'm telling you it was one of the most terrible shocks when I couldn't get in here in drafting. You don't know how that hit me—I tell you I was just no good for a couple of months because it seemed like everything, you know, that I'd wanted to do like a guy does—he hopes for things and I could just see all that and never happening to me—boy, it made me feel terrible and it makes it all the worse because I don't know now just what I want and if I did know it would still be hard to find out how to get what I want.

. . . . .

"That's the whole damn trouble—my mind's in a whirl—I just don't feel like I'm getting anywhere—the things I've really wanted, I can't get to them, and I get to feeling sort of disgusted every once in a while —I get encouraged and hopeful and, boy, I felt way up in the clouds when I got called back here—I really did. Now that I'm here longer I see that it's going to take years before I can hope to get anywhere. Boy, when you get to thinking that way it really makes it tough. Oh, I don't want to say that I don't like it here at all—I'm awful glad to be back—

as long as they keep me here I'll still be glad *but the thing I'm worried about is how long are they going to keep me here? I was going to go up and talk this over with the boss and then we started hearing about layoffs and so I decided to keep my mouth shut.* That's just the trouble, see. If I felt like I was going to stay here for a while, then that would be different but I can't—things are beginning to settle down—if I could find out where I stood—what I ought to do, then it wouldn't be so bad but it just seems like I don't know what I want at all.

.   .   .   .   .

"This job, it's a job, see—I can't brag about it—people ask me where I work—I tell them over at Western but if I just tell them I'm an assembler what the heck, that's all I am anyway. I've got to do so many parts—not much, you know—well, I just can't see where I'm going to be and I like it here—I'm glad they called me back—it's just that everything just seems so, oh, dark and sort of mixed up and, well, I suppose I'll get over it—I shouldn't have to tell you all these things but that's about the way I feel now."

Comments on the interview

Here we see a young man about the same age as Mike but with quite a different orientation toward himself and his career. He wants to get ahead, of that he is sure. He had hoped to get into drafting work, this would assure him of an opportunity to develop and practice a skill, it would get him out of the shop into a white collar job and provide him with more room for progress. The importance to him of achievement is suggested by the long hours he spent going to evening school. This might indicate that he was oriented toward achieving task competence.

But something seems to have deflected the direction of this need. He is now willing to settle on a job somewhere in between drafting work and assembly work, perhaps relay adjusting. This, he feels, would provide him with the amenities of life and free him from the uncertainties his father and brother experienced. We see him becoming oriented away from intrinsic rewards toward extrinsic rewards. Why this shift in direction?

One possibility is that from Henry's point of view the difficulties of rising to the top of the task structure may have seemed simply insurmountable. We must remember that his job placed him at the bottom of the social structure in the plant and from that position the jobs toward which he tentatively aspired were a long way off. Also the position he occupied made him vulnerable to displacement because he was easily replaceable. So, if we consider his need to keep his job (he was concerned about this), in conjunction with the problems of rising in the task structure and in the community— keeping up with his classmates, buying a car, and establishing a home of his own—we can see how, together, these pressures might divert his achievement needs toward extrinsic rewards.

So in the case of Henry we also see a close connection between his personal and job development. His goals are not clear to him. He thinks he knows what he wants to get away from but he is not clear about where he wants to go. His mind is in a whirl; he has so many things crowding in on him that he doesn't know where his interests lie and he can't make up his mind.

The Case of Charlie, a Semiskilled Worker

Portions of this interview were quoted in Chapters V and VI. It may be recalled that Charlie was a young man in his mid-twenties, with about five years of service. At the time of the interview he had recently been transferred to a new inspection job from one he had mastered and enjoyed. The new job represented a downgrading with a reduction in his hourly rate of pay. On his old job he was paid average earnings, the reasons for which are not brought out in the interview, whereas on the new one he was on a system of financial incentive for inspectors. The reduction of his hourly rate was taking place in small steps over a period of time in accordance with Company policy in movements of personnel involving reductions in earnings.

COUNSELOR: Hi 'ya Charlie, how are you?

EMPLOYEE: Glad to see you. We all set to go?

COUNSELOR: Sure, any time you're ready.

EMPLOYEE: Well, I'm ready any time to get out of this g.d. place. *You know, you get shoved around from one place to another.* One day I'm on this job and another day I'm on another job. I never have settled down since I moved up from the first floor.

COUNSELOR: You mean you don't have one steady job.

EMPLOYEE: Steady, hell. When I came from the first floor I was supposed to do this one particular bank job. I stayed on that for two or three weeks, not even long enough to learn it, then I got transferred up here. Well, inasmuch as I've never done either one of them I had to start learning the second one all over again. Well, I was only here for about three weeks and I got moved again. Now, I'm back up here again. Seems as though every time they need a sucker to fill in, I'm it. I was doing all right down on that frame job. I had that really under control and after being on that for well over a year I had all the angles straightened out, I knew what could be used and what couldn't be used, I had been helping the operators and helping the engineer, helping everybody, maybe that was my trouble. I was trying to help everybody too much. Of course you know what I got. It got me nothing, just this job here which was a cut.

COUNSELOR: Then all that work didn't pay off?

EMPLOYEE: Pay off, hell, there's no pay off at all. A guy goes along and does a good job, tries to work hard, and look what it gets you, nothing. So then I come up stairs and I figure well, I'll try it again. But I tried two weeks here and two weeks some place else, gee, you can't learn a job like that. *It won't be too long before I start having that quality check on me* and I can't learn that job that fast—unless I'm at it. See, here's the hooker. You're given six months to learn the job. Well, the job isn't really too tough, but I'm expected to learn it slowly. If I learn it too fast they will figure the job is too easy, and how come the rest of the boys aren't doing it. So, I'm having trouble with them. If I go too slowly then of course it's my own neck. *So I got to watch my step pretty carefully and not get my boss mad at me or get the boys mad at me.* Because either way I'll need both of them at one time or another.

COUNSELOR: You want to stick to the middle of the road.

EMPLOYEE: Yeah, I suppose you could call it middle of the road. It's really trying to satisfy two things which kind of overlap a little bit. *But right now I could put up with almost everything if I figured I wasn't getting pushed around.* You know, this business of one job one day and another job another day. Never knowing ahead of time what I'm really going to do.

While I was downstairs, I not only knew what the job was, but I felt pretty safe in it. As soon as I was told I was going to have to move up here I took it pretty hard because now, not only have I been moved once, in other words from that job to this department, but I'm moving around to do a lot of jobs up here and I really don't know any of them too well. I don't suppose I'll be getting another cut in pay but that's a possibility. Down there I was going along on average earnings and everything was fine but up here it's a different story. *Like I didn't have a quality check for a year and a half. It won't be too long now before I do have one.* It isn't that I'm afraid of being quality checked or that I haven't been doing a good job on my part, but it's one of those things you get used to, then you get out of the habit of it and then you have to get used to it again. And there are so many darn things you can get checked on. You watched me check out one of these sets—three hundred terminals to test and you have to test all three hundred with a five hundred volt break-down. They go through and see that all the points are in place and have good connections. It isn't easy you know, there are so many little spots where you can get caught. As a matter of fact, I don't think there's an inspector down here who couldn't get caught by the quality check man on one of these sets if the quality man wanted to catch him. There are just too many things you can get caught on that really don't interfere with this set working, but the layout calls for a particular way so that's it.

COUNSELOR: In other words, you're kind of over the barrel on these jobs depending upon how your quality man feels.

EMPLOYEE: Yeah, more or less. If I go along with them and these fellows, because I haven't been checked yet. But if they go along and the boards look clean he's not too tough on us. But there's always that possibility. Now I moved to this job and took a cut, went along for, oh, maybe a week and this department put in a little over-time. Well, for a week or two before my cuts went into effect I was actually making more money on the new job than I was making on the old one by the amount of the overtime. Then after the interval I started taking my first ten cents an hour cut and then I got the balance. Well, now it's beginning to show up pretty heavy although as I say it was offset somewhat by that extra money.

But all that aside I still don't like the way this place operates. You know the company policy always says that you work hard and you'll do all right, and I wish I could say it worked out that way in my case, but I don't think it has. True, I didn't have too much service on the other job and there were fellows with a lot more service than mine, but I knew the job because I started with it. As far as qualifications for doing the job, I'm actually doing it. I couldn't be beat, but inasmuch as this place seems to think another five years' service is worth more than an energetic man I guess I'm out of luck. *All the times I look back on it I think I've been treated pretty well for having that job, keeping the percentage for that year and a half when these other fellows started to take cuts, not being quality checked, and being my own boss up to a certain point, and I liked that and know that I got a better break than others. If I did such a good job down there I still feel that I should have hung on to it instead of losing it to a twenty-five year man.* Maybe if I had the twenty-five years I'd feel the same way he did, but I don't so I'm out. Downstairs it was quality they were looking for, up here it's straight production. Downstairs I didn't have anybody particularly to compete with as I was the only one. *Up here we got a variety of people, including some old timers who know all the short cuts, know how much you have to do to get the job done, and know how you can make the thing look tough and really not be, in other words, know how to get by with the least amount of effort and the most amount of recognition.*

Well, that's okay except it's a little tough on the newcomer because they're not at all willing to show you anything because they figure you'll come out there and take it away from them. They're not particularly interested in doing a real good job, they're just interested in getting along.

COUNSELOR: Then you think there's something more to the job than just getting along on it.

EMPLOYEE: Well, according to the way some of them think that's about it. For me, I could never operate that way. On my old job I was never satisfied with just seeing that the part was able to meet the gauge. I had to know why it had to meet the gauge. I had to know how far off it could be and still be used. In other words, when a man makes a drawing of a part he has to put down some dimensions. Even if you're making a bracket to hang a frame on, the bracket doesn't have to be any particular size or shape or length or anything as long as the thing will hang up. In other words, it's strictly utility. Or these little round bent wire things that hold a kind of a rope of wire on a bank. Now if they weren't perfectly round or if they were a little too wide or a little too narrow it wouldn't make a bit of difference in the world. Because all they do is hold some wires, so I would know, if I were on that job, that I could get away with almost any kind of work. Some parts on this frame, where the boys are drilling or tapping, I know the parts that go in there are pretty small and they require close tolerances. At least as close as the drawings say. So we watch those pretty carefully. On some other parts where I know it doesn't make a bit of difference one way or another, I just make sure that the hole is in there and that's it. But up here you don't have the same kind of inspection at all, although I suppose it would be the same as soon as you find out how good these connections really have to be to be acceptable, not only to the quality man, but to the man doing the installing. As soon as I find that out and can kind of work that into my job I guess I'll be all set.

COUNSELOR: Then it's a case of knowing what you really have to do and what you can overlook.

EMPLOYEE: That's about it. As soon as you learn the job well, then you don't have to work so hard of course, but even so it's pretty dull by comparison. Because as I said, it's all production, you don't really need any brains up here at all. You need good eyes and you have to work fast, but you don't have to know very much. Oh, yeah, that's another point. Take a look at the g.d. lights up here. I don't ordinarily work over at this table, but today I have to. But today is one day like any other day, it's the day I have to get a job done. How the hell am I supposed to work with no light? Today I've had four aspirin tablets, I got a headache and my eyes hurt, I'm supposed to break my neck and look at the layout I have to work with. If I had to work on this spot for a couple of weeks, I'd go blind. Hard enough to see these things when you got plenty of light, properly spaced so it shines right down on these parts. When you got a setup like this, no wonder the guys scream and moan about it. I don't suppose this will be a permanent setup or if it is, they'll probably install some lights. A guy goes nutty doing this—I couldn't take it.

COUNSELOR: You figure the strain on your eyes would be too great.

EMPLOYEE: Yeah, it would start out with a strain on my eyes just like all these things, they get something that kind of irritates you and then the whole thing starts going poorly, and the madder you get at it, the harder the job gets. Some of these jobs aren't particularly easy anyhow. When you put all these hazards in the way it really makes a poor job.

COUNSELOR: The thing sort of snowballs then.

EMPLOYEE: It's sort of like days when you come down to work feeling like a million bucks. *Like the day after I got a little extra money for a suggestion. Nothing could go wrong that day,* I was buddies with everybody. Somebody could of hit me on the nose that day and it wouldn't have made a bit of difference. On days like today just watch out. Just watch your step and no funny business because I'm in a rough mood. I just hope before today is over that nobody says a cross word at me or I'll probably blow my stack right up through the roof. *If my boss should come down here now and tell me I'm working too slow I'd feel like picking up one of these things and clubbing him over the head.* You know I don't get worried too much or get excited too much but today is the day.

COUNSELOR: You could really get up a good head of steam today.

EMPLOYEE: You're damn right I could and I don't have a bad head of steam right now. Fortunately, these guys around here, they're too busy doing their own work to bother too much about me or I'd be impossible to get along with even now. I suppose if I can hang on until five o'clock when a lot of these people will be going home and it will be a little more quiet in here and not so many distractions, I suppose I'll make it okay, but I'm telling you if I would get shifted at five o'clock to another job, then I'd really be mad. Not because I would like it or dislike another job but it would be just one more thing in a long series of things that got me teed off today.

You know, I kind of dread staying down here when we have a day like this. I can just smell when he's coming, and I get down here and everything starts to go wrong. I guess it's partly me because when I figure they're going wrong I don't help them very much and instead of trying to straighten out a few right at the start I begin squawking about it. And, of course, the more I scream the worse it gets. I guess I'm just a problem to myself. Even when I know that things aren't going to change because I'm complaining about it I still complain. *I know I'd be a lot better off if I'd go back to work and try to figure out and see if I couldn't find a way to really cut down on this job, that is, cut down on the work and still get the same amount out, kind of make a game out of it. See if I really couldn't think of some way for it to become so simple that it would almost be cheating the Company. Not really cheating them because I'd be doing the work but making the system so easy that by comparison with the way I'm supposed to do it, it would almost seem like I was taking money under false pretenses.* I may not be able to find a thing like that but I'm sure going to try and I suppose if I go back feeling that way it won't be so hard to put up with all this stuff, because then I can say to myself, "You really got them by the tail now." One more slick idea like that and you can get your eight hours' work in about three or four hours, maybe it will take longer, maybe I can only cut an hour off of the the thing. Maybe I could cut a couple of hours but whatever it is it would be plain gravy. I'm not especially looking for a way to just cut the time down, because my big job is to find some way so I don't get so mad at the thing. Still if it serves the purpose of cutting down on the time required and also satisfies my desire to get something done up here, then I'd be all right.

Look, it's almost five o'clock, what do you say we get back? I still have some frames to put out, you know.

COUNSELOR: Okay.

Comments on the interview

In the case of Charlie we see a semiskilled worker who appears to be oriented toward task achievement but who is having a difficult time mastering his job because of too frequent job changes. In this respect his interview resembles the interview with Marie who became distraught because of too frequent changes, quoted in Chapter VIII.

We might note that being pushed around is principally a hazard encountered in the lesser skilled occupations. One of the distinguishing characteristics of a highly skilled job is that the worker, while perhaps performing a variety of assignments some of which may not utilize all his skills, is generally assigned the work called for by his trade. Liability to arbitrary job change increases as the learning period decreases. So here we can see one significant difference between the work of Charlie and that of Marie who was subjected to many more arbitrary job changes than Charlie. Charlie was very much concerned about his change in jobs. He knew he could do his work better if he were not concerned but, as he said, his feelings were always getting in his way. Let us see whether by examining his concerns in terms of the need hierarchy and comparing them with Henry's, the unskilled worker we considered before, we can identify the constraints to his development on the job in the direction of task competence.

Considering first his safety needs, it is quite apparent that they have been activated. Henry's safety needs were also activated but he was concerned about being laid off whereas Charlie is concerned about meeting the standards for the particular job he holds.

Henry was still in the process of searching for an occupational group with which he would like to be identified. Charlie had made this determination but he has encountered a dilemma in relating himself to them. He feels pulled in opposite directions from his desire to establish a good performance record and the pressures placed on him from the group not to learn his job too fast. The old timers are seeing that he doesn't do so by refusing him help and keeping their trade secrets from him. While his concerns about belonging are different from Henry's, the underlying need has been activated in both cases.

Charlie's interview is strewn with felt injustices. He says there's no pay-off for doing a good job, all it gets you is nothing. He feels that his rewards have been unjustly reduced through no fault of his own and that service counts too much compared to ability. He apparently takes great pride in the quality of his work and the judgment he exercises in performing it but he feels that these attributes are being overridden by emphasis on output and rigid conformance to standards. He feels so unjustly treated that he is even considering how he might reduce his investments and get away with it. Henry, on the other hand, appears to feel indebted to the Company.

Considering dependency needs next, we can infer that Charlie is extremely dependent upon the Company but finds himself continually rebuffed by too frequent and inconsiderate job changes. He evidences a generalized apprehension of authority reflected in his concern about the check inspector, his desire to be able to use independent judgment instead of blindly following the layout in accepting or rejecting work, and in his comments about his supervision. One wonders why he doesn't try to get help from his supervisor. It is possible that he is afraid to confess his need for help. This apprehension obviously has a restrictive effect upon his development of job competence.

What are the similarities and differences between Henry and Charlie? In terms of the constraints to the achievement of task competence, they are remarkably similar. Both are having difficulties, but whereas Henry seems to have given up the struggle, Charlie seems to be still struggling to achieve it. It looks as if Henry has settled for the extrinsic rewards his job offers, while Charlie is still struggling for the intrinsic rewards he may some day get. But the difficulties in his way toward this achievement, principally his vulnerability to transfer and job change, are rather formidable and we can only speculate as to whether he will persist in this direction or shift toward seeking more extrinsic rewards.

The Case of Jim, a Skilled Worker

This interview was held at the employee's request at the time he had decided to leave the Company for a better position working for a former acquaintance in a new enterprise. While unusual in this respect, it nevertheless highlights a significant aspect of the syndrome we are considering. Jim was in his mid-twenties and had completed the Company's tool and die training course four years prior to the interview. We have included only those parts of the interview bearing upon his career and his personal development. The interview is the fourth in a series held with him during a period of ten months. He refers to the counselor as "Si."

EMPLOYEE: You know, Si, I'm going to have some regrets about leaving here. I don't think I've ever been in a place that's given me as much opportunity to learn things as this place here.

COUNSELOR: You gained an opportunity here that you hadn't had anywhere else.

EMPLOYEE: I'd done a lot of different things before I got here. I worked first as a clerk in a trucking company, but you know, I couldn't seem to get the hang of it. I worked there several weeks and I still couldn't seem to make out the bills properly and get things right. Well, I guess they let me go because I wasn't doing too well. It was all right though. Then I went to work for a packing company doing about the same thing there, making out bills and figuring out the cost of things that were sold and that sort of thing. I didn't like that very well either. You know, some of the fellows down there seemed to be able to remember things without even trying. They seemed to remember the price of all the things that were made, but I couldn't remember them at all even though I worked there six months. Well, I didn't stay there any longer than six months. I just didn't seem to be interested in it. You know, Si, if you're not interested in something, you certainly can't get anywhere in staying there.

COUNSELOR: You have to be interested in something in order to make a go of it.

EMPLOYEE: Yeah, well, after the packing house I worked on a hard-road gang for a while pouring cement. I was one of the fellows that stood below the mixer and whenever it would dump its load of mixed concrete, then I would be one of those fellows that would shovel the concrete into a corner, sort of laid it down smooth. That was a pretty good job. That got me out in the open and I was able to enjoy that a little bit. But that was still just manual work. It wasn't anything that you'd want to do all your life. Of course it was good for me all right. I'll admit that, but not as a steady diet. Then I went to work for the Electric Eye Company down there. That was when I first got a glimmer of what it was I really wanted to do. At this Electric Eye

Company, where I worked, was this other fellow. That's the guy I'm going to work for down in Charlestown. He and I both worked there. Well, I didn't know very much about machines or anything but I enjoyed it a great deal and I used to work down around the tool room they had there so I kind of got the feel of the machines and got to look around and see what it was like. Well, what I saw there I liked a great deal. It seemed to me that that was something I could do pretty well, and *I decided then that if I could get a chance I'd certainly like to get into tool work.* That's when I got the opportunity to come to Chicago and go to work here.

You know, I was lucky that I was able to go here. So many of the training schools only teach specialized lines, but when I came here I was taught all the lines. Jigs and fixtures, punches and dies and gauges and a little bit of everything. All of the machines, the different machines, the grinders and the mills and the jig borers and lathes. *You know, when you take the training course here, Si, you really get a good training. It's pretty thorough business.* You know, when a fellow gets out of here with a little experience he really knows what he's doing so far as this sort of work is concerned.

COUNSELOR: This kind of training gives you confidence in the kind of work that you're able to do.

EMPLOYEE: *You know, Si, I feel that I can go down there to this new job I've got and I don't feel there's anything about it that I won't be able to take care of. It's a responsible job and it's a big one and I think I can either make or break myself on it. I haven't the slightest doubt that I can go ahead and do it successfully and without any kind of hitches. I just feel I know my work so thoroughly and so well that there can't be any doubt as to how I'm going to come out with it. You know, confidence in yourself is something important. It's something I always haven't had a great deal of.* You know, there used to be a time when I wouldn't even do anything in order to be heard. I wouldn't talk to anybody and I wouldn't . . . *I was always afraid to express myself. I was always afraid to speak up or talk.* That wasn't so long ago either, Si. You should have known me then. You probably could have helped me. You know, it wasn't until I took this course in Industrial Psychology at Northwestern that I really began to get on to myself so far as this thing was I was telling you about is concerned. I was always able to get along with the fellows all right, but *when it came to talking to some of the boys farther up, that's when I had trouble.* I wasn't always too well prepared in class, because I didn't have much time to do any studying. You know, that was about the time when the baby came along, and he was doing a lot of yelling and it wasn't very easy for me to study so I'd either have to do it late at night or early in the morning, and the result was that in general I didn't get a great deal done. But we had a discussion one day in class—I didn't join in particularly, but we had a discussion concerning a theory by a man named Dalton. Well, Dalton gave an example of what he meant by saying when he was typewriting he always committed the error of writing the word "the" as h-t-e instead of t-h-e, and he couldn't break himself of the habit. He'd go along and decided the only way to cure himself was to deliberately go ahead and make that error, that is, just try and force himself to make the error of writing the word as h-t-e and it wasn't long before he was able to write it t-h-e without any difficulty at all. Well, you know, that kind of set me on fire. It just made me tingle to think that here was a man who had deliberately committed the error in order to get away from it. Well, I decided I would try that out.

You know, I used to be a very nervous individual. I used to fidget and get all excited and then I couldn't do anything and I'd get so emotional I could hardly stand it, so I decided from then on, whenever I felt that I was getting that way, I'd tell myself to go ahead and get excited, "Go on, what are you waiting for," I'd drag myself on that way and it wasn't long before I didn't have to egg myself on anymore. I was able to go ahead and remain calm. I was having to do that less and less often. For example, one time when I was in the church I was supposed to help serve Communion and I felt myself getting all flustered, and you know if you shake those trays with all those little glasses on it, why you get so excited and nervous that it sounds like a bell factory, so I just went ahead and said, "Go on now, get excited, go ahead and get all fussed up." By the time I was trying to serve Communion, I was all right, I was just as calm as anything; I didn't have a bit of trouble at all. Well, that's the kind of thing I think that helped me a great deal in that psychology course. I didn't tell anybody how I thought or how I arrived at that. I just went ahead and did it.

COUNSELOR: By deliberately committing the error or goading yourself, you found you could get over whatever it was that was bothering you.

EMPLOYEE: That's right and you know, Si, *I've been able to talk to the big shots successfully ever since that.* You know, when we went up and talked to the superintendent about our labor problem, well, I was all right up there. Now whenever I go and talk to the department chief I never have any difficulty in that respect either. When

my group chief called me over after that meeting with the superintendent and began bawling hell out of me I was able to keep just
as calm and unemotional as anything. You know, that was a funny
business. *As a matter of fact, Si, that's what decided me to leave the
Company.* You see, we were up there as I told you to check into
our labor grade, and I was wondering then if I was going to have
any repercussions from it. Well, I really got it. You know the group
chief and I went at it for two hours and both of us were pounding
at each other about this business. He was accusing me of being lazy
and not paying attention to my work and all those other things.
Well, I was pounding right back at him, just that I had a perfect right
to try and better myself and it was just the way I worked, that I
didn't work all the time, eight hours a day. I had to work when I
was able to do my best work and I pointed out to him that all the
fellows around me were complimenting me on the way I was getting
my jobs out and the way I was able to do my work so fast.

Well, the group chief didn't like that at all and he and I really
went at it that day, but he finally told me I was either going to have
to get down to business and work all the time or else he was going to
look into it and I told him that if he didn't leave me alone and quit
nagging me, I was going to ask for a transfer and get out of there.
Well, that's the way it went. *I was able to talk to him and not get
excited. I was able to just tell him the way I felt and the way I had
to work and he got all excited and fussed and fumed around about
it,* but it didn't do any good. Well, finally he got pretty peeved with
me so when I went home that night I got to thinking over all these
things and the opportunity that had been offered me, so right there
I wrote a letter down to the guy and told him that I was very much
interested in his offer and that I'd be glad to consider it.

COUNSELOR: The discussion you had with your group chief pretty
much settled in your mind what you wanted to do.

EMPLOYEE: It surely did. That convinced me that I'd be better off on
my own. I didn't want to have to work in that kind of atmosphere.
Well, I got a phone call the next day from this fellow to know when
we could get together. He thought he might be in Chicago that weekend and then we could get together and talk then, so we left it at
that. But somehow he had to miss that trip and so he didn't get to
make it.

Well, he called the next week to find out about it and I wasn't
there, but my wife answered the phone and she said that we were
going to come down there and talk to him. And that's what we did

that weekend. We went down there and talked to him, and I listened to his proposition and it sounded so good to me that I told him I thought it would be swell and that I'd be glad to come down. We settled on May 1st as the date that I would start. And you know, all the time I've thought about it, I still can't find anything wrong with the proposition. There isn't a single flaw in it. It's a wonderful place for hiking, boating, fishing, and swimming and I think we're just going to find it's a wonderful thing to have happen to us.

You know, Si, I'm going to miss something a great deal when I go down there. *I'm going to miss the gang up there.* You know, the gang I went to school with here was a pretty swell bunch. We could have parties and we never had a single fight or quarrel in all the time we had our parties. Everything seemed to work out so well. That was a pretty good gang. Of course, when the war came on and we began drifting apart, then the gang broke up and we weren't able to have as many get-togethers but I will miss them.

Comments on the interview

Here we have a young man who has achieved a high degree of task competence. He has many more years to go before he reaches the proficiency of older and more experienced toolmakers but he has achieved a solid background of training and experience. Let us compare his interview with that of Charlie and Henry.

We can infer that because Jim is voluntarily quitting his job he is not concerned about holding it. Had he remained on the roll it is unlikely that he would have been much concerned about it either. For he has achieved the status of a craftsman in his own field, and if for some reason he were separated from the roll he could readily obtain employment elsewhere. He has achieved a measure of independence from a particular employing organization and in this respect stands in marked contrast to Charlie and Henry.

Jim has assured membership in a recognized reference group. He is a member in good standing in his craft and in the union. Although not brought out in the interview, when he met with the superintendent to review the appropriateness of the grade assigned to his work, he did so as one of several spokesmen for the toolmakers in his grade of work. Here again he stands in marked contrast to

Henry and Charlie, neither of whom has assured membership in any immediate work group.

Jim evidences no feelings that he has been unjustly treated. His comments about the Company are favorable and he feels that the time and effort he spent in his training have been rewarded. His is not a case of quitting because he feels his investments have not been sufficiently rewarded, rather he feels that he can increase his rewards and perhaps better utilize his training and experience in another place of employment. His decision is a rational one arrived at after weighing alternatives.

Jim as with Joe, the Rebel (cited in Chapter VIII), had an altercation with his boss but unlike Joe who threatened to quit, Jim did quit. We cited Joe's case as an extreme manifestation of dependency needs but in Jim's case we feel that his argument with his boss was more of an expression of a feeling of independence. Although there is a superficial similarity in these two episodes, there are several significant differences.

The general similarity is that both Jim and Joe were sensitive to authority and in both cases the dispute was about wages, but here the similarity ends. Joe's dispute was personal, it was about his rate of pay; whereas Jim was a spokesman for a group, he was not protesting for himself but for the toolmakers in his grade. A second difference is that Joe became emotional and angry, whereas Jim, as he says, was able to talk calmly and logically and was in command of himself at all times. A third difference is that Joe seemingly was inviting more intercedence or structuring from his boss whereas Jim was asking that the supervisor recognize the professional status of his craft. Here Jim was in effect asserting the norms of his reference group—that competence should be respected and the craftsman should be the judge of how to implement his skills. In short, Joe's problem was more personal, Jim's was more in terms of the tradition of his craft.

Considering the direction of Jim's drive, we can see that he is clearly oriented toward intrinsic task rewards. We note that he worked hard to get his training and willingly underwent personal sacrifices in order to get it. Like most young men he wasn't sure of what he wanted at first, but when he happened upon a type of work that excited his interest he set his course toward a well defined goal. He wasn't diverted from his course by his marriage and family but got through his courses by studying late at night and early in the morning.

His orientation toward himself is best expressed in the way he feels about undertaking his new job. He feels on top of his job and fully competent in meeting any job challenge that might arise. He has a skill, his capability resides in his head and his own two hands, he has become a self-reliant, autonomous craftsman.

Finally, let us consider the relation between Jim's personal development and his job development. We note that as a youth he was shy, sensitive, unsure of himself, and afraid to make himself heard. Especially when in the presence of someone higher up he tended to become agitated and distraught about his lack of confidence. Yet when the interview took place he said he could then talk to the "big shots" with assurance. This was indeed a dramatic change for him. He attributes his growth in self-confidence to what he learned from the psychologist and we don't want to discount that. But there remains the probability that his personal development was also greatly assisted by his development in his craft. In point of time his personal development and his job development went hand in hand, and it is reasonable to surmise that one stimulated and reinforced the other.

Review of Four Interviews

Let us review the four cases we have examined—Mike, Henry, Charlie, and Jim. In the case of the first three, it can be seen that there is no substantial difference in their expressed concerns. Both of the two unskilled workers, Mike and Henry, and the semiskilled worker, Charlie, are still concerned with the satisfaction of their lower order needs. Not until we reach the case of Jim, the skilled toolmaker, do we find the need for task competence being fully realized and rewarded. Then the change is dramatic.

It looks as if the lower in the structure the worker is, the more he is threatened by changes originating in the external environment and the more his behavior is circumscribed by rules and regulations. Not until he reaches the safeguards to his security in the skilled crafts at the top of the job structure is he relatively freed from these constraints. When these constraints are present, as they

FIGURE 9.5

OUTCOMES OF THE DEVELOPMENT SYNDROME

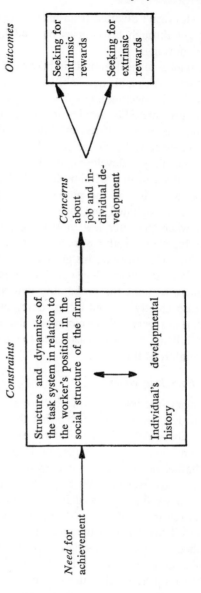

were even in the case of Charlie, the semiskilled worker, he remains still more concerned with the extrinsic than the intrinsic rewards from the job.

In all four cases we saw a close connection between job and individual development. Each can stimulate and retard the other. Becoming a person and becoming more competent on the job seem to go hand in hand and one can facilitate or impede the other.

GENERAL SUMMARY

We can summarize the main points developed in this chapter with reference to Figure 9.5.

We have been looking at the need for achievement in relation to the opportunities and constraints to its realization in the industrial setting. When activated, this need, the highest order we postulated, takes the direction of task competence, individual growth, and autonomy. Although the opportunities for the realization of this need are present at all levels, we found that they were often overridden in importance by constraints from another source. This source we identified as the broader social structure of which the task structure is a part. The lower the individual's position in this structure is, the greater his degree of subordination and the more exposed he becomes to the hazards of technical and economic change and the constraints of rules and standards. These serve continually to activate his basic needs and direct his energies toward coping with them. As a consequence the need for competence becomes increasingly diverted from seeking intrinsic task rewards of skill and competence to seeking social status rewards such as salary and interpersonal relations. With this shift the need for competence which normally is expressed in terms of individuation, independence, and autonomy is arrested and he seeks his satisfactions from a reward system which places a premium upon dependence and conformity to social norms. His forward thrust to grow as an individual is thwarted and becomes dissipated in coping with the problems of security and status.

PART III

Contributions of Counseling

CHAPTER X

The Personal Resolutions
of Concerns at Work
and Their Organizational Outcomes

In Part III of this book we will be looking at the contribution of counseling to the personal resolutions of the workers' concerns. In this chapter we will look at how these concerns are usually resolved and the functional and dysfunctional consequences these resolutions can have for both the individual worker and the organization. In the following chapter we will look at what difference counseling can make to their resolution which would be more satisfactory for both the individual worker and the Company.

Perhaps we can state most clearly the point of departure for this chapter by summarizing in Table 10.1 the situational analyses we made of the workers' concerns in Part II. In each chapter of Part II we looked across each row in this table. In this chapter we want to look down the columns of this table and see what they add up to.

What the Worker Expects of the Organization

If we look down column 3 we can say that the expectations that the worker brings to his job are something as follows. He wants

–a job.
–a steady, secure job.
–satisfactory relations with his fellow workers, i.e., the opportunity to establish such relations.
–to feel he belongs to or has the opportunity to establish a position in the work group.

TABLE 10.1

SUMMARY OF SITUATIONAL ANALYSES OF WORK CONCERNS

Needs and Values	Concerns	Constraints	Common Alternate Forms of Resolution	
			1	*2*
I. Physiological and safety	1. Keeping and losing a job	1. Business conditions 2. Plant relocation 3. Transfer of work 4. Technological change 5. Output and quality standards	(a) Meet minimum standards (b) Spin out the work (c) Resist change	(a) Excel in output (b) Make good impressions (c) Do more than required
II. Friendship and belonging	2. Satisfactory work relations	6. Company rules 7. Movement of personnel	(a) Restriction (b) Socialize (c) Conformance	(a) Rate buster (b) Isolate (c) Nonconformance
III. Rewards should be proportional to investments	3. Felt injustices	8. Company provisions for rewarding employees — Job evaluations — Wage incentive plans — Performance appraisal	(a) Demand more rewards for perceived investments (e.g., make complaints) (b) Decrease investments relative to rewards (e.g., goof off)	(a) Demand less rewards for perceived investments (e.g., not complain) (b) Increase investments relative to rewards (e.g., take more responsibility)
IV. Dependence	4. Satisfactory relations with authority	9. Supervision	(a) Dependence (b) Submission	(a) Independence (b) Rebellion
V. Task competence	5. Job development	10. Task structure	(a) Seek for extrinsic social rewards from the job	(a) Seek for intrinsic task rewards from the job

–to have satisfactory relations with his supervisors or the opportunity to establish such relations.

–his dependence on the organization to be recognized but not taken advantage of.

–his investments in his job to be recognized and rewarded; for example, his age, service, and experience to count and be recognized.

–a job in which he can develop skill and competence that is recognized by his co-workers and his superiors.

–a job that leads somewhere and enables him not only to meet his developing financial needs but also

–to develop himself as a person in his own right, i.e., to be somebody, going and getting somewhere.

These conclusions are not exactly "news"; that is, they have been commented upon before by many persons who have been concerned with employee behavior. However, many investigators have tended to treat one or another of these needs primarily or exclusively. We have not done this. Rather, we have chosen to assume that they are all present, even though some may be present only in a latent sense, and that until the worker's lower order needs (e.g., for safety and security) have been satisfied, his higher order needs will not tend to emerge.

Moreover, we assumed that in this hierarchy of needs, the worker cannot be differentiated from the president of the Company. No matter at which level of the organization the individual is, from worker to president, this hierarchy of needs exists. In this regard it is assumed that the worker and the president are both human beings, are both members of the human race, and are both sharing similar common yearnings and the same fundamental human conditions. Each has to differentiate his personal objectives, goals, aims, or purposes from the objectives, goals, aims, or purposes of the organization. Although the goals of the individual and the goals of the organization are never identical, we are not assuming that they are so incompatible that the individual cannot identify with them. Instead we are assuming that under certain conditions he can, and we are making this assumption for the worker as well as for the president.

What the Organization Expects of the Worker

However, even though we did not posit a set of needs for the worker which differentiated him from any other member of the organization or excluded him from the human race, we did look at the particular environment in which his needs were to be realized. So we did put him in his own industrialized world in the U.S.A. at the Western Electric Company in Chicago at the Hawthorne plant. So let us look down column 2 in Table 10.1 and see what this adds up to.

Here we can see the reverse side of the coin—the highly structured constellation of expectations that are being made of the worker, which become the constraints and opportunities for the realization of his needs. These constraints and opportunities in the worker's environment for the realization of his needs we treated as arising in turn from the requirements of the organization to survive in and cope with its external environment. So behind them we posited a reality just as brute and as stubborn as man's yearnings for a better life.

In terms of this reality we can now state what management as the representative of the organization expects of the worker. Management wants the worker

-to work hard.
-to be efficient; to meet standards.
-to do what he is told.
-to interact with his fellow workers only when the job requires it (which in terms of work simplification it seldom does).
-to understand the logics behind the task structure and the reward system and to see why they are equitable.
-to have an elementary understanding of economics so that he has at least an intuitive appreciation, if not a complete logical understanding, of why marginal costs should equal marginal revenues if the firm is to operate at an optimal level and why this may result sometimes in his being laid off.
-to understand why this is all so without complaining but instead
-to be responsible and mature.
-to be cooperative, and above all
-to be loyal, i.e., to identify with the goals of the organization.

So as we look down column 2 in Table 10.1 we can see that there are many aspects of the worker's environment which are not too favorable for the realization of what either management or the worker expects. Because of changing business conditions, techno-logical change, and organizational controls of many kinds, the worker's safety and dependency needs are easily activated. At the bottom level of a complex structure he is being acted upon and reacting to a set of powerful forces to which he can do little else than to accommodate and there seems to exist little opportunity for self-actualization.

Again these observations are not exactly "news"; they have been made before by many other researchers on employee behavior. Ob-viously at the worker level, the environment is not the best for the realization of man's higher order needs. But what environment is? It seemed to us that in this respect history has revealed no Utopia. Man finds himself through trying to cope with the actual environ-ment which by fate or by circumstances he is placed in.

So although we feel that some environments are more or less fa-vorable to man's individual development, we are not making any judgments about this—at least not as yet. From our point of view at the moment a person can discover himself in many different en-vironments. To state our position extremely we would say that it is possible that a person can realize himself in a concentration camp, or in a slum neighborhood, or on Park Avenue, or at the Hawthorne plant, or at the Harvard Business School, even though in some as yet undefined aspect, some of these environments seem to be "tougher" than others.

So without getting sidetracked now into questions about how management might create an environment more favorable to the worker's higher order needs, because this is a book primarily on counseling and only secondarily on management, let us return to our question and the data we have. What has counseling to con-tribute to the resolution of the worker's concerns that would help him better to realize his needs at work?

To us this question was at the heart of the problem. If the coun-seling program had nothing to say on this problem and was merely providing an opportunity for workers to talk about their family and marital problems outside of work, this to us—although important

—was still only a fringe benefit the Company could afford. But as we explored the origins of the program in Chapter II, it seemed to us that initially it had had higher aspirations than that. To us there was no challenge in writing about counseling as a fringe benefit; this was too easy. It would be only too easy to concentrate our story on Hank's or Susie's quarrels with their respective spouses and how counseling had helped in some cases to mend up their broken homes. Not that this was not important. It was extremely important to Hank and Susie. But we wanted to talk about these problems in a different way. And to us the challenge was not to rationalize counseling as a fringe benefit but instead to show that it might be addressing itself in a very realistic way to the fundamental concerns of employees that we outlined in Part II.

So let us return to the tough questions our analyses thus far have raised. Under the conditions of modern industry, has the worker a chance of realizing his higher order needs or are all the cards stacked against him? Has he any opportunity to make choices and decisions or are all these made for him? Is he just a passive instrument to be rewarded for doing what he is told or can he also influence management? Can his needs be satisfied only passively by management or can he learn to satisfy them too?

How the Employees Resolved Their Concerns

What do our data tell us about these questions? Let us look down column 4 in Table 10.1 and see what this column adds up to. Here it can be seen that each of the concerns we considered in Part II ended up often in two rather extreme alternative resolutions. At first glance they seem to add up to two extreme pictures of the worker. On the one hand we have the extreme picture of Worker A who

   —wants to play safe, to do the bare minimum required to keep and hold his job.
   —wants to be liked without having to do anything in return.
   —wants the company to treat him as a child and yet as a responsible individual too.
   —wants to dump his problems on someone else's lap—the company's or the union's.

–wants more pay and a better job in general as a matter of right.

–is extremely sensitive to "injustices."

–has no plans or ideas for his own development.

–has no idea of what he has to do for what he wants.

–feels that he should be rewarded for just giving his time to the job and the company, in short

–tries to get something for nothing, i.e., without any cost.

On the other hand we have the picture of Worker B who

–starts doing what is expected of him in order to learn his job better.

–sees what skills and knowledge are required in order to get a better job.

–tries to fit into the work group in order to make his work activities more pleasant.

–tries to establish a relationship with his supervisor so that he can accept help and learn something.

–tries to learn about the values and norms of the group so that he can receive and give help.

–tries to develop so that when he is older and has more service his contributions will count more.

–gets a more clear and specific notion of who he is, where he wants to go, what he must do to get there, and how to cope with situations to achieve his goals.

But let us look at these two pictures more closely. Not only are they "loaded" in the direction of the "baddie" and the "goodie," but also they are confusing certain aspects of the resolutions that our data suggest. Obviously Worker A, as described above, would not last at the Western Electric Company, or any company for that matter, very long. Let us see if we can create a classification of resolutions that does not present us with this false dichotomy.

In our abstract Worker A we have in fact three different resolutions mixed up. We have (1) the worker who *accepts* the situation he is in but who tries to cope with it passively. We also have the worker who *rejects* the situation he is in and who reacts to it either (2) *passively* or (3) *actively*. In our abstract Worker B we have a type of a worker who *accepts* the situation he is in and tries to cope with it *proactively,* i.e., realistically. These four resolutions are depicted in Figure 10.1.

FIGURE 10.1

FOUR KINDS OF PERSONAL RESOLUTIONS

	Accept	*Reject*
Active	A (realistic worker)	B (trouble maker)
Passive	C (minimal performer)	D (withdrawal)

Let us look at these four resolutions to which we have given certain labels.

1. Box A represents the worker who accepts the situation he is in and believes that by his own efforts he can improve it. However, the way in which he tries to improve it differs radically from the way in which Worker B represented by Box B tries to do it. Unlike B, he does not seek his autonomy and independence by protest and aggression against forces that seem to him to be in opposition to their realization, but instead he seeks to gain them by trying to cope actively and realistically with the problems he faces, and, unlike B, he does not see these problems as unsurmountable.
2. Box B represents the worker who fundamentally does not accept the situation he is in. For him his personal goals and the goals of the Company are antithetical. So he "resolves" his conflict by making as much trouble as he can for the forces, most often persons, whom he perceives as preventing his growth and development. The common term for this person is the trouble maker.
3. Box C represents the worker who, like the worker in Box A, accepts the situation in which he finds himself and tries as realistically as he can to cope with it. But his definition of being realistic differs from that of Worker A. For him it means "proceed cautiously": go slow, don't rock the boat, and don't work yourself out of a job. This attitude is well expressed by the Scottish word "ca' canny." No one who has read our Part II carefully can quarrel too much with this worker's definition of his situation. It has an overwhelming reality. But unlike our worker in Box A, his resolution is essentially passive. Like A, he accepts the situation in which he finds himself, but fundamentally he does not feel he can do anything about im-

proving it. He can only grin and bear it and protect it from becoming any worse.

4. Finally in Box D we have the fourth resolution. This worker not only cannot see any possible integration of his needs with the goals of the Company but also he does not feel he can do anything about it. So he withdraws and becomes an embittered and unhappy loner.

FUNCTIONAL AND DYSFUNCTIONAL CONSEQUENCES OF THESE RESOLUTIONS

It can be seen that these four resolutions have consequences both for the individual and for the Company. For the individual they are all "satisfactory," in the sense that they "work" for him and take care of his present needs at a given stage of his development. But in terms of future growth, it can be seen that resolutions B, C, and D are achieved at some cost to such a development. From this point of view, each of these resolutions is one that prevents the further development of his career in the organization. So from this point of view they are unsatisfactory or dysfunctional. Many interviews with employees attested to this kind of dissatisfaction; they were not too happy with the resolutions they had made.

Obviously, from the point of view of the Company, resolutions B, C, and D are "unsatisfactory" or dysfunctional. One has only to look at our previous listing of what management expects of workers, in order to see that resolutions B, C, and D fall far short of management's expectation of how workers should behave if the optimal level of organizational effectiveness is to be realized.

So within the framework of the organization it can be said those resolutions that are satisfactory for the individual from the point of view of his personal development are also satisfactory for the effective operation of the Company and, vice versa, those resolutions that are unsatisfactory for the individual from the point of view of his growth are also unsatisfactory for the Company from the point of view of its effective operation. But it is also well to remember that sometimes there are some B's and C's whose future growth and development are achieved through the union organization with whose aims they can identify more easily.

Personal Resolutions as Latent Social Roles

It should be stated that the above four kinds of personal resolutions are not intended as fixed classifications of workers but as four types of accommodation to the situations in which they find themselves. So it is well to remember that a given individual worker in the course of his life cycle under certain conditions may move out of one of these boxes and into another. We will have more to say about this later because it is extremely important to the difference counseling can make.

But now we would like to point out that these personal resolutions can also be thought of as "latent social organizational roles." By this we mean that they are not formal occupational roles such as a relay adjustor or tool maker. A person in any one of these occupational roles can appear in any one of our four boxes. He or she can be "ca' canny," withdrawn, a trouble maker, or concentrating more on improving task competence. So we also mean that some of these personal resolutions can and do become well recognized and accepted ways of behavior in industrial life. Being "ca' canny," for example, can become an accepted norm of behavior for certain social groups that cut across formal occupational lines.

We would like to concentrate now more on this aspect in order to develop a more extended typology which will take this aspect into account. But we also want to do this in order to show that some of these personal resolutions become crystallized into latent social roles by a myriad of personal choices made by the individual worker over an extended period of time. They are not just personal resolutions; they are also social organizational resolutions that are more or less viable and that come about through time.

Personal Resolutions as Precipitates of Choices Made Over Extended Periods of Time

March and Simon in their book, *Organizations*,[1] identify and analyze two major decisions employees face. The first is the decision

[1] James G. March and Herbert A. Simon, *Organizations* (New York, John Wiley and Sons, Inc., 1958).

to stay or quit; the second, assuming the employee stays, is whether to produce or not to produce at the rate demanded by the standards of the organization. Because we are interested in March and Simon's model which treats workers not only as "passive instruments" to be manipulated (the oversimplification of the "scientific management" model) or not only as having passive attitudes, values, and goals to be satisfied by management (the oversimplification of the "human relations" model) but also as "decision makers" and "problem solvers," we decided to utilize it in order to conceptualize better the problem we want now to consider.[2]

In Figure 10.2 we have constructed a very rough and probably oversimplified decision (or choice) tree which might lead to certain personal and social types of resolution. Let us examine this tree and see how these outcomes may come about through a number of personal choices which in time become commitments of one kind or another. We have to start with a dissatisfied employee.

He can choose either to quit or to stay. If he decides to quit, this chart bids him farewell and hopes that he has arrived at his decision proactively (i.e., in order to improve himself) and not reactively (i.e., not because he is mad at the Company). If he stays, he can either accept the situation in which he is and try to do something about it or he can reject this alternative and choose either to withdraw or to make trouble. If he decides to do something he can choose either to try to improve his situation actively or to accept it just passively. If he decides to improve his situation he can choose to improve either his technical competence or his interpersonal competence. If he decides just to live with his situation he can choose to become either a minimal performer or a good Joe.[3]

That this way of conceptualizing our problem leads to some familiar social types that any person acquainted with modern indus-

[2] Although we wish to acknowledge our indebtedness to their ideas, we also wish to free them from any culpability, should we have utilized them incorrectly.

[3] If the reader is disturbed at this point by the fact that some of these choices seem to be a bit false (i.e., the worker can choose both), let him relax; we shall discuss this point not now but later, because we want to get our model off the ground before it gets grounded.

FIGURE 10.2. PERSONAL RESOLUTIONS AND ORGANIZATIONAL OUTCOMES

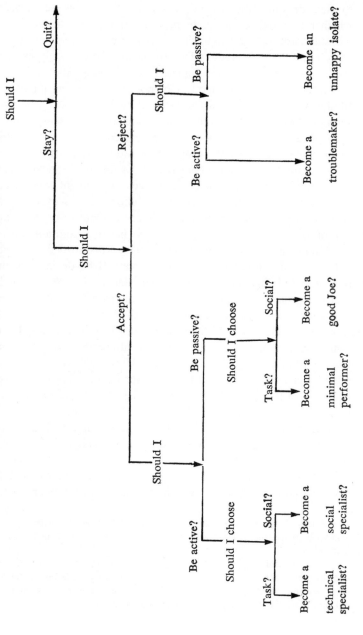

try will be able to recognize lends some credence to our approach. But what is lacking in our computer-like model by which these outcomes are reached are the decision rules which our decision maker, the unhappy employee, uses to arrive at the decision he reaches. So let us program them in.

Each of these choice points can be viewed as an answer to the question, "How much am I willing to pay in order to get what I want?" For each worker—and in fact for all members of any organization—this is a matter of personal choice and a sticky wicket. It is a matter of what his goals and values are, that is, what is important to him and what he wants. Of course we would like to program in our model what the worker's values should be and what he should want, but, as we saw from the scientific management model, this is not cricket. As we do not want to do this, the decision rule for our decision-making worker will be therefore only that when he meets one of the unhappy choices in our diagram, he should make up his mind about whether he is willing to pay the price for going down this road. If the answer to this question is "yes," the decision is "go"; if the answer is "no," the decision is "no go." The assumption behind this rule is that no one gets too seriously into trouble who is willing to pay the price for what he wants; the person who gets into trouble is either the person who wants to get something free or keeps squabbling about the price he has to pay. If this sounds highly moralistic, let us state again that we are not putting the values the worker should have in our decision rule. If he wants to commit larceny and is willing to go to prison for it, the decision rule says "go." But if he wants to commit larceny and not go to prison for it, then the decision rule says "no go."

Although, as an induction from experience, the decision rule is as clear as a bell, it is often difficult to apply in many particular situations because it depends upon (1) what in a particular moment of decision the worker perceives the alternatives to be (about which he often has not too much information), (2) what he perceives the consequences of the different alternatives to be, i.e., the price he has to pay (about which he often has difficulty in making accurate probability estimates), and (3) his individual goals and values, i.e., what he wants (about which he often is not too clear) in terms of which he evaluates the alternatives and comes to a decision.

Now this is where later we will plug a counselor into our model because this is just what his function is. It is to help the worker in a moment of decision under these conditions of uncertainty to perceive more clearly the alternatives available to him, their possible consequences, and what he really wants so that he can assess them before and not after he has gone down one of the primrose paths in our diagram. In this way it is to be hoped that he will do his complaining about the price he has to pay for going that way instead of the other before and not after.

But before we bring this human agent into our model, let us see how these personal decisions roughly but remorselessly over time work themselves out into the six outcomes at the bottom of Figure 10.2.

The Technical Specialist

Let us start with the worker who has decided to increase his task rewards by improving his skill, by improving his output, by meeting the technical challenge his job offers, and by trying to get jobs which offer more intrinsic rewards. At this point in his career he has made already a large number of personal choices. He may have had to choose to pay the cost of ostracism by his work group whose output norms he may have violated. He may have had to choose between being an output specialist—a rate buster—and a quality specialist. He may have forfeited the acquiring of the social skills upon which his promotion into a supervisory rank might depend. But we hope he has paid these costs cheerfully in order to achieve the task competence he values and through this route earn his group's respect if not their total social approval. In time he may also learn to share his technical competence with others by helping newcomers, for example, and by this means increase his status in the group. Hand in hand he builds up his own self-respect as he earns the respect of the group for his technical competence.

In this manner, if he so chooses, he may become a first line supervisor. In the case of Jim, the skilled worker, discussed in the previous chapter, we saw Jim tussling with some of these choices.

The Social Specialist

When Worker B decides to accept and improve his situation by seeking the social rewards he can get from the group (approval) more than the rewards he can get from management, he too has made a number of personal choices. In many work groups in order to get the social approval he seeks, he may have to abide by their output norms. He may have to forfeit the intrinsic rewards his job offers. But in time he may become the informal social leader of the group. In this position he can protect its members, his flock, from too much outside interference and too much rapid change. He may give the members of his group the personal encouragement and support the supervisor may be unable to provide without arousing their feelings of dependence. In this way he increases his social status in the group.

In time he may learn to develop his social skills in trying to improve his relations not only with his co-workers but also with supervision and management. In this process he may become in time less conflicted in loyalties. Like the task specialist who achieves his identity through the development of his task competence, so does this worker achieve his identity through the development of his interpersonal competence. In time, should he so choose, he may become an accommodative supervisor, or even in time a more transactional one and a valued member of management. But many of them never become supervisors. They pay this cost cheerfully because the alternative cost they would have to pay in terms of becoming alienated from the work groups with whom they identify would be far greater. Such workers often provide an invaluable function at the work level that any good manager will recognize.

The Fusionist (*not specified in Figure 10.2*)

In talking about the technical and social specialists, we have tended to talk about this social role specialization primarily at the work level. Only secondarily have we brought in the worker's aspirations for advancement and a career in the ranks of management. Were we talking more about this, we can see that this choice between task and interpersonal development can be a false one. A worker with aspirations for advancement would have to take into account both, and the development of both is not an impossible achievement. But for many supervisors this is a difficult integration to realize. The production-oriented versus the people-oriented supervisor is only too often a very common dichotomy.

So this third alternative—let us call him a "generalist" or "fusionist," i.e., the man who tries to integrate and not choose between these false alternatives—we did not include in our Figure 10.2 because he is a rare bird and only after much supervisory experience at higher levels does he tend to emerge. Were we talking about the career development of managers instead of workers, we would have to spend much time on the price a person has to pay for this achievement. But fortunately we are spared from this discussion. It is filled with the most subtle of nuances to which a whole book could be written. But as many books and management development programs have been devoted to this subject, we can for the time being ignore it. We will only return to it in Part V, our conclusion.

The Minimal Performer

So now we come to our worker who accepts his situation but who does not want actively to improve it. He too has made a number of personal decisions to arrive at this conclusion. In order to protect his investments in the job, he has to see that not only he but others obey the output norms, the exceeding of which he feels might cost him and them the loss of their jobs. So he becomes the watchdog and policer of these norms. He tries to maintain the establishment and resist its change at the worker level. Through these procedures in some work groups he may become an informal leader, but unlike the social specialist, his social skills are employed only in the direction of maintaining the status quo. So he never gains the approval of those members of the group who do not share to such a degree his values for security and conformity.

For obtaining the security and safety this worker values so highly, he has had to pay a high price. He has had to renounce all his latent desires for advancement, for bettering his lot, and even for satisfying his own self-esteem. Not many can achieve this personal resolution without some occasional tinges of bitterness and resentment. He exemplifies the adage, "Nothing ventured, nothing gained." He makes no investment in his job or career for which there is not a high probability of coming out safe, and when under certain conditions he loses his job through layoff, his sense of justice, as one can imagine, is outraged.

As we have said before, there is much in the industrial environment to encourage this personal resolution so that we cannot put all the blame on the worker who makes it. But it is an uncomfortable bed to lie in, particularly as one gets older and begins to reflect upon what might have been.

The Good Joe

Good Joe is a term in common usage in industry to designate a highly valued type of employee frequently encountered in offices and shops. He knows his way around, is well liked, and gets along with everyone. Social approval from everybody is the value he needs. He wants to be popular and accepted. Toward this end he readily accepts authority and will go out of his way to be helpful. He neither seeks nor resists change too much, but he is passive about improving his or the Company's goals. He has many of the social skills of the social specialist but he employs them only at the level of gaining friends and influencing people for his own needs. He feels that it is whom you know and not what you know that counts.

Because this kind of resolution is frequently associated with a low aspiration level, he is often willing to pay the costs this kind of resolution entails. For him—at least a part of him—these are not perceived as costs. Getting along and not getting ahead is what he wants. So he is willing to settle for his satisfactions from general increases in pay, occasional merit increases, friendship, fringe benefits, and pleasant working conditions—all the extrinsic rewards his job affords.

Those who are more task oriented or socially mobile may feel that the good Joe has paid too high a price for the popularity he seeks. But let us remember our decision rule. If he is willing to pay this price, the decision is "go" down this path. And quite a number do. Some may even move up part way in the supervisory structure because of their surface social skills. Every organization has them and no organization can get along without some of them.

But some good Joes turn sour. And a bad good Joe is a sorry (incongruous) sight to see; and here the counselor can help.

The Troublemaker and the Unhappy Isolate

In the last two resolutions we come to our problem cases. Because of their attitude of rejecting any possibility of being able to integrate their system of needs into the goals of the organization, they are in basic conflict. This frustration has only two outlets: to attack or to withdraw. Because both resolutions are self-defeating these are never very happy workers. The assumption underlying the first resolution is that the world is hostile and he must attack it; the assumption underlying the second resolution is that the world is dangerous and he must placate it. Every large organization has some of them but not too many. These were some of the counselors' most difficult problems. Many of their attitudes spring from unfortunate early experiences as children and adolescents which they have not been able to resolve satisfactorily. So in these last two cases we do have more personal resolutions that do not evolve so clearly into social organizational resolutions as in our previous four cases. Obviously these workers are paying high costs in terms of personal growth and development for the road they have chosen to take in order to resolve their inner conflict. For them our decision rule makes the least sense because they are making incompatible demands of their environment. They want to have their cake and to eat it too. As they want to go down one path but obtain the rewards of the other, they become immobilized at the fork and this is why in our Figure 10.2 there is no development at the lower end.

Probably no worker needed more the services that counseling could provide than these two kinds of workers, but curiously or ironically enough they were the ones who sometimes resisted most the counselor's advances in this direction. So many counselors spent much time in wooing them and sometimes they succeeded in being able to get them to accept the help they so badly needed.

SUMMARY

In this chapter we have tried to set the stage for the counselor's intervention. Where and how can he intervene to make a difference to the workers' concerns? Obviously he can do little to change the object of their concerns—the nature of their organizational environment. But he can do something, perhaps, about the way the worker goes in resolving his concerns in this environment. So we decided to look first at how the worker goes about this and the consequences it has for both him and the Company.

In this exploration we toyed with three models of man: (1) man as striving for self-actualization,[4] (2) man as a decision maker,[5] and in the realm of personal decision making (which we think is something different from organizational decision making), (3) man as trying to figure out rationally the price he has to pay for what he wants.[6]

Starting with the first model we explored what the worker expects of management and, vice versa, what management expects of the worker. What impressed us here was that from the point of view of self-actualization they both seemed to be wanting the same thing but they did not seem to know it. Management wanted a mature, self-reliant, responsible, competent worker. The worker also wanted not to be treated as a child but as a self-respecting, mature, and responsible person. Why was this extraordinary state of affairs so? As we looked at the way management had organized its human resources in order to operate most efficiently, it looked as if it had created an environment which made for the development of dependency, passivity, conformity, and apathy more than for the development of independency, proactivity, innovation, and spontaneity.

We decided not to explore the question this raised in this chapter but to save it for later in our conclusions. So we looked at how the employees resolved their concerns in this kind of situation. Here again we were impressed with the fact that the resolution that seemed to be good for the individual also seemed to be good for the Company.

At this point we thought our model of man as striving for self-actualization was playing tricks on us, so we decided to change our

[4] Maslow, op. cit.

[5] March and Simon, op. cit.

[6] George C. Homans, *Social Behavior: Its Elementary Forms* (New York, Harcourt, Brace and Company, 1961).

pair of glasses and conceive of man, in the best fashion of the day, as a decision maker. We now conceived of his personal resolution as the outcome of many individual personal decisions made over an extended period of time and how at each moment of decision he had to perceive what the alternatives were, make a probability estimate of what the perceived consequences of each alternative would be, appraise what he wanted, and in terms of the latter, re-appraise the different consequences and decide then what to do.

So we created a little toy model in Figure 10.2 to see how this worked. And up to a point it worked very well. One of the sticky wickets in this model was that man did not seem to know how to evaluate the consequences of the different alternatives that faced him in order to arrive at a rational decision. So we plugged in a decision rule to the effect that before going down a particular road he had to answer the question, "Am I willing to pay the price for what I want?"

Here we were playing a bit of dirty pool, we admit, but we had to get our model off the ground. It should be noted that we still treated, as we did in our first model, man's wants as fundamental. In this respect we did not differentiate the worker from the man-ager. We said, "Do what you want—satisfy your needs—there's nothing bad with your wants as wants—the more you satisfy them the better. Just don't belly ache about the price you have to pay for realizing them. Moreover, don't expect us to tell you what you want. That's your problem. You and you alone know what you want. Don't expect us to tell you. Only you and you alone can plug this into our model."

So what we mean by playing a bit of dirty pool is that we could not program into our model what man's wants were in terms of which he had to evaluate finally the consequences of the different paths open to him. We left this up to him. Although this salvaged our conscience a little bit, it grounded our model, computer-like speaking, a good bit.

So now we began to toy with the idea of trying to hitch some of Maslow's ideas about what man wants [7] with some of March and Simon's ideas about how to go about realizing them rationally [8]

[7] Maslow, op. cit.
[8] March and Simon, op. cit.

and with some of George Homans' ideas, some very old ideas, which he has resuscitated in modern form, about how man in exchange with his fellow men has to pay the price for what he wants,[9] and thus in this manner try to get our model off the ground.

With the help of all three and just a few psychological sleight-of-hand tricks of our own we finally were able to do this. Using all three, we feel we made a plausible case for how the personal resolutions of workers with their organizational outcomes might have been reached.

But now, having done this, we had a few qualms. Because although by this approach we began to see more logically how the counselor might intervene in order to realize a resolution of the worker's concerns that would be more satisfactory to him as well as to management, we felt that we might have created for the lay reader an image of the counseling process that was more logical than psychological and which even the counselors in the counseling program at Hawthorne would not recognize. In fact in the first draft of this book, which we passed around to many of the remaining counselors of the program at Hawthorne for suggestions, the overwhelming concensus of responses was to the effect, "We don't recognize ourselves in your picture. From our point of view this is not quite what we were up to. What are you doing, writing a fairy tale?"

For example, the counselors could argue that the notions of an interview which a layman could get from the picture we had drawn could go something like this.

Hypothetical Interview Number One

EMPLOYEE: I'd like to punch my supervisor in the nose.

COUNSELOR: Have you considered the consequences of this course of action?

EMPLOYEE: Well, yes and no.

COUNSELOR: What do you think your chances would be of losing your job if you punched your supervisor in the nose?

EMPLOYEE: About ninety-nine in a hundred.

COUNSELOR: You don't want to do it under these conditions?

---

[9] Homans, op. cit.

EMPLOYEE: No.

COUNSELOR: Well, what about if there was a fifty-fifty chance? Would you do it then?

EMPLOYEE: No.

COUNSELOR: Well, what if the chances were only one in a hundred? Would you do it then?

EMPLOYEE: Well, if there was only one chance out of a hundred that I'd lose my job if I punched my supervisor in the nose, I'd take a chance. Frankly speaking, I'd get a helluva lot of satisfaction out of doing this under those conditions.

COUNSELOR: Well, you are not what I would call an entrepreneur—a big risk taker—you seem to be playing it safe—you don't live dangerously.

EMPLOYEE: You're right.

COUNSELOR: Have you thought of any alternatives to your course of action?

EMPLOYEE: What do you mean?

COUNSELOR: Well, why do you want to punch your supervisor in the nose?

EMPLOYEE: Well, it would give me a lot of satisfaction.

COUNSELOR: Why?

EMPLOYEE: Because he treats me like a child.

COUNSELOR: But if you punch him in the nose, will this stop him from treating you as a child?

EMPLOYEE: I don't know. At least I would have told him off.

COUNSELOR: You don't seem to me to be behaving very rationally. You have told me that in your rational opinion there exists ninety-nine chances out of a hundred of losing your job if you punch your supervisor in the nose. You don't want to take this chance and yet you keep wanting to punch your supervisor in the nose. I don't get it. Moreover, I don't get what you expect to gain by punching him in the nose. You don't want to be treated as a child by your supervisor but you seem to me to be behaving childishly toward him and provoking the very kind of behavior you don't want. This seems to me nonlogical. Do you get what I mean?

EMPLOYEE: I'm not sure.

COUNSELOR: Well, think it over and we will discuss it more tomorrow.

So we hunted through the files in order to see if we could find an interview like this. And the counselors were right. We couldn't find *one*. But we could find interviews that resembled this one.

Hypothetical Interview Number Two [10]

EMPLOYEE: I'd like to punch my supervisor in the nose.

COUNSELOR: So you'd like to punch him in the nose? Why?

EMPLOYEE: Well, he treats me like a child.

COUNSELOR: You don't like being treated as a child?

EMPLOYEE: No.

COUNSELOR: Well, why don't you punch him in the nose?

EMPLOYEE: I don't want to lose my job.

COUNSELOR: You like your job.

EMPLOYEE: Yes, I like my job.

COUNSELOR: And you don't want to lose it?

EMPLOYEE: Yes sir, that's right.

COUNSELOR: Why don't you want to lose it?

EMPLOYEE: Well sir, you know I'm the breadwinner in the family and you know I don't want to deprive the family and the kids.

COUNSELOR: This is important to you.

EMPLOYEE: Yes sir.

COUNSELOR: You got angry at your supervisor.

EMPLOYEE: Yes sir.

COUNSELOR: What did you do?

EMPLOYEE: I told him I'm through, I'm quitting.

COUNSELOR: So you decided to quit.

EMPLOYEE: Well, in a way, yes, but . . .

COUNSELOR: But did you want to quit? I thought you said you liked your job.

EMPLOYEE: Yes, I like my job but I don't like my supervisor.

COUNSELOR: So you like your job but you don't like your supervisor. Why?

EMPLOYEE: Well, as I told you, I don't like being treated like a child; I'm no longer in school.

COUNSELOR: You don't like being treated like a child.

EMPLOYEE: That's right. You know I'm a man, not a mouse.

COUNSELOR: So you want to be a man instead of a mouse.

EMPLOYEE: Yes sir.

COUNSELOR: Would punching your supervisor in the nose be behaving like a man or a mouse?

EMPLOYEE: I don't know. At least he'd know he can't push me around.

[10] This is a highly condensed and somewhat altered version of an interview whose full blown form we will show and discuss in the next chapter, in the case of Joe, the Machine Helper.

COUNSELOR: But are there other ways in which you might behave more like a man than a mouse?

EMPLOYEE: What do you mean?

COUNSELOR: Well, I gather you feel a bit mousyish now, after having told your boss you're quitting when you really don't want to quit and you can't tell him so.

EMPLOYEE: I suppose so.

COUNSELOR: Is there anything you can do about that?

EMPLOYEE: Well, I could have a man-to-man talk with my supervisor.

COUNSELOR: Would you want to do that?

EMPLOYEE: I don't know; I don't want to knuckle under that bastard.

COUNSELOR: Will you be knuckling under that bastard, as you say, if you tell him what's got you down?

EMPLOYEE: I don't know. Do you think I should speak with him?

COUNSELOR: I don't know. Would you like to try?

EMPLOYEE: Yes sir, I think I will.

If we look at the logical and psychological structures of these two interviews we can see quite a difference. The logical structure in both cases is not too different. Each one is exploring alternatives, trying to assess the consequences of them and what the employee wants, but the psychological structures are quite different.

In the first case the assumption is that the employee will be influenced by the logic of the situation, while in the latter case the assumption is that he will be influenced more if one tries to understand his situation from *his* own perceived psychological point of view. As this was important in *how* the counselor should intervene in these matters of personal decision making, we decided to explore this in the next chapter and see what difference, if any, this would make.

In summary, too, it should be pointed out that this chapter is woefully lacking in cardinal numbers. Probably many readers would like to know how many of each of the six kinds of personal resolutions were made in the plant. Unfortunately, we have no data to answer this question; it can only be answered by future research. In our opinion such an appraisal might be more useful to management than many of the attitude surveys it often gets, and we will have more to say about this in Part V, our conclusion.

CHAPTER XI

The Difference Counseling Can Make

IN THIS CHAPTER many of the strands of the counseling story, which we wrote sequentially, since we could not write about them all at the same time, come together with a dramatic impact. Finally the encounter between the worker and the counselor is to take place. For the worker it is the moment of decision, of adaptation, and of choosing which path in his career development and his development as a person to take. For the counselor it is the moment of intervention at which his skill is to be exercised and tested and when finally, if at all, he will make a difference.

THE COUNSELING PROCESS

So in this chapter we will be reducing the "big picture" of counseling to an interaction between two persons—a counselor and a worker—at a moment of time, that is, to an interaction covering a short duration of time in the life cycle of the two parties. We will be also reducing our focus in another sense. We will be speaking only about the 40% of employees in the plant population who expressed concerns in any one quarterly period, as described in Chapter IV, and we will be choosing from this segment of this plant population for our examples only those (about 10% of the plant population) which we identified in Figure 4.1 of that chapter, as those whom the counselors thought had been helped by counseling.

We are narrowing our focus to this moment of time for a selected group of employees quite deliberately. In the next chapter, in Part IV, we will take up the question of the 60% of the plant population who expressed no serious concerns and also the factors which may have contributed to the fact that only about a third of the employees with serious concerns had in the opinion of the counselors been helped by counseling. But in this chapter we will concentrate our attention solely upon trying to make alive and meaningful the difference counseling can make to certain employees under certain conditions and not to any employee under any conditions.

The Worker at the Moment of Personal Decision

In the last chapter we built a toy model of the choices a worker might encounter and the factors which might influence, among different alternatives, the particular path he chooses to take. But what triggered off these alternatives? Let us consider this question.

In Part II of this book we spent considerable time in describing the work environment from which some of the workers' concerns emerged. In this description we hoped to show that any changes resulting from changes in business conditions, technology, or control systems intended to improve efficient operation could and did result in changes at the work level in the worker's job (to the point sometimes when there wasn't any), changes in his job assignment (involuntary transfers), changes in his shift arrangements, his seating arrangements, his position in the flow of work, his work group, his amount of pay, his differential of pay, his investments in his job, his supervisor, his new supervision's different interpersonal style, his capacity to develop the intrinsic rewards from the job, and so on and on, all of which resulted in some cases in felt injustices.

At these moments when the worker felt that he was being asked to accommodate to the requirements of the organization without due regard for his own personal needs, he was not an unemotional but a highly emotional decision maker. All the choices we depicted in Figure 10.2 in the last chapter were activated: "Should I stay or quit? Should I take this lying down or should I protest? And how should I try to exert my influence? By playing within or outside of the framework of constraints I am in?" and so on.

Obviously the worker did not frame his questions this way. They were more of the order: "Should I seek for a transfer, ask for a raise, tell my supervisor off, go to night school, try to get on the day shift, complain to the shop steward, complain to the union, complain to my immediate boss, complain to the big boss, talk to my wife, punch my supervisor in the nose, say to hell with it (not produce so much)?" and so on and on. In short, the big alternative choices along the major dimensions depicted in Figure 10.2 were now reduced to their concrete, particular, minute, multivarious (and to what to an outside observer sometimes might appear trivial) alternative forms.

But these sorts of questions involving personal decisions were not only triggered off by changes in the worker environment; they were also activated by changes in the environment outside of the plant. And here they took the form: "Should I get engaged? married? divorced? live with my in-laws? Can I afford children? How can I make enough money to buy the things my wife and children want or send my kids to college? How do I do what my wife, children, friends, and neighbors expect of me? How can I live on my pension? and so on.

And then there were those questions involving personal decisions that were generated by the individual himself at certain periods of his life cycle when he started to do a bit of soul searching. All of a sudden, for example, he begins to question whether if by just conforming passively to what is daily expected of him (just being a good boy), he will fulfill his career expectations. He sees others moving ahead while he is being passed by. He finds himself one day reporting to a person who at an earlier period had been his subordinate. He finds himself getting old and unable to do the things or get the satisfaction from them that he had done earlier. These changes that occur slowly over a long period not only stimulate an odd assortment of ill-defined and vague questions of "Where am I going? Where have I been? What might have been? What's it all about?" and so on, but also they generate certain kinds of behavior, such as excessive drinking, abusive language, chronic complaining, embittered withdrawal, and so on.

But let us remember that regardless of whether these questions involving personal decisions arose from factors inside or outside the plant, the worker who confronted the counselor was essentially the same person. The needs he had outside the plant were the same needs he carried with him into the plant, even though his social roles and obligations in these different environments were different. Worker A who was having difficulty in relating himself to others outside (his wife, husband, in-laws, children, neighbors, etc.) was the same person who often was having difficulty in relating himself to his co-workers and supervisors at work and often for the same reasons. The good Joe inside the plant was the same person who often outside the plant was the life of the party. The technical specialist inside the plant had often at home his workshop outside the plant. The social specialist inside the plant was also taking care of his social obligations outside the plant. The trouble maker was displaying often in union halls and stockholder meetings the same basic attitude he manifested in the plant. The minimal performer was just as cautious about living dangerously outside as inside the plant. And the unhappy isolate was often just as much alienated from the members of his neighborhood as he was from his co-workers and supervisors at work. So it was the concrete person that the counselor encountered in the interview—not a worker bifurcated between home and work concerns but a full-blown person with all his concerns in a highly charged emotional state resulting from one interrelated and interdependent constellation of needs (what he wanted) and roles (what was expected of him both inside and outside the plant).

At this moment when he encountered the counselor, he did not know the decision rules of how to live rationally under conditions of uncertainty. He was often not even in a problem-solving posture. He was often not "searching for" or "scanning the environment" in a binary go or no-go fashion, as a computer would, for a solution to his problem. More often than not, he was seething with strong, if not too clarified, feelings. He was reacting to these feelings and not being proactive to them. Or, to put it in less social science language, he was feeling either angry, frustrated, anxious, or dejected, and venting these feelings. At that moment he was not the rational decision maker we posited in our toy model in Figure 10.2 in Chapter X; he was then often ready to do almost anything regardless of the consequences. We say "at that moment," because at a later moment, when his feelings have been more thoroughly aired, he might feel differently and consider the posture we assumed in Figure 10.2 in the last chapter. But this assumption could not be made by the counselor at the first instance when he met the angry or dejected, reactive, conflicted, nonproblem solving, non-logical—sometimes irrational—concrete worker.

The Counselor at the Moment of Intervention

In Chapter II we armed the counselor with a role model that had been derived from previous researches. One of the components of this role model we called "the listening-helping-communication component." This component prescribed for the encounter the way the counselor should intervene at these critical moments of personal decision. It said, listen—don't talk; don't argue; don't give advice; listen to what he wants to say, what he does not want to say, and what he cannot say without help, i.e. the conflict between what he wants (his needs) and what is expected of him (his role in the given situation). Help him to clarify and accept his feelings; and above all try to understand him from his and not from your own point of view. Do not evaluate and make moralistic judgments from your point of view; do not approve or disapprove of his feelings; help him to understand them, and finally help him to make his own personal decisions—do not make them for him.

Most of these rules, as can be seen, were rules for the counselor to follow in order to prepare the emotional worker for the more rational decision-making process later. Before this latter process could be evoked, however, other things had to happen first. The counselors learned that it was ineffective to say to a highly concerned person that he should not be concerned about what he is concerned about. This was the best way to provoke a fresh torrent of feelings and to retard rather than to facilitate the more rational process of constructive search behavior. Only after his strong feelings were understood and accepted, would he, perhaps, be ready to do this. So in this process of letting workers get things off their chests, as it was often expressed at Hawthorne and is often said in the popular vernacular, the counselor played a cathartic role.

But it would be incorrect to believe that the counselor was only a *passive listener* to workers who wanted to get things off their chests. Far from it. The prescription said: "Don't listen passively; listen proactively; listen for the implied as well as for the expressed feelings. Develop your third ear." (Had he not done this, all of

Part II of this book could not have been written. All we would have had would have been an endless list of attitudes without any matrix or meaning, such as an endless string of beads but no necklace.)

The Personal Encounter—The Interaction Between A and B in the Interview

So this popular image of the counselor as a passive door mat on whom people relieved their feelings is not the whole story. In the encounter he was supposed to play a catalytic role. As this role is too often misunderstood, let us see if we can clarify it.

In ordinary social behavior when B expresses certain feelings to A, A often reacts to them with an expression of his feelings about the feelings B has expressed. He tends to say something to the effect that these are good or bad feelings or "I approve or disapprove of your feelings." To speak more concretely he says, "You shouldn't feel like that," or "Buck up, old man, things can't be as bad as that," or "Let me tell you about my case," for example, and make statements like that or to that effect.

These statements are all intended to be reassuring from A's point of view. And the more B expresses negative feelings, such as, for example, "I hate my wife," or "The company is one goddamned big jail," the more A tends to make these reassuring noises or tries to argue B out of them such as by saying, "Your wife or the company can't be as bad as that."

Now if A, as a counselor, behaves like that, it should be noted that A is *reacting* to the sentiments B has expressed; that is, his feelings are being acted upon by B's feelings and he is reacting to his own feelings instead of B's feelings. By his responses he is implying, "Please don't express feelings like that. They make me feel uncomfortable, uneasy, embarrassed, etc." So B hears, "Please stop expressing such feelings, I can't stand it." So B stops.

This may be good ordinary social behavior; it is not good counseling behavior. As a counselor he does not react to his own feelings which the feelings B has expressed have aroused. Instead he takes a proactive posture toward B's feelings; and when he does this he becomes the catalyst we previously mentioned. What is this proactive stance?

It is a very difficult stance to take and is acquired only by long arduous experience. Although all the prescriptions of the counselor's role model implied it, they are often not heard or their implications not understood. Before the counselor can take it, he has to learn to differentiate his feelings from the feelings of the person he is counseling. He has to keep saying to himself: "These are B's feelings—not my feelings. They belong to B, not me. I am curious about them and why B has them. I will try to understand why B has them. But I'm not going to get sentimental about them or let them get under my skin and get angry about them, and if I do, at least I will try to recognize the fact that I feel sorry for or irritated by this troubled person. But in the last analysis these are B's feelings and if he is to be helped, he has to learn to accept and live with these feelings himself. His feelings are his responsibility—not mine. He has to learn to take responsibility for them."

So the proactive stance of A in the last analysis goes something like this. It implies, "Mr. B, these are your feelings. What are *you* going to do about them?" Slowly but surely, step by step, in every act of intervention by the counselor in the encounter, he is making this essential communication.

Now this is where rules and words fail us. Because a rule can be practiced by a person without as well as with some understanding of the phenomena with which he is dealing, it is here where counseling transcends a skill and becomes an art. No books can teach it. It can't be learned without experience, but even then some persons cannot seem to learn it. But for those who do, a great transformation takes place. They become skilled artisans or artists of their trade (i.e., of a particular class of phenomena). They are not verbal artists; they are not employing verbal skills such as those we are manifesting now when we are writing about them. Many counselors are verbally inarticulate but they have a feel for the human materials with which they are dealing—the subtle world of sentiments and feelings and some of the basic uniformities (not of chance and probabilities or of logic and optimalities but of love and of compassion in man's encounter with his fellow man) which resides in them. They latch on to these uniformities like mad and, lo and behold, a change (a transformation) takes place in B. By their own transformation they transform others. This is the meaning of the catalytic role and the wizardry of change agentry, about which we will have more to say later in our conclusion. They change B's behavior, not by directly trying to change B but by first changing their own behavior.

With this insight they finally internalize the positive Hawthorne effect we discussed in Chapter II. It will be remembered there that some persons were disturbed by the "contaminated data" which the early Hawthorne experiments had produced. From these early researches two insights had resulted. One—the high road in the search for truth—was, "Let us escape from this contamination at all cost." The other—the low road in the search for truth—was, "Let us accept this contamination and build on it." The counselors took the low road and tried to build on this second insight.

So the counselor did not try to escape from his involvement. He accepted it and tried, as well as he could, to use the contaminated data his behavior produced and the uniformities that resided in them. And with that acceptance of the phenomena of human interchange as they were and not as they should be, a miracle was wrought. However, because we have an aversion to miracles and even though words are a sorry substitute for the human reality that now confronts us, let us try to unveil this mystery and look at some of the simple uniformities the counselor was latching on to.

One was that negative feelings, if freely allowed to express themselves, will tend to take on in time a more positive character, well stated in the old adage that hope springs eternal. This is not because the counselor is *doing something*. He is just allowing (what in the old days was called a law of nature but what we are now just calling) a uniformity of human nature to express itself. And what is the great wizardry he exercises? He just does not do anything to prevent this from happening. He just removes the constraints which are preventing the natural uniformity from expressing itself. And how does he remove these constraints? Well, look at the "reassuring" behavior we described before. This is not the miracle of pulling a rabbit out of nowhere (the kind of miracle we have an abhorrence of); it is the miracle of not preventing what is by nature in the uniformities of the phenomena (and not in himself as a wizard) from happening. Now this is the function of a good catalyst. The function he performs sounds passive but in human affairs it is the highest form of proactivity that can exist and unfortunately it is manifested rarely.

But now let us look at how this extraordinary proactivity of restraint on the part of A produces a proactivity on the part of B, our worker, who up to now is refusing to accept his feelings and instead is just wallowing in them. All of a sudden, if not prevented by too much soothing syrup, an alternative appears. He begins to feel, *"I can do something about them."* Note the proactive stance. Without it, the counselor can do little except not to prevent it from emerging. But once it rears its head—no matter how slightly—the counselor is over the hump. Now he can render the only kind of help he is capable of giving and B recognizes this, well expressed by the old adage, "You can't help people who are not willing to help themselves." *Finally B is going to do something, and it is B and not A who is doing it.* A is just on the cheering (catalytic) stand, letting what is become what ought to be.

With this fusion of what is with what ought to be, a counselor sometimes reaches his greatest insight. He becomes a discoverer. He shouts, "Eureka," and sometimes this discovery goes to his head and he feels that he is the first one who discovered it. But this sin of pride the counselors at Hawthorne were not guilty of. They noted that constructive *search behavior* was back in the saddle again.

And then they noticed another curious thing. This small spark of proactivity on the part of B was often expressed in very small ways. It did not manifest itself in some great heroic act or in some loud-mouthed, table-thumping, fist-shaking gestures. It often just expressed itself in some small, simple, almost obvious first step, such as, for example, "Perhaps I can talk this over with my supervisor or wife or someone."

Again no great miracle had occurred. All that had occurred was that now the troubled employee felt that he could do some "little" thing about his concern, such as talking to his wife (or husband) or supervisor or shop steward or fellow worker about it, and that this might help. And this simple realization—this little step in reestablishing communication with his world had an effect out of all proportion to the simple stimulus that had originated it. This, to the counselors, was also the meaning of their function as catalysts.

They were the experts on the big difference a little difference can make.

ILLUSTRATIVE CASES

We now should like to give some examples of some of the matter we have been talking about. There is some risk in doing this because the raw data of an interview can be interpreted in many different ways, depending upon what the reader is attending to. So in all these instances in which we present a raw interview, we will follow it with a discussion of what the counselor heard and what difference, if any, he thought he had made.

It might help if, when reading an interview, the reader would try to listen for the expressed and implied feelings and not get too enthralled with the logics of organization of the Western Electric Company, such as, for example, its piece-work system. We hope that Part II of the book would have provided him with enough understanding of these logics so that he can put his primary attention on the worker and his feelings.

The Case of Anna, the Married Worker with Three Children

We will start with the case of Anna where we will commingle the raw data with our interpretation of them. Anna was the mother of three children; two older girls in high school and her youngest, a son, in grade school. Her husband worked in the same department as she did. Anna had been working on the day shift but now it was her turn to go on the 3 to 11 shift.

For Anna this precipitated a crisis of decision: (1) should she do what she was supposed to do according to her contract of employment, namely, go on the swing shift, or (2) should she go to her supervisor and try to get approval from him to stay on the day shift, or (3) should she quit and stay at home and take care of her children?

But why had these particular alternatives been evoked? Let us look at what bothered her about these three alternatives. In the first interview she spoke at great length about the friction which had long existed between her husband and the children and of her role as peacemaker in this friction. In this interview she said,

"This is the first time I've mentioned these difficulties to anyone."
So what was bothering Anna about the first alternative was her
apprehension about the possible unhappy consequences she thought
might happen between her husband and children if she went on the
3 to 11 swing shift.

So why didn't she go to her supervisor and try to stay on the day
shift? Well, she had considered this but she was reluctant to do it.
Why? Because since her husband worked in the same department
and he was a worker in good standing with twenty-one years of
service, she did not want to say anything which would go against
him in any way. So this was not a satisfactory alternative, i.e., an
alternative the costs of which Anna was willing to pay.

Well, what about quitting the job and taking care of the children? Anna considered this too in the interview. But then there
were the extra earnings her employment brought which allowed
her and her husband and children to satisfy their wants more than
they would otherwise have been able to do.

So here was Anna tussling with a difficult decision. The counselor said in effect, "Gee, Anna, this is a tough decision to make
but it is yours—not mine. Let's talk about it and see if you can
make up your mind."

So through three interviews Anna talked through this problem
and finally she said, "I'm going to go on the 3 to 11 shift and see
what happens. Perhaps my fears are groundless; if I take the 3 to 11
shift perhaps this is the best way to find out if this is so." (Note
how proactivity in this case takes the form of "reality testing.")

So Anna finally decided to go on the 3 to 11 shift, which was
what she was supposed to do in the first place, and let us see after
the first week what she said to the counselor.

"I never was so surprised in all my life! I declare a miracle must
have happened. Everything's going along beautifully—can you imagine that? My girls say they don't know what's got into their father,
but he seems to be a changed man . . . Maybe this was just what
they needed, a chance to work things out by themselves."

There is probably little need to discuss this case, the role the
counselor played is fairly obvious. However, we should like to
point out that Anna illustrates well the difficulty of distinguishing

a work from a personal problem. She was concerned about both her job and her family.

The Case of Joe, the Machine Helper

The counselor was walking through the department, when he heard Joe, an employee with whom he was previously acquainted, talking in very emotional tones to another employee. So the counselor went up and said:

(1) COUNSELOR: Well, hello, Joe. What's been going on?

(1) EMPLOYEE: Oh, hell, Bill. These goddam bosses around here, they aren't worth a dam. They . . . you have a raise coming and they won't give it to you. They give other guys raises all around you and they won't give you a raise. This goddam place stinks. The sooner I can get out of here the better I'll feel.

(2) COUNSELOR: Well, gosh, Joe, this apparently has got you pretty much upset. What do you say we go upstairs and have a smoke and talk it over till quitting time.

(2) EMPLOYEE: Oh, hell, that won't do any good. If those guys can't give me a raise you can't give a raise. There's no use talking about it. Hell, I might as well get out of here, take my tools and quit. Hell, you can't do me any good, Bill. I know you have always been fair with me, but this is something that I don't think you guys can handle.

(3) COUNSELOR: Well, Joe, maybe I can't do any good, but at least we can talk it over, couldn't we? Hell, shut your machine down and let's go up and sit down and have a smoke for a little while.

(3) EMPLOYEE: Well okay. I don't think it will do a damn bit of good, but we will go up and have a chat. That goddam department chief—he is an s.o.b. Do you know what he told me?

(4) COUNSELOR: No, I don't. As a matter of fact, I don't know what it is all about, Joe.

(4) EMPLOYEE: Well, I'll tell you, Bill. I heard that some of the boys around here got a merit increase in their pay so I simply went up asking for a raise and he tells me that getting a raise around here is a matter of luck. Boy, that burns me up. I am working for the Western Electric Company, I'm working, I'm not gambling. If this goddam thing is a gamble, I don't want any of it— I don't want to gamble. I can go across the street here in these dives and gamble my money. I came here to work, I didn't come here to gamble. If it is all a matter of luck, I don't want any of it. I want to get a job where I can work and get ahead

on my merit. Yeah, it seemed to me as if I had a reasonable squawk why I should get a raise. I simply asked the department chief for a raise and boy, he just flew all over me. A guy that talks like that to me . . . why I haven't any use for him . . . I won't work for him at all. I told him too that he wasn't the Western Electric Company, that he was only a representative of the Western Electric Company, and that I was working for the Company and I wasn't working for him, but by God, if I can't convince a man like that that I deserve a merit increase, why how in the hell am I ever going to get ahead? He tells me that I am at the top of Grade 34 and I can't get any higher, that's as far as I can go. Then I said, "What the hell is the matter, I'm working on screw machines down there—that is Grade 35—I have been working on them for some time now so why don't I get the upgrading so I can get some more money?" Well, they tell me that those jobs down there are Grade 34 because we are only helpers on the screw machines and there will be some time before we can be upgraded to a better position to get more money. I said, "What the hell do you mean, those other guys get raises and they are at the top of their grades and over the top of their grades and I know damn well they are, Bill. (pause) Well, there is one guy down there maybe that isn't at the top of his grade yet.

(5) COUNSELOR: You think there are some at the top of their grade and they still get a merit increase, Joe?

(5) EMPLOYEE: Sure, I know that's what happened, and he is trying to give me the old bull that I can't get any more money on my day rate because I'm at the top of my grade. Well, my God, Bill, at that rate I may be around here until the war is over and I still wouldn't get any more money. I can stay around here for ten years and I still wouldn't make any more than I am doing now. Well, I can't afford to do that. This is war time and you have to make the money while the making is good—you know that.

Hell, he sure burned me up. He tells me that if I think I'm due for a raise, I'm in the wrong place. Well, that sure is a hell of a way to talk to a guy simply because he asks for a raise, he tells me I'm working in the wrong place. I know that my bogey sheets have been up to everyone else's down there and I also know that those helpers get shoved around a lot because when one machine breaks down or when one machine has to be cleaned up, they will send you over there to clean it up and do the dirty work while the machine setters get all the gravy, and they also told me about the fact that I was learning it, that I was in training while I was down there, that he wasn't running a training school, that he was paying me while I was learning.

Well, I never did care about working in that department, but I went in there because they told me that was the best they could do for me and I didn't like that machine work at all and never did do it, but now I come around to the point where I kind of like it, and I've been really working at it. When a guy talks to me like the department chief did, I can't work for him at all. I wouldn't work for the s.o.b. at all. He has no business talking to me like that whatsoever. Anybody around here, if they don't get a raise the way I look at it, has got a right to go up to the boss and ask for a raise without catching hell. He says he is not running this training school and he can't afford to run a training school down there, and that he is paying me while I work, and that I'm getting two-hundred dollars' worth of education. Why hell, Bill, we don't learn anything. Those darn machine setters won't tell you anything—they won't explain anything, they shove you out of the way, they do everything they can to keep you from learning anything, and it is a hell of a hard racket. You know how those machine setters are, especially screw machine men, they won't tell you anything.

(6) COUNSELOR: I see. They seem to be pretty selfish about their knowledge of screw machines.

(6) EMPLOYEE: Selfish isn't the right word. They are absolutely tight. They won't tell you anything. As a matter of fact, if you try to learn anything, they try to hide it from you. Take for example, when I got in there, I wanted to get some books on this subject. Now, there is another case too, if the department chief had been on the up and up he could have gotten me some books on that stuff, so I could learn, but no, he sits you down there and leaves you cold. He never would make any attempt to get you to study. The only way I got my books was that another department chief that I used to work for came through our place one day, and he stopped me and he said, "Oh, so you are working on screw machines now." I said, "Yes," and I said, "I would like to have some books so I could read up on this stuff." He said, "Hell, come down and see me some day, and we will fix you up." So one day I went down after work and I saw him and he fixed me up with some books and was really helpful.

Well, hell, this department chief that I'm working for, he never did that. One time he came down there, and he went over to the machine setter and he got a book. I didn't know where he got the book. He brought it over to me and told me I could use it, to take care of it, and to bring it back when I got through, so I took the book and put it in the desk drawer there. Pretty soon, the machine setter comes over and says, "What the hell did the department chief do with that book?" I told him, "Well, I put it in my drawer, I was going to take it home." The machine setter said, "Who in the hell does the department chief think he is anyway! That book belongs to me. I'm not going to let you guys tear it up." Well, I said to this machine setter, "The book is over there in my drawer." Well, that night when I went to get it the book was gone, so I went back and saw the machine setter and asked him if he took it. He said yes, he took it. Well, I I thought it was kind of a small thing to do, not to let me read the book. I told the section chief about it and the section chief thought it was pretty darn small too, but then the department chief—I don't know whether he heard about it or not—but he didn't offer to get me any other book, I had to get them myself.

The other department chief I used to work for, he would give us all the information he could, and I'll tell you, Bill, I've been working hard in studying these machines and trying to do my best to get ahead on them so I could learn something, and then he comes around and tells me that if I want a raise, I'm working in the wrong place. How in the hell can you get a raise around this place anyway? I used to think that if a guy works hard and does the right kind of work that he can get a raise, but hell, now you just get to the top of the grade and when you are there you can't get anywhere. Hell, that may mean that I'll be making the same money that I'm making right now from now on. Well, I'm too young a guy to do anything like that. I've got to get out where I can make money, especially right now.

(7) COUNSELOR: Well, tell me, what is the top of Grade 34?

(7) EMPLOYEE: Top of Grade 34 is 76 cents an hour.

(8) COUNSELOR: I see. Are you making piece rate in there?

(8) EMPLOYEE: Yeah, we get 30% by the week and I think the department pays 35%.

(9) COUNSELOR: I see. That's about a dollar an hour that you make.

(9) EMPLOYEE: Yeah, that's right. About a buck an hour, and there are plenty of guys down there making a whole lot more than that. I wouldn't care so much about a big raise. I would like to have a little raise. A three-cent raise would be all right with me because I haven't gotten a raise at all in about a year. Every

time I've been transferred here lately, I've been transferred four times this last year, I've taken a cut, not in day rate. I have always held my day rate, but I have taken a cut in percentage. You know, that certainly eats into your take home, you know that. Day rate isn't important when you are working on piece rate, it is how much you take home and every time you are transferred you have to take a cut—well, you are just making less money all the time.

That's another thing, the department chief said to me, "Well, you got the advantages in the raises a year ago here." I said, "Yes, those were smear raises, those were raises that everybody got." They weren't for the work I was doing or what I merited. Everybody in the Company got those. I don't see why I should be penalized for that. The way it looks now, it would have been better if I hadn't taken those smear raises and gone ahead on my merit raise. Anyway, most of them have been taken away anyhow due to my transferring around, taking a lower piece-rated job. Yeah, the department chief tells me that due to those smear raises I'm at the top of my grade, and he can't do anything for me. I know that just isn't so, because he has given other fellows down there raises that have been above their top rate. I don't think they deserve it a damn bit more than I do. (pause) Well, yes, they have got a little more service and service is worth something—I know that.

(10) COUNSELOR: You see a value there?

(10) EMPLOYEE: Yeah, it just makes me sick to give it up too, and to leave the Western Electric Company. Understand, Bill, I haven't got anything against the Company—they have always, as a company, as a whole been fine to me and I never in my life have had any argument with any boss wherever I worked. I always went along swell. I never had to ask the boss for a raise in my life. I always figured that if I did my work, they would see to it that I got my raises. Up until now that's the way it has worked, and when I come along with this guy, boy oh boy, I'm not going to work for a guy like that at all. He simply made me quit, that's all, because I wouldn't take that kind of stuff from anybody. You ask a guy for a raise and he comes out with all such silly talk as he came out with. Why, that is ridiculous.

(11) COUNSELOR: It's something you don't feel is worth living with and it's kind of got your cork out.

(11) EMPLOYEE: (At this time, the three o'clock whistle blows which is the quitting time for this employee. The employee makes a

move to leave the room and to go home.) I kind of hate to leave in this way, but that's the way it is. When a guy has made up his mind, he has made up his mind. What the hell can I do?

(12) COUNSELOR: You're wondering where to turn.

(12) EMPLOYEE: There's no place to turn. I've got to get out of here. I was up to the Placement three or four times in the last year when I got transferred, but what the hell can they do about it? Anyway, Bill, it is too late now. I already told that guy I was quitting. He has already made out my time. I told him to have my time ready at three o'clock. Well, I don't figure that there is much use in talking to anyone. I don't feel that I can possibly get out of it now. I don't see what anyone could do to fix it up.

(13) COUNSELOR: You feel as though you've definitely burned your bridge beyond repair.

(13) EMPLOYEE: Well, the fact is, I don't have any job lined up at all. That's the heck of it. I never thought about quitting the Western Electric Company, and Bill, I don't really want to quit because I like it here. I always have liked it here. I have had a good job ever since I've been here, until this job here. Well, this job isn't so bad. I like the job, but that department chief, why that s.o.b., I wouldn't work for him at all.

(14) COUNSELOR: It's not so much the company as the individual that you feel you want to get away from.

(14) EMPLOYEE: Well, I'm satisfied with my job all right, I like the job. There is nothing wrong with it at all. I would like to stay there, but I won't work for that department chief. If I could talk to the guys in Placement, maybe they could fix it so that I could work for someone else. The hell of it is that s.o.b. probably won't let me go up there. Maybe he will tell me to get out. I wouldn't like to do that. I wouldn't like to ask him for any favors. (pause) Even if he would let me go up I wouldn't know what I should tell them anyway. I was all ready to quit, I hadn't thought about going up and talking it over with those guys, at all. I don't know what to say to them whatsoever. I don't—I don't know how to handle them or anything. I haven't any idea what kind of job I want or where I want to go or anything about it. As a matter of fact, the job I have is perfectly all right. Are they going to transfer me around just because I don't like my boss? They'd probably tell me I'm crazy—that I lost my head, but then again they might see it my way—my record's good and I've never squawked before.

(15) COUNSELOR: Your point is that they'd probably take a better look inasmuch as it's never happened before and. . . .

(15) EMPLOYEE: Maybe I'll do that then, maybe I will go up and talk to those fellows. Do you think I ought to talk to the department chief before I go up there?

(16) COUNSELOR: You're wondering if you should tell him first. . . .

(16) EMPLOYEE: Well, I say that because he will know the right place to send me, he will know the right Placement man to see.

(17) COUNSELOR: I see. . . .

(17) EMPLOYEE: Damn it, that's what I'm going to do. That might fix it all up. (pause) Well, Bill, I certainly thank you a lot for doing this. Yes, I thank you a thousand times. I didn't know that I saw the chance to get back in here at all. I thought that when I told the old man that I was through that I was through and that was the end of it. But one thing yet, if I don't get transferred out of there, or get some other kind of a job, or get some satisfaction, I'm still going to quit.

(18) COUNSELOR: You can still quit but you believe that you ought to take this chance here now before you do quit.

(18) EMPLOYEE: Well, I don't see why not. I don't see what I have to lose. I might as well do that—tell those fellows how I feel about if. If I don't get a job I can still quit. If I do get a transfer, well, I guess I'm about as good off as I was before I ever came into this department.

(19) COUNSELOR: You figure there's nothing to lose.

(19) EMPLOYEE: Okay then. I'll go down and talk to the department chief. I will have to change clothes though before I go up to the Placement Department. I don't want to go up there in these old greasy clothes.

(20) COUNSELOR: Freshen up a bit, eh?

(20) EMPLOYEE: Are you going back with me?

(21) COUNSELOR: Yes, I think I will go back down there.

(21) EMPLOYEE: Oh, well, hell, I'll tell the department chief myself what I want to do. I'll tell him that I want to go up and see the Placement man, and if he gives me a pass up there, I'll go up and talk to him. That's what I'll do. Gee, Bill, thanks for talking to me—thanks a million times. Thanks for everything. I feel pretty bad about this. I really do hate to leave the Company. As a matter of fact, it would break my heart if I had to leave here because this is about the only place I have ever worked for any length of time and I really like the Western Electric Company.

I don't have anything against it at all. Thanks a lot for what you have done.

(22) COUNSELOR: Not at all. I hope everything comes out all right, Joe. I'll see you tomorrow sometime and we can talk over what happened.

(22) EMPLOYEE: Sure thing. Come on down and see me in the morning, Bill, or some time tomorrow. I'll let you know what went on—see how it came out.

(23) COUNSELOR: Sure, fine. Good luck then, Joe.

After this interview Joe had a talk with his department chief. What happened in this talk we do not know, but it is likely that he was able now to express his feelings to the department chief in a less exaggerated form than he had stated them to the counselor. Anyway, as a result of their conversation Joe decided to stay on his present job. The counselor contacted Joe several times after that and Joe seemed to be satisfied with the decision he had reached.

What the counselor heard and what difference he made

During the interview the counselor was hearing and observing the following:

1. Joe had had a dispute with his department chief over an increase in pay, which had upset Joe enough so that he had said, "I'm quitting."

2. In talking to the department chief, Joe had taken his complaint over his first two levels of supervisors (group chief and section chief) so to Joe he was talking to the big boss—a very important and influential person—to whom one is expected to speak somewhat more deferentially than Joe did.

3. Joe seemed to be a bit confused about how the grade structure and the incentive system worked and this was what the department chief wanted to straighten Joe out about. (However, except for one remark—No. 7—the counselor was not too concerned with straightening out Joe's confusion about the workings of the incentive system or his labor grade or pay as such because he was hearing what Joe had to say.)

4. Joe was concerned more about his hourly rate than his piece-work earnings (take-home pay) with which he seemed satisfied. What Joe wanted was a "three-cent *merit increase* in hourly rate and not one of those goddam smear raises" that everyone got. He wanted a raise (recognition) for what he, Joe, was doing and *merited*. Joe felt that he was not being rewarded justly for his perceived investments.

5. After Joe had vented a lot of negative feelings about his department chief (which the counselor did not say tut-tut to) he began to express some positive feelings. He began to weigh the cost he would have to pay for quitting, such as his seniority rights, a job he liked and on which he felt he was learning something.

6. It was that "silly talk" of the department chief that, according to Joe, had *made him* quit. He hadn't wanted to quit; the silly talk *made him* quit which was Joe's way of stating (quite inaccurately) the feelings that, as yet, he was not able to express, such as "Perhaps I've made a bit of a fool of myself by shooting my big mouth off."

7. Joe felt that he had been treated like a school boy by the department chief and quite naturally had resented this and had become so overwhelmed with these feelings that he had finally done something he now wished he had not done. Now he wondered if he had burned all his bridges, if all was lost, and if he was at the end of his rope, etc. (feelings which the counselor reflected). Could he recoup without having to crawl on his knees and ask the big boss for his job back? (These are the implied feelings and not the expressed feelings the counselor heard and which he did not, quite appropriately, reflect as such at once.)

8. But in the latter part of the interview the counselor decided to try to help get them expressed (see responses No. 12, 13, 14, 15, 18, 19) and finally Joe felt he could talk to the department chief as man to man and not as an apologetic, beaten down, crawling on one's knees, school boy; and the curious part is that it worked.

In terms of the counseling process there are a few further observations that are interesting to note.

1. In terms of the number of words recorded, the counselor listened while Joe did 90% of the talking.

2. Of the 23 responses the counselor makes to Joe, they are all,

except No. 7, in the direction of trying to get Joe's feelings amply stated and clarified, to reflect the feelings Joe had difficulty in expressing, to clarify the decision alternatives implied by these feelings and to get Joe to take responsibility for his own feelings, and finally to take a small step toward coping with them better.

3. There are no moral admonitions, no attempts at reassurance, no pieces of advice, no great words of encouragement, no evaluations to the effect that "You were a fool to speak to the big boss like that," no attempts to steer, to direct or to manipulate Joe in the direction of where to turn, that is—go to placement, go to the shop steward, or go to his supervisor. All these alternatives were Joe's choice. From the point of view of counseling, he could have made any one so long as this was what he wanted to do and was willing to accept the consequences.

4. Had Joe made the right decision? Would it have been better for him if he had quit? We don't know. From the point of view of counseling the important matter was that Joe had reached his own decision and was willing to live with it. He had not been treated as a school boy but as a responsible adult—a treatment which, one does not have to be a psychiatrist in order to hear, was important to Joe.

5. Might Joe have come to the decision he did without the help of the counselor? Yes, many persons do. Most of us have said things in anger that we did not quite mean and then recovered our perspective without help. But then too, some persons don't. Some persons, with feelings like Joe's, have quit their jobs and then rued their decision later.

6. Did the department chief listen to Joe well and hear what he was saying? No. Could he have? Yes. Why didn't he? He was defending a decision.

7. Could the department chief have conducted an interview with Joe just like the counselor did, had he had the counselor's insights? No. Why not? Because his role relationship was different. We will discuss this later in Part IV and not now.

The Case of Mary, the Lead-Off Operator

As we said in Chapter II, the counselor spent a good deal of his time on the floor as well as in the interviewing room. Here he could familiarize himself with the job setting, become acquainted with everyone in the group, and observe their daily interactions and relationships with one another. From these activities he became aware of the organizational context in which often a problem arose and he could relate it to that setting. So sometimes the counselor was dealing with a group problem instead of strictly an individual one. Let us see how the counselor intervened in this kind of setting and the difference he could make.

In telling this story—a fairly complicated one because it involves a number of people and their relations with one another—we will tell it from the counselor's point of view, after having established a few facts common to all the parties. The counselor in this case was a woman. When we make some observations of our own, we will put them in parentheses. The problem centered around the efforts of a new supervisor, Dick, to gain the acceptance of a well-established group of older women who had developed restrictive practices under a former supervisor who knew of and had sanctioned them.

Work layout and pay arrangements

In this situation there were two groups involved, A and B. Each group consisted of a feeder conveyor, and a final assembly conveyor. Both groups were part of a common payment system, i.e., their pay was determined by the collective efforts of both A and B. In order to maintain maximum efficiency between the two groups, units had to be exchanged between them. Perhaps a schematic diagram would help. As can be seen from this diagram, if the feeder conveyor of group A produced more units than the final assembly of group A could process, while the feeder unit of group B produced less units than the assembly conveyor of group B could process, then it made sense (i.e., was more efficient) that some of feeder A's units be given to B's final assembly. Also if B's feeder conveyor was more efficient than A's, then the reverse was true, i.e., some of feeder B's units should be given to A's final assembly. Also this made sense from the point of view of the workers, since the more the total output in terms of final assemblies for both groups was, the greater the total earnings of the workers of the combined groups, constituting one payment system, would be.

SCHEMATIC DIAGRAM

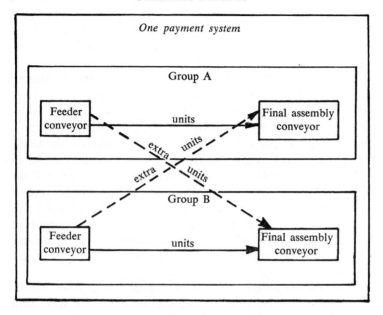

Dick's story to the counselor

1. When he was assigned to group A, Dick had said that he had been told by his boss about the restrictive practices that had developed there under the previous supervisor and to do everything in his power to bring about the kind of cooperation essential to the best progress of the job.

2. When he got on the job he found that the feeder conveyor of Group A was more efficient than final assembly and was producing from 100 to 200 more units than the final assembly girls could process and that just the reverse was true in group B so that extra units were tending to flow in one direction, i.e., from feeder A to final assembly B and that the girls in A—in spite of all his explanations to the contrary—felt that the girls in group B were robbing them of their efforts and often concealed pans of units which should have gone to the final assembly in B.

3. But more than this, he found a rather reserved and some-what negative attitude on the part of the older women in group A toward him, which puzzled him because the previous supervisor, his predecessor, had been a very rough spoken and abrupt sort of person while his own approach, comparatively speaking, was tact-ful.

4. One of his chief problems was Mary, the lead-off operator on the final assembly conveyor in group A. Three instances had oc-curred which disturbed him. One day a quarter of an hour before quitting time, he noticed that the first twenty fixtures on the final conveyor were empty and that Mary was not processing any work. When he asked her why, she said that she wasn't feeling well. When he told her he would be glad to give her a pass to the hospital, she said, "I'm not feeling badly enough for that." So he said, "Well, if you are well enough to remain at the conveyor, I must insist that you continue your work because you are holding up the work of the entire group." To which her reply was, "Well, you are not go-ing to bluff me and neither is your department chief." This remark puzzled and disturbed him.

5. But more than this, after he had moved her to an intermedi-ate station on the feeder conveyor, she still continued to control output. Several times she went to get a drink of water without see-ing to it that she was replaced by a relief operator. So each time he had to remind her that relief should be obtained before leaving the conveyor. The last time he so instructed her, Mary ceased to have any further conversation with him. She stopped talking with him and any instructions given her requiring a reply were an-swered in monosyllables. A similar attitude, although not as pro-nounced, pervaded all the women in group A. But still more than this, the output level of group A had gradually dropped to a point below that of group B.

6. It was at this point that he decided to ask the counselor for help. Would she talk to Mary?

The counselor's interpretation of Dick's talk

The counselor was well aware of some of the things Dick was talking about. She knew that a rivalry between the two groups ex-isted and that some restrictive practices were occurring which in part had been generated by the past relations between two of the supervisors: (1) Supervisor C—the predecessor to Dick, as supervisor of group A, and (2) Supervisor B—the supervisor in charge of group B who at one time had been outgoing Supervisor C's boss but who had been demoted and placed in charge of group B, and which had resulted in an animosity and competition between them.

But she was puzzled about Dick's treatment of Mary. Was it because he did not know that Mary had enjoyed a position of informal leadership under former Supervisor C and therefore he had just unknowingly walked into a human problem or was it because Dick did know this and was trying to undermine Mary's influential position in the group—a practice frequently resorted to by supervisors in trying to break up restrictive practices and establish higher levels of output.

Not only had he moved Mary from her influential and high status position as lead-off operator in final assembly and assigned her on a less influential and intermediate station on the lower status feeder conveyor; but also the counselor had noted that when Dick came on the job, he had ignored Mary and cultivated Ethyl, another girl in group A whose job was soldering, who had less service than Mary, who was considered to be less efficient than Mary, and yet whose hourly rate, because of her previous work history, was the highest in the group. But in addition Ethyl was generally noncommunicative and did not enter spontaneously into the group's activities. (In short, unlike Mary, Ethyl was not an enthusiastically accepted member of the group.)

In Dick's talk to the counselor, he had not brought up clearly his attitude on this question of just what he was up to, and the counselor had not raised it in the talk. Although our data do not allow us to answer the question of why she did not do this, let us assume that she felt that the appropriate time had not come, as yet, to do this.

However, her (the counselor's) first size-up of the situation was that Mary's informal leadership position in group A was too well established to be broken up by either Dick's ignorance or his tactics (she did not know which) and that they had only succeeded in solidifying the whole group against him.

The counselor's strategy of intervention

So let us look at how the counselor intervened in this very complex situation and see some of the alternatives open to her. (1) She could have had another talk with Dick and tried to clarify what, if anything, he was up to. (2) She could look up former Supervisor C and talk to him about how he had wittingly or unwittingly encouraged the restrictive practices. (3) She could talk to Supervisor B in order to see if he understood how his demotion had affected his behavior and the resulting outcome. (4) She could talk to Mary and see how the undermining of her position had affected her. (5) She could talk to Ethyl to see if she understood what the new interest of Dick in her meant. (6) She could talk to nine other operators in group A who were also involved in the problem in some fashion or to some degree or other.

Had the counselor been doing research, she would have done all these things. But she was a counselor (a practitioner) and not a researcher (exploring or testing a hypothesis). Here is where intuitive familiarity, judgment, skill, art—call it what you will—come in.

The counselor decided to spend the next few months circulating around group A and making herself easily available to anyone who wished to talk to her. She cast a wide net and finally each one of the important characters to the drama (except Supervisors B and C whom she decided to ignore, because, let us assume, she felt they were no longer strategic variables in the present here and now situation) walked into her net one by one—Mary, Ethyl, the nine other girls, and finally Dick. In each encounter she adopted the posture we described in the early part of this chapter. She expressed a great interest in understanding their side of the story; for example, why they felt that their efforts were being robbed by group B, and why they felt it necessary to hide their pans of parts. (She did not explain why as one payment system this was a difficult position logically to maintain.) Her attitude was, "How non-logically thrilling, tell me more about it!"

But, of course, she was interested in Mary, the lead-off operator, whose influential position in the group Dick had unwittingly or knowingly undermined. So when Mary came into the net she had a long interview with her.

The counselor's first interview with Mary (in the interviewing room)

In the interview with Mary, which lasted all afternoon, Mary talked mostly about Dick, how he differed from his predecessor, Supervisor C; how he had let group A down by cooperating with group B, and particularly about what she felt were his attempts to belittle her. The last time she had left her position momentarily unattended on the conveyor it had been merely to show her friend across the aisle an article that had been written up about her in the plant newspaper. (Mary was prominent in employee club activities.) When Dick reprimanded her for this and when she had protested, he had said, "I tell you what to do, I am a supervisor and you are an operator." For Mary this was the last straw in what she construed as his attempts to subordinate her and put her in her place. She, a good worker, well accepted by her group, and a prominent employee in Hawthorne Club activities, was not taking this kind of behavior from any young upstart supervisor. So she decided to have nothing more to do with him and stopped talking to him and went to her department chief to ask for a transfer.

After pouring out her injured feelings at great length, she recalled that she had once helped to straighten out a supervisor in another department in which she had worked by frankly pointing out to him some of his shortcomings. In that case, however, she had not been directly involved, so she was able to act as peacemaker. But as she was directly involved in this case, she asked the counselor to perform this function.

"You could help us out," she said to the counselor. "You might talk to him like I talked to the supervisor in the other department. I know you wouldn't tell him right out and out to be human, but you might get him to thinking about a few things that he might do. I think I myself have given him a lot to think about. If he does start to change, we'll meet him half way. This is a 50–50 proposition. If the department chief has forgotten about my asking for a transfer, I won't bring it up again. I really like the girls and I've worked here for so long that I would just as soon stay where I am. I always have turned out as much work for Dick as I would for anybody, even when I haven't been speaking to him. After my talk with the department chief I felt much better. You have made me feel still better. I am so glad that we could come out here and talk."

(Whether or not the counselor clarified to Mary that, as counselor, she could not perform this function, we do not know, as we have no data. But let's assume she did, as it was a problem a counselor frequently met—i.e., requests for help the role could not give —and we will discuss it in the next chapter.)

The counselor's second interview with Mary (*on the floor*)

But in this case it made little difference as the very next day, when the counselor met Mary on the floor and asked how she was:

"Swell," Mary said. "I had a talk with Dick. It came about when he was away talking to the department chief and another operator needed some help. She asked me to come over and help her so I did. I no sooner started than Dick came over. I did not want to get in bad with him any more so I told him what I had done.

"He said that was the right thing to do and he was glad that I had used my initiative. Somehow when he said that I asked him why he was always so serious and why didn't he try to understand us. I told him he should smile a little and not walk around with such a serious look on his puss. When I said that to him, I looked out of the corner of my eye to see how he was taking it. He was taking it, so I went on. I said he had the best posture of any of us but he walked like a king and we were his subjects. I said everything to him nice and pleasant like. I could see that he was really interested. I wasn't the least bit sarcastic.

"I told him that when he talked with me, I would appreciate it if he didn't stress the fact so much that he is a supervisor and I am just an operator. I mentioned to him how he could have talked to me that day when he came up to me and told me that I was taking too much liberty and that as he was the supervisor, I should remember that, and I said if he had only said, 'If the department chief had seen you walking around the conveyor it would have been hard for both of us and it might be better if you didn't do it.' He said he could see how I had something there and he didn't seem to realize how many times he had said he was a supervisor and I was an operator, but he said he was very glad that I had pointed this out to him.

"Then I talked to him about understanding us and entering into our fun and how if he did we would all be happier at our work.

"After lunch he was back again and I said, 'My goodness, are you back for more?' You know, I just feel sorry for him. He's been having such a hard time. He told me that he would appreciate any help I could give him and I told him I would help all that I could. I also told him that the girls would cooperate too. I told him about the other supervisor—the one I mentioned to you—and he was quite interested. I also told him not to get discouraged, that the girls might not accept any change in him right away, that it might take two months, but just to keep right on and everything would be all right. He came around late in the afternoon and told me again that he would appreciate anything I could do to help him. I told him I was going to cooperate 100% with him. I really feel sorry for him. He's trying so hard."

Dick talks again to the counselor about what he heard Mary tell him

Dick said that after Mary had had the interview with the counselor, Mary seemed in a much better frame of mind. He had had an opportunity to talk with her about some part of the job and it was obvious that her attitude had changed quite radically. "You know what she said to me":

"You know, you're not such a bad guy, as a matter of fact, you shouldn't have any trouble getting along with our gang. The only thing is that we feel you use too many big words. The bunch also feels that you're stuck up because you never join in any of our risque conversations."

I was surprised to hear all this and particularly that I had given the impression of being highly educated. So I told her:

"You know, as people go around here, I don't have much of an education and I never gave any thought to the use of big words. However, I do know that it is considered bad taste to use a big word when a simple one will do, and I'm glad that you have called this to my attention. In so far as risque conversations are concerned, I enjoy a good joke regardless of whether it is smutty or not. However, I have always felt that it was not my privilege to enter into such discussions when there might be employees present in the groups who might resent such action and not feel at liberty to express their objections."

The counselor's subsequent observations of the relationship between Dick and Mary

After this conversation, the counselor noted that a more friendly relationship developed between Dick and Mary. Dick assigned Mary as utility and relief operator on the feeder conveyor where her gifts for natural leadership could be exercised. But the counselor also noticed that whereas these capacities had heretofore been exercised in the direction of controlling (i.e., restricting) output, they were now being exercised in the opposite direction. Not only did she proceed on her own initiative to make the daily minor adjustments on the conveyor that were necessary without instruction, but also she began to haze those employees who lagged in output.

The counselor continued to have talks with Dick whom she met every day and frequently several times a day on the floor. The conversations took on more the character of an interview in which Dick began to express more and more his desires to improve his methods of supervision. At one time the counselor gave Dick some books to read on the subject.

Part of Dick's statement to a counseling supervisor much later

Several years later Dick was assigned to the counseling organization as a step in his development as a supervisor. As part of his training he wrote up his experiences in this situation which he felt had been a great learning experience for him. It might be interesting to quote the latter part of his written statement.

With Mary's restraining influence replaced by a constructive influence the output of the feeder conveyor began to rise to new heights. A comparable rise also occurred on the final conveyor to which her influence apparently still extended. Meanwhile, a cordial relationship had been established with group B and there was a constant exchange of parts and units where such action was helpful, and in return considerable help was received from the supervisor of group B by way of advice in connection with manufacturing difficulties based on his many years of experience and job knowledge of the equipment involved. The over-all result was a sharp and sustained rise in output for the entire section which was reflected in improved quality and the cleaning up of several thousand dollars' worth of defective apparatus that had accumulated previously. The improved situation also was reflected in a pronounced reduction in supervisory load so that shortly thereafter it was found possible by management to transfer one supervisor from that assignment and combine the units under one supervisor.

It should be kept in mind that during the period that this incident took place, many forces of management were at work and all these forces contributed their full share to the efficient management of the project. However, it was evident that accelerated group integration was accompanied by an accelerated rate of rise in the efficiency of the unit. The highly cooperative force involved which now processed a relatively large volume of work in an atmosphere that was pleasant and obviously giving them considerable satisfaction, would hardly have been recognized as the same group of individuals who shortly before protested and gagged at comparatively light loads.

As a further illustration of the changed attitude on the part of the key employee involved, some weeks after the improved relationship had been established, a hand operation involving bending a piece part to change an angle was introduced on the job. I laid out this job on a motion economy basis and estimated the hourly output, using time standards. As I realized that an expected hourly output, such as this, should compare rather closely with an actual piece rate and knew that it might take many months to attain the expected hourly output, I proceeded to show the employee what I had done in connection with this job. I instructed her on how to proceed, told her what the expected hourly output was, but also indicated to her that I had no way of telling how quickly she could attain that output and realized that it might take some lengthly period but asked her to proceed at a normal pace and to be the judge of what was a fair day's work. Within two weeks a piece rate was set on this job. The expected hourly output set by the piece rates people was approximately the same as that set up on the estimated basis, and within the same two-week period the employee had attained the expected output level. This person was the same individual who not long before had not only been restricting her own output but influencing an entire group in the same direction. Based on this and other parallel experience, it is the opinion of the writer that counseling of both supervisors and individuals can greatly accelerate the integration of working groups and the boosting of morale and thus rapidly accelerate the attainment of peak efficiency in manufacturing operations.

Authors' comments

We have taken up the case of Mary, the lead-off operator (which could have just as easily been called the case of Dick, the young supervisor) at great length in order to try to illustrate what we meant by what a big difference a little difference can make. Even then we covered only a small portion of the many interventions the counselor made. Her interventions covered a period of about two months. We did not provide, for sake of brevity, the interviews the counselor had with the nine girls who were also partially involved in this interacting web of human relations. But in each case the counselor's intervention was of the same character. She was intensely interested in the human drama presented before her and in the feelings the girls had. She never reproved them for these feelings and for restricting output. From their perceptions she understood why they did so. From her point of view their responses were human (i.e., functional), even if from the point of view of the incentive system and their weekly earnings they were not logical (i.e., dysfunctional).

It should be noted that although counseling, as originally conceived, was confined primarily to employees at the worker level, in this situation it extended to the supervisory level. Dick became an important factor in the developing situation. As this happened, the counselor adopted toward Dick the same attitude that she had displayed toward Mary. She never said to Dick, "How dumb (humanly speaking) can you get? Don't you see what your behavior is doing to Mary?" She was just as interested in how logical (i.e., functional) Dick's behavior was in relation to his needs as it was nonlogical (i.e., dysfunctional) in relation to Mary's needs, and she allowed Dick to achieve this insight for himself.

One can see that Dick became intrigued with the counselor's attitude. He had never met it before. As a result he focused his attention less on Mary and more on himself—his own interpersonal supervisory style—and he got more curious and proactive about it—i.e., maybe I can improve this?

One can begin to speculate, "Does this happen in all cases?" The answer is no. If Dick had not been Dick and Mary had not been Mary (from the point of view of their needs at a particular moment in their respective life cycles) all this might not have resulted. If both Dick's and Mary's needs to make trouble were paramount, the counselor would have had a much tougher time. But on this occasion these particular needs were not the critical variables.

But of what import are these speculations? Just matters to argue about? Or are they matters for further research to be done by people interested in matters of personnel? We shall speak about this more in Part V, our conclusions. All we are saying now is that in the opinion of the different particular parties involved in this particular situation, these particular results obtained. Is this evidence the *whole story,* of *no value* or of *some value?* Our position is the latter. It is telling us *something.*

The Case of Henty, the Demoted Group Chief

The following are three on-the-job interviews with a supervisor about to be demoted. Probably nothing is more heart-tugging than to see a man's status in the Company and the community and his investments in the job gradually disappear. Let us see how the counselor intervenes in this situation. We will comment after each interview.

First Interview—12/27/48
SUPERVISOR: What do you say there, Bill? Can I see you a minute?
COUNSELOR: Sure, Henty. What can I do you for?
SUPERVISOR: You going this way? Let's walk down a ways.
COUNSELOR: Okay.
(Supervisor and counselor walked approximately fifty yards from his desk in the office to a place around the corner where they could not be seen by anyone in the office.)
SUPERVISOR: I hear from the underground that I'm going to be busted.
COUNSELOR: Is that right?
SUPERVISOR: Now don't let on that I told you because I'll get into a lot of trouble. I'm not supposed to know about it either, I just heard about it from the underground.
COUNSELOR: Do you feel that I would say anything, Henty?
SUPERVISOR: No, but I just don't want it to get out because as I say, I'm not even supposed to know about it and I'd just get this other guy and myself in trouble if they did find out that I did know about it. But that's what he told me. What do you think of that?

COUNSELOR: It's taken you somewhat by surprise and you don't quite know what to do about it?

SUPERVISOR: Well, there's nothing I can do about it because I'm not even supposed to know about it. I can't go up to my boss and say, "Look here, what the hell's the idea?" because I'm not even supposed to know about it.

COUNSELOR: Your hands seem to be tied.

SUPERVISOR: Yes, they're tied because I can't say anything to my supervisor nor can I go around looking for another job because if they would ask me, "Well, what's the matter with your present job," I wouldn't be able to say I'm going to be out of it pretty soon. What do you think of that, isn't that a dirty rotten trick?

COUNSELOR: You don't feel as though you're being treated fairly.

SUPERVISOR: Well, Jesus Christ, would you after 29 years' service, then they start kicking you around like this? Can you imagine, they've got a bench job picked out for me on a test set. Why, I'll quit before I'll take a job like that. Imagine after all these years working on a supervisory job I'm supposed to get on a job where I've got a bogey to make and on top of that to take a cut like I have to. I just won't be able to take it, that's all.

COUNSELOR: You don't see where you'd be able to go along with something like that.

SUPERVISOR: My god, no. That just goes to show you what kind of guys I'm working for. I told you that right along, they're no good blankety blanks. They've been kicking me around ever since I came into this department. I've never been satisfied from the first day I've been in here and they transferred me out to ————, and they transferred me back here and I get stuck with the s.o.b. again.

COUNSELOR: It's never been a very pleasant experience for you.

SUPERVISOR: Pleasant? Huh, I never had a pleasant day in this place. I'm sorry I ever walked into this place 29 years ago. If my son ever comes here to apply for a job I'll break his back.

COUNSELOR: You can't see anything good about this place.

SUPERVISOR: No, I don't. I can't see what in the hell you're hanging around here for either. Why don't you wise up and get the hell out of here before you get too many years under your belt? I told you that a long time ago. You've got too much to offer to be hanging around here. You'll never get any place until you find the right guy's ———— to kiss. That's all you'll be in for if you stick around here, a bunch of politics—you've got to know the right guy. The same old story. If your bosses take a liking to you and they're white enough to see that you get something for it, well, they'll do something for you. If they don't care for you, why they'll see that you don't get any place. I only wish I was in your boots, I'd show you how fast I'd get out of here. It's just too bad you couldn't have your age and my experience in this place because then you'd know.

COUNSELOR: You're not too satisfied with the way you've seen things done around here.

SUPERVISOR: You bet your sweet life I'm not. People talk about crooked politics, I've never seen more crooked politics than they have in this place. Boy, I just wish I could get out of here, that's all.

COUNSELOR: You'd like to get out of here and go some place else.

SUPERVISOR: I sure would. Just let them give me my pension, just let them tell me that I can have a pension and I'm going tomorrow. As it is I can't even get a class C pension out of them. I have about another two years to go. Oh, well, what the hell, I guess we'll just have to wait and see what happens, that's all. In the meantime I'm sure going to lose a lot of sleep over it.

COUNSELOR: The whole thing has got you pretty well disturbed.

SUPERVISOR: That's putting it mildly. Now don't let on that I said anything to you. I didn't say it to you . . . that is, my reason for telling you is not because you're a counselor but because I consider you a friend of mine and I just thought I'd say something to you about it.

COUNSELOR: I'm glad you did, Henty. I'd certainly like to get together again with you soon if you'd care to.

SUPERVISOR: Well, I'll see you again. I'd better get out there before that goddam s.o.b. comes along and starts hollering his head off again.

COUNSELOR: Okay, Henty, take it easy then. I'll see you.

SUPERVISOR: I'll try.

In this case Henty feels that he must talk to someone so he seeks out the counselor. The counselor provides him with the opportunity to express his concern and is careful not to approve or disapprove of any of the assertions Hentry is making. He treats them as an opening phase in an interview and ends it with an expression of interest in continuing it if Henty wishes to do so. Three days later the counselor in walking through his territory was hailed a second time.

Second Interview—12/30/48

SUPERVISOR: What do you say, my friend? How is the world treating you?

COUNSELOR: Oh, not bad. How about yourself?

SUPERVISOR: Well, you know. You going this way? I'll walk with you.

COUNSELOR: Okay.

SUPERVISOR: Well, I haven't been able to find out anything more about what I told you the other day. I did hear though that there are supposed to be four or five other guys busted. I felt right along for a good many years now that this place was going to the dogs. It doesn't matter what kind of a job you hold around here, it just seems like you don't know from one day to the next if you're going to have the job.

COUNSELOR: You've not been able to feel too much security in your job.

SUPERVISOR: No, that's what I say and I don't think anybody can actually be sure of his job. Look what they did to Bob—33 years and they busted him and he was one of the first interviewers up in your outfit, he was a moderator for a good number of years, conducting meetings, even taught the stuff over at Morton. And from all indications he was doing a good job but they broke him anyhow. What's a guy supposed to do?

COUNSELOR: It seems to you like whether you're doing a good job or bad job you're still subject to being broken.

SUPERVISOR: That's sure the way it seems to me. I've always done a good job, I've had a number of commendations on the job I was doing. Even during the war when I went out to ———, why I got all sorts of recommendations that they sent back to ——— about the job I did for them. Of course, this crazy goon I'm working for now has got no appreciation for anything but what he thinks is right and wrong. He's chewed my ears a number of times but that doesn't mean anything, he does that to everyone. He just doesn't have an ounce of sense in him; he's a maniac, that's what he is.

COUNSELOR: You've never been able to get along too well with him.

SUPERVISOR: Hell, nobody can get along with him, all he knows how to do is holler and spit tobacco juice at everyone he talks to. He comes down here without a shave and goes around goosing all the women. Let one of us try that, why we'd be fired right away. I'd like to know who's in back of him.

COUNSELOR: You don't feel that he has the proper qualifications for his job.

SUPERVISOR: Well, you know the guy, what do you think? You see how he acts and talks. Don't try kidding yourself out of it, it's just like I told you, sure somebody's behind him—somebody's behind two-thirds of the supervisors around here. They're certainly not qualified to do the job that they're doing, so they just back them up and get them in there, that's all. I've been telling you that right along—unless you can get somebody to sponsor you around here you won't go any place. I know he's the guy that's trying to make it tough for me, his boss, too—neither of them like me. I just don't do things their way, that's all, and I don't have them up to the house for dinner and buy them drinks and anything.

COUNSELOR: You feel if you would do those things you would win their favor.

SUPERVISOR: Well, I don't know, maybe yes, maybe no. They're the kind of guys that you don't know how the hell you should deal with them. The whole trouble with them is they never let you know how you stand with them.

COUNSELOR: It's important to you to know how you stand.

SUPERVISOR: I think that's important to everyone, not only me. For instance, in this other matter, if they'd be man enough to come out and say, well, we don't have enough work around here to keep you on so we feel it necessary to put you on some other job, then I'd feel a lot better about it, then I'd be able to do something about it. Or if they get me off the supervisory role then I can go to the union. I've got a lot to fight for in my case. *I don't see any reason why I couldn't get my old job back.* With 29 years service with the company I've got more service up there than anyone else as far as service with the company, and service on the job, that is on that particular job. Hell, I did that kind of work for 20 years before I was made a supervisor. I think I'd have a pretty good case there, don't you?

COUNSELOR: You feel that you have enough reasons to warrant them giving you back your old job.

SUPERVISOR: Well, if this goddam place would ever wise up they'd see that I'd be more valuable up there than on some dirty old testing machine down here. It seems they don't like to take advantage of your best qualifications. Ninety-nine per cent of the guys here are only interested in their personal welfare anyhow, they don't care how this is going to affect me. Why, do you realize that's going to mean an $18 to $20 cut a week for me.

COUNSELOR: That's a sizable cut.

SUPERVISOR: You're damn right that's a sizable cut. I just won't be able to take it, that's all. I guess I shouldn't say I wouldn't be able to take it because if I have to I have to, that's all. We'll just have to learn to live on less because we'll be forced to. Boy, I sure wish I knew more about all this, then I could tell what I ought to try doing about it. This way I can't do anything.

COUNSELOR: Your hands are pretty well tied.

SUPERVISOR: Well, I don't care, let them do whatever they want to do, I don't have too many years left before I get out of this goddam hole. They've been kicking me around for so long now I should be used to it but I guess I'm not. They just never give me anything to shoot for.

COUNSELOR: You feel you've been limited.

SUPERVISOR: Yes, because I don't play the game their way, I just don't care to play that kind of politics, that's all. They can throw me out tomorrow and I won't start playing politics with those guys. Oh, what the hell's the use? What's the sense of trying? You can't do anything that's any good around here. They're going to do what they want to do anyhow, I haven't got anything to say about it, so why should I let it worry me.

COUNSELOR: There doesn't seem to be anything you can do about it but yet it does worry you.

SUPERVISOR: Yeah, I guess you're right, it does. I guess I have to admit it. I don't know why I should let it worry me though. I guess maybe it's just the principle of the whole thing. I know I'm not the only one that's involved but it still doesn't make me feel any better. It still is going to affect me the way it is, that's all. I guess maybe I'm just like a lot of other people around here; I don't care how it affects them, I only care how it affects me.

COUNSELOR: You're looking out for your own welfare.

SUPERVISOR: You have to. For Christ sake, if you don't, nobody else will. I've got a wife and kid to think about, too, so it's really not only my own welfare but it's the welfare of my family that I'm thinking of. Well, I didn't mean to keep you from your work so I guess I'd better let you go. I'll be seeing you then. That is, I think I will if they don't fire me in the meantime.

COUNSELOR: Okay, Henty, I'll be seeing you.

SUPERVISOR: Now remember what I told you, if I were you I'd be thinking seriously about getting out of this place.

COUNSELOR: Okay, Henty.

In this second interview we can see somewhat clearer than in the first one how completely dependent Henty feels upon the organization and how he tends to attribute all his difficulties to his supervision. He expresses a feeling of being alone and that no one is concerned about him; everyone is concerned only with himself.

We can also note a slight shift in his thinking. He seems to have accepted as fact that he will be demoted and is now thinking about where he will be placed. He has considered the various placement possibilities and indicates a preference for the job he had held for many years before he became a supervisor. The third interview takes place about a week later under the same circumstances as the first two.

Third Interview—1/5/49

SUPERVISOR: What are you saying, Bill, do you have a couple of minutes?

COUNSELOR: Sure, Henty. Why don't we go upstairs where we can sit down and be comfortable?

SUPERVISOR: Naw, I'd like to but I'd better stay down here, or that old s.o.b. boss of mine will be looking for me and raise hell because he didn't find me.

COUNSELOR: Is there any way we can notify him that we're going up there?

SUPERVISOR: Oh, hell, no, he'd have a fit if he heard that. Well, I still don't know what they're planning to do with me. That is, I don't know for sure, but I know what I want.

COUNSELOR: At least you know what you'd like to see happen.

SUPERVISOR: Yeah, I thought about it a lot and of course what I'd like to see happen and what's going to happen might be two different things but all I want out of them is to get my old job back, that's all. I'll be satisfied.

COUNSELOR: You'll be satisfied if they only let you go back to your old job.

SUPERVISOR: Yeah, that's right. I don't care if I have to take a cut, all I want to do is go back up there to the ——— department. I know the job, I spent 20 years doing it, I'm familiar with the surroundings, there I'd be pretty much my own boss, I wouldn't have to be under this constant pressure all the time from that s.o.b. that I'm working for. I know I can handle the job because I did handle it for a long time. I don't see any reason why they shouldn't let me have it. As I told you before, I have more service with the company and more service in that department than any guy that's up there now, certainly they ought to have at least that much consideration. And as far as the money is concerned, well, I suppose I could get back at least my old grade which was grade 39. Sure, I'd be making about a buck eighty-five an hour where now I'm making over two dollars an hour; it might be tough at first but we'll just have to learn to live on it, that's all. I won't be able to do as much for my kid as

I wanted to but we'll just have to make the best of it, that's all. He wanted to go back to school and I know it would cost me some dough but he'll just have to make his own dough and send himself through school. And as for the old lady and myself, well, we got the building paid for and we don't need too much to live on. And although we haven't been carrying on an expensive social life, we could even cut down on that, too. And who knows but what things might pick up shortly again anyhow.

COUNSELOR: How do you mean, Henty?

SUPERVISOR: Well, I mean maybe I'd get the next higher grade or maybe put in some overtime and make some extra dough that way.

COUNSELOR: Oh, I see, I thought maybe you meant they'd make you a supervisor again.

SUPERVISOR: Oh, Christ, no. I wouldn't take it if they gave it to me on a silver platter. I just want to finish out the rest of my time here, after that I want to get out of here the first day I possibly can. You know, Bill, wih me it's a little different than it is with you. I spent too goddam long here already in this company without getting any place. If I haven't gotten any place in 29 years, I sure as hell aren't going to get any place in the next five or ten, so I might as well just pull up stakes and get out of here. My best days are over, your best days are still to come. But I'm warning you, you either better start brown nosing around or else you'd better get out of here.

COUNSELOR: Henty, that's the only way you see it possible for a guy to get ahead around here, isn't it?

SUPERVISOR: Well, Bill, you should know that better than I do. You get around here a helluva lot more than I do, you can see how things are being run. Haven't you seen that yourself? You know yourself in a place like this where there's 33,000 people, why, unless you've got somebody to stand by and recognize your efforts, why, nobody will see them and you'll just stand still. *We're all just like a bunch of lost sheep around here, unless somebody picks you up and brings you in the barn where it's a little warmer, pays a little attention to you and pushes you along, why, you'll never get any place, you'll be out in the cold all the time.* That's why I say, if they only let me go back up into the ———, why, I'll be satisfied. That's a very interesting job, there's nothing monotonous about it. You get a motor in there and you have to find out what's wrong with it and then you figure out how to repair it and there's nobody standing there and raising the roof off the place and hollering and spitting all over telling you that you've got to get this and goddam it, why, don't you do that, and s.o.b. this and what not. You can go along as fast as you want or as slow as you want and get it done as ever the best you can. At least that's the way it was when I was there before, it might have changed some since then. One thing I do know, it certainly couldn't possibly be any worse up there than it is here. I've never been more dissatisfied or unhappy since they sent me down here.

COUNSELOR: This place has only caused you grief and unhappiness.

SUPERVISOR: Certainly nothing more to speak of. Look, when I first came down here they put me out in building ———, put me on a job I knew absolutely nothing about. They gave me no chance at all to learn the job before they put me in there as a supervisor. Well, what did the guys do, they laughed at me because they knew more about the job than I did and I was supposed to be their supervisor. What the hell else could they expect? I never saw the stuff before, how am I supposed to know how it works? I don't blame the guys for laughing at me. Here I am their boss and they know more about the job than I do. I tried to learn the job when I was on 3 to 11. I used to sit down at one of the benches and try to learn how it's done and they used to laugh at me for that, too. What the hell was I supposed to do, I didn't ask to be put in there.

COUNSELOR: You tried to do your best.

SUPERVISOR: Well, I wouldn't say I did my best all the time but there were times when I wasn't quite so disgusted that I went ahead and I tried some of these things, but none of them seemed to work.

COUNSELOR: You didn't get much satisfaction from your efforts.

SUPERVISOR: To be honest with you, no, I didn't, and as a result I just stopped trying, that's all. I didn't get any cooperation from supervision out there either. The other supervisors were on the job much longer than I was and they knew what they were doing but they certainly didn't go out of their way to help me to find out what was to be done. If I asked them something, they would tell me, sure, but they'd never go out of their way to show me that it could be done better this way or maybe I'd better watch for this or whatever the case might have been. You know, when you get on that old monthly roll there's more cutthroat business than anything else around here. Everybody else is looking out for their own hide and how they can hurt you in order to better themselves. It is just too much of a struggle, that's all. Just like a guy in the water trying to keep his head above water when everybody else is trying to push it down. I put up with that crap long enough, now I'd be satisfied if I get out of there and get up to my old place and be happy like I was before.

COUNSELOR: You feel that if you can get away from all these things such as the pressure, the competition, and the responsibility, if you just get back up to where you can do a job at your own speed and a job that you know, why, you'll be much happier.

SUPERVISOR: Yes, I really do. I've thought a lot about it and I think that's the only thing I'd like out of this place before I get out. Don't worry, I've done a lot of thinking about it ever since I was told by my friend about their plans and even before that, because you know from what I've told you before this isn't the first time I've said anything about wanting to get out of here, I've been wanting to get out of here ever since a month after I first came in, that's why I'm a little worried as to whether or not they'll let me get out now because the dirty s.o.b.'s wouldn't let me off before, I think they just want to make it tough for me, that's all. I requested I don't know how many times to have placement or someone look up another spot for me to get me out of here but they wouldn't release me. I think they were just waiting for the day that they could do something like this to me.

COUNSELOR: You feel that they were maliciously trying to do you harm.

SUPERVISOR: Well, I can't say for sure but that's the way it looked to me. They certainly never did anything to show me that they were happy that I was here.

COUNSELOR: In other words, they never really made you feel as though you belonged here.

SUPERVISOR: Yes, that's right, I never really did feel that I belonged here because I never felt that they wanted me here. *They always made me feel like I was an outcast.*

COUNSELOR: It was important to you, as I think it's important to all of us, that we have a feeling that we are wanted and that we have a feeling of personal worth for the job we're trying to do, so that the worth is also recognized by others besides ourselves.

SUPERVISOR: Why, sure we do. We all like to have a pat on the back when we did something good and be talked to decently at least when we fouled up some place. It makes us all feel good, it makes us feel that we want to do more. When you don't get it you just say the hell with it. Then I think it's because they made me feel that way down here is why I maybe don't feel too bad about leaving. I only hope I can. I certainly don't want to get out on one of those testing machines down here, I want to get as far away from this place as possible.

COUNSELOR: And forget it if possible.

SUPERVISOR: That's right. Just skip those two years of my life completely. Here comes the old bastard now, I guess I'd better be getting back. Drop over and see me sometime when you've got a few extra minutes.

COUNSELOR: I sure will, Henty. Take it easy.

SUPERVISOR: Okay. See you.

In this third interview Henty begins to express for the first time his feelings that he may not have been successful as a supervisor. For two years he had felt unhappy because of his lack of job knowledge and nonacceptance by others in the organization, and for the first time in the three interviews he expresses this to the counselor. His need for warmth and support is eloquently expressed in his statement that they are all like lost sheep and need to be taken into the barn where it is a little warmer. Perhaps he feels that he will recapture some of this warmth on his old job where he had worked so long. At least he has prepared himself for this demotion if it occurs and he seems now to feel that he can accept it with some equanimity.

The contribution of the counselor in these interviews was to help Henty express and clarify his concerns. The counselor could do nothing directly to help him maintain his supervisory rank; possibly this might have resulted if the counselor had been able to interview Henty much sooner, but he did provide Henty with an opportunity to express himself and he lent some support during the initial phases of the adjustment to his demotion. One can imagine that this was a difficult interview for the counselor, whose heart must have been wrung by Henty's plight. Very few persons could have stopped themselves from commiserating with Henty; but it is doubtful if this would have helped as much as what the counselor did.

The Case of Freddie, the Newlywed

As we mentioned before, the processes of maturation and personal growth are going on for an individual both inside and outside of the plant. Sometimes the precipitating factors arise from changes outside.

The case we want to consider now is Freddie, just recently married, who is having difficulty in coping with his wife while still living in his parents' home. As Freddie represents well a certain kind of problem that the counselor frequently encountered, we would like to put his problem in a broader perspective.

The personal crises of decision that occur in the life cycle of an individual as he goes through the various stages from the family of orientation to the family of procreation are innumerable. Should he stay with or leave the family? Should he marry or stay single? If married, should he stay married or get divorced? Should they have children and how many? Moreover, illness and death can always unexpectedly happen to change relationships. The wife becomes a widow; the husband becomes a widower; the children become fatherless or motherless, and so on and on. In these respects management shares the same fundamental human condition as the worker.

Each stage of personal development has its unique problems. What one has learned from each stage of the life cycle, after one has gone through it, becomes difficult to communicate to those who have not, as yet, reached it. From this arises the problem of the generation. One generation has difficulty in passing on to the next what has been learned from experience.

However, it can be noticed that these personal crises reactivate all the major dimensions of personal decision making that we depicted in Figure 10.2 in relation to work. Should I *stay* (married) or *quit* (get divorced)? Should I *accept* (my wife) or *reject* (any reconciliation)? Should I adopt an *active* or *passive* form of resolution (i.e., should I get a divorce reactively or proactively?)? Do I take responsibility for my feelings or don't I? Do I learn or don't I? Do I grow up or don't I?

So there exists a very close relationship between these processes of growth as they occur outside as well as inside of the plant. In reading the case of Freddie, the case we now want to present, let us see how Freddie's stage of maturation in marriage bears a very close resemblance to his stage of maturation at work. They are inextricably intertwined. We shall comment on this more later but first let us have the interview.

EMPLOYEE: Golly, I'm in a heck of a mess. I don't know what's the matter, but things aren't going along too good with my wife and myself. I don't know what to do, we can't seem to get along. Maybe you can give me some advice, maybe tell me what to do. Golly, I don't know.

COUNSELOR: What seems to be the trouble, Freddie?

EMPLOYEE: Well, don't you think a wife should go a little out of her way to try to please her husband? To learn about some of the things that he likes, and go out of her way to learn how to do these things? We've been arguing back and forth at the house for a couple of weeks, and the other day my father broke in and told us that he didn't want any more of this arguing, he was tired of hearing it, that we better learn how to get along together. Well, she took offense to that. I know he shouldn't have broken in, he wasn't right there, but after all, it's his house, and he wants everybody to live harmoniously. He doesn't want to hear this arguing back and forth, we can't seem to agree on anything.

COUNSELOR: Just one argument after another.

EMPLOYEE: One of the things we've been arguing about was a wedding last Saturday, but I didn't want to go. I told my wife I didn't want to go. The whole darn trouble is that her father said that we should go. Well, shucks, I wasn't going to let anyone tell me that I should go. I didn't know the person getting married, and my wife didn't know the person, but just because her father knew him, we should go to the wedding. That doesn't make sense to me. Anyway, they told my wife that we should go, so my wife was arguing with me that we should go. I said no, I didn't want to go. We didn't go, but we've sure been having a lot of argument over it. It seems to me that we have an argument over anything we do now. My gosh, we've only been married three weeks! Two people ought to be able to get along better than that. I don't know what to do. What would you do? What do you think I should do?

COUNSELOR: You don't like to be told what to do?

EMPLOYEE: That's right! I think that the man should wear the pants in the family. My gosh, if I let them tell me what to do all the time, I wouldn't be able to do anything on my own. I think a wife should go out of her way to try to do things that her husband likes. When they get married, their first duty should be toward their husband and not toward their folks or anything like that. A lot of little things come up.

You know, we're married and living at my parent's house now. You'd think that a person would go a little bit out of their way to learn a few things, like going down and learning how to cook certain things that I like, and how to take care of my shirts, and stuff like that. My wife doesn't do anything. She has a job, but all she does, she comes home and we wait for her for supper. She eats and washes the dishes, and that's about all. You'd think that on Sundays she'd go down in the kitchen and watch my mother cook, and learn to cook a few things. My mother told her that she would teach her anything she would want to know. When she came in my dad told her to just make herself right at home. Anything that she wanted to do in the house she sure could because my folks have known her since she was a real little girl. That's the way it should be, but she doesn't do anything. Don't you think that she should learn to cook a few things the way I like them? I was going around with a Polish girl at one time, and I learned how to eat the things that she knew how to cook, but I think that she should learn maybe one day a week or something like that to cook some of the things that I like; but my wife doesn't seem to want to do anything like that. The other day I asked her to bake me a cake, and she said that she didn't want to bake and cook in somebody else's house. She wanted to wait until she got in her own. Well, now, that's foolish because my folks told her to do anything she wanted. That's no excuse. So I don't know, she don't seem to want to take any interest in anything around there.

The trouble is, her folks are always telling her this and that. Her father is always telling her what to do, and I don't know where I come in. For gosh sakes, it's no fun going on that way. There's no sense in it. Life is too short to be unhappy all the time, and what are you going to do if you have children or something like that. I sure as heck don't want to go ahead and have children when I don't know how I stand with my wife. The same with a place of our own. We're supposed to get an apartment in the near future, but I don't know. I don't want to go ahead and spend a lot of money on furniture, and that; and then have everything bust up. I kind of like to know right now what the score is. I don't know, maybe the only way out is to get a divorce now. Her folks are always making cracks to her about me. Like I told you last week I bought her a watch, and it cost me $150. I paid part of it, and I still have $75 to pay, and her father told her one day, "Oh, I saw a watch just like yours in the jewelry store for $55." Then she told me that. Well, she knows darn well I'm still paying on the watch, and what I paid for it. Still she takes stuff like that.

Her folks have always been that way. I don't know they're just dumb, they're just a couple of dumb Dagoes. You can't tell them anything, you can't sit down and talk to them. That's the trouble, if I sat down and talked to them I'd probably get sore and slug the old guy. They're always wanting to argue, they are always different. Instead of sticking up for me, my wife always sticks up for them. Like the other day we stopped in the store to get a couple of bottles of ginger ale to fix a couple of drinks at home, and we ran into my wife's father. I shook hands with him, asked him how he was, "Hi Pop," and all that stuff. We got talking about cars. He said, "Just across the street is my Buick. I wouldn't have any other car, it's the best car on the street today." I told him that I had a 1949 Packard, that the Packard was a better car all the way around. You could take it part by part, it was a more expensive car. I told him to go down here to ———— Garage, and see the number of Buicks being worked on there, and then go across the street to the Packard place and see how many Packards. Buick has always had trouble with their clutches, generators, and all that. So then my wife pipes up and says, "Well, there's more Buicks on the street than there are Packards." You know, taking sides with her father against me. I don't know, she doesn't seem to stick up for me in anything. It's stuff like that that gets me. I don't know what to do, I want to do right. I want to make a go of it, but still I'm not going to give in all the time. My gosh, you give in once, and the first thing you know they take everything.

COUNSELOR: You're afraid she'll take advantage of you if you give in a little bit.

EMPLOYEE: Sure, just like my mother told me. She said that all these arguments are up to us to settle, but she said if you give a woman a foot, she'll take a yard. She said that's what she does to my father. So you see, my own mother told me that. Another trouble is the fact that her father is awfully strict that way. I think that's one reason why she's the way she is. She's seen her mother being told what to do all the time by her father. She's probably afraid that she's going to be the same way if she lets me tell her what to do. Her father puts his foot down, and if he didn't feel like doing something, he told her and that was all. I think that's the big trouble right now. She's afraid that might happen to her, and she doesn't want it, and that's why she's always trying to tell me what she wants to do.

I don't know, the whole thing's a mess. Just like our wedding. I didn't want a big wedding, I just wanted a little supper at some hotel downtown, and a nice quiet wedding; but her father wanted a big wedding. So naturally what could we do, so I said, "Well, okay, go ahead if you want to." But I told him after we were married and settled down I was going to do what I wanted to do. He says, "Sure, that's right. After you're married and living alone, you're the boss.

Do anything you want." The trouble is that it's not that way. They're trying to influence everybody too much. Sure, I know my father did the wrong thing when he butted in the other day, but that's his home and he wants everybody in it to get along. None of this arguing all the time, he can't take it any more.

I don't know what to do. I know one of these days I'll lose my temper and beat her up. Well, if things like this keep up, heck, I'd just as soon have a divorce. I'm young yet, I can marry somebody else because I'm not going to go through life this way. Divorce, though too, you don't know how much it would cost or what it would take—I wonder if I would have to pay alimony, but then again I probably couldn't get the divorce cause I didn't have any grounds. I don't know what grounds you need. There's something I might bring up. We were married the 9th of November, and then the 21st she got a letter from some soldier. She told me about it. This letter says, "Darling, I love you and I want to marry you." Well, that was after we were married. I could tell the judge that my wife was unfaithful. I don't know just what you'd do in a case like that. That's why I don't want to have any children if we can't get along now, there's no sense in having a family, and just have to break it up. If you break it up then, you've got to pay extra money to support the kids. You're losing all the way around.

I want to get along with my wife, but I think she ought to do things that I like. After all that's part of the wife's duties, don't you think, to learn to do the things her husband likes to do. I know she wants to drive my car, and I told her she couldn't. The first thing you know, she'd be using it to take her mother around all over. I can't see that stuff either. Let her stay away from her family. I know every time I go over there I get in an argument with her old man, and I have all I can do to keep from hitting him. Maybe the only solution of it would be to quit my job and leave town, and go a thousand miles away and get a job where there wouldn't be any in-laws. But I don't want to do that either because we both got all our friends here, and I've got seven years' service here I don't want to give up. Suppose I did do something like that and it still didn't work out. Where would I be? I'd be out some place, I wouldn't have a job, wouldn't have a job here, and we'd be worse off than we are now.

COUNSELOR: This way out doesn't seem to be too good.

EMPLOYEE: No, I don't want to leave here, I want to stay. If you leave town you probably couldn't get a place to live, maybe live in a hotel. I've always had a home, and I may be funny that way but I always wanted to have a home of my own. This idea of living in some hotel or boarding house, I don't like that idea. I think that maybe divorce is the only way out. Maybe I could tell her that I was going to quit my job, and we were going to some other town to live. She'd have to follow me, wouldn't she? Doesn't the wife have to go wherever the husband wants her to go?

COUNSELOR: You think that this might be one answer?

EMPLOYEE: Yeah, but what would I do if my wife said she wouldn't go? Then what kind of a spot would I be in?

COUNSELOR: You're looking at that in terms of her refusing.

EMPLOYEE: Sure! Maybe that could be grounds for a divorce. I don't know. What if I hit her or beat her or something? I suppose they could use that as grounds for a divorce, probably get a lot of my money. I was wondering if they could take that money away from me, that I got saved up. You see, I've got a couple of thousand dollars put away I thought we might build a home with, but with all this coming up I don't know. I'm kind of leery that if anything happens she's liable to get a hold of it. You know there's a young widow living down the street. I could go out with her any time I'd like to. That's one thing, I haven't cheated on my wife yet. I could marry this widow, and take over her business. I was wondering if they could get something like that on me. They could say they saw me in the company of another woman and build up a case like that. Maybe get it to court, and take all that money away from me.

COUNSELOR: If it went to court, they might take all your money away from you?

EMPLOYEE: Yeah, then I wouldn't have a dime. You know it's hard enough, a guy's got to have a little extra money to buy nowadays. Just to support a family and all that. Like I say, probably the smart thing to do would be to quit my job and go some place else, but I don't want to quit my job. When it comes right down to it, I think more of my job here than I do of my marriage. I figure that my dad's job here was able to support a family and a wife for 30 years working here at the plant, and I want to stay here and make something of it too. So I say I'd rather give up my marriage than give up my job here.

You know, I can't understand the whole thing. Take when we got married, the honeymoon, and then the first week, we were so happy, everything was just perfect, and now everything's the opposite. It's getting so that we just can't stand one another. I'm getting so that it's affecting my work down here, I can't work very much any more, I've got this on my mind, and I don't know what to do. I don't know just what the answer is to it. If only her folks would quit tell-

ing her what to do, and leave her alone, and let me decide a few
things. It would be all right. Like this cooking, if that was all it was
it wouldn't be bad. Anything she cooks, well, I can eat it. After
eating all that slop in the Army for four years, I sure as heck can
eat just about anything. I can overlook that, that's just a minor thing.
There's all this other stuff, like last week, her brother and sister and
a niece made their confirmation, so we went and I got cards, three
cards for them, and I put $3 in each envelope and gave it to the
kids. The next day, her dad comes up to me and says, "Didn't they
give you $20 when you got married, and you only gave her $3 for
confirmation?" So I told him when she got married, I'd give her
$20 but my gosh, this is just a confirmation, and I can't afford to
be giving that kind of money out. I don't know, I guess maybe he
figures just because he can afford it, I can. He's been married for
30 years. I've been married for three weeks, I don't know what he
wants. That was one of the troubles, remember I told you I was
going with this gal before, and couldn't get along with her folks, then
the last minute we got together and got married. Things sure have
changed. I just don't know what to do, I don't know where to turn,
or what to tell her. If somebody would only tell her what to do, and
what to expect.

(There was quite a long pause. The employee just sat and seemed
to have little left to say. They had talked through the employee's
lunch period, so the counselor suggested it might be a good idea to
terminate the interview and make a date for the next morning.)

COUNSELOR: (Looking at his watch) Say, Freddie, we've gone right
    through your lunch period. When are you going to eat?

EMPLOYEE: Oh, forget about it, I don't feel much like eating. I'm not
    too busy around here, maybe I can grab something later.

COUNSELOR: Let's say we make a date for tomorrow morning, and we
    get together and continue this discussion.

EMPLOYEE: Sure, that's swell. There's not too much work around here
    now, I'll be able to get away. That's a good idea. I'll be looking
    forward to seeing you tomorrow morning then.

    Swell, tomorrow morning then. See you later.

The next day:

EMPLOYEE: I had a long talk with my wife last night.

COUNSELOR: You did?

EMPLOYEE: Yeah, I thought that that was the best thing to do. I told
    her that I had talked it over with my counselor during the day,
    that I told him all about it, how things were going. I told her we sat

down and talked about it, in a very calm way and that I had decided to sit down and talk with her to decide just what the score was on this whole thing. I told her that a divorce wasn't the way out of this, and if I quit work and left town, that wouldn't be the answer either because neither of us want to leave our friends. I told her that we've just got to learn how to get along with each other. I told her some of the things that I expected, I wanted her to do these things for me. I told her that I want to go out of my way to do things to make her happy, too. This wedding the other night, I said I didn't want to go to that because she wouldn't like me around there with a long sour face. I wouldn't have enjoyed myself; and I told her I didn't think she would either. I told her it was just up to the two of us to look after each other; after all, it was our affair.

COUNSELOR: You thought it was something that the two of you had to work out together.

EMPLOYEE: Sure, I told her that we shouldn't pay any attention to what all these in-laws are telling us to do. I told her that she was no dummy, that she was 20, that she had a good education; and that we're both smart enough to be able to work out something like that ourselves. I told her I'm 25, and I've had a lot of experience in handling money, and know all about that stuff as far as handling the money. I told her that probably these other little things like working around the house and cooking was her responsibility. I told her as soon as we could get into a place of our own, then everything would work out a lot better. You know, my dad told me that both of us had to get adjusted to one another, and learn to know what each other was like. He says that sometimes it's hard to get adjusted, but that almost everyone goes through that period. Yeah, he told me that after they got married, there was a certain period where they had a lot of little differences. Then I found that out about my sister and her husband, too, so I guess it's something almost everybody goes through. I thought maybe it was just because of us, but I guess everybody goes through it. We're not any different than any one else. We should want to sit down and get to know each other better. That's what I told my wife. We've got to learn what the other person likes, and know each other better so we can work this thing out.

COUNSELOR: You've found a satisfactory way of working this thing out.

EMPLOYEE: Yes, I think everything will turn out all right. You know, when I sat down talking with her, I was calm and kept my head. I was very reasonable, didn't get angry or lose my temper. I told her that there's no sense of yelling at one another, or me losing my head. I told her that I didn't want anything like that to happen and didn't want to get a divorce, and I didn't think she did either. I told her, though, she's young, she could probably get married again if anything ever did happen. Then you know we're Catholics. Say we went ahead and got a divorce, and she met another nice fellow, and he'd want to marry her. Then his folks would say that she's a nice girl, but she's been divorced, she's a Catholic and they don't recognize divorces. The same would be true from my side of the story too. Like this widow I told you about yesterday, you know at the bakery shop. I could maybe marry her, but our religion doesn't recognize divorces and it's just like being a marked man. Like going around with a number on your back or a sign on your back, "I am divorced!" (Pause) Say, have you heard anything about a 12½ % raise going through?

COUNSELOR: No, I haven't.

EMPLOYEE: Well, my dad told me something about it. He said it just went through the last day or so. So I told my wife last night. I said, "Honey, if that raise goes through I'm going out and buy you a sewing machine. That's what you always wanted." You know, she's always said that she wanted a sewing machine, and we don't have any other debts right now. The only one we have is that watch like I told you yesterday, but outside of that we don't have any at all. I could have paid cash for that watch, but I figure there's no sense in taking the cash out. I can have that cash on hand and pay for the watch on time. Everybody else is doing it, so I might as well do it. So if this raise went through, I'd buy my wife the sewing machine. She said, "Oh, it isn't necessary, we can wait." But I told her no, I wanted to buy it if we had this extra money cause I told her that I wanted her to be happy, and I told her that I was going to try to make her happy. (Pause)

Yeah, you know the way I look at it, I think that the woman should go out of her way a little bit to make her husband happy, but too, the fellow probably owes something himself towards trying to make his wife happy, I know I've been away from home for three and a half years, and I know what it is to be away from your folks. Like her, she's away from home too. I can understand, I told her I know it's hard for her to get used to living with somebody else, so I told her just as soon as we get to living alone everything would be all right. I told her until then what we should do is try our best to get along with each other, and not pay too much attention to what the others want us to do. I guess it's always hard for a daughter and a mother-in-law to get along, you know what I mean with my wife trying to get along with my mother. Don't you think there's always a feeling of jealousy around there? A lot of times things are said that really don't mean anything, but I told my wife that if anybody ever says anything to her, I hope it don't happen, but if it ever did happen to just forget about it and not say anything about it. In that way we'll get along a lot better. I told her that I would have to do the same thing. Like when we go over to her house and I get so burned up at her dad. He always thinks he knows everything, and I get hot. I told her that I'd just take that stuff and wouldn't say a word about it. That way everything is easier all the way around. You don't hurt anybody's feelings.

Well, you know living with somebody else, there's always something coming up. My mother probably feels that she wants to do these things for me. You know my mother's been doing everything for me for 25 years, and then to have somebody else come in the house and take care of my stuff is hard. There's probably a little bit of jealousy between them, and you can't blame them. I guess all mothers are alike. Your wife and your mother probably feel that same way. There's a lot of times when they don't get along, but probably the best thing is not say a word. I suppose her mother feels the same way. She probably wonders sometimes why her daughter married a fellow like me, and I guess it's only natural. Every mother thinks that there's no fellow good enough for their daughter.

I know a little thing happened around our house the other day in the bathroom. My wife goes in the bathroom and stays in there a little longer than usual to clean up the bowls and that. Well, I guess my sister wanted to go in and was waiting around. Instead of telling my wife to hurry up, that she wanted to go in there, she waited around and when my wife came out my sister gave her a funny look. I told my wife to just forget about that, not to pay any attention to it, just to worry about me, and I'd worry about her. That's all the two of us should bother with now. I think after having this talk that everything will turn out all right. I hope so anyway.

COUNSELOR: This makes you feel pretty good about the whole thing.

EMPLOYEE: Boy, I'll say it does. You don't know what it means to be able to settle down and be able to get that stuff off your mind. I'm able to at least do some work around here now. For a couple of days I couldn't do a thing. People would come up and ask about something, and I couldn't get my mind on my work, and didn't know what I was doing. You know I've got a pretty good job around here, I think I can make something out of it. I've got the reputation of being able to get the work done, and people come to me when they want to get things done right. You know, that's why I don't want to give up my job around here because I think I've got a pretty good start and a pretty good bunch of fellows to work with. I know a lot of jobs around here. If somebody comes up and asks about a job that I don't know anything about, I'll go up to my boss or find somebody that does know something about it. I'll always go out of my way.

Well, going back to my wife, I told her the same thing. I told her that if there's anything she wanted to know that she should come to me and ask me about it. I told her that if I couldn't tell her, that I'd find somebody that could tell her. Say, I guess it's pretty close to the time for lunch. Let's start heading back.

(They got up from the bench and started heading back to the department. Just before they got back, they stopped and the employee turned to the counselor and said:)

EMPLOYEE: Say ———, I want to thank you for all you've done for me. You sure helped me an awful lot. If there's anything I can ever do for you, let me know because you've helped me more than my dad has. You've been more of a help to me than my parents. I don't know, there's just something about this whole thing that kept building up and building up. I didn't know what to do, it was beginning to affect my job, and it was beginning to affect my entire system. Like I said to my wife, I've seen enough excitement, I can't stand all this excitement, cause when I do my stomach goes bad on me. Well, gee, the last couple of days all this excitement has been building up inside of me. My whole system has been on the bum. I haven't been able to do much of anything. You've really helped me an awful lot, and I just had to get all this stuff off my chest. So I want you to know that if there's anything I can ever do for you, I just want you to say the word.

COUNSELOR: Well, thanks, Freddie, but you see we were doing only what the company wants me to—to be around here for when a person has things on his mind and wants to find somebody to talk to about it. That's why I'm here.

EMPLOYEE: Yeah, I think that's good. You know there's a lot of fellows have things on their minds and talking it over with you might do something for them. I think that's very good. Well, I'll be seeing you around a lot. Thanks a lot!

What the counselor heard and what difference he made

Depending upon his age and stage of development, the reader may perceive these interviews with Freddie quite differently, from being tragic, to comic, to trivial. So let us see what the counselor heard.

From his point of view he was listening to the feelings of a young man, recently married, generated by the transition from his parental family to his own and the difficulties he was having in coping with them. In the first interview Freddie keeps bemoaning the fact that his wife does not come up to his conception of an ideal wife. To Freddie it was incredible that his young wife should not have the same concerns about him that his parents had. It sounded as if Freddie wanted his young wife to be like a mother to him, or perhaps a mother he wished he had had.

So in the first interview he toys with the ideas of divorce, quitting his job, moving out of town, cheating on his wife and thus having revenge for her maltreatment of him. He does not seem to consider seriously moving out of his parents' home. But he does think of his job. "When it comes right down to it," he says, "I think more of my job than my marriage."

But what does Freddie's job and the Company mean to him? The Company had allowed his parents to earn a living and raise a family. Shouldn't it provide him with the same opportunities (dependency needs)? He wants to live in his parents' home (dependency needs) but also wear the pants in the family (counter-dependency manifestations), and the first interview ends on the dependency note to the counselor—"If only somebody would tell her (his wife) what to do and what to expect."

There is a long pause and the counselor muses, "I wonder who that somebody will be?" But the counselor does not express his musings nor, it should be noted, does he reflect many of the implied feelings he has heard. Many of these implied feelings, if reflected too soon or too baldly, he feels might damage his relation with Freddie. So he reflects only the most obvious expressed feelings without twisting (interpreting) anything Freddie has said.

Nevertheless part of the counselor's message must have gotten through to Freddie, and in the second interview we see Freddie trying to apply it. He *tells* his wife what their relation *should* be. It does not sound as if his wife had much chance to express what she would like her relations to her new husband to be. But undaunted, Freddie keeps trying; he's not surrendering or throwing in the sponge as yet.

Still the counselor, who may have felt some slight sense of futility at this point, keeps up his basic posture. He doesn't say to Freddie, "How stupid can you get." He recognizes Freddie's striving—no matter how futilely expressed—to cope with his situation. He feels that in the main, Freddie wants to make a go of it with his new wife, but his balled up (ambivalent) feelings are making this difficult to accomplish.

So the counselor keeps trying to get these feelings out in the open where they can be looked at and coped with. But mostly Freddie keeps looking in the opposite direction, i.e., not at his ambivalent feelings but at the object of them—his wife and his job, for example. However, a few occasional notes of a different direction do creep in, such as "a fellow probably owes something himself towards trying to make his wife happy."

Obviously no great miracle occurred in these two interviews. Freddie does not come out of them a fully matured and responsible person, capable of coping fully with his dependency-independency needs. But the counselor's motto is "sufficient unto the day is the problem thereof." If Freddie has taken one small step in the direction of maturation and gotten some satisfaction from it, this, the counselor feels, might reinforce Freddie's desire to take another step in that direction again someday. Moreover, the counselor has the statement from Freddie that the interviews had helped him. How much more evidence do many doctors have for their treatments?

What has all this to do with the Western Electric Company? Well, just this. Someday—we do not know quite when—if Freddie does not take more responsibility for his feelings—the Company is going to fail Freddie in the same way that his wife did. At that point the Company no longer will be ideal. Can one imagine what his interview would sound like then? The counselors had hundreds of them.

Summary

In this chapter we have tried to clarify the counseling process and how the counselor tried to perform his catalytic as well as his cathartic roles. We tried to illustrate this process in five examples, the cases of Anna, Joe, Mary, Henty, and Freddie. Although these cases fall far short of the many different kinds of situations the counselors met, we tried to cover a fairly representative sample. In each case we tried to show how the counselors intervened and the difference it possibly made.

In many cases the reader may have heard more catharsis (on the part of employees) than catalysis (on the part of the counselors) going on. He may have heard and felt that the counselors in their catalytic role seemed to be confusing proactivity with conformity to management dictates and the so-called power structure. He may have felt that the counselors interpreted all protestations against the existing values and norms of the Company as trouble making and all personal resolutions as having to accept (in the sense of resigning oneself to) the power structure. The counselors, in short, seemed to be soft on the power dimensions.

It is true that, in every case, we did not dwell on the opposite side of the coin. We did not dwell on the silly talk of Joe's supervisor which Joe felt *had made* him do what he did not want to do. If Joe had wanted to organize an anti-silly-talk-of-supervisors-club, the counselor would not have objected. But it is true that he did not encourage this form of protestation. He felt that supervisory training might be a more problem-solving resolution of this silly talk.

But these idealogical issues of counseling we would like to postpone for our conclusion in Part V. Although important, they are very difficult to talk sense about. Moreover, we have not finished with our analyses of the counseling program which might put some of these issues in a clearer perspective. So let us now turn to the problems the counselors had in implementing their program in the industrial structure.

PART IV

The Ambiguity of the Counselor's Role

CHAPTER XII

The Organizational Problems of Counseling Employees

In Part IV we will be considering the problems of implementing the counseling program in the industrial structure and we will be dealing primarily with another segment of the employee plant population. In Part II we dealt primarily with those employees who expressed concerns at work in any one quarter and of this segment in Part III we dealt primarily with those employees who had been helped by counseling. (See Figure 4.1.) Now in this chapter of Part IV, we will turn our attention primarily to the remaining employees with no serious concerns, as well as to those employees with serious concerns who had not been helped by counseling. Together this constitutes about 90% of the plant population in any one quarter. But with regard to these problems of implementation we will not confine our attention only to the employee level; we will consider them also in relation to supervision in Chapter XIII and in relation to management in Chapter XIV.

How We Propose to Deal with the Problems of Implementing the Counseling Process

As we do not want to present these problems of implementation in a piecemeal but rather in a systematic fashion, we will state first how we propose to go about it. Again, as we did in the last chapter, we will pick up several analyses we have already partially developed for other purposes and point them in the new direction we now want to take.

But first we will have to become clearer about the concept of a role. So far we have used the word rather loosely, hoping that the generally accepted current usage would convey our meaning. But now we want to state more precisely the way in which we shall use it. In Chapter II we say that any person in an organization has a *position* in a system of social relationships, which we called a social structure. Around each of these positions in this structure there is defined and there emerges a set of expectations. This set of expectations is an evaluative standard which says *how that person is supposed or expected to behave in that position*. In that system of social relationships these prescriptions constitute "his role"— that is, to repeat, these prescriptions state the way he is supposed or expected to behave *in that position*. So the role should not be equated with the actual behavior of the role incumbent; it is what his behavior *should be*.

In relation to any set of role prescriptions for any position in any organization there are social controls which reward the role incumbent when he conforms to the role prescriptions and which withhold these rewards from him (i.e., in this sense punish him) when he does not conform to them. In sociological literature these are referred to as sanctions by means of which rewards are given or withheld from the incumbent of the role by the persons or categories of persons who have defined or who feel that they have something to say about what his role should be.

Although there is a certain set of expectations around a certain position in any organization, there is often not complete consensus from different parts of the organization as to what is expected of the person in this position. Although in a well-established traditional society such a consensus can be assumed without getting into trouble, in a more adaptive, innovative, and industrialized society this consensus cannot be assumed without getting into very serious trouble. So now let us turn to what we have said about the counselor's role thus far.

In Chapter II of Part I we stated the counselor's role model, that is, the prescriptions of how he *should behave* in this *new* position of *counselor* as derived from the Hawthorne researches. Because these prescriptions had been derived from research and not from the nature of industrial organization, we called it a role model. We stated these prescriptions in instrumental terms, that is, the way the counselor *should behave* in order to achieve certain kinds of results. In the last chapter we illustrated these kinds of results in the personal encounter of the counselor with the employee, that is, in the two-person or dyadic relationship. In the future we shall refer to this aspect of the counselor's job as his intrinsic task role or the in-counseling role relationship, that is, the way the counselor should structure his relationship with employees under these conditions. It should be noted that the prescriptions for this task role, as specified in Chapter II, said nothing about how the counselor should behave or structure his relationships outside of these conditions, that is, in any other role relationships he might have with employees or other persons in the organization.

In Chapter III of Part I we specified the formal organizational conditions under which the counseling program was supposed to operate, that is, how the counselor was *structured into* the existing system of role relationships of the Company, and how he should behave under these conditions. For example, he was supposed to conduct himself so as not to interfere with the prerogatives of supervision or with the employees getting their work done. But just how he was to do this was not too clearly specified. This was left to the counseling organization to work out. In the future we will refer to this aspect of the counselor's job as his organizational role or the outside role relationship, that is, how the counselor worked out his relationships with all those other persons with whom he was also involved in the performance of his task function.

So now the question arises, "Where did the sanctions for the counselor's role model—his task role—come from?" It would be difficult to say they came from the Western Electric Company management at Hawthorne or its New York headquarters or even from the American Telephone & Telegraph Company and its Bell Laboratories. So for a while we will have to house them in a reference group—a set of persons called social scientists, living in 1936 outside of the Western Electric Company and the Bell System, and personified for them perhaps by a person such as Elton Mayo. Of course, to the extent that the values of this reference group became internalized by the counselors and by those who would be in charge of the counseling program, they would reside there. Their first place of residence we will take for granted; their second place of residence remains still hypothetical until we take a look and see.

But what about the sanctions for the counselor's organizational role? As we have seen, the organizational role was not too clearly specified; it was something to be worked out. As a result, as we shall see later, there was never any consensus in the organization as to what the counselor's role should be. Different groups in the organization—from employees to supervision to management—had different expectations as to what both his task role as well as his organizational role should be. In many cases these two different aspects were not clearly differentiated. Even among the counselors themselves there was no complete agreement as to what their role outside of the two-person relationship should be. Obviously the counselor required the active support and cooperation of others in the performance of his task function. But how was he supposed to obtain it?

It will be around these different expectations of what the counselor's role should be—what we shall call the ambiguity of the counselor's role in the industrial structure—that we will focus our attention in all three chapters of Part IV. Around this focus we will state the problems of implementing the counseling program; that is, we will treat all the problems of implementation as symptomatic of this underlying ambiguity.

However, it should be pointed out that these problems of implementation from the point of view of the counseling organization were matters of daily operating procedures and administration. Had these problems not been coped with somewhat satisfactorily at this level, obviously the program would not have continued for twenty years. We shall look therefore at the way these problems were dealt with at this level by the counseling organization, that is, why they did what they did in order to deal with them. But also we shall look in order to see how, if at all, in a more fundamental sense, these daily operating procedures resolved the problem of the underlying ambiguity.

Why are we setting up such a stiff hurdle? Why are we not willing to settle this question by making just a good case for the way the counseling organization dealt with these problems at the operation level? Because this is too easy. At this level a very good case could be made. But in the process what would have been learned? We believe not very much.

To us the counseling story presented a far greater challenge.

Here was an innovative role, derived from social science, cata-
pulted into an organization based upon certain traditional principles of organization. In the process a whole set of assumptions
about the motivation, productivity, and satisfaction of workers
were brought into question. Only by driving the counselor's role
model to its limits would we be able to see how it fell short, that
is, what factors about organization behavior it was not taking into
account.

In carrying out one set of assumptions to its limits one can be
foolhardy, stubborn, or courageous, depending upon one's point of
view. But in this process can one perhaps also learn something? Being optimists, we think so. So this is the premise on which we shall
proceed. In this connection it may be well to repeat what we said
in the first chapter. "The counseling program will always remain
for us a very real and genuine attempt to address a very real and
genuine problem. No one can take this achievement away. But that
it also provided all the answers to this problem is too much to ask
and no such claims will be made."

So now let us return to our task. We shall look at these loosely
housed organizational sanctions for the counselor's role model as
the counselor walks into the territory where he will meet other
groups, who organizationally speaking are much more securely
housed than he is; that is, for whom much better organizational
sanctions exist, and who may feel they have something to say about
what the counselor's role should be.

Figure 12.1 below shows the four major organizational catego-

FIGURE 12.1

THE COUNSELOR'S FOUR MAJOR RELATIONSHIPS

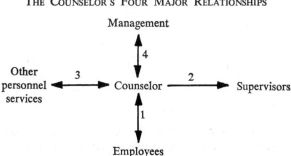

ries of persons with whom the counselor had to interact in order to perform his job. We will take up each of these relationships in turn: (1) in relation to employees, (2) in relation to supervisors, (3) in relation to other personnel services, and (4) in relation to management.

PROBLEMS OF IMPLEMENTING THE COUNSELING PROGRAM WITH EMPLOYEES

The program, as first designed, was directed exclusively to counseling the employee group. It was thought that the formal procedures, as outlined in Chapter III, would allow the counselors to do this without intefering with the functions of the supervisor. So the practical problems of implementing the program in its early stages were concerned almost exclusively with the employee group. Employees were the counselor's chief concern and in an intrinsic job sense remained so during the twenty years of the program's existence. In trying to counsel employees the counselors faced four problems:

(1) living up to and living with the prescriptions of *not* giving information, advice, and direction (see the prescriptive rules in Chapter II, page 42);

(2) in terms of these prescriptions, gaining the acceptance and understanding by employees of the counseling activity;

(3) developing a counseling relationship with all employees; and

(4) dealing with the reluctant employee.

Problems About Giving Information, Advice, and Direction

Probably we can see how these problems arose by looking first at the kinds of questions the counselor was asked by the employees. Figure 12.2 shows four general categories of questions frequently asked of him.

Although the counselor's role prescriptions in a literal sense provided no specific rules as to how the counselor should deal with each of these four categories of questions, they did provide a general orientation. For example:

(a) To Category A questions the role prescriptions said: Although obviously some simple explanation will need to be

Figure 12.2

KINDS OF QUESTIONS ASKED OF COUNSELORS BY EMPLOYEES
(Directly and Implied)

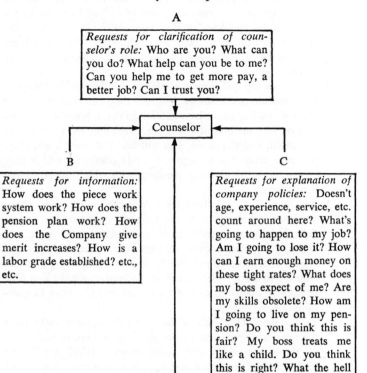

A

Requests for clarification of counselor's role: Who are you? What can you do? What help can you be to me? Can you help me to get more pay, a better job? Can I trust you?

Counselor

B

Requests for information: How does the piece work system work? How does the pension plan work? How does the Company give merit increases? How is a labor grade established? etc., etc.

C

Requests for explanation of company policies: Doesn't age, experience, service, etc. count around here? What's going to happen to my job? Am I going to lose it? How can I earn enough money on these tight rates? What does my boss expect of me? Are my skills obsolete? How am I going to live on my pension? Do you think this is fair? My boss treats me like a child. Do you think this is right? What the hell is going on here?

D

Personal decisions I face at work and outside of work: Should I stay on or quit my job? Should I get another job? a transfer? How do I get a better job? more money? How can I get along with my s.o.b. boss? Should I punch him in the nose? How do I get along with my fellow workers? Should I be a job killer, a rate buster? Should I get a divorce? Should I live with my in-laws? Should I take night courses? Should I be a man or a mouse? Tell me, what should I do?

given, do not get trapped into an over-logical elaboration of the counseling program. Probably the basic questions the employee wants to know are, "Are you a guy I can trust with my personal problems, and if you are, have you the competence to deal with them, i.e., help me?" These questions will not be answered by an over-logical explanation of the counseling program.

(b) To Category B questions the role prescriptions said: Although these questions cannot be ignored, they can become booby traps if you pay exclusive attention to them. Keep your attention on why the question is being asked, why the information is wanted, and if you do, you will find Category B questions will turn often into Category C or D questions, which may be the more troublesome questions with which the employee is concerned.

(c) To Category C questions the role prescriptions said: These questions are going to be the toughest questions for you to field. Here you are going to be seduced the most easily into approval or disapproval, agreement or disagreement, and logical explanations and justification of Company policy. So here try to clarify the underlying feelings expressed and wait until these questions can be translated into Category D questions.

(d) To Category D questions the role prescriptions said: Now the questions are coming from the right end up. In such cases (1) the employee not only wants to gripe (Category C); he also wants to do something; (2) to such questions even the social conventions prescribed that one does not rush in with a lot of free advice, and (3) here the counselor can demonstrate his professional skill and the beneficial results that might follow from a talking-out process where new alternatives for reaching a decision can be considered.

Let us state these role prescriptions at a higher level of generality. What they were saying were:

(1) You (the counselor) cannot ignore questions on the B–C axis. But on the other hand, try to avoid keeping the interview at this level. At this level the questions are coming to you from the wrong end up; they will be the most difficult for you to field; where you will most often drop the ball, i.e., have the most difficulty in practicing your role model.

(2) On the A–D axis the questions are coming to you from the right end up. At this level the practice of your role model will be the most congruent, rewarding, and satisfying and will make the most sense to both yourself and to the employee. Here you can demonstrate the kind of help you can provide and not just talk about it.

Let us admit now that we have packed many clinical insights into these statements. Obviously the two categories of questions: (1) those coming up from the right end and (2) those coming up from the wrong end are not logically operational categories. They are distinctions involving clinical judgment and hence they will make more sense to a person who has practiced counseling than to a person who has not. So if the noncounseling reader will accept them for a while on faith, it will allow us to proceed with the business at hand.

In terms of these categories, about 10% of the interviews started or became translated easily in terms of the A–D axis; about 90% of them did not reach this stage during the interval considered. (See Figure 4.1.) So let us consider first a case where things were coming from the right end up, that is, where the practice of the role model was working with the least amount of friction.

The case of Jim Evans, who wanted to be transferred

Jim Evans, an employee, approached a counselor and asked him what he could do to obtain a transfer for him. He said that he was not satisfied with his present assignment, that it did not offer enough scope for future development, and that there must be other jobs in the company more suited to his capabilities.

He added that he had made a similar request of his immediate supervisor who had referred him to one of the placement specialists. The placement specialist had reviewed his work history and, after going over the available job openings, had concluded that the employee was well placed on his present assignment. "He told me," said Jim, "my work experience does not qualify me for a higher grade of work, and my earnings are better in my present department than in any other to which I might be transferred." "So," Jim continued, "I am coming to you (the counselor) as a last resort because I really need to get another job."

The counselor informed him that he was not in a position to recommend job assignments, but that he would be glad to arrange an interview in which Jim might explore the problem in more detail. To this, Jim agreed. The interview started out with Jim elaborating upon his reasons for wanting a job transfer, but as the interview progressed, he began to bring out some other factors underlying his request.

During the depression of the thirties, some 15 years ago, Jim had been asked by a first-line supervisor for whom he was not then working to assist him in putting up his storm windows in the fall and taking them down in the spring. At that time Jim was in need of more money, and so he had welcomed this opportunity. This arrangement had continued on down to the present time.

In this interval, however, certain changes had taken place: (1) the supervisor for whom Jim did these chores had been promoted to the superintendency of the shop in which Jim was now working, (2) Jim also had been upgraded in pay several times, and he felt that he was no longer in need of outside work, (3) Jim's co-workers (who had become aware of this arrangement) kept kidding him about being "buddies with the big boss," and (4) Jim, who had thought of telling his superintendent that he no longer wanted to help him with his chores, was afraid to do this because he feared that the superintendent might be offended and would construe this request as an act of ingratitude on Jim's part.

As Jim continued to tell his story, he brought out that he really liked the work he was on, that the only thing that bothered him was the incessant kidding of his co-workers, and that to avoid this uncomfortable relationship, he wanted to get into a new organization where he would have a fresh start. He also brought out that he always had had difficulty in establishing a free-and-easy relationship with people around him. Here the interview ended.

Although at this point the counselor, at Jim's request, arranged for several subsequent interviews, Jim never availed himself of them. After reflecting upon his first interview, Jim decided himself that he was better off where he was and that the action he should take was to explain to the superintendent how he felt. So, as he told the counselor later, he had arranged to see the superintendent. He had told him that he now had a home of his own to care for and was so fully occupied that he would not have sufficient spare time to help him with his storm windows. He had had a very pleasant interview with the superintendent who readily understood his situation. Jim felt quite elated about having resolved a problem of long-standing and thanked the counselor for having helped him.

As we have said, we have chosen the case of Jim Evans to illustrate where things were going well. As it contains certain features which many such interviews had in common, we should like to point them out.

1. Obviously this was not a world-shattering problem but it was a problem very important to Jim. He faced an uncomfortable personal decision. "Should he solve his problem by getting another job or by telling his big boss that he did not want to put up and take down his storm windows any more with the possible consequence that this might be misconstrued and jeopardize his relationship with him?"

2. Without too much reflection, perhaps, of the possible consequences of these two different courses of action, Jim started by taking the first course but without any success, so he finally went to the counselor with one of those questions—Can you help me to get a transfer?—which the counselor's role model said, "This is not the help I can or should give."

3. Without any long discourse about the counselor's role, that is, with out an elaborate explanation by the counselor to Jim of why he could not do what Jim was asking him to do, a few simple words suggesting another alternative, "Would you like to talk to me about it?" seemed to be enough. Nor did the counselor have to provide Jim with an elaborate explanation of why talking about his problem might help him. So two big hurdles were jumped over "with the greatest of ease" and the interview proceeded on the right track (the A–D axis) because Jim wanted help and was willing to accept the kind of help he could get.

4. During the interview the counselor demonstrated the help he could give by clarifying for Jim the decision Jim faced.

5. With this clarification Jim decided himself to talk to the boss. He did and, lo and behold, Jim's personal problem was resolved. What brought Jim to this decision we do not know, but let us speculate that it might have been of the character, "What do I want to be— a man or a mouse?" He decided to risk his job investment by being a man. The superintendent probably responded more favorably to Jim—the man—than he would have responded to Jim—the mouse. "It feels good to be a man" (speaking symbolically), says Jim with elation to the counselor after his talk with the superintendent. "Thank you, Mr. Counselor."

6. Jim felt good (he felt like a man); the superintendent felt good

(he acted like a man and not like a stuffed shirt); Jim's supervisor
felt good (his authority was not undermined); the placement man
felt good (his specialist knowledge was not undermined); the counselor felt good (he really was of help); the counseling supervisor
felt good (here was a kind of outcome he could show management).
Everybody was happy! The role model was working.

But the yield from the counseling program of this kind of outcome, as we have said before, the counselors estimated averaged
about 10% per quarter for a changing population. Let us remember that whether or not under the given conditions this was a high
or a low yield, we do not know, because no standards for making
such an evaluation exist. But this does not stop us from exploring
what else was happening in the case of about 90% of the other
employees during the interval considered.

Cases where an explanation of the counselor's role was required

Probably no aspect of the counselor's role was more difficult for
others to understand than the prescription that he should not give
information, advice, direction, or explanations of Company policies. As a result on this issue there were wide differences of opinion among different groups, such as employees, supervision, management, and other personnel services as to what the counselor's
role should be. So a good amount of the counselor's time was spent
in explaining his role, that is, in providing the reasons (i.e., the
underlying logic) for why he behaved as he did.

Let us look first at the questions raised by supervision and management. By looking at Figure 12.2 their queries can be stated as
follows:

(1) In relation to requests for information (Category B), for example, why should the counselor not correct employee misin-
formation with correct information? Would this not be beneficial? Dissatisfactions with his rate of pay, for example, might
be corrected if he understood better the payment system and
the logic of its application to him. Or, for example, would it not
help if the employee was better informed about the nature of
the free enterprise system and the way it worked.

(2) But this argument applied even more strongly to Category C
questions. Here the employee was viewing the situation too

narrowly—merely from his point of view—the way the shoe was pinching him. He did not see the problem also from management's point of view. Hence, would it not help to provide management's side of the story, that is, management's rationale for why such policies, rules, regulations, etc., existed?

To these kinds of arguments, the counseling organization gave two general types of explanations.

(1) One stemmed from the rationale of the counselor's role. The gist of the reply was, "To do what you suggest would not be in keeping with our role model and the beneficial results that follow for employees from its practice." Any further explanation as to why this was so would require an elaboration of many of the matters discussed in Chapters II, X, and XI, and this, as the reader will remember, was not an easy communication to make. Or a further elucidation could take the form: "Let's look at the case of Jim Evans; don't you see that all your suggestions are beside the point. Jim Evan's problems are the kinds of problems we are interested in and trying to help."

(2) But another kind of explanation took a different form. Here the gist of the reply was, "Don't you see that to do what you suggest would do the very thing organizationally that we—and that even you would agree—are not supposed to be doing, namely, taking over and interfering with the prerogatives of supervision."

Around this last explanation a very sharp differentiation between the counselor's role and the supervisor's role was made by the counseling organization. From the point of view of the counseling organization the counselor's role had to be dissociated completely from all those activities and functions normally performed by persons in positions of authority. As the common way by which authority is exercised is through direction-taking functions, the counselor had to be dissociated from all such functions. In every way he had to stay clear of these authoritative activities. So to the counseling organization the prescription not to give information, advice, and direction was important from the points of view of not only, (1) the theory of counseling (the prescribed task role), but also (2) the way counseling had to be organizationally implemented, if they were to keep their relations straight with supervision.

We shall come back to this later in the next chapter but now let us look at the problem from the employees' point of view. This can be best seen by examining how the counselor went about to gain their acceptance and understanding of the counseling activity. In these activities the counselor spent about 30% of his time.

Problems of Gaining the Acceptance and Understanding by Employees of the Counseling Activity

In the territories to which they were assigned, it will be remembered, the counselors engaged in two activities, (1) on the floor and (2) in the interviewing room. The counselors were not sitting in an office to which employees went who wanted and needed counseling help. The rationale for setting up counselors on-the-hoof instead of solely in an interviewing office had derived in part from the two sets of role prescriptions outlined in Chapter II—his observer-research-diagnostic role (see pages 40–41) and his listening-helping-communication role (see page 42).

These two roles, it was felt, could be fused by having the counselor on the floor where he could exercise his observation and diagnostic skills in assessing individual and organizational needs. He could make use of these evaluations for allocating interviewing time. Moreover, his understanding of the departmental situation would provide a useful context for more effective listening. But in addition by having the counselor visible on the floor, it was felt, the employee could see what kind of a person the counselor was; the counselor would be in a better position to explain and demonstrate the kind and nature of the service he could provide and so the employee would be more likely to avail himself of this service if he needed it. It is this latter aspect of the counselor's activities that we now want to consider because in relation to them he spent about 30% of his time and his role model prescriptions were the least clear.

It is now that we need to distinguish the counselor's task role from these roles which he developed on the floor to gain the employees' acceptance of counseling. As we said before, the role model prescriptions applied to his task role; they specified his orientation on the floor as observer and in the interviewing room as listener. They did not specify what his organizational and social roles on the floor should be. Thus, the latter became a source of great preoccupation to the counselors. Many hours were spent on this aspect of their jobs and in time the counselor's role, that is, the way this word was used by the counseling organization, became equated mostly with their social-organizational roles on the floor and their preoccupations were about the ambiguities that existed between these roles and their task role.

The preoccupation of the counselors with this problem never ceased from the very beginning to the very end of the program. In fact the evidence we have would suggest that it increased instead of diminished throughout the twenty years. For some counselors— perhaps a greater proportion—a viable and manageable fusion of their task with their organizational and social roles occurred. But this fusion was not easy; it never could be taken for granted; at the slightest provocation its viability would crop up. So let us look at some of the underlying forces of which this problem was a symptom.

In Figure 12.3 we have tried to summarize three general kinds of responses made by counselors to the question, "Who are you, what do you do, and what help can you be to me?" From this figure it can be seen that:

(1) Category B-type responses were in the direction of differentiating sharply the counselor's job from all other organizational jobs. They lead to a curious anomaly of having to define themselves "outside of the Company structure."

(2) Category C-type responses were in the direction of trying to present a nonthreatening self or image of the counselor's activities to the employees.

(3) Category D-type responses were in the direction of trying to get acceptance by the employees of the counselor's sphere of competence where he could be of help.

(4) Category E-type responses were in the direction of more lengthy explanations of the rationale of the counseling program, i.e., how it was supposed to work.

Let us look first at how these different aspects of the counselor's role did fuse together into something which made sense to both

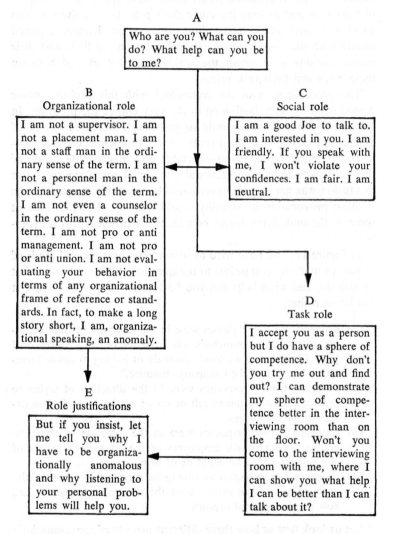

FIGURE 12.3

KINDS OF RESPONSES OF COUNSELORS
TO QUESTIONS A BY EMPLOYEES

A

Who are you? What can you do? What help can you be to me?

B
Organizational role

I am not a supervisor. I am not a placement man. I am not a staff man in the ordinary sense of the term. I am not a personnel man in the ordinary sense of the term. I am not even a counselor in the ordinary sense of the term. I am not pro or anti management. I am not pro or anti union. I am not evaluating your behavior in terms of any organizational frame of reference or standards. In fact, to make a long story short, I am, organizational speaking, an anomaly.

C
Social role

I am a good Joe to talk to. I am interested in you. I am friendly. If you speak with me, I won't violate your confidences. I am fair. I am neutral.

D
Task role

I accept you as a person but I do have a sphere of competence. Why don't you try me out and find out? I can demonstrate my sphere of competence better in the interviewing room than on the floor. Won't you come to the interviewing room with me, where I can show you what help I can be better than I can talk about it?

E
Role justifications

But if you insist, let me tell you why I have to be organizationally anomalous and why listening to your personal problems will help you.

counselors and employees. The presentation of a nonorganization self—even though if carried too far raised the issue of "Who are you, organizationally speaking?" into bold relief—did fuse with a nonthreatening self. It said: "I am evaluating you situationally as a person and not just organizationally as a worker in terms of management standards of performance. So don't get scared. I am interested in you and your individual development as a person and I am only interested in you and your performance as a worker to the extent that this bothers you."

Moreover, as in the case of Jim Evans, an elaboration of B, C, and E was often not required. Jim did not require or demand an explanation or justification of the counselor's role but entered easily and quickly into the D role where he was able to be helped.

But there were instances where these different roles did not fuse automatically and did present conflicts for the counselor. For example:

(1) How far do I define myself outside of the formal organization of the Company until my identity becomes so diffused that I would be representing myself falsely to the employees?

(2) How far do I play along the dimension of being a good Joe until my sphere of competence becomes nullified?

(3) How much time should I spend in trying to get employees to go with me to the interviewing room?

(4) How much time should I spend rationalizing and justifying the counseling program? How does the prescription of not rationalizing the Company policies to employees coincide with this emphasis on rationalizing the counseling program to employees? Is there not a discrepancy here? Why should the counseling program receive a treatment by the counselors different from any of the other personnel functions authorized and supported by management?

As was said in Chapter III, many reports and papers were written by the counselors on this aspect of their job. Latent in these reports were many of the conflicts we raised above. Read from the point of view we are now taking, they seem clear. But again we must remind the reader that they were not researched at the time from this point of view. So to this extent the reader should be warned that we are interpreting data that were generated for purposes other than those for which we are utilizing them now. From the point of view of the counseling organization these were problems which could be solved or resolved by greater counseling insight and skill. The burden for their resolution was placed upon the counselor. It was in this direction toward which all their discussions and reports went. The organizational consequences of these resolutions were minimized; it was thought that satisfactory personal resolutions by individual counselors could be made. We shall discuss this point further after we have discussed all the problems of implementation with employees.

Explanations given to employees of the counselor's role

Let us look first at some of the explanations of themselves and of counseling that were given by counselors and see if we can hear some of the forces operating in Figure 12.3 and how the counselors resolved them.

C_1: We are called personnel counselors. We don't know whether that is such a good name or not because *ours isn't personnel work as people usually think of it.* That is, we don't have anything to do with placements or transfers or personnel records.

*   *   *   *   *

C_2: Our job is *different* in that we just talk to people about anything we may care to talk about whether home or hobbies or something on the job—*anything we may both be interested in.*

*   *   *   *   *

C_3: I know how I feel sometimes when I have something on my mind, and I can just sit down and talk it over with somebody. If I try to explain it to them, I find it comes out a lot clearer for me.

That is the way I hope you will feel about my job—I'll see you often—but *if something comes up and you feel it would help if we talked about it, I hope you'll let me know, because that's what I'm here for.*

*   *   *   *   *

C_4: And another thing about our talks, whether they are on the job or up here or anywhere, we always consider them confidential. We don't tell anyone, people you work with or your supervisors, what we talk about. *We make no reports to the supervisors.*

Of course, you may see us talking to the supervisors too, but we regard our talks with them in the same way we talk with you. *Sometimes they have things on their minds they want to talk over and we try to be useful to them in the same way we hope to be useful to you.*

I hope I've made this clear. If I haven't and there is anything you don't understand now or later, just ask me any time and I'll be glad to explain. I ask you questions about your job and it's only fair that you know what I do.

*   *   *   *   *

C_5: My name is Ethel; I'm from the Personnel Counseling Department.

E_1: And my name is Mary.

C_5: I'm glad to meet you, Mary. I don't suppose you've met any personnel counselors here yet, have you?

E_1: No I haven't. Just what is your purpose?

C_5: Well, to put it simply, Mary, I'm going to be the kind of *friend you can talk to about anything at any time.* I don't have anything to say about your work. But we can *talk about all sorts of things,* whatever you may care to. Sometimes that kind of talk helps, etc. . . .

*   *   *   *   *

C_6: I want to feel that *I am helping people think out the things they are troubled about.* We feel that people are perfectly capable of attending to their own affairs; that's why we don't presume to give advice or anything like that. We do have a real service to offer, however, in that we provide a place where people can think out their personal problems and decisions, whether they be about work or outside.

*   *   *   *   *

E_2: (who has been asked by his supervisor to see the counselor) Well I don't know what your exact desire is here, I guess I'm supposed to talk about the situation upstairs there, so I might as well get on with it. Or do you have anything in particular that you want me to talk about? I would assume the way I was told about it and everything that you know all about the situation that I'm in so that I don't see that I need to talk about that very much.

C_7: Well, I'll tell you, Ed, I'd better give you an idea of how we might be using this time together because I realize that what we're *going to try to do may be a little different from what you had expected.* I don't suppose you have anything that you do expect too clearly clarified from our conversation on the telephone.

E$_2$: No, I don't have too much of an idea, except that I can guess from
   what's been going on upstairs there, but then you were going to tell
   me what your position was here.

C$_7$: Yes, I was going to say that our job around here is one of presenting *a spot where a person may talk about anything he wants to
   talk about.* I was called out to your department by your department
   chief; he felt that there might be a possibility that you and I might
   be able to talk about things that you may have on your mind relative
   to your job there, because he had some kind of a feeling that *you
   were not able to tell him what was on your mind.* He felt that there
   was something that you didn't want to tell him and so he suggested
   that possibly someone *outside of the organization* like myself might
   be able to talk with you and that you would feel a little freer to talk
   with me because I'm not connected with your department in any
   way, but at the same time I am interested in being of any help that
   I can be. Our talk will be *confidential;* I won't be reporting anything
   that we talk about here to supervision upstairs; it's merely an opportunity that you can take or leave, as you like. I do not know much
   about your situation upstairs, Ed, because I'm not interested in that
   in the sense that *I'm only interested in the way you see it and feel
   it and that's the only interest to me.* The supervision upstairs did tell
   me a little bit about the fact that they had been talking with you
   about some of the difficulties you've had here at work and I let it
   drop there, and today I'm going to forget everything they have said
   because I'm just interested in what you think about that situation
   or whatever it is you'd like to talk about.

E$_2$: I suppose then I might as well start out and tell you just what I
   am thinking about. (This is the beginning of a two-hour interview.)

Problems of Developing a Counseling Relationship with All Employees

The phrase "counseling relationship" was part of the shop talk
of the counseling organization. Counselors as well as counseling
supervisors used the phrase again and again in their discussions,
reports, and studies and for them it came to have an accepted common internal meaning. But for our purposes here we will need to
"extentionalize" this phrase because the organizational prescription "to develop it with all employees" carried with it a great deal
of organizational significance. Let us remember that the task role
prescriptions as derived from research had been concerned with
the quality and not the quantity of the counselor's service; there-

fore this prescription must have been derived from some other source.

Let us start with what it did and did not mean on the extreme poles of a continuum.

(1) It did not mean on the one hand that all employees who did not wish to be counseled had to go to the interviewing room and get the counseling treatment or even on the floor be forced into a conversation they did not wish to have with a counselor. Counselors respected the rights of employees who did not wish to talk to them.

(2) Yet it did mean something more than that the counselor would make himself just available for those who *wished* and asked for his services.

It was something more "in the middle" and like all things in the middle it becomes more difficult to specify. From the point of view of the counseling organization it was important:

(1) To make sure that the counseling service reached everyone who *needed* it.

(2) To acquaint those not needing it with its purposes so that if they had problems later they would know that this service was available.

(3) Neither (1) or (2) above they felt could be achieved unless the counselor talked with or tried to talk with each employee in his territory. Only in this way they felt could the counselor explain his services and find out who *needed* them.

(4) But more than this, only if the counselor was on the floor would the employee avail himself of this service. According to them, "It wouldn't work otherwise."

So counselors did invite all employees to the interviewing room where they could explain and demonstrate their services in the case that in the future the employee needed them. This notion of coverage created some problems for counselors and they revolved around four dimensions:

(1) There were those employees who were willing to talk and those who were not. Among those willing to talk, there were those who were willing to talk on the floor but not in the interviewing room.

(2) Among those who were willing to talk, there were those who did or did not want counseling.

(3) Among those who did not want counseling, there were those who, in the opinion of the counselor, did or did not need counseling.

(4) Among those who needed counseling, there were those who were and were not helped by it.

From some estimates made by the counselors in their reports about the numbers of employees in some of these categories, and from two studies made by counselors of the employees in their territories who expressed work and personal concerns which in the counselor's opinion needed counseling and were helped by it, and from studies counselors made about the utilization of their time over a three-month period, we constructed Figure 12.4.

Obviously these figures are crude but we thought that some rough estimates would be better than none. Moreover, all we are going to use from these data are the four categories A, B, C, and D (the bottom row of Figure 12.4) that they roughly generated. Perhaps one more word of caution about these data is needed. Estimates on the number of employees who did or did not want counseling were made by us on the basis of their behavior regarding where they wished to be interviewed.

So, taking these limitations into account, let us see what little light Figure 12.4 can throw on the question of what were the results from trying to develop a counseling relationship with everyone.

(1) About 10% of the employees wanted and needed counseling and were helped by it, taking up roughly about 35% of the counselor's time (A).

(2) About 25% of the employees needed counseling who were not helped by it, taking up roughly about 40% of the counselor's time (B).

(3) About 55% of the employees did not want or need counseling, taking up roughly about 20% of the counselor's time (C).

(4) About 10% of the employees were not willing to talk to the counselor, taking up roughly about 5% of the counselor's time (D).

Can we interpret these categories in a way which will throw some light on the kinds of relationships that the counselors developed with employees? From their endeavor to establish a counseling re-

FIGURE 12.4. EMPLOYEES WILLING TO TALK AND WANTING AND NEEDING COUNSELING

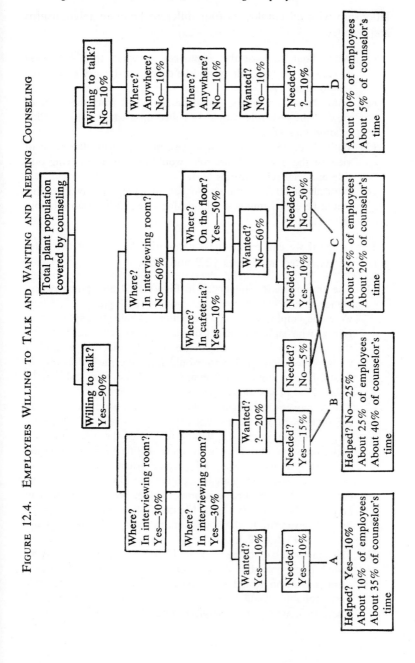

lationship with all employees four different kinds of relationships had resulted:

(1) With about 10% of the employees, in what, from the point of view of the task role, would be called satisfactory counseling relationships (A).

(2) With about 25% of the employees, in what, from the point of view of the task role, would be called unsatisfactory counseling relationships (B).

(3) With about 55% of the employees, in what, from the point of view of the organizational role, would be called satisfying outside or social relationships (C).

(4) With about 10% of the employees, in what, socially speaking, would be called minimal relationships, i.e., little or no relationships (D).

Let us see if we can relate these categories to some of the categories we generated in Figures 12.2 and 12.3.

(1) The employees in category B in Figure 12.4 bore some resemblance to the employees in category C in Figure 12.2. These were the employees who were willing to talk, to express their gripes, who suffered most from a sense of felt injustice, who the counselors felt needed counseling help and with whom, as we expected, the counselors would have the most difficulty in establishing a counseling relationship. They were asking the wrong kind of questions and asking for the wrong kind of help.

(2) The employees in category C in Figure 12.4 were those who in the opinion of the counselors expressed no serious work concerns but who were quite willing to engage the counselor in a social conversation. They were quite willing to share common interests and experiences and become friends with the counselors. In these engagements—unlike the B's—the counselors encountered no barbed questions. Things were most pleasant and congenial. So the C's in Figure 12.4 were most rewarded by and rewarding to the counselors in their social role of category C in Figure 12.3.

(3) The employees of category B in Figure 12.4 we might expect would offer probably a great challenge to the task-oriented counselors, who would want to convert the B's into A's while they probably would have a tough time in relating to the C's where their professional services were not required.

(4) On the other hand the B's in Figure 12.4 we might expect would present a tough assignment for the counselors who cultivated their social role as the B's wanted someone more than a good Joe to talk to.

Problems of the Reluctant Employee

There is another way of talking and thinking—probably a more useful one—about the problems the counselors had in gaining employee acceptance. In their endeavor to establish a relationship with each employee in order to assess his needs for counseling, the counselors met employees who could be arranged in a continuum from those who on one extreme end (1) refused to talk to those (2) who on the other extreme end talked freely. So far we have assumed that this may have had something to do with whether or not they wanted or needed to be counseled. But there were other factors operating which had something to do with their willingness or reluctance to talk freely.

In the territories of each counselor, as we have seen, there existed a pattern of social relationships among the workers which emerged from their formal conditions of work. There existed small social groupings whose members had social interactions over and beyond those required by the work. In these groups there existed accepted norms of behavior in terms of which workers gained or did not gain membership. Those who abided by them belonged; those who didn't didn't belong. In terms of them, therefore, workers had a social position or status—different sometimes from the position or status they occupied in the formal organization. These social positions or informal statuses can be arranged roughly in a continuum from those (1) who not only were well accepted influential members—let us call them informal leaders—to (2) those who were well accepted but not key members—let us call them regulars—to (3) those who were partially accepted because sometimes they did and sometimes they did not abide by the group norms —let us call them deviants—to (4) those who were not accepted— let us call them isolates.

As we said, these membership or informal status designations could not be deduced from the formal organization; they did not appear on any official records of the Company; employees did not wear any name tags saying, "I'm Jim Evans, a regular." These membership designations could only be obtained by observation from following the prescriptive rules on page 40 in Chapter II. One could hear them, for example, when Jim Evans minded the ridicule from his fellow employees because he was putting on or taking off the big boss's storm windows, meaning, "My dear fellow, in our group we don't like this kind of behavior, it smacks of getting into the big boss's good favor by means of which our group doesn't approve. Mind your behavior, Jim, if you want to belong—to be one of us."

Because these phenomena could only be observed where they took place was one of the reasons why counselors had been put on the hoof instead of solely in an office. Only by being on the floor could he assess the group structure—its values and norms in terms of which individual workers had different social positions. From such data about the norms of acceptable shop behavior he could learn one of the important pressures on the worker, namely, (1) what kind of behavior the work group was expecting and demanding of him. Together with what the counselor knew (2) about what kind of performance management was demanding and expecting of the worker (by far more explicitly spelled out) and what he could learn in the interviewing room (3) about what the individual worker was demanding and expecting of his work, a better appraisal of the individual worker's total situation could be made, as we saw in Part II. But also it would provide the framework for more intelligent listening. This, it will be remembered, was the way in which the prescriptive propositions on pages 40–42 were to complement each other in implementing his task role. And along this dimension of his job, they did work well together. But what about the counselors' role in relation to gaining the employees' acceptance of counseling? This is what we want to consider now.

Obviously these norms of acceptable shop behavior were critical to the group's acceptance of the counselor and counseling. Although it is sometimes tried, it would be the trick of the week for a person to become accepted by a group whose norms he flouted. So let us look at some of these norms of acceptable shop behavior. Many of them emerge from trying to keep their world steady in an environment of rapid technological change. They emerge sometimes, for example, in the form of certain unauthorized procedures, methods, tools, layouts, and short cuts of one kind or another which the workers develop themselves and which become their most precious secrets, for which the norm is, "Don't be a squealer." They emerge in implicit understandings of what constitutes a fair day's work in which the norm is, "Don't be a rat-buster." They specify how a worker is supposed to behave when a rate setter is timing his job in which the norm is, "Don't kill the job or be a job killer." They specify what things a worker talks or does not talk to his boss about and what things he does and does not do for his boss in which the norm is, "Don't squeal but also don't suck up to him." (If the reader didn't hear it when he read the case of Jim Evans, let him reflect now upon how powerful this norm was operating on Jim Evans who would rather try to get a transfer to any old job than be accused of sucking up to the big boss.)

What being called soft on communism is to a politician, so being called a squealer, job killer, rate buster, and the like is to the industrialized worker. He just does not like these category identifications and he will do almost anything—sometimes even against, as in the case of Jim Evans, his own economic interests—to avoid them.

If we reduce all these norms to the activity of talking, they can be boiled down to norms about to whom you talk, when, where, how, about what, at what level, and for how long. And in relation to authority figures they can be reduced even further to, "Just don't talk," or "Act dumb," etc. So here we have the counselor in a territory trying to listen to workers who, even though personally they might be garrulous, were influenced strongly by norms which said, "If you want to belong (be one of us), you better keep your fat mouth shut."

It would be strange indeed if these norms were not influencing those workers who were more or less reluctant to talk freely to the counselor, and particularly powerful when the worker was talking to the counselor on the floor and visible to his fellow workers. Any worker whose position in the group was not too secure and could be jeopardized by talking to the counselor and by this activity per-

ceived as violating this norm by his fellow workers would be reluctant to talk to him.

It was for these reasons in part that the counseling organization
had stripped the counselor of all authority status symbols and defined him outside of the structure and presented him to the workers as a nonthreatening figure, that is, as Joe Green, a good guy to
talk to. But the worker was asking of Joe Green, "Are you a guy I
can trust with these group secrets?" Until he finds this out, "mum's
the word," or the conversation is likely to be about baseball and
fishing (or in the case of women, about babies and cooking) or in
any other forms of innocuous chit-chat.

To the seasoned counselor it was obvious that gaining employee
acceptance was not just a matter of being a good Joe, a one-shot
proposition, or something that could be obtained merely by logical
explanation. It was a long, arduous, time-consuming task requiring patience and a basic understanding of why employees might be
reluctant to speak with him. His understanding of these norms was
critical and in some terms he had to come to peace with them.

(1) He had to understand why gaining the acceptance of himself
    as a guy to be trusted by the informal leaders might help him
    to gain acceptance more readily from all the regulars of their
    respective groups.

(2) But with greater depth he had to understand also why these
    informal leaders (the regulators and policers of these norms)
    were the very ones who had the most to lose by talking with
    him, that is, of losing their high status and position in the
    group, and so might be most reluctant to talk to him.

(3) He had to understand why deviants and isolates might have
    less to lose by being counseled and that sometimes in fact coun-
    seling might provide them with a mechanism for getting even
    with the group which had rejected them.

(4) He had to understand that there were two quite different kinds
    of isolates, (a) the self chosen and (b) the unhappy. The former
    were the workers who were quite willing to pay the cost (isola-
    tion) for nonconformity to the group's norms but who some-
    times gained the group's grudging respect for their task com-
    petence, even though they did not have their social approval.
    The latter were those who did not want to pay the price of
    flaunting the group's norms. They wanted to be liked and

accepted by the group while still not conforming to their norms. They wanted to have their cake and to eat it too.

(5) He had to understand why he could not approve or disapprove of these norms (see prescriptive rules, page 42) and why this was more difficult to practice on the floor than in the interviewing room.

(6) But with greater depth he had to understand that while he tried to remain neutral (a phrase often used by counselors toward these norms), he in turn too could be neutralized by them, that is, rendered ineffective by them. He had to understand that these norms were double-edged swords.

Now these insights do not come quickly or easily. They came more easily to some counselors than to others. Some of them, as they became more seasoned, could learn to utilize their understanding of these norms in doing a more effective job, not only in the interviewing room but also on the floor. Such understanding, for example, could help them in scheduling their interviews more intelligently, in assessing better individual and group needs (as we saw on the part of the counselor in the case of Mary, the lead-off operator in the last chapter), in trying to behave as naturally and congruently as they could on the floor by doing as well as they could what was required by the total situation in which they were involved.

This kind of understanding was not in the direction of indiscriminate interviewing, that is, of trying to get everyone to take his or her hair down, to maintain equal coverage, or to be fair and equal to everyone. Instead, it was in the direction of highly discriminating behavior based upon an understanding of the situation in which as counselors they were involved and, along this dimension, being as competent as they could. Such counselors did not eschew social conversation, but neither did they cultivate it nor utilize it as the main source of gaining acceptance. They did not strip themselves of all status symbols and define themselves outside of the structure. They realized they were part of the Western Electric culture as well as involved in the subcultures of the small groups whose norms they might not share but toward which they could try to be at least intelligently understanding. And so they saw why it was difficult to be congruent and natural on the floor and they longed to get in the interviewing room where they could be more at peace and of a piece with their role model.

THE COUNSELORS' RESOLUTIONS OF THEIR ROLE AMBIGUITY

As we have examined the problems of implementation in relation to employees we have uncovered in each case an underlying lack of clarity between the counselor's in-counseling task role and his outside, gaining-of-acceptance-of-himself-and-of-counseling role. It was not so much a conflict between the two roles as an ambiguity between which one he should cultivate more or most and how they could be fused into an acceptable, integrated, and viable pattern for him.

As we have said, some counselors were able to make a more satisfactory personal resolution than others. Let us look first at the four kinds of role resolutions that were possible. We have depicted them in Figure 12.5.

FIGURE 12.5

FOUR POSSIBLE ROLE RESOLUTIONS OF THE COUNSELOR'S AMBIGUITY

		A Professional counselor	D Integrated counselor-researcher
Task Role	(+)		
	(−)	C Conflicted counselor	B Social counselor
		(−)	(+)

Outside (Social) Role

A. There was the counselor who wanted a task and professional identity. He emphasized the task aspect of his role. He was the one who chafed at his outside on-the-floor, gaining-of-acceptance social activities. He was the one who recognized more acutely that although he did not have organizational authority, he had to earn the respect of employees and gain the authority for a competence, skill, and knowledge that stemmed from "science" and a "professional orientation." For him, being a Joe Green, a good guy to talk to, was not enough. If he got seduced into presenting himself to employees too much at this level, he felt that it would be at the expense of presenting himself as, "I'm Bill Brown who happens to know something and can be of professional help to you." One might notice the resemblance to the technical specialist in Figure 10.2 in Chapter X but now at the staff and not at the operating level.

B. There was the counselor, who emphasized the "I'm Joe Green, a good guy to talk to" aspect of his job. For him this outside role was more rewarding than being an observer-listener, that is, cultivating either his diagnostic skills as an observor of human behavior or his catalytic function in the two-person encounter as described in the preceding chapter. For him gaining the acceptance of counseling and of himself (often not too clearly distinguished) was of paramount importance. At this level he could gain approval and acceptance and often continue to conduct "social conversations"—not "interviews" as described in the last chapter—in the interviewing room. One might notice again the resemblance to the good Joe in Figure 10.2 in Chapter X, but now at the staff and not at the operating level.

C. Obviously the counselor in category C did not remain long in the counseling organization as a counselor, because he was too conflicted. Some of them had reservations about the purpose of counseling. For example, was it an antiunion activity? Was it ideologically viable? Should management be concerned with such problems? Were not the interests of the worker and the interests of management incompatible? Should not management accept this fact and deal with it organizationally via an equally strong union organization, and so forth? Because it has been published and therefore is public information we can cite one example of this orientation [1] and we shall return to those problems in the conclusions.

D. But now we come to the last resolution which we were beginning to consider at the end of the last section. This resolution was difficult to achieve because it depended upon not only a fusion of the task and social roles but also a conceptual integration of the two task components in the counselor's role model itself: (1) the diag-

---

[1] Jeanne L. and Harold L. Wilensky, "Personnel Counseling: The Hawthorne Case," *The American Journal of Sociology*, November 1951, pp. 265–280. The first author, who had been a counselor for a period of time at Hawthorne, writes with the help of her husband (a sociologist) about her experiences as a counselor and her evaluation of the program as a whole.

nostic and research role and (2) the catalytic role as described in Chapter XI.

Let us see how this problem manifested itself. For many counselors who became dedicated to their catalytic role in the personal encounter, there existed a strong aversion to attempting to classify persons or their problems, such as, for example, we are doing now and did in Chapter X of this book. In the personal encounter they felt that such evaluations impeded instead of facilitated the process of communication. Even though they were intended to be descriptive, most labels or typologies, they felt, took on a normative connotation of good or bad and in the personal interview this was harmful. So for many counselors the research component of their role model, as stated in Chapter II, did not fit well with their catalytic role as change agents and counselors. Let us hear this orientation from a former counselor.

> In reading your manuscript, I react somewhat negatively to this component of the counselor's role (diagnostic-observer-researcher). Perhaps I'm too much oriented to the *process* in which the interviewee and counselor are engaged and which results in employee growth. The counselor is not a problem-seeker: a person without a problem can benefit through understanding his values, goals, and needs through the counseling experience.

Any counselor who has become dedicated to his catalytic role, where in the process of trying to describe it in Chapter XI, it will be remembered, words failed us, becomes almost by definition anti-labeling, anti-classification, anti-problem, anti-evaluation, anti-typological, etc. Why? Because these intellectual processes and their products can become so easily instruments of misevaluation instead of proper evaluation. They make for premature closures instead of for dynamic openness. They deny man's existential condition, that he unfortunately exists before he knows what he can become. For man's becomingness there are no answers at the end of the book. *Process* is all; *substance* is illusion. So it is not strange that many "good counselors" often tend to become kinds of mystics (remember, we are using this word descriptively and not evaluatively) who eschew substantive knowledge about human behavior and wisely, perhaps, do not write books about it.

THE VIABILITY OF THE ROLE RESOLUTIONS

Perhaps we can clarify further the problem we have been analyzing by looking at the viability of these role resolutions for the individual and for the organization. We shall use the word "effective" for a person who realizes the technical standards of expectation of his job; we shall use the word "efficient" for the person who receives satisfaction from doing his job, i.e., fulfilling these expectations.[2] To be viable in the long run we shall mean that the role incumbent has to be both effective and efficient.

FIGURE 12.6

FOUR ROLE RESOLUTIONS OF COUNSELORS WITHIN THE
IN-COUNSELING RELATIONSHIP

(+)	D Counselor- researcher	A Professional counselor
Effective		
(−)	C Conflicted counselor	B Social counselor
	(−)	(+)

Efficient

In Figure 12.6 we have placed these four role resolutions in terms of the four combinations of effectiveness and efficiency for the dyadic, in-counseling, task relationship. From this figure it can be seen that:

1. *Resolution A* was both effective and efficient for 10% of the plant population. The continued existence of twenty years of the counseling program plus the genuine satisfaction that such counselors felt imply that this role was viable within the dyadic counselor-counselee relationship and so long as there was a career opportunity for professional counseling in the organization.

[2] We are using the concepts of effective and efficient in the same sense as they were used by Chester Barnard in his book, *The Functions of the Executive* (Cambridge, Harvard University Press, 1938).

This counselor understood why in order to optimize self change on the part of the one counseled and to avoid dependency upon the counselor, the role prescriptions were necessary. He did not rationalize his role prescriptions in terms of his outside role.

Within this relationship the satisfactions for the person being helped and the counselor fitted; their perceptions of the counseling role coincided. The counseled one felt that he had been helped on the road toward independence; the counselor felt that he had been of help in facilitating this direction.

Both the counselor and the counselee were congruent with the development of the need hierarchy posited in Chapter IV. One was not satisfying his needs at the expense of the other. Both were learning and developing together.

2. *Resolution B* was efficient but not effective, so in the long run not viable. This counselor often rationalized his role prescriptions in terms of his outside role. Although he gained satisfaction from his role, it could not be justified by the counseling program. To the degree that the counseling role was perceived this way by employees, supervision, and management, the counselor's effectiveness was diminished. Moreover in this resolution the satisfaction of the counselor's needs for acceptance was at the expense of helping the one being counseled toward satisfying his higher order needs for independence and competence.

3. *Resolution C* was neither effective nor efficient and so this counselor did not stay in the program long.

4. *Resolution D* was effective but was it efficient? Theoretically it could be both, but in fact was it? As it is here that we keep meeting again and again the underlying ambiguity we are trying to state, let us examine it carefully. In terms of the way the counselor's task role was originally designed, it had two components, (1) research and (2) counseling. So the counselor who met the prescriptions for both these standards was more effective. However, for many counselors these two roles were in conflict; the prescriptions for good research were not congruent with the prescriptions for good counseling. So the resolution of this conflict may have required a division of labor within the counseling organization itself, about which we will have more to say in our conclusion.

But as a matter of fact, as the counseling program became more and more a service organization and less and less research-oriented, the fusion of these two roles was no longer required.

However, as the counseling organization expanded and became more and more a service organization, the counselor's outside social role became more and more critical—not for purposes of research but for purposes of coverage and employee acceptance. For the professionally-oriented counselor (A) this made his job less satisfying. So although in the dyadic relationship he was both effective and efficient; in his total job as it developed he was effective but not so efficient. In the actual organizational situation, as it developed therefore, these role resolutions from the point of view of effectiveness and efficiency looked more like those shown in Figure 12.7 which resembles Figure 12.5 again. The split was along the A–B diagonal between the professional and the social counselor.

FIGURE 12.7

FOUR ROLE RESOLUTIONS OF COUNSELORS FOR COMBINED
INSIDE AND OUTSIDE ROLES

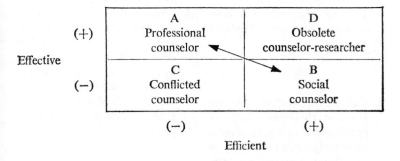

THE SELECTION AND TRAINING OF COUNSELORS

Many of the problems of counselors that we have been discussing were dealt with by the counseling organization through selection and training.

Criteria for the Selection of Counselors

From a statement issued by the counseling organization about the characteristics of the effective counselor, we prepared Table 12.1. From this statement it can be seen that the counseling organization placed a high value (1) on being interested in the daily lives and problems of *shop people,* (2) on being *emotionally mature* and *self reliant,* (3) on being *socially adjustable,* and (4) on understanding *the function of counseling.*

TABLE 12.1

CHARACTERISTICS OF AN EFFECTIVE COUNSELOR

Plus	*Minus*
1. Is interested in shop people.	1. Is interested in people just to be popular.
2. Is interested in the ordinary daily lives of shop people and in helping them with their problems.	2. Is interested in people just intellectually, that is, in making cases of them just in order to verify theories of human behavior.
3. Has a realistic attitude toward adaptation to life situations; his own as well as others.	3. Takes a highly personalized view toward life situations; his own as well as others.
4. Is capable of taking a non-evaluative view toward unusual behavior.	4. Places a high positive value on the new, the unconventional, and the shocking or, on the other hand, is overly disturbed by unconventional forms of behavior and thought.
5. Can relate well to different kinds or classes or groups of people (both younger and older or of a higher or lower rank or of different backgrounds from his).	5. Can relate well only to certain kinds or classes or groups of people.
6. Can exercise initiative in planning his work day.	6. Requires close supervision in planning his work day.
7. Learns from his mistakes and experiences.	7. Justifies his mistakes and cannot seem to learn from them.
8. Understands the peculiar and important therapeutic functions of his counseling role in the dyadic, helping relationship.	8. Tends to keep discovering and reporting conditions which management *ought* to change or the solutions that the employee *ought* to arrive at or treating the interview as an information-gathering procedure in order to be able to offer suggestions, admonitions or advice.

The last value, perhaps, deserves comment. That the counselor should understand the nature of his task role one might think would top the list. But here we have to put the counseling program in its historical perspective. In the early years of the program, the counselors were made up of persons who had become dedicated and committed to counseling through their experiences with the original Hawthorne researches. Many of these men and women had a wealth of shop and personnel experience; they were not psychologists but the catalytic role of the counselor intrigued them. In this role they saw a new approach to personnel practices. In later years many of them became counseling supervisors.

As the program expanded three different groups of new counselors were brought in, (1) younger men or women who were college graduates with a liberal arts background and in some cases with a major in the social sciences, (2) employees within the plant who were looking for a permanent transfer to counseling, many of whom had only formal education through high school, and (3) employees who came to the counseling organization on a rotational basis as a phase in their development, most of whom had little formal education and no training in the social sciences.

During most of the existence of the program, the counseling organization was made up of these three groups of counselors. The criteria for selection varied somewhat for these different groups. Although there was no rigid age or educational qualifications, as time went on the counseling organization preferred younger to older people and college graduates with a liberal arts background and preferably with a major in the social sciences to noncollege graduates with only work experience. But at any one time there was about an equal distribution of both.

The Counseling Supervisor's Training Function

This situation placed the burden of the training of the counselor in his task role primarily on the counseling supervisor. After an indoctrination period, the counselor was assigned a territory and the remainder of his training took place on the job.

In the early years the indoctrination lasted about a month. During this period the counselor was given information about the company, its history, personnel policies and practices. He talked with experienced counselors. But for the most part the training consisted of group discussions of readings, cases, and problems that a counselor met frequently both on the floor and in the interviewing room. The counseling orientation in the dyadic relationship was stressed.

As time went on, however, this indoctrination period was shortened to a week because the counseling organization found that many new counselors became so concerned about anticipating their first interview that they became nervous wrecks. So they were put in the territory almost at once and told to try to make their interview with the employee an interesting and rewarding experience for themselves as well as for the employee, to record their interviews, and to discuss them with their supervisor as soon as possible.

After the indoctrination period, the on-the-job training for the new counselor consisted primarily of frequent discussions with his supervisor about the problems he was having and how he might deal with them better. This phase was very intensive during the first six months and gradually diminished as the counselor became more experienced. In these discussions the counseling supervisor attempted to establish a counseling relationship with the new counselor, as it was felt that only by coming to understand himself better could he become aware of his own attitudes and responses which might be affecting or blocking the employee's responses to him.

Besides these discussions with individual counselors, weekly conferences were held where the counselors pooled their experiences and where cases and problems encountered in implementing the program were discussed. At various times role playing was used as a training device.

The Self Learning of the Counselor

In reviewing these selection and training procedures, it can be seen that the responsibility for dealing with and resolving the ambiguities of his role, as described in the last section, was placed on the individual counselor. He was assisted toward this resolution by being counseled by his supervisor who, as a counselor, did not tell him what to do so much as to let him work out a resolution which was congruent with his own interpersonal style as well as being effective for his task role. But in the last analysis the responsibility for making a satisfactory adjustment was his. By selection procedures the counseling organization tried to select counselors with sufficient emotional maturity, self reliance, and social skills to perform their duties both on the floor and in the interviewing room.

SUMMARY

In this chapter we have tried to examine the problems that the counselors had in establishing their organizational and professional identity with the workers. We examined the barrage of questions with which they were confronted and the problems these questions presented for the practice of the counselor's role model in relation to not giving advice and direction. We used the case of Jim Evans to illustrate the kind of help counseling could provide and did provide for about 10% of the employees.

We saw how in order to gain the acceptance of the employees and not to interfere with the prerogatives of supervision, they had to dissociate themselves more and more from any managerial, supervisory, or authoritative functions. This in time became more and more the justification for their role model. Employees would not speak to them freely if they did not divest themselves of all status symbols and present themselves to workers as nonthreatening figures. This reinforced the development of their social role, but this in turn made it difficult for them to establish both their organizational and their professional identity. It increased the amount of time they had to spend in explaining who they were, what help they could provide, and how this help would benefit the workers.

We examined the endeavor of the counselors to establish a relationship with all workers in order to explain their services to them and to find out who needed their help. We saw how about 70% of the employees were reluctant to go off the floor and to the interviewing rooms and as a result why many contacts, conversations, and interviews took place on the floor.

We examined some of the powerful factors—the norms of shop behavior—which might be influencing the reluctance of employees to talk freely, and saw how the counselors had to work with or through these norms, and realized why this might be difficult to do.

We examined the way in which the counselor resolved the task and social functions of his job and looked at four possible role resolutions and their viability.

Finally, we looked at how counselors were selected and trained for their job, with particular reference to the way they were helped in making satisfactory personal resolutions to its complex and ambiguous demands. We saw that they were helped to learn but the responsibility for learning was theirs.

In examining the counselor's role so far we have taken only one leg of our four-legged journey. So in the next chapter we will take our second and third steps and see how counseling related itself to supervision and supervisory training.

CHAPTER XIII

Counseling and Supervision

IN THIS CHAPTER we want to look at the problems the counselor faced in his relations with supervision. However, we do not want to look at them as just an additional set of problems separate from those which he had with employees, but instead in relation to the problems he had with employees. So our unit of analysis will be the set of relationships as shown in Figure 13.1 below.

FIGURE 13.1

THE COUNSELOR'S ROLE VIS-À-VIS SUPERVISION

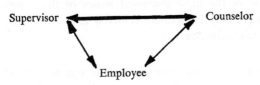

THE COUNSELOR'S ROLE SET

In sociological literature this would be called a role set. The focal person we are considering in this role set is the counselor. The more complete role set which we will consider finally will be composed of all those occupants of offices related to his in the work flow and authority structures with whom he has to interact in order to do his job. This more complete role set for the counselor, for example, we showed in Figure 12.1 which included his relations to other personnel services and management as well as his relations to employees and supervisors. As we go on we will have to include still other relationships, that is, those he had with the shop steward and the union.

But because we cannot talk about everything at the same time, we will take one relationship at a time; but each time that we add a new relationship, we will build upon the relationship we have considered before. As we add each new relationship, therefore, our unit of analysis will become the role set including the new relationship we added until finally we will have the complete or as nearly complete set of relationships we want to consider and to make some meaningful statements about. In this role set we will not include, for example, the counselor's relation to his wife or to her husband. We will assume that in their home there was love and understanding. So to the extent that this assumption was not true, our model will be inadequate.

If the reader will keep our unit of analysis—the role set—in mind, we hope now to be able to proceed more rapidly by not having to repeat all over again everything we said before. Probably no problem vexed the implementation of the counseling program more than the question of what was the counselor's role *vis-à-vis* the role of the supervisor in relation to employees. This became one of the most discussed issues of the counseling program; it was never completely resolved over the twenty years of the program's existence.

THE COUNSELOR'S ROLE VIS-À-VIS THE SUPERVISOR'S ROLE IN RELATION TO EMPLOYEES

Questions Asked of Counselors by Supervisors

We will start our analysis in the same way as we did with the employees by looking at the kinds of questions which the supervisors asked of counselors. At times he asked questions of the same order as employees. As shown in Figure 12.2 in the preceding chapter, he wanted information (see Box B). He also wanted to know, "What the hell is going on here?" i.e., why he was demoted or not promoted?, etc. (see Box C). He also faced personal decisions at work and outside of work of practically the same character as the worker, "Should I stay or quit; how do I get promoted?" etc. (see Box D).

Among the supervisors there were also persons very much like Jim Evans where the questions were coming from the right end up and where counseling could help. But in addition to these questions there was a particular set of questions, which we now show in Figure 13.2 and would now like to consider.

FIGURE 13.2

KINDS OF QUESTIONS ASKED OF COUNSELORS BY SUPERVISORS
(Directly or Implied)

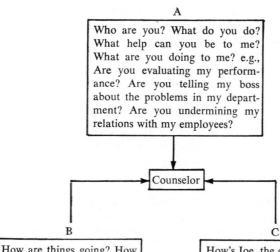

A

Who are you? What do you do? What help can you be to me? What are you doing to me? e.g., Are you evaluating my performance? Are you telling my boss about the problems in my department? Are you undermining my relations with my employees?

Counselor

B

How are things going? How do things in my department look? What kind of records do you keep? How do you use them? How can you help people without telling them anything? How can you help me without telling me anything?

C

How's Joe, the guy I referred you to, doing? He's a joker, isn't he? How can I do my job with some of the lemons I have in my department? How can I do my job with the s.o.b. boss I have? Are you just getting their side of the story? Whose side are you on—my side or their side? Don't you see the tough spot I'm in? Can I trust you to get a fair picture of the situation in my department?

It will be noticed that all these questions pertain to, "What is my role, as supervisor, in relation to your role, as counselor, with regard to *my* people in *my* territory, which, by the way, Mr. Counselor, you keep calling *your* territory?" They are all questions pertaining to the role set we showed in Figure 13.1.

From Figure 13.2 it can be seen that:

(1) The supervisor was concerned not only with, "Who are you? What do you do? and What help can you be to me?" but also and far more with, "What are you doing to me, particularly in my relation to my employee and my boss?" (see Box A).

(2) He wanted information about what the counselor was finding out about the human problems among the workers in his department (see Box B).

(3) He wanted understanding from the counselor about *his* role set; that is, his man-in-the-middle role-bind (see Box C).

Examples of misunderstanding of the counselor's role

Probably some examples would help. At the conclusion of a series of conferences on counseling with line supervisors, the two counselors who held the meeting summed up their impressions as follows:

"Many of the supervisors expressed surprise over learning that the counselors would not take any direct action as a result of their interviews with the employees. Some of the supervisors thought that some change had taken place in their status following an interview with the counselor. They assumed that the counselor must have played some part in bringing this about or in recommending that this change be made."

*   *   *   *   *

"Many of the supervisors expressed a strong interest in the kind of records we keep as well as the uses we made of them. The counselors talked freely about these records and indicated that for the most part they provided a means through which the counselors could review their own participation in the interview and thus could improve their skills. One supervisor in particular said that he was glad the counselor had brought up this discussion of records since he had often had questions about our recording procedures but had never had enough courage to ask us about them."

*   *   *   *   *

"Some of the higher ranking supervisors who attended the conferences said that they were always under the impression that the chief purpose of the counselors was to report trends on what they observed to upper management. They were surprised when told that while the counselors did from time to time report general observations with regard to employee attitudes to higher management, this was considered to be a somewhat incidental part of the counselor's job."

*   *   *   *   *

"Some of the newer supervisors in the conference felt that in spite of the counselors' protestations to the contrary, they (the counselors) had always talked over the results of the interviews with line supervision. In view of this they had expected that they would be similarly favored by counseling now that they were serving in a supervisory capacity themselves."

*   *   *   *   *

"It was implied that some of the indirect ways in which resistance was expressed toward the counseling activity was through ignoring the counselor's presence by constantly being too busy to see him, by making appointments and then not keeping them, and by resisting the counselor's taking employees off the job on the grounds that they were always too busy."

Early Statements of the Role Relationship

When the counseling program was first started, the activity of counseling was stated almost exclusively in terms of employees. No mention was made that the supervisors would be counseled too. The relations of counselors to supervision were not specified except in terms of (1) don't interfere with his duties and responsibilities and (2) don't violate the confidences of employees.

The counselors were well aware that they should not do anything to come between the supervisor and the workers reporting to him. Yet in the early developmental stages of the program, they thought that some of the problems they encountered should be brought to the supervisor's attention in some form but they were not sure just how this could be done without violating the employees' confidences. In the early records, for example, frequent references were made to "working through the supervisor" or "indirectly counseling the supervisor," but there were no prescriptions as to how this could be done without infringing upon the supervisor's role or violating the confidences of employees. In these early records, statements of this order appeared.

"He (the counselor) will not assume any of the duties or responsibilities of the supervisor. He should be considered as a specialist in human relations, free to devote his entire time to study of employee problems. It is therefore thought that in addition to interviewing employees it may be a distinct help to supervisors *in counseling them with regard to the human aspects of their supervisory jobs.*"

*   *   *   *   *

"The counselor should interview employees and where the problem resides in the individual's attitude, the counselor's course of action is to interview. But where the problem is one where it requires some direct action of some sort, he should find ways of *indirectly counseling the supervisor.*"

*   *   *   *   *

"I talked to the department chief in the assistant superintendent's office. *I outlined our interpretation of the problem* pointing out that the employee had been babied for several years while he was out sick, and then placed on a job paying him much more than his performance would warrant. *I then pointed out* that he had been transferred and downgraded too many times since the depression started—each one meant that he, who already believed himself partially disabled, had to learn a new job and adjust himself to work for which he was not suited. Each one of these adjustments was difficult in itself, and in addition to that, they carried with them a reduction in his rate of pay. The real basis for the employee's complaint was a protest against being moved around too much. On the surface he could not accept the explanation that has been given him about his hourly rate, as 'they' had been able to pay his predecessor six cents more an hour than he was being paid."

*   *   *   *   *

"I happened into the assistant superintendent's office today and he inquired about the progress we were making in the experiment. *I told him* that overall we were going along very nicely, but I was beginning to get a little concerned because employees were asking questions of me regarding hourly wages and piece rates that I thought *would be very difficult for supervisors to answer.* I felt that these questions should be answered but I didn't believe that the situation had stabilized sufficiently to give the answers. *I told him* that we did not want to antagonize the supervisor needlessly. *I also pointed out* that the individual employee has to be very much upset before he takes a problem to the supervisor."

* * * * *

"Mr. D., the department chief, stopped me to inquire about our progress. *I told him* that I was getting a lot of talk about piece rates and hourly rates. *I also pointed out* that I believed they would have to get a much better statement ready for employees regarding the new piece rates than they have at the present time."

* * * * *

"I talked to the department chief and said that some supervisors were worried about my getting information that might be used against them. *I told him* (the department chief) that I hoped we *could work with this condition informally,* that is, I would give all of the supervisors plenty of opportunity to know what I was doing and whether a problem concerned only them and their people. I hope to be able to work out some kind of a plan with each individual. *I also told him that I did not plan to take anything up the line for discussion without first talking it over with him.* The department chief pointed out that this might not always be possible but seemed to appreciate the thought at any rate."

* * * * *

"I spent quite a bit of time with Mr. L. in his department. I have a feeling that he believes that this experiment is another brain-trust idea and that it won't last long. He does not see how it can accomplish anything unless we are lucky enough to find an operator who needs some help such as a job for his boy or financial advice. He feels that he knows the problems of his operators as well as anyone and there is nothing much we can do to help them."

Problems of New and Inexperienced Counselors

In the early days of the program the counselors were few. They were mature men with a wealth of shop experience, so the counseling supervisor was not too worried about this rather wide interpretation of working through the problems and indirect counseling of supervision without violating the confidences of employees or interfering with the supervisor's role. But as the program expanded and new and younger counselors with more counseling theory and less shop experience entered the counseling organization, new problems appeared. For example:

The new counselor would approach the supervisor with a statement that one of his employees wished to talk with him. Some supervisors would react by saying, "Why doesn't he come to me himself?" Or they might approach the employee saying, "The counselor told me you wanted to see me. What's on your mind?" In some instances, the employee would respond by denying he had made such a request, particularly if he sensed hostility in the supervisor's attitude. He would feel reluctant to say what was on his mind because of a fear that the supervisor would misunderstand him or misevaluate his meaning. In other instances the supervisor would take something the counselor said out of context and defend himself or do something based on only a partial understanding of the problem which only made matters worse.

To the early counseling supervision, the mere act of informing a supervisor that one of his employees wished to talk to him and had asked the counselor to pass this word along to him did not appear to be a serious violation of confidences. However, if the supervisor subsequently said or did something that had an unfavorable consequence for the employee, the employee might infer that the counselor had gone beyond the simple request made of him and had talked over his case. Thus merely relaying a simple request could be construed as a violation of confidence by the person originating it. For the new counselor this presented very serious and difficult choices about what should and should not be transmitted.

This dilemma became even more acute when supervisors asked them such questions as, "How do things in my department look to you now that you have been in here for a while?" To such questions, what should his attitude be? Should he brush them off by saying that conditions looked pretty good and thereby run the risk of appearing to be ill informed when he knew there were problem situations of which the supervisor was well aware? Or, if he mentioned that there were problems, how far should he go in discussing them? How could he be sure that anything he said might not, from the employee's point of view, be a violation of confidences?

Redefinition of Role Relationship

Experiences such as those cited forced the counseling organization to re-examine the counselor's role in relation to supervision.

Attempts to indirectly counsel or work through supervision could not be accomplished without violating his role prescriptions, particularly those relating to the confidential aspects of his activity. To pursue this course of action threatened to destroy the solid foundation upon which the counseling activity with employees was being built. What then was the solution?

One approach woud be to think of the counseling program as being confined exclusively to employees. This removed the necessity of contacting supervisors except to get their permission to interview their people. This approach, which some of the counselors adopted for a short time, left all the problems of communication with supervisors unsolved and to the counseling organization seemed untenable.

Another approach, and this also was practiced by some of the counselors for short periods of time, was to present themselves to the supervisor in the role of a *helpmate*. For example,

COUNSELOR: (to supervisor) I feel I'm getting on to the lay of the land pretty well here. I was wondering if there are any problems from your point of view upon which I could be of assistance.
SUPERVISOR: Yes, I wish you would interview Mary; she keeps pestering me all the time. Maybe you could see what lies behind it.
COUNSELOR: Why, I haven't met her yet, but I'll see her right away.

This approach sought to gain supervisory support by conveying the impression that the counselor was in effect a willing and helpful worker on the supervisor's staff. The danger in this approach, as the counselor found out, was that the supervisor could construe this in the same way as he would any other task assignment and would expect some sort of feedback on the counselor's progress which would violate the confidential aspect of the program. Also this approach placed the counselor in a subordinate role to the supervisor and this would threaten to undermine his position in the organization.

Throughout the early developmental period of the program, it seems clear in retrospect that the counselors were operating from one point of view toward the employee and from quite a different one toward the supervisor. They did not feel it was a part of their function to correct employee misunderstandings or in any way intercede in their behalf. Yet they also felt that there were some situations in which some outside action should be taken, and they were not too happy to leave this to chance. Since the supervisor was the duly appointed representative of management charged with the responsibility of taking all action pertaining to employees, the counselors concentrated their attention upon the supervisor and the various ways in which he could be stimulated by them to take such actions as they thought were required without violating the confidence of the employee. They kept trying to find some way in which to intervene in the supervisor's role without making it obvious.

The problem with which we are concerned here is encountered by counselors everywhere who are involved in a role set. It is seen in school situations where a student is referred to a counselor because of some problem encountered with the teacher. The counselor, let us assume, as sometimes happens, finds that the teacher was himself responsible in part at least for the student's problem. How should the counselor proceed in such a situation? Should he go to the teacher and review his work with the student? Should he tell the teacher that in his opinion the problem resides at least in part with him? Should he plead with the teacher to try to see the student in a different light and give him another chance? In short, how should he intervene?

At Hawthorne much thought was given to this problem and various approaches to it were tried. But each approach, while it solved some problems, created others. For the Hawthorne counseling organization the solution *lay in redefining the counselor's job as being that of developing a counseling relationship with the supervisor in exactly the same way as he did with all the employees.*

From this point of view the counselor would in no way try to interfere in the relationship between the supervisor and his subordinates. The effectiveness of this relationship was to be determined by the voluntary interactions between the superior and his subordinates. By having the counselor address himself solely to the improvement in the respective attitudes of the two individuals in this superior-subordinate relationship, it was assumed that there would be a resulting improvement in the relationship between them.

This restatement of the counselor's role, it was felt, would remove the ambiguities encountered by the counselor in trying to counsel supervision indirectly and would enable him to adopt a consistent point of view in dealing with everyone in his territory regardless of the position he held.

Perhaps we can clarify how this new approach was supposed to work and did work in the case of Frank Jones.

The case of Frank Jones, according to the supervisor, a lemon

Frank Jones was transferred into the machine department only a few days before his supervisor spoke of him to the counselor in the following words: "It looks as if we've got a lemon in this guy, Frank. He is supposed to be a good man; that is what my boss said, so I put him on stamping. You should see the job he did, he got the letters all out of line. Then I asked him if he could read blueprints; he said he could. I showed him one of our equipment drawings and he said he had never seen anything like that before." (The supervisor continued to mention the various work assignments he had given Frank in the few days that he had been in the department, saying that Frank had been unable to do any of them satisfactorily.)

Two weeks later, according to the counselor, the relationship between Frank and his supervisor deteriorated further. Typical of the supervisor's attitudes were statements such as the following: "We're going to get rid of this guy Frank. I got burned up plenty Saturday. I talked to a guy who used to be a group chief in the place we got Frank from and he said they were sure glad to get rid of him up there because he was such a lemon. They preach to us supervisors that we shouldn't transfer lemons. They should have gotten you counselors in on it before they even transferred a guy like that."

The supervisor then went on to talk about several jobs Frank had botched up. He concluded by suggesting that the counselor take Frank out for an interview and this the counselor arranged to do.

A few days after the interview with Frank, the counselor met with the supervisor in the interviewing room to review the situation. In this discussion the supervisor again launched into a long tirade against Frank, pointing out that his work would not pass inspection and he didn't know how to sharpen his tools, that he was unable to read blueprints, and that he couldn't even get down the correct order number for the jobs he had worked on.

"He puts the micrometer on a part and then holds it way out from himself to take a look at it. *I don't know, maybe the guy's eyes aren't good. You know another guy spoiled a lot of work a while ago. I gave him particular hell. I asked him whether he wasn't able to see. He said he couldn't see very well. We sent him down and found that his lenses were loose. Say!! maybe Frank has got some trouble like that. I'm going to ask him and see what he says."*

The supervisor talked to Frank who said his eyes did bother him and that he had had quite a few headaches and that he would have mentioned it to the supervisor but "things hadn't been going so well between us." The supervisor then arranged for him to be fitted with new prescription goggles.

Later the supervisor told the counselor that Frank was doing much better and Frank himself said he felt much better. "You know," the supervisor said, "we really got a lot of good out of that smoke we had the other day. You and I sat up there smoking and all at once something popped into my head and I thought maybe the guy's eyes aren't so good. You know, all week until you and I started talking about him, I was so mad at him that I didn't pay much attention to what he was actually doing. When I got through with him today he was smiling just like a kid."

But this "redefinition" of the counselor's role (the new policy of the counseling organization) was a unilateral one; the supervisors had not been involved in it. Nor had it been discussed with management from which a policy statement had been issued which said that now counseling was available to supervision. It came in slowly by the back door, so to speak, without anyone seeing too explicitly its organizational significance. In fact it was not until the late 1940's that the counseling organization included lower level supervision in their written and spoken statements concerning the scope of their counseling activities. As a consequence, the counselors were attempting to develop a counseling relationship with supervisors without explicitly saying so. The supervisors did not know they were being counseled because the talks they often had with counselors in which the counselors "listened" were not, from their point of view, "counseling."

Let us review again slowly the changes which came about, each of which alone made sense but which when put together made for a kind of organizational ambiguity.

1. When the counseling program first started, it was addressed to non-supervisory employees. It was thought that supervisors "solved" problems; unlike employees they didn't have them.

2. As they interacted more with supervisors they found this picture was not true. Supervisors had concerns of the same character as employees in which counseling could be of help.
3. But as the program expanded, the counselors felt an increasing need to clarify their role *vis-à-vis* supervision. After getting themselves involved in unsatisfactory kinds of situations from the point of view of maintaining the confidences of employees, they finally decided that a consistent attitude toward both supervision and employees was required. This consistency they felt could be achieved by maintaining a counseling relationship with both parties. They would clarify only for each party his respective attitudes and problems.
4. In this way they would not only help those supervisors described in point 2 above, but also communication between supervisors and employees would be improved indirectly, that is, with no direct intervention by the counselor to facilitate this process.
5. This new policy was reached by the counseling organization itself with little or no attempts to clarify it with supervision or management. This happened because in a sense it was not a new policy at all; it was merely reaffirming the need to maintain consistency in the role set in which they were involved with the role prescriptions set out in Chapter II and finding it difficult. So it was one thing to state this new policy; it was quite another matter, as we shall see later, to carry it out, because this new policy solved nothing about the underlying ambiguity of the counselor's role *vis-à-vis* supervision.

Let us see if we can clarify this in Figure 13.3. Here we show the kinds of responses made by counselors to the questions by supervision for the clarification of the counselors' roles *vis-à-vis* them, that is, the responses to the questions we showed in Figure 13.2. (This is the same kind of analysis we made in Figure 12.3 of the kinds of responses by counselors to the kinds of questions employees asked of them that we showed in Figure 12.2 in the previous chapter.)

We realize that Figure 13.3 can be easily misinterpreted, so let us say what we are trying to communicate by it.

1. Let us start with the new policy. Its purpose was to outlaw very clearly responses C_1, C_2, and C_3 and to state as *ideal* responses D_1, D_2, and D_3.
2. But with the vague definition of establishing a counseling relationship with supervisors and with no explicit policy from management

FIGURE 13.3   KINDS OF RESPONSES MADE BY COUNSELORS
TO SUPERVISION ABOUT THEIR ROLE RELATIONSHIPS
(Explicitly or Implied)

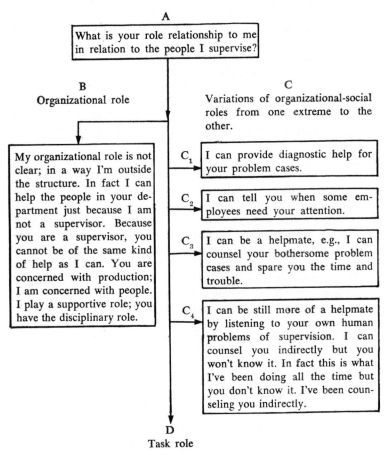

A

What is your role relationship to me in relation to the people I supervise?

B
Organizational role

C
Variations of organizational-social roles from one extreme to the other.

My organizational role is not clear; in a way I'm outside the structure. In fact I can help the people in your department just because I am not a supervisor. Because you are a supervisor, you cannot be of the same kind of help as I can. You are concerned with production; I am concerned with people. I play a supportive role; you have the disciplinary role.

C₁ I can provide diagnostic help for your problem cases.

C₂ I can tell you when some employees need your attention.

C₃ I can be a helpmate, e.g., I can counsel your bothersome problem cases and spare you the time and trouble.

C₄ I can be still more of a helpmate by listening to your own human problems of supervision. I can counsel you indirectly but you won't know it. In fact this is what I've been doing all the time but you don't know it. I've been counseling you indirectly.

D
Task role

I can counsel you explicitly

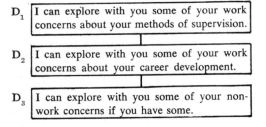

D₁ I can explore with you some of your work concerns about your methods of supervision.

D₂ I can explore with you some of your work concerns about your career development.

D₃ I can explore with you some of your non-work concerns if you have some.

about counseling being available to supervision, a constant gap between C_4 and D_1, D_2, and D_3 was maintained. From the point of view of the counselors, much help could be given and was given by indirect counseling, i.e., by just listening to the supervisor's problems of supervision and where the supervisor, in his terms, was not aware that he was being counseled. That such beneficial outcomes occurred in fact in some instances we are not questioning; we are questioning the underlying ambiguity that still remained.

3. Nondirective counseling is a technical term in psychotherapy. It means addressing the expressed or implied feelings of the client's discourse instead of its manifest subject matter. In such counseling the client knows he is being counseled. This is what we mean by Box D in Figure 13.3. The phrase "indirect counseling" is a layman's word; it has no technical meaning in counseling theory; so Box C_4 is our attempt to state what we think it meant.

4. Referring to Box B in Figure 13.3, there was an implication that the social maintenance functions of supervision were being turned over to counseling while supervision was left with primarily its task functions. The counselor was supportive, nurturing, and permissive; the supervisor was disciplinary, evaluative, and authoritarian.

5. For some supervisors this division of labor was satisfactory. But for some supervisors who were trying to reconcile these two functions, it was not. At the outset, but later modified by experience, they felt that the chief avenue by which they could influence their employees was taken away from them, in spite of all the good intentions and reassurances by counselors that they were not. This cleavage showed up again in relation to the counselor's role *vis-à-vis* the trainer's role in matters of supervision and so to this we will now turn.

Counseling in Relation to Other Personnel Services

Placement and Medical

But before we do, let us consider first briefly the counselor's relations to some of the other personnel relations units, such as, for example, employment, placement, medical, safety, etc. In the early stages little attention and thought were given to these relations and how counseling might have been viewed from their point of view. The whole attention of the counseling organization was focused on establishing the counselor's role with employees and lower levels of supervision. But as time went on, it became obvious that the understanding and acceptance of counseling by these other personnel services were also as important in some cases as its understanding and acceptance by employees and lower levels of supervision.

It was not until 1944 (eight years after the program had started), however, that a series of conferences were arranged with the representatives of all the different industrial relations units in order *to explain* and *define for them* what the counseling role was *supposed to be* and *how they needed to relate their activities to it.* (Informal discussions had, of course, been held with them from time to time before this.) We have underlined the one-way character of this communication because we wish to return to it later.

But first we will need to understand the position the counseling organization had reached regarding their role relations *vis-à-vis* these other personnel services and thus what they were trying to communicate to them. Let us review briefly some of the problems they encountered in terms of which their position became formulated.

1. Take, for example, *placement.* The counselor could not intercede directly in placement problems any more than he could with supervisory problems (see the case of Jim Evans). There was no direct referral from counselors to placement people because the formal procedures required that the employee go first to his supervisor. For the counselor to refer an employee directly to placement would therefore interfere with one of the supervisor's prerogatives. On the other hand, placement people could call the counselor's attention to placement problems which were of concern to them or the counselor could ask for this service which would be of great help to him. But were this arrangement entered into—as it was at times—the counselor was in the same helpmate or handmaiden role he had been with supervision. One good turn deserves another. How did the counselor return the favor of the placement man when the latter asked the counselor, "How are you getting along with Jim (my placement problem)?" By indirect counseling, i.e., by treating the placement man in the same way as he did the supervisor? But this did not coincide sometimes with placement's notions of reciprocation.

2. Take, for example, *medical*. Counselors often encountered employees who thought they required medical attention. Counselors could not refer them directly to the medical office because the formal procedure required that they obtain first a pass from their supervisors. If the counseling organization tried to establish a relationship with the medical organization—as was tried—by asking them to provide them with names of employees on the repeater sickness list (information that would have been very helpful to them), the medical organization could respond by saying—as they one time did— "This should be a two-way street; as a return for this favor, you should provide us with the names of workers interviewed who require medical attention." When the head of counseling had to say —as he did—"But these interviews are confidential, the counselors are not qualified medical diagnosticians, and moreover referrals need to come from line supervision," the medical department in turn had to respond—as it did—"but medical information is also confidential and medical people enjoy the same right of privileged communication as does the counselor" (and, it could have added, which is far more institutionally sanctioned than the counselor's). Had the counseling head responded to this by saying—*as he did not*— "But we can counsel you indirectly and you might find this helpful"—even an elementary student of human interactions should be able to predict the response of the medical organization.

From these examples it can be seen how step by step the counseling organization came to the conclusion that it had to develop the *same kind of relationship* with each of the units of personnel relations as it had developed—or tried to develop—with supervision. But when this *same kind of relationship* was worked out in terms of establishing a counseling relationship with them, paradoxes appeared, of which one of the most extreme forms appeared in relation to the medical department.

As we have said, in 1944 the counseling organization did organize a series of meetings with the various units of personnel relations in order to explain to them the logic of their activities— that is, the reasons why they could not violate the confidences of employees. But there is no evidence in the recordings of these meetings that anyone discussed explicitly how the counseling organization was doing violence to their conventional notions of reciprocity and of fair exchange, i.e., the kind of return that is deserved by a good turn. So the counseling organization came to a position of *defining* not only the kind of help that it could provide, but also of *defining* the kind of help that they (the other personnel services) ought to want from them, if they understood counseling correctly. This is a difficult communication to make.

Supervisory Training

It was in relation to supervisory training, however, where the role relationships between counselor and trainer became acute. In Figure 13.4 is diagrammed the role set that we now want to consider.

FIGURE 13.4

THE COUNSELOR'S ROLE VIS-À-VIS SUPERVISORY TRAINING

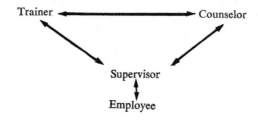

Again the question came up about the role of the trainer *vis-à-vis* the counselor in relation to the help that each could provide to the supervisor with regard to his relation to employees. Supervisory training was the one personnel activity in the counselor's role set with which an opportunity was provided for working out a cooperative and mutually reinforcing relationship without violating employee confidences or interceding in another's organizational mission. Yet the full potential of this relationship was never realized.

There was some exchange of ideas and concepts. In their training sessions with supervision, the training organization spent some time on the ideas underlying counseling; they prepared a very well-received brochure on "Complaints and Grievances" based on counseling concepts and experiences. The counseling organization in turn supplied some carefully edited case material for training discussions and in later years provided guest speakers and discussion leaders. There was some interchange of personnel between the two activities. Yet supervisory training reported to the man who also headed up counseling during only half of the twenty years of the program's existence and then only intermittently. Essentially, the two activities tended to develop separately. Why was this?

The major force making for this separation was the very same cleavage that had developed between counseling and supervision while trying to work out their respective roles in relation to employees. If supervisory training was to enter the field of human relations training for supervision, it would have to operate quite counter to the one upon which the development of counseling was based. The latter was based on the premise that the supervisor would be primarily concerned with matters of production and discipline while counseling would take care of the human side; obviously the development of human relations training for supervision would be stunted by such an assumption.

So two different orientations developed in the Company with regard to the supervisor's role in relation to his employees as people. Counseling and supervisory training (and later management development) brought the difference into focus.

The Development of Two Different Orientations with Regard to the Functions of Supervision

Let us show these different orientations by stating first their underlying assumptions, and then modify them later in the way they were resolved.

The underlying assumptions of the counseling orientation

1. Supervision cannot do the job of counseling because of its authority relations with employees.
2. As a result supervision cannot take care of many of its human problems, as in some ways they are the cause of them.
3. To take care of them a third party called a counselor has to be introduced.
4. The counselor will not interfere in any way with the supervisor's authority and task functions, i.e., getting out production.

5. The counselor will not violate the confidences of employees.
6. The counselor will not try to change the Company's formal structure; he will only work through it.
7. The counselor will help the employee to solve his own personal problems, make his own personal decisions, initiate his own personal action, etc.
8. This is the road to constructive and enduring social changes.
9. Self-initiated change is the "best" change; all other changes tend to become manipulative. Change comes from within and not from without.
10. This self-initiated change is generated by the counselor's catalytic role in the two-person encounter.
11. By also developing a counseling relationship with all the parties with whom the counselor has to interact, the counseling organization will allow each party to *change itself*. And by doing so it will maintain consistency and congruence with its role model.

The underlying assumptions of the training orientation

1. The supervisor's behavior (his interpersonal style of leadership, his sensitivity about people's feelings, his social skills, his production-orientation) has something to do with the work concerns of employees.
2. Human relations training addressed to improving the supervisor's sensitivity, social skills, and interpersonal competence should be introduced.
3. Although the supervisor cannot counsel the employee in the strict sense of the term, he should supervise his people in terms of the same overall conceptual framework of counseling regarding the determinants of worker motivation, productivity, and satisfaction.
4. The supervisor's task function and his social-human function (his people function) cannot remain bifurcated. The supervisor cannot be left with only his task functions to perform. These two aspects of the supervisor's role have to become integrated.
5. Without intending to, the role of counselor is not helping to resolve this problem of integration.

SUPERVISORY PARTICIPATION IN COUNSELING

In our analysis of the counselor's role in relation to that of the supervisor we have oversimplified the actual situation that obtained between them at different times in order to clarify the underlying organizational problem that was present throughout the life of the counseling program. We would now like to correct for this oversimplification. The question we will be addressing is whether the supervisors, through their actual interactions with the counselors, came to perceive counseling as a help to them and if so in what ways. The data presented in Figure 13:5 will help us to consider this question.

FIGURE 13.5

SUPERVISORY PARTICIPATION IN COUNSELING*
(Averages based upon counseling activity reports
for four quarterly periods in 1949)

N = 1,000

26% or 260 supervisors	*Level A* Came to perceive the counselors as a possible source of help to them in resolving their own concerns. — 16% were helped — 10% were not helped	680 or 68% sought the counselor's help — 31% were helped — 37% were not helped
42% or 420 supervisors	*Level B* Perceived the counselor as a possible help to them in dealing with employee problems. — 15% were helped — 27% were not helped	
28% or 280 supervisors	*Level C* Passively accepted the program	
4% or 40 supervisors	*Level D* Resisted the program	

* The criteria for the discriminations made in arriving at this chart were of the same order as those used in compiling Figure 4.1. The supervisors whose participation in the program was appraised averaged 1,094 per quarter and included all those in the three lower levels of supervision in the counseling territories except a small number, ranging from 53 to 127 per quarter, who could not be included because of shift changes, transfers, demotions, etc. Comparable data for each year from 1947 through 1951 support the findings of the 1949 study but could not be included because of slight differences in their compilation.

Figure 13.5 can best be thought of as representing the emergent perceptions of the counseling program developed by supervisors over varying periods of time. If we assume that before the program was introduced supervisors had no perception of it at all, then we can say that this figure represents, as accurately as we can with the data we have, how they saw it in 1949, thirteen years after it was introduced.

We see that in 1949 the supervisors in the counselors' territories were, according to their perceptions of the program, at four different levels. These ranged upward from those who resisted the activity, level D (4%), to those who passively accepted it for their employees, level C (28%), to those who saw it as a help to them in relation to their employees, level B (42%), to those who perceived it as being of some possible help to them personally, level A (26%).

The movement of individuals between these levels we would assume was generally upward because the counselors were striving to influence them in that direction. We want particularly to comment upon (1) those at level B and (2) the emergence of those at level A from level B.

As the program was formally structured, level B represents the optimum condition sought. It was presented to supervisors as a program for employees, and to the extent that supervisors saw it and used it in this light, their participation was considered satisfactory. This meant that they would lend their support to the program, take the initiative in explaining it to their employees, answer employees' questions about it, introduce counselors to employees, cooperate in arranging interviews, keep the counselors informed of changes in personnel, changes in work schedules, and other changes which might affect them, and call the counselors' attention to employees who they thought would benefit from counseling and to group situations which were disturbing to the supervisor. At this level the program was conceived as a service to supervision and, in 1949, 42% of them perceived it and used it in this light with positive outcomes for 36% of them (15% of total supervisors) in any one quarterly interval. But these supervisors, be it noted, thought of counseling as being for someone else, it was "out there," so to speak, on the same basis as any other personnel service. For these supervisors a counseling relationship did not exist.

As noted previously, the counselors came to realize that level B performance was not satisfactory in many cases because the supervisor himself, his attitudes and methods of supervision, were a part of the problem with which the counselor was dealing and there needed to be some change in him before a satisfactory resolution could come about. Thus the counselors strove to influence as many supervisors as they could to move up to level A. But, again, as previously noted, they tried to do this indirectly, that is, without formally extending the program to include supervisors on the same basis as employees.

One of the main arguments for why the supervisors were not formally included within the scope of the program was the counselors' belief that this would be presumptuous of them and would possibly antagonize those who otherwise were cooperating at level B. At issue here was a subtle but important status factor. In terms of formal status the counselor was subordinate to the supervisor and to include him in a program which he pictured as being designed for his subordinates, the counselors felt, might be humiliating to him and cause him to feel that his status with his subordinates had been lowered. (Supervisors didn't have problems, they solved them.) Acting on this premise, as we have said, the counselors tried through indirect counseling (that is, without a direct confrontation, "I am a counselor, you are my client") to keep the status factor unmolested while developing an unspoken but mutually understood recognition of how talking things out might be as beneficial to the supervisor as to the employee. They did this by listening attentively to everything the supervisor said even in a casual chat and by displaying an interest in him as a person. The outcome of this activity is reflected in level A, 26% of the supervisory force moved upward from level B, and for 62% of this group (16% of the total supervisory force) indirect counseling seemed to be helpful.

There is one further point that needs comment. It will be noted that a larger percentage of supervisors were, in the opinion of the counselors, helped by interviewing than were employees, 16% compared to 10% (Figure 4.1). Various factors may be involved here: (1) The supervisory force were a more select group, their educational level was generally higher than those in the work force, and they were more experienced in solving problems and making decisions. (2) They comprised a smaller and relatively more permanent group, thus affording the counselors more time to develop a relationship with them. (3) The requirement that supervisory approval was needed to take employees off the job, the handling of time tickets, and other arrangements brought the counselors into frequent contact with them. (4) Unlike the worker, many supervisors who had both men and women counselors in their organizations could talk to either a man or woman counselor, and a good many men preferred to discuss some of their personal problems with women. These factors together with the counselor's first concern upon entering an organization to establish a favorable relationship with each supervisor could help to account for the difference in the percentage of those helped noted above.

In summary, while the underlying ambiguity in the role of the counselor in relation to that of the supervisor was never resolved, through their policy of nonintervention and indirect counseling the counselors were able to be helpful to some 31% of the supervisors in any one quarterly interval. At level B, in Figure 13.5, no counseling relationship existed so the ambiguity in their role relationships was less than at level A where a counseling relationship of sorts was implicit. Whether a more formally structured relationship, which presumably would have resolved the ambiguity, would have led to increased participation of the supervisors at level A is an open question. If higher status and more professional counselors were provided for supervisors, this might well have been the case. But for the program as it was structured, with all its attendant status problems, the ambiguity in the counselor's role *vis-à-vis* the supervisor's was not entirely dysfunctional. In the opinion of the counselors many supervisors who responded to their suggestion that they go out for a smoke would have bridled at the suggestion that they go out for an interview.

Participation of Other Personnel Services in the Counseling Program

As the counselors conceived their role, there was no need to establish a counseling relationship with other personnel services as there was with supervisors. The supervisor was a part of the primary group to which the counselor was relating himself whereas other personnel services were regarded by the counselor as being peripheral to it. Consequently the counselors, as we have indicated, were slow in examining their role in relation to these other services and when they did, it was with reference to the question of what communications could be made to them which would not violate confidences or short-circuit the supervisor. The only answer they could come up with was to encourage referrals from these agencies.

As time went on an arrangement was worked out with placement, safety, and medical whereby they did make referrals to the counseling organization and the counseling organization did attempt to follow through on these cases and report their progress or lack of progress to those making the referrals. However, the requirement that confidences be observed limited such feedback to rather general observations, a communication of doubtful value in many cases. Furthermore these arrangements were informal and subject to change at the discretion of either party entering into them. The outcome was far short of an organizational solution.

In principle or in theory the positions of counseling and training in relation to the supervisors were not irreconcilable. Both parties in a theoretical sense realized the merits of the other's position. But in organizational practice the integration of these two positions is sometimes difficult to achieve, as the development of the counseling program indicated.

Had this not been so, it would be hard to explain why the counseling person in charge of both counseling and supervisory training in its early period would have relinquished this position and the opportunity which it gave him for influencing this integration. Would he not have stated strongly the need for this integration? The records available to us show no such concern. Although the collaboration between them (counseling and supervisory training) fulfilled the formal requirements that organizational collaboration required, the real differences between them were never explicitly discussed nor a more active collaboration between them sought. Each went on its own separate way.

With this resolution, however, the possibility of achieving a better coordination (integration) of counseling and supervisory training between themselves was relinquished. The problem now became the responsibility of the new executives to whom both counseling and supervisory training formally reported. Someday they and their supervisors would have to take a stand on this issue and reach a decision.

SUMMARY

In this chapter we have tried to show the problems the counselors had in clarifying their role *vis-à-vis* supervision, supervisory training, and other personnel services. That the counselor's role was unique and quite different from theirs as time went on became clear. What was not clear was how the counselor's specialized role could be integrated with the more traditionally differentiated roles of supervision, training, and others which were also concerned with the human problems of employees. The more the counselors tried to differentiate their role, the more they highlighted the problem of integration—the integration of the roles comprising their role set whose members had also something to say and do about employees and their concerns.

Stating the problem at a higher level of generality, it looked as if the total positive outcomes that the counseling program was seeking required a noninstitutionalized role for their manifestation. But how to do this, that is, how to introduce a noninstitutionalized role in a highly institutionalized setting was the organizational problem that the counseling organization was facing, and that it was having difficulty was not surprising. But about this, we shall speculate more later after we have completed our pedestrian walk around the circuit and considered the last, but not least important, member of the counselor's role set—management.

CHAPTER XIV

Counseling and the Logics
of Organization

IN THIS CHAPTER we want to look at counseling in relation to the Company's (1) communication structure, (2) job structure, and (3) control structure, and finally (4) to the union structure.

COUNSELING IN RELATION TO THE COMMUNICATION STRUCTURE

In Figure 14.1 below we have diagrammed schematically the relations we now want to consider.

We are calling the diagram schematic because all we want to show is that (1) the Company had an extended line organization of many levels of supervision and management (just how many need not concern us; it changed during the twenty years of the program; let us say it was about six); and (2) in this extended communication chain, the lower levels tended to be called supervisors; the upper levels tended to be called management. (Just where this division occurred need not concern us here; when we split it between the third and fourth levels we are being somewhat arbitrary.) The point of the diagram is to show the relations we will be considering. Although we will be considering primarily the counselor's relation to the upper levels of management, we shall not be doing this apart from his relation to lower levels of supervision and employees and to their relations to each other. Our unit of analysis will be the role set made up of the four parties, as shown in Figure 14.1.

FIGURE 14.1

THE COUNSELOR'S ROLE VIS-À-VIS MANAGEMENT

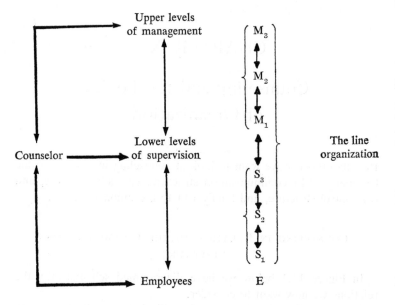

Reports to Top Management

In Chapter III we mentioned the nature of the reports which the counseling organization made to top management. During the early years of the program they consisted of reports on general topics which were issued at the time the counseling organization thought them to be of current concern to both management and employees, such as attitudes of long-service employees, short-service employees, women workers, first-level supervisors, etc. At the end of the year these reports were consolidated in an annual attitude survey of the entire plant. As these interim and annual attitude surveys were based upon the problems which concerned employees and supervisors brought up in their interviews with counselors, they were not attitude surveys in the strict sense of the term. However, it was felt that the counselors were in a strategic position to sense the prevailing attitudes and sentiments of employees and that this kind of information, without violating the confidences of employees, could be provided and would be of use to top management.

Although reports of this character continued during the twenty years of the program, as time went on they became fewer in number and more general in character; that is, only the most general uniformities of employee attitude and sentiment which would not identify any particular individual or shop were reported. This development arose from the same set of forces which turned the counselor's relation to supervision in the direction of maintaining a counseling relationship. Let us look at these forces.

In the early years of the program, far more than in its later period, management consulted the counseling organization with regard to the probable consequences for employees of certain proposed technological or organizational changes. In such cases, as in the case of Jim Evans, questions were coming from the right end up and counseling could be helpful. But also, just as a lower-level supervisor could ask the counselor for a report of progress on a lemon that he had referred to him; so could the upper levels of management ask the counseling organization for a report on a specific problem in one of their particular shops. In the beginning these requests were a little more difficult for the counselors to turn into a counseling relationship with the manager. They became involved in such situations as the following.

The Case of Manager White

In a newly formed shop in which a new product was to be manufactured, great care was taken by the piece work department to establish equitable labor grades and piece rates for the jobs to be done. Only employees had been transferred into this shop who had been on what was considered to be similar work in another shop. However, many of the employees on their new jobs in this new shop felt that their piece rates were too tight and that they could never get their earnings back to their former level.

When they came into this shop, management had pegged their earnings at a level equal to their previous average hourly earnings. The difference between what they were paid and what they actually earned on the new rates was to be made up by what was called an executive allowance. This was an amount added to the earnings of a group in order to assure them of the same level of take-home pay. It was understood that after a specified period of time for learning and gaining proficiency in the new jobs, the allowance would be reduced by small amounts over a period of time until it reached zero. At this time it was felt that the efficiency of the workers would have increased sufficiently so that the take-home pay on these new jobs would be the same or even more than it had been on their old jobs.

In this situation the employees complained that the piece rates were not properly set, that they were too tight, and that they would never get their earnings back up to their previous level. The supervisors reviewed these complaints with the piece rate people who concluded that the rates were properly set. The employees then turned with their complaints to the union, but the union representatives felt they could not do anything about them. The management refused to change the rates on the grounds that they were fairly established and would yield earnings as high or higher than the rates on their former jobs, if the workers would apply themselves. In this situation pressure mounted, and while output rose, the increase was not sufficient to offset the scheduled reduction in allowances.

Employee complaints became more vehement. When the higher levels of management conferred with the lower levels of supervision, they got the impression that the supervisors who were directly in charge also thought that the rates were too tight. From this they inferred that the first-level supervisors might not be putting forth a sincere effort to convince employees that the rates were fair. Because of the conflicting points of view expressed with respect to the fairness of the piece rates, Mr. White, the manager in charge, *requested that the counselors provide him with an objective appraisal.*

The report prepared by the counseling organization described the attitudes of the employees in detail, emphasizing the point that the employees could see little difference between the work that they were on before and that performed in the new shop. The activities of the supervisors were described as positive in support of management's objectives. The report concluded that the main problem was to develop more positive employee attitudes toward the job and to get the employees' attention off the rate question. In order to do this, the report suggested that a small improvement in some of the rates would relieve the pressure, indicate the sincerity of management's intentions, and induce a more constructive approach to the job. This was substantially what the lower level supervisors had been recommending.

After preparing the report, the counselors reviewed it with every supervisor in the line so that they would not feel they were being short-circuited, and so that when the report reached the manager who had requested it, it would have been approved, in effect, by all the supervisors in the shop.

After reading the report, Mr. White, the manager, said that he thought it was a fair description of employee attitudes, but he took issue with the suggested remedy, saying that it looked as though the counselors were in league with the employees. He also suggested that the counselors by reviewing the report with his line supervisors had crystallized supervisory sentiment in favor of the employees.

Adjustments were eventually made on some of the rates with the result that output rose and earnings not only reached the level to which the employees were accustomed in their former shop but surpassed them. However, this result did not endear the counseling organization to Mr. White. He now began to question whether they could be trusted in the achievement of management objectives.

From the recommendations the counseling organization made, it can be seen that they could have been accused of being in league with the lower levels of supervision just as well as in league with the employees. Moreover, had they highlighted in their report the opinions of lower level supervision, they might have confirmed the manager's suspicions and justified him in bringing greater pressure to bear on the line. In this way the counseling organization could have been accused of being in league with the manager by the lower levels of supervision.

In attempting to report on employee attitudes in such situations, and to get caught up in the dynamics of an organization undergoing change, the counselors ran a grave risk of jeopardizing their role completely and becoming cast in the role of a contender. Although some more instances could be cited to show how the counselors got their fingers burned, the above illustration is sufficient to show the nature of the problem confronting the counselors in their relations to the role set we are now considering.

In this respect the counselor's relation *vis-à-vis* top management was as ambiguous as his relation *vis-à-vis* supervision and *vis-à-vis* supervisory training. Nobody seemed to want to talk about this. And the processes of counseling—as such—could not get it on the table. Unintentionally the counselors themselves and their orientation seemed to be pushing the problem under the rug. Let us explore this possibility further.

The solution by which the counselors resolved these problems for themselves was once again to *define for themselves,* without any explicit discussion with the other parties in the role set, what their role should be. As they met each new relationship—supervisor, other personnel services, and now top management—and became entangled in requests for a kind of help which they could not provide, they had to redefine their role in each of these new relationships in a way which was consistent with what the role model had prescribed their relations to employees should be. But with each new relationship this redefinition became more difficult. They thought they had solved it with supervision, but then it became more difficult with supervisory training, and now finally it reappeared all over again with top management.

In their endeavor to maintain consistency with their role model in all of the relationships with which they were involved, the lines of communication in the organizational system got clogged up. It was difficult enough to develop a counseling relationship with the workers, still more difficult with supervisors, still more difficult with other personnel services, and almost supraorganizational with management. All the questions from management were coming from the wrong end up. And to get them from the right end up was an organizational anachronism. Let us see why by taking up one management question at a time.

THE COUNSELOR'S POSITION IN THE JOB STRUCTURE

What was the counselor's labor grade?

Let us start by examining the counselor's position in the payment structure. For purposes of payment every job in the company was either (1) hourly rated or salaried and (2) graded or ungraded. As practically all hourly rated jobs were graded, these categories generated primarily three instead of four groups, as shown in Figure 14.2 by Boxes A, B, and E.

For our purposes here, however, we have added another distinction to Box E; that is, (1) jobs where job evaluations were made and where it was found difficult to establish a labor grade,

FIGURE 14.2

WAGE AND SALARY CLASSIFICATION

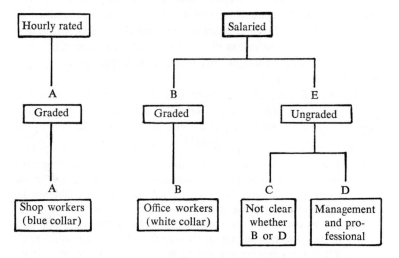

and so in this sense remained ungraded but where nevertheless a labor grade was arbitrarily assigned as a benchmark (see Box C), and (2) jobs where a job evaluator would fear to tread and so were unequivocally ungraded (see Box D).

Looking at Figure 14.2 we have added still other distinctions as follows:

(1) Jobs A, B, C, and D can be thought of as going in the direction from low to high status in organizational-social space.

(2) Jobs A and B roughly correspond to shop and office workers in socio-technical space; also they correspond roughly to blue collar and white collar in social space.

(3) Jobs D are clearly upper management or professional jobs.

If the reader would like to play a game, he might try to predict what kind of a job counseling was—A, B, C, or D? Well, he guessed it the very first time. Counseling was an ambiguous C job. It had an ungraded grade.[1]

[1] For an explanation of the labor grade system, see Chapter VII, pp. 139–140.

Although counseling was assigned finally the top labor grade as a benchmark, let us see how this came about. After counseling became an established personnel function, several attempts were made to grade the counseling activity. The first attempt resulted in a labor grade which put counseling one step above a departmental secretary and the equivalent of a technical specialist. As the counseling organization thought this grade was inappropriate, it was never used.

The second attempt was more serious. An experienced labor grading engineer studied the counseling activity with great thoroughness for a month or so. At the end of this period he concluded that counseling could not be graded because:

(1) The criteria for some job dimensions, such as education, experience, analytical ability, judgment, ingenuity, responsibility for monetary loss, etc., by which a job was scored could not be applied to counseling in their conventional sense.

(2) For example, did the counselor exercise judgment? According to the conventional way of looking at it, because the counselor's job did not involve the giving of advice, direction, etc., it involved no judgment or decision making. According to the way the counselor looked at it, however, he was making very important judgments and decisions.

(3) For example, did the counselor exercise ingenuity? From the conventional point of view, passive listening to an employee did not seem to require any particular inventiveness, novel solutions, or ingenuity. From the counselor's point of view, proactive listening which entailed the making of appropriate responses to employee questions required considerable ingenuity.

(4) Moreover, the counselor had no responsibility for monetary loss, such as making a mistake that might ruin an expensive piece of equipment. He had no responsibility for others; he was trying to get others to assume responsibility.

These problems sorely vexed the labor grading engineer. In all his experience at Western he had never met a situation like this, so after two months of looking at and discussing with the counselors themselves the activity of counseling, he decided to say that counseling was ungradable, but for purposes of rough reference to salary administration, they should think of themselves as being in the top grade. As this grade was assigned to only a few specialized oc-cupations in personnel relations, counseling enjoyed a favorable position in the salary scale.

Where did counseling fit into the flow of work?

But the problem of fixing the counselor's job in the organiza-tional structure had far more serious difficulties than that of as-signing it a labor grade. Where did it fit in the flow of work?

An industrial organization can be conceived as a coordinated system of activities or jobs. The activities or jobs come into being by the division of labor and specialization of function. They are coordinated by what can be thought of as two primary systems of interaction: (1) the flow of work, that is, how the jobs are related to each other as materials and parts flow through the plant from their raw to their finished states (the horizontal or lateral system); and (2) the supervisory hierarchy, that is, how the jobs are ar-ranged in terms of supervisor-supervisee relations (the vertical system). According to "good organizational principles" every job should have a clear place in both systems. Let us look at counsel-ing in relation to the horizontal system first.

Obviously, all productive jobs can be arranged easily in terms of this flow of work sequence. But also most service fuctions can be thought of in terms of keeping goods flowing through the plant. The maintenance people come into play, for example, when a ma-chine, conveyor belt, or assembly line breaks down and the flow of work is impeded. Production control people see to it that parts and materials are at the right place at the right time so that the flow of work is smooth and efficient. Employment people see to it that the required amount of people with the required skills are there in order to perform the required jobs so that the work gets out. When vacancies in jobs occur, either through quits, illnesses, accidents, etc., services are set up to provide new or temporary workers for the vacancies and services are provided for workers who are ill or hurt. In brief, a service function arises whenever a problem interfering with the efficient flow of goods becomes suf-ficiently identified so that a group of people can be assigned to deal with it, instead of leaving it just to chance or the supervisor.

It was very difficult to put counseling in this horizontal or work flow system. Had there been, for example, a large number (i.e., a large enough number to impede the flow of work) of alcoholics, newcomers, war veterans, chronic absentees, quits, accident-prone people, delinquents, or neurotics to which it could have been said that counseling was exclusively directed, counseling would have fitted into the horizontal system. But in its population of employees, counseling had all these things and many more but not any one exclusively.

Many of the ventures of counseling can be viewed as abortive attempts to get into this system, e.g., when they asked supervisors for their problem children, when they asked placement people for their placement problems, when they asked the medical office for their chronic cases, when they asked the safety people for their accident-prone people, etc. Many of their reports to management too were directed to these topics. Moreover, it can be noted that counseling enjoyed its greatest expansion (1942–1948) when there did exist identifiable categories of workers (e.g., newcomers, minority groups unaccustomed to factory work, returning war veterans, and so forth) in terms of which counseling could be rationalized.

But counseling never fitted smoothly into the world of technological space. It was hard to show just where and when it intervened in the flow of work and just how it shortened the time interval from t_1, when the raw materials entered the plant, until t_2, when the finished product left it. Had a red light flashed whenever counseling services were needed, this would have made sense in technological space. But counseling was an activity in which the counselors and not management decided who wanted and needed their services.

But to make matters still worse, counseling not only did not fit into the time dimension of technology; it also did not fit into its spatial dimension. In technological space jobs are done not only at a specified time but also in a specified place. But where was counseling done? All over the place—on the floor, in the interviewing room, in the toilets, in the cafeterias, in the supervisor's office, in the placement man's office, and even sometimes in upper level management's offices.

So counseling had a hard time fitting itself into this world of technological space.

(1) It could not specify where it did its work except by saying, "everywhere" or "anywhere."

(2) It could not specify when it did its work except by saying, "any-time."

(3) It could not specify at just what point it intervened in the pro-ductive process and flow of work except by saying, "at every point."

(4) It could not mention a specific problem of management concern to which its function was directed except by saying, "you name it, we got it."

In the world of technological space, in which a good part of management dwells, these answers were most unsatisfactory in-deed. So the pressure on the counseling organization to justify its activities in these terms was very great. But the more they tried, the more talk got generated which sounded as if counseling was a good thing for everybody, everywhere, anytime, any place, and under any conditions.

THE COUNSELOR'S POSITION IN THE CONTROL STRUCTURE

Let us see now how counseling fitted into what we referred to previously as the Company's vertical system, which comprised its communication and control system. As we have been around this problem in bits and pieces for a long time, we shall proceed more rapidly.

In any organization each subunit has a subgoal which can be or should be related to the total overall goals or purposes of the en-terprise. So for each subunit there are generally specified practices and routines approved by management by which these subunit goals are to be achieved as well as standards of performance set and approved by management by which the achievement of its sub-goal can be evaluated. This is management's major system of control; it evaluates the performance of people in terms of speci-fied standards of performance.

How did the counseling activity fit into this system? Let us divide this, as we did before, into a number of subquestions which management could ask and did ask.

What were the organizational objectives of counseling?

The counseling organization had great difficulty in answering this question. As we look through the records, the plethora of different answers is the major uniformity which meets the eye. Although its most general goal was to improve the motivation and satisfaction of workers and their relations to supervision and management (which, it was hoped, would improve their productivity), it could not specify the unique function it performed which was different from and complementary to other groups involved in the same general objectives. So the organizational objectives of counseling were stated in the most general terms, such as, for example, (a) to aid in the processes of individual adjustment, (b) to improve supervisor-employee relations, (c) to improve management's understanding of the human problems existing at the work level, (d) to conduct research on problems encountered in the course of achieving these objectives, (e) to develop a more stable and responsible work force, a more cooperative spirit, etc.

Who set them?

The counseling organization did and they were approved by management.

By what methods were they to be secured?

By developing a counseling relationship with employees and in time, as we have seen, with everyone in their role set.

Who set the standards for the counselor's performance?

The counseling organization.

What were these standards?

Not clear. It depended upon which aspect of the counselor's role was under consideration.

How could management evaluate the results of counseling?

They could not because,

What information could counseling provide management?

Very little, without violating the confidences of the employees.

In short, as the counseling organization itself had said, they were outside of the structure. They set their own goals, methods, standards, and communication system; they defined their own role. All the questions which management conventionally asked, that is, all those questions which made management *management,* were by counseling defined as improper and illegitimate. To such questions they could only answer, "Don't ask me that, don't you see I can't answer you; be forebearing. We're not part of your communication network and control system. You judge our work by the productivity, satisfaction, and cooperation of others. Don't judge us, sir."

These statements by the counseling organization generated about as much static in management's vertical system as its previous statements had generated in its horizontal system. Activities whose results could not be evaluated, communicated, controlled, or coordinated were about as unsatisfactory to management as activities which could not be assigned a specified place, time, or technology. They were out of this (management's) world.

Where was the one place in which the counselor's position was clear?

There was just one place where the counselor's job was clear and unambiguous. Every job in the company structure could be classified as (a) direct or (b) expense. To the question, "who are you," the one clear unequivocal answer the counselor could give was, "I am expense"—with all the connotations of being "expensive" and "expendable." From this world the counselor could not escape. In this respect, for better or for worse, he was in the structure; he was no longer in the stratosphere, he was back to earth.

Without going into the logics of cost accounting by which jobs are classified as direct or expense and which are as complex as the logics of wage and salary administration, let us just make a few general statements which will be sufficient for our purposes here and for the reader who may not be too well acquainted with these matters.

1. All jobs whose wages can be charged directly to the cost of the finished product are direct so that generally all hourly rated employees are direct.

2. All jobs whose salaries cannot be so charged are expense so that most clerical, office-type occupations are classified as expense.

3. In general most service organizations are expense so that all personnel jobs are generally classified as expense.

4. As the volume of business goes up or down, direct jobs go up and down proportionately, i.e., in a straight linear fashion. Direct people are hired or laid off as the volume of business goes up or down.

5. As the volume of business goes up and down, expenses go up and down too but not in a straight linear fashion, because as business goes up, more expense people are not hired right away and as business goes down, expense people are not laid off right away.

6. So for any profit center (department, division, etc.) there is a ratio which can be expressed by the number of expense employees divided by the total number of employees.

7. As managers of profit centers are evaluated in part by the expense ratio, they tend to watch it with an eagle eye.

8. When the volume of business goes up, the expense ratio tends to go down, if no more expense people are hired; but when the volume of business goes down, the expense ratio goes up, unless some expense people are laid off too.

So all expense people spend a great deal of time generating good reasons for their existence, particularly when business is bad. Sometimes they go so far as to say that their services are more essential when business is bad than when business is good. But these good reasons are looked at with a jaundiced eye by a manager whose expense ratio is out of line with the expense ratio of another profit center. Also, line organizations which had counseling had a higher expense ratio than line organizations that did not.

So although from the standpoint of cost accounting, "expenses are expenses," there are other factors which tend to make some expenses more expensive than others. This happens because some expenses are more difficult to justify in terms of the horizontal and vertical systems of management about which we talked earlier.

All personnel activities, for example, have had to fight to get accepted in these systems. Employment, placement, and employee training had a fairly easy time. But let us take, for example, medical and hospital services, safety work, benefit and pension plans, savings plans, suggestion systems, restaurant operations, employee club activities, civic relations, informational services, real estate services for transferred employees, supervisory training, personnel counseling, and management development. Here is a continuum of expenses (which we have enumerated only for purposes of illustration) in which it becomes increasingly more difficult to state where they fit into the productive process, i.e., to state just how and where they fit into the flow of work except in very general terms. So over the past fifty years each has had to gain acceptance with a bit of doing.

Because the further along this continuum an activity is, the more it can be said roughly:

1. The greater amount of time that is spent in generating good reasons for their existence, and the greater the number of words, and the more general and vague the words become,

2. The greater the number of words are used which appeal to values residing outside of a business organization's strict horizontal and vertical systems. They appeal to values which reside, so to speak, in the wider society and so which all executives of organizations share, because they belong to society too, but which, strictly speaking, do not have their real homes in these organizations, because they are values which executives bring there but which are not put there by them.

It has taken us a little time to establish the background for the few simple points we now want to make about counseling in relation to expense. It can now be noted that:

1. Counseling was at the far end of the continuum; it was an expensive expense.

2. In its early period it tended to justify its existence in terms of the values of science and research (see Chapter II) which even in 1936 no one could be against.

3. But it was a peculiar kind of research. It was related to people instead of to products. The official home for the values represented by this kind of research was outside of the company. So counseling in the beginning had informal sponsors but no formal sanctions.

4. But as counseling expanded and became more and more of a pure service organization, it became more vulnerable to the "expense ratio."

COUNSELING AND THE UNION

In 1936 when the counseling program was introduced, there were no unions either at Hawthorne or at any other unit of the Western Electric Company. An employee representation plan had been established in 1933, however, and when the introduction of the counseling program was discussed with the employee representatives, they made no objection.

When the Wagner Act, which outlawed "company unions" and "employee representation plans," was declared constitutional in 1937, an "independent union" was formed by the leaders of the employees (not those in the old representation plan). When this union was formed, at an early meeting they requested that the counseling program be discontinued on the grounds that it was in direct competition with their organization. The management committee assured them that this was not the case and asked them to confer with the man in charge of the counseling organization.

As a result of this, the man who was in charge of the counseling organization at that time organized a series of meetings aimed at acquainting the union representatives with the origins and purposes of counseling. He traced its history (in simpler terms than we did in Chapter II) and pointed out that this research had occurred long before there was any thought of unionism in the company. He assured them that the counselors were concerned with the problems of individual employees and with their relations with supervision.

At the conclusion of this series of meetings the head of the union said: "If that is what you are trying to do, I am all for it. Anything you can do to improve supervisory relations is good." He added this provision: "We will watch this operation very carefully and we have many sources of information, and if at any time in our opinion you are transgressing upon our jurisdiction, we will take this up as a grievance and insist that your program be discontinued." The head of the counseling organization said: "I understand how you feel and if in your opinion any occurrence justifies such an action, the management will welcome your views."

On the basis of this understanding the program continued and no complaint was ever lodged against it during the existence of the "independent union." But was this "independent union" in fact a company union? This issue was brought before the National Labor Relations Board. They decided that it was in fact independent and not company dominated, so now we shall remove the quotation marks.

In other manufacturing locations where counseling was introduced, the employees were represented by various unions. At only one location was opposition expressed to its introduction. The head of that union at first opposed the program but then later acceded to it and there was no further objection. When the International Brotherhood of Electrical Workers came to Hawthorne in 1952 to represent the workers, they accepted the program.

Counselors and Shop Stewards

So much for general history. But how did the counselors relate themselves to the shop stewards in their territories? Obviously they knew who they were and this made a difference. But in general, they tried to relate to union stewards more as employees of the company than as representatives of the union. The counselors said that their interviews with shop stewards were practically indistinguishable from those of other employees. As to whether shop stewards were more reluctant to talk to counselors than other employees, we have no data. We suspect that this might have been so; nevertheless, when they talked, they talked about their jobs, their future in the company, their personal problems, and their outside obligations in the same way as other employees.

But there was one difference. They also talked about certain individuals, whom as shop stewards they were representing, and with whom they had great difficulty. There were some individual employees who kept pestering them with all sorts of requests and grievances. They felt that these complaints and grievances resided more in the person and would not meet the test of the formal grievance machinery. So sometimes they asked the counselor to interview such workers in order to see if counseling would be of some assistance.

The counselors treated these requests in the same manner as referrals from supervision, the placement organization, etc., and so far as we can tell from the data available, the extraordinary thing was that the shop stewards seemed to demand less feedback on their problem cases than supervision and these other organizations did. Could it be that the union understood the functions of counseling better than management did? Let us explore this question.

The Functions of the Union Compared with the Functions of Counseling

It will be remembered that while the counseling organization was, counseling-wise, outside of the structure, it was in reality (i.e., expense-wise) inside the structure. But the union structure was in fact outside the company structure, as shown schematically in Figure 14.3.

In looking at Figure 14.3 there are some interesting parallels and differences between the union organization and the counseling organization in terms of purposes, methods, sentiments, and ideologies.

1. Although it was the alleged purpose of the counseling organization to improve upward communication in the company's line organization, it could not be said that this was the purpose of the union. Yet, in terms of sentiments, both were trying to get something about E to the attention of M_3. But they were using quite different methods.

2. The union, it could be said, was intervening with a big stick; it was trying to represent employee grievances and it was not treating them confidentially. It used its own line to get these grievances up and it specified direct procedures to get them across.

3. The counseling organization was using the counseling method to get E to become a big boy and to choose for himself which line organization—the company's or the union's—he wished to take his complaints and grievances through. Because, according to the counselor's role model, if the employee decided that his personal interest would be better served by going through the union rather than management, this was up to him. The counselor was helping him to decide but not what to decide.

4. The union by its methods got things on M_3's table more quickly and directly than counseling did by its methods. But while the union got things on M_3's table, they were often in a form of demands about as difficult for M_3 to pick up as management's questions about counseling were for the counseling organization to pick up. They were

took too much interest in the human side of its enterprise, it would undermine the union's function. Its (the union's) function—speaking in terms of sentiments—depended upon management remaining, so to speak, s.o.b.'s. If they became too interested in human conditions of work, the union would lose its function. This was, in part, back of the union's initial objection to counseling. If counseling reduced employee complaints and grievances, the union would have less ammunition with which to go to M_3's office.

6. Interestingly enough, counseling was operating in part upon a very similar assumption. If management and supervision improved their interpersonal competence and leadership style, where would counseling be? Counseling in part depended upon supervisors sticking solely to their production functions while counseling picked up the human pieces.

Obviously we are speaking at a symbolic level so, to reassure the reader who may fear that the counselors were in some way in cahoots with the union, let us say that there was another dimension in terms of which all of the Company's employees were classified. Regardless of whether they were individuals or supervisors, every employee was also management or nonmanagement. This determination was made in hearings before the National Labor Relations Board, who decided what jobs were to be included in the bargaining units of the union. This Board decided that counseling was a management occupation and hence to be excluded from any bargaining unit. This confirmed the fact that counseling was under the direct control of management and not interceded for by any collective bargaining agency. Legally and formal organizationally, they were part of management.

As a part of management counseling could now be accused, as some have done, of being a union-busting activity. In terms of intent this would have been a difficult case to prove; in terms of the sentiments aroused by the jurisdictional assumptions previously mentioned, this would have been a difficult case to deny. Through counseling, management was trying to improve its human conditions of work. That through such an activity, work dissatisfactions might decrease was highly probable. But that the intent of this outcome was to break the union is one of those ideological oversimplifications about which some persons like to speculate but which we do not. Such conclusions follow from oversimplified assumptions about matters of human motivation which in our experience are exceedingly complex. As a result they generate only futile controversy.

There is, however, one more point about Figure 14.3 about which we would like to comment. It will be noted that the counseling structure was truncated at the top. Its highest official representative was a department chief or assistant superintendent. In terms of the Company's extended hierarchy, this was not very high up, that is to say, this person at this level was still not in the inner councils of management. He was still a *counselor* and not a *councilor*. Had the logic by which counseling had been extended to the lower levels of supervision been followed through consistently, it would have resulted in an extended counseling structure paralleling the company's extended line organization. Every level of management would have had a counselor of equal status to whom he could go for counseling service. But this never happened. We mention it now because it will help us to understand later an important dimension limiting the influence of the counselor's role in the total company structure. The counselor, as a change agent, not only had little professional sanction and identity but also little organizational power or influence. He had to achieve his effects from a position not very high in the supervisory structure.

SUMMARY

In this chapter we have tried to show how the counseling organization tried to maintain consistency with its role model with the last but not least important member of its role set—management. Step by step it was driven in the direction of a policy of complete nonintervention (which is another way of saying maintaining a counseling relationship with all the members of its role set). We are now ready to state our conclusions.

PART V

Conclusions

CHAPTER XV

The Criteria for the Conclusions

IN THE CONCLUDING part of the book we will follow the same procedure we did in each previous part, namely, to state first the framework from which we will proceed. Our rationale for this procedure is now particularly relevant in the conclusions.

THE RATIONALE FOR THE FOUR PARTS OF THE BOOK

It is needless to say that because we were both involved in the counseling program our account was open to bias. For this reason we felt obliged to process our data not through a black box, but out in the open—so to speak—where the reader could see what we were up to.

In the process of going from the original raw data to this chapter we met essentially four problems: (1) the problem of the uncommunicative files, (2) the problem of whose questions should be answered, (3) the problem of what questions should be answered, and (4) the problem of the contaminated data. A few words in review about what was done about each of these problems will suffice.

The Problem of the Uncommunicative Files

In the beginning we were faced with many green file cabinets filled with dusty, inert, and dead materials. For a year or more we poured through and stared at these files, hoping that somehow miraculously an "objective" book would spring forth. But the files remained singularly mute; they would not speak for themselves; they were just downright uncooperative. So this was the first problem we met. We had to become engaged with our data. If the files would not woo us, we had to woo them. We had to tease out their hidden secrets. But how? The answer seemed clear. By asking some simple questions of them. But whose questions? So this is how we ran into our second problem.

The Problem of Whose Questions Should be Answered

It arose not because we were lacking in questions; to the contrary, we were surfeited with them. Everybody seemed to be asking different questions about the counseling program—employees, supervisors, personnel, management, social scientists, the counselors themselves, and even the authors had a few of their own. But whose questions should we try to answer? Like good counselors, we felt we should not prejudge these matters. Anybody had a right to ask any questions he wished—no matter how unanswerable they were—but we were not obliged to answer them. So for the most part we treated these questions, not as questions to be answered, but as part of our data; that is, we asked ourselves why these different people were raising these questions.

The Problem of the Unanswerable and the Costly Questions

Although this got us out of our second problem, it created in turn our third. We now had to decide what questions we and not somebody else wanted to ask and have answered. This was tough. So we took all the questions we raised and divided them into two subsets: (1) those questions that were answerable empirically and (2) those questions that were not. The second subset we decided to put back in the uncommunicative files and consider them no longer. But of the first subset we decided to divide them still further into (1) those questions that the data we now had could answer to a first rough approximation and (2) those questions that would require more data, i.e., would require more research in order to answer them. From rough estimates of what outputs we thought we would get (in terms of better answers) in relation to what inputs we would have to pay (in terms of time and money) in order to get them, we decided to stick with the data we had. And this is how we finally arrived at the four questions which in time became the four parts of the book. But our problems were not quite over.

The Problem of the Contaminated Data

Just how good were the data we had? The more we looked at them, the more we realized how contaminated they were. From beginning to end the data had been contaminated by the effect of the observer on the observed, i.e., the Hawthorne effect, but now as authors and not as counselors we were stuck with its negative effect.

But here again we decided to accept the problem we were stuck with and do the best we could. (The reader might want to refer to Figure 10.2 for a shorthand version of the procedure we are following.) We thought we could process these contaminated data through some decontaminating procedures that would make them more *comme il faut*. So this is why we preceded each part with an analytical scheme which said not only what questions we would be asking and what contaminated data we would be looking at but also how we would analyze them. So in each part we were engaged in a kind of analysis which in effect was saying "This is the counseling program from *this* perspective or *this* frame of reference or *this* scheme of analysis." We kept reiterating—we hope not too often—that we could only speak of one thing at a time. We were very careful not to say, "These are the pure, pristine, ungarnished, unadulterated, and complete facts that constitute the whole truth and nothing but the truth about the counseling program." We only felt that some analysis had to precede some somewhat unbiased synthesis. All these precautions we realized would tend to make the book wordy, lengthy, and tedious, but in view of our involvement and the possibility of bias we saw no other alternative.

The Problem of Meaning or of Ultimate Subjectivity

So now in this chapter we come to the last but not least of our problems—the problem of meaning. What do our data mean? Up to now we have postponed this question. Unfortunately our decontaminating procedures had not completely solved it. All that they had done was just to generate more data—something like findings—but they still did not say what they meant. Were we stuck with this problem too? How involved could we get? All that had been provided us had been those green files with their contaminated data. *We* had to provide the questions; we had to provide the schemes of analysis; and now we had to say what the data generated by these different schemes meant. Something peculiar was going on here. We just could not seem to stay neutral, aloof, and objective. How subjective could we get?

As much as we would have liked the reader to take this next step for us and tell us what our data meant, we were unfortunately authors and not counselors (i.e., in a different role relationship to him). As authors the dictates of the academic world were clear. "From this last and final step there is no escape. Take it or else close up shop." So again we decided to accept and make the best we could out of the intolerable situation that, as authors, we were stuck with.

The Problem of Dual Authorship or of Togetherness

But now we would like to relax a few of the constraints. The authorship of this book was two—not one. We had voluntarily *stuck together* through all the preceding parts. We had faced together, worked through together, and reached an agreement together about the problem of the uncommunicative files, the problem of the unanswerable and costly questions, and the problem of the contaminated data. But did we have to take this last step together? Were we stuck with this problem too? Did we have to remain stuck together to the bitter end? In spite of differences of opinion between the business and the academic communities about this question of togetherness, we felt not. But should we each write separate conclusions? Again, after much deliberation we decided not. We decided to write the conclusion in the plural first person according to an agreed upon general plan, but whenever a statement was made to which one of us felt some modification should be made, that is, something should be added, subtracted, underscored, or restated, he would feel free to do so by means of a singular first person initialed footnote.

THE PROBLEM OF THE HARMONIOUS SYNTHESIS

So now let us state our general plan for this last part of the book. How did we propose to relate and tie together some of the separate pieces our analyses have generated? What harmonious concluding music did we now want them to produce? We were stuck with this question too, and we met it face on too. We thought we could state our criteria for the symphony we would like to produce by looking first at some examples of what we thought would constitute more noise than music.

The Problem of Explaining the Program's Discontinuance

Let us start with a question that hovered over this book since its inception like the sword of Damocles. Why was the counseling program discontinued? This above all others was the question which everyone wanted a simple answer to. Whenever anyone heard that we were writing up the story of counseling their very first query was, "Why was it discontinued?" When we said, "This is a difficult question to answer; it is not susceptible to a simple cause-and-effect analysis," and so on and on, the next response took one of the following forms depending upon "you know who."

Response 1—"Come on, save that for the book; you're among friends now. Give us the scuttlebut. Who was the s.o.b. responsible for its demise? The program could not justify itself in terms of dollars and cents, could it? So it got bumped off, didn't it?"

Response 2—"It looks to me as if the counseling program couldn't counteract the forces of bureaucracy. Having got so involved with human relations, it overlooked and abdicated power and so it couldn't or wouldn't resist them. Whether from idealism or from stupidity—I don't know which—it committed organizational suicide, didn't it?"

Response 3—"It looks to me as if the original germinal ideas of the Hawthorne researches got packaged and transplanted too quickly. It got so involved with implementing itself that it lost track of the main ideas it was implementing. In the process it got hardening of the arteries. It died of old age, didn't it?"

Needless to say, these oversimplified responses bothered us. Although, if properly interpreted, there was a grain of truth in each, there was also in each a gross misrepresentation. But what constituted proper interpretation? Here again was one of those questions with which we were stuck and for which we felt we would have to establish our own criteria. It was obvious from the above responses that other people had already made up their minds. But what kind of an interpretation or evaluation of the counseling program did we want to make? Let us see now how this question about explaining the discontinuance of the program can help us.

In the analyses made in this book, we never put our big guns directly on this question of why the program was discontinued by management. This was because we thought it was not a too meaningful question in the first place and certainly not the question to be asked first in the second place. So this is why we organized the book in the four parts that we did.

It seemed to us that first we had to understand the underlying ideas that had generated the counseling program as a new approach for dealing with problems of employee morale (Chapter II). Second, we had to get some idea of those matters about which the workers were concerned (Part II) before we could see, third, what counseling, if anything, could do about them (Part III), and fourth, we had to understand how counseling fitted into the division of labor that the logics of organization specified, so that we could see how it was coping with its organizational environment (Part IV).

Obviously each part raised a possible underlying reason that might have contributed to the discontinuance of the program. Part I, for example, raised questions about the underlying ideas of the program. Were they accurate, realistic, workable, practical, and so forth? Parts II and III raised the question of what counseling could do about what the employees were really concerned about. They raised the question of whether that twisteroo of "what a big difference a little difference can make" (the catalytic effect) was a piece of magic with which hard headed managers should be concerned. Part IV raised the question of the viability of the counseling role in the organizational setting in which it had to survive.

But notice that these analyses were not directed exclusively at explaining why the program was discontinued by management. These analyses could have been made, and all the questions that they raised could have been asked, before the program was discontinued. But were they? This we do not know. We never interviewed the top management of the Company to find out how they arrived at their decision to discontinue the program. This was one of those questions we had decided previously was too costly (not only in a monetary sense) to research. What we mean is that such an investigation would have sidetracked us into an examination of the decision-making processes of the Company and how effective they were. No matter how interesting this study might have been in itself, this was not the point of this book. We were concerned with how effective the counseling program was and we wanted to settle this question ourselves regardless of how management had reached the decision to discontinue it.

From our point of view the Company had a very important and difficult practical decision to make. This was *their job* and we assumed that they knew *their business*. In this book—thank goodness—we were not facing this tough practical decision. We wanted to evaluate it from another point of view. This was *our job* and we assumed that we knew *our business*. To us it was important to keep these two jobs and businesses straight and not get them mixed up. They were different.[1]

It is true that in the last chapter we took a quick look at some aspects of the organizational environment in which the decision was reached. That these organizational logics played some part in the decision reached, we have little question. How much again we don't know. But again this was not the reason for making this analysis. We wished to see for ourselves how and how well the counseling organization was coping with its environment. This was *our concern—our question*. Whether it was management's concern—to repeat—we do not know. Should it have been their concern? We do not like to keep repeating—we just were not investigating this question. It had a nonanswerable flavor about it. It was dead-end, that is, it lead only in the direction of heat (controversy) instead of light (inquiry).

So what were the concerns dictating our questions? One does not have to be Sherlock Holmes to detect that we were interested in the germinal ideas underlying the Hawthorne researches and what had happened to them, or, even to put it more sharply, why what had happened to them had to happen to them? These were the kinds of uniformities we were looking for; we were not hunting

[1] As an academic this was a very important distinction to me. Unto each his own business and about this let there be no monkey business. F.J.R.

for villains, fools, heroes, or wisemen. We were looking for uniformities residing in the processes of human interaction where, interestingly enough, the original Hawthorne researches had told us to look (see Chapter II).

The counseling experience had both a terrible fascination and frustration for us. We had experienced before in other similar human relations ventures (a) a period of excitement and of discovery, (b) a period of inability to communicate and of misunderstanding, and (c) a period of frustration and of failure. This cycle was not confined to the counseling program at Hawthorne. We had seen it and personally experienced it before, so we had had in our minds for quite a long time the questions: Why do such promising ideas, when applied, seem to take this direction? What are the factors making for this uniformity? Was there something wrong with the ideas themselves? Or was it in the way they were applied, understood, treated, or all three? If we could throw a little light on these questions, we felt that something worthwhile might be learned. So this is what the examination of the counseling program meant to us—an opportunity to examine these ideas with some concrete data.[2]

[2] I am expressing here probably my own concern more than my co-author's. Whether or not the counseling program could justify itself in terms of dollars and cents—let me be honest—never interested me too much. In the counseling story there were ideas at stake that were just as important to me as the dollars and cents involved. That as an academic I take ideas seriously should not sound too strange. Also that it was the Company's dollars and not my own that were involved should help to make my attitude even less strange. Anyway, the total outcome of my attitude, strange or not strange as it may seem, was to skew the account of the counseling program in a certain direction and I alone was responsible for it. For this skewing I take full responsibility. Obviously the counseling story could have been written in many other ways than the one we finally chose, but to me they were all deadly dull in comparison.

The idea probably originated at a luncheon meeting to which I had been invited by Douglas McGregor and his group at M.I.T. some few years ago. The point of the meeting I forget but I remember that the conversation finally turned in the direction of discussing: "Would it not be interesting if we reviewed a number of human relations ventures that had been written up in the literature as so-called success stories and looked at what has happened to them?" We named about five or six of such ventures among which the Hawthorne researches and the counseling program were mentioned as

This is how the problem of trying to explain why management had discontinued the program became a dead issue to us, that is, how it became a dead-end and ennervating question and how a more exciting and challenging question arose.[3]

one. At the time—because academics think in terms of books—we began toying with the idea of a book in which all these ventures—not just one—would be analyzed. I was intrigued by this idea.

At about this time Bill Dickson was asking me to join with him in the writing of the counseling story. With this idea in mind I could get involved and excited; short of this idea I couldn't. I didn't want to make a case for or against the counseling program. As the saying goes, "I couldn't care less." I could do either but so what? With this new spirit of inquiry introduced by Douglas McGregor, however, I could go along. This seemed to me exciting.

So as a result, what happened? I urged my good friend and co-author to conceive of the counseling program as one of those cases illustrating the same sort of three-cycle uniformity I mentioned before. I put it in a class of "both success and failure stories" which needed further analysis. So I pressed Bill in this direction very hard. But it will be remembered that in the original idea of Doug's we were all going to "level" together. One wasn't going to claim that he had succeeded any better than the next fellow. We were all in the soup together.

But the book, as envisaged, didn't result. So by luring my friend, Bill Dickson, to do to his program what others had not as yet done to theirs, I put him in a vulnerable position. I have spent many a sleepless night about this. F.J.R.

[3] This may be as good a place as any to state briefly what was done by the counseling organization in response to requests from management that we provide them with information in terms of which they could appraise the activity. These questions do arise and must be answered to the best of one's ability. Also, they were of concern to counselors and counseling supervisors as well as to those higher up in the structure who had to approve budgets and justify expense ratios.

They were of course provided with information about the purposes of counseling, about the counseling technique used and why it was used, and about the beneficial effects which were expected to follow from its implementation. From time to time illustrative interviews and studies of counseling in group situations, carefully edited to assure anonymity, were also provided and discussed with those who were interested and some of them were intensely interested. Periodic attitude surveys, as indicated in Chapter XIV, were also provided the heads of all the major functional divisions. Reports were also prepared showing organizations requesting counseling coverage and our progress in providing it. Numerous special studies, as indicated earlier, were also provided. Beyond this we always encouraged the interested line supervisor or manager to ask his first line supervisors whether they

The Problem of Implementing the "Perfect Solution"

But there was still another set of questions filled with static which we would now like to consider. These questions all revolved around the issue: was there not a simpler and more effective way for the counseling organization to have organized itself to do its job, and which would have solved the ambiguity in which it got itself involved? For example:

Why did they not just set up counselors in offices to which employees could go voluntarily if they wished their services? Why did they not man these offices with trained clinical psychologists or trained professional counselors who knew their business? Why did they allow themselves to get so entangled with supervision? But if they did, why did they not set up a separate department for counseling supervision with a similar set of offices manned by a trained professional personnel of senior status? And why did they not restrict their activities so that no feedback to management was required and so, as in the case of medicine, they could exercise more easily the sanction of privileged communication? Why did they not set themselves up under the medical department and so forth? Why was this seemingly simpler and more logical alternative not chosen? Did not the analysis of the counselor's role in Part IV imply such a solution? Let us discuss these questions because in this manner we can establish another criterion for selecting the kind of concluding statements we want to make.

To the counseling organization this alternative way of going about their business was anathema. It was never ever seriously entertained. The mere mention of it would provoke hurt feelings of "You don't understand" and put the questioner in the "outgroup"—a barbarian. Why was this so?

To the counseling organization this form of organization just wouldn't work. In the first place under these conditions employees would not avail themselves of the counselor's services. It would put them in the eyes of their fellow workers as problem children. But not only for this reason but by the very nature of the way their

---

thought the program was worthwhile and what kinds of benefits they saw in it. This, in the opinion of the counselors, was the most realistic way in which a manager could satisfy himself about the program. W.J.D.

problems were conceived, the logics of organization dictated they go elsewhere. Take the case of Jim Evans who wanted a transfer. The logics of organization said, "For the solution of this problem, Jim, you go to placement." Would Anna, the married woman with three children, Joe, the machine helper, Mary, the lead-off operator, and Dick, the young supervisor (all discussed in Chapter XI) have gone to these antiseptic offices? It is very unlikely; only Henty, the demoted group chief, and Freddie, the newlywed, might have considered it, but even this is assuming that they saw their problems quite differently from the way they did. Only because the counselors were on the floor and had had prior relationships with the employees were they able to be of help.

Also, although trained clinical psychologists or professionally trained counselors might know personality theories better than the Hawthorne counselors, would they know as well the culture of the factory—its technology, logics, norms, and values? Would they not because of their background and training tend to make personality problems out of interpersonal problems—the very thing the counseling program was trying to counteract?

But the alternative solution had still further difficulties. In spite of its simple and logically seductive appeal, it was in fact just a verbal, paper, textbook solution to the problems the workers had and the counselors faced and saw all around them. It would look nice on a table of organization. But it would reduce all the original ideas with which the counseling program had started to a narrow and circumscribed sphere of specialized activity—professionally more respectable, institutionally more sanctionable, organizationally more logical and less ambiguous but, phenomenologically speaking, more sterile. It would not be addressing the phenomena but the table of organization. Such a solution would be a complete abdication of all the values the counseling organization stood for and which they were trying to implement.

So the counseling organization would have rather lived with and died for their ambiguity than to switch to such a conventional and sterile compromise. For them their ambiguity was not a minus factor; it was a plus factor; it was the secret of the success. It was why they had been able to be effective for twenty years.

We have stated this issue in value laden terms, not just to be dramatic, but because these values were present in the issue we are discussing. We are not putting them there; they were there. Unless we can make some sense out of the counseling organization's resistance to this perfect solution of all their difficulties, we are in bad shape. Our hands tremble at the task that now faces us, as we approach the mysteries of implementing the perfect solution. Perhaps a dialogue between one of the authors (F.R.) and an imaginary proponent of the perfect solution (P.S.) might help.

P.S. I just don't see why the alternative solution I proposed wouldn't work. It just seems to me they were making things hard for themselves. What gives?

F.R. You think their way of going about things was nonlogical?

P.S. That I do.

F.R. But do you see why your solution disturbs them?

P.S. No, I don't. That's got me baffled.

F.R. But do you see that your solution does disturb them?

P.S. That I do; it makes them sputter like a firecracker.

F.R. They don't like it.

P.S. That's putting it mildly.

F.R. You don't like this response?

P.S. I sure don't.

F.R. Well, why don't you stop reinforcing this response by your perfect solution?

P.S. Well, I'm just trying to be helpful.

F.R. But does your solution help?

P.S. They won't even consider it; they just give me reasons as to why it won't work.

F.R. Seeing that your alternative hasn't been tried, you see that the reasons that they gave you as to why it won't work are the same reasons for why they did it their way instead of your way in the first place. So your perfect solution hasn't moved things off dead center one small fraction of an inch or millimeter. You are still wallowing in the same puddle you started in.

P.S. That's a fact.

F.R. Well, why do you continue doing this? You don't seem to be getting anywhere fast. What would be the perfect solution for the impasse you are now in?

P.S. I don't get you.

F.R. Well, why don't you shut up?

P.S. I don't like your attitude.

F.R. You mean you can't implement my perfect solution.

P.S. I don't get you.

F.R. Well, don't you see how my perfect solution makes you sputter just as your perfect solution made them sputter? You can't implement my perfect solution any better than they can implement yours. So you both sputter. It looks to me as if you are more similar to than different from the counseling organization.

P.S. You're getting too deep for me. You tell me to shut up—that's not a nice thing to say.

F.R. But it would be a perfect solution to your problem. You don't want people to sputter like firecrackers; you see how your perfect solution tends to provoke this response and get you nowhere. You see how, if you shut up, you would not provoke this response. But you keep doing it. It sounds to me as if you are being as nonlogical as you accused the counseling organization of being in the first place.

P.S. You're getting me all tangled up with your verbal tricks. If I shut up, there's nothing left for me to do.

F.R. You could listen.

P.S. What good would that do?

F.R. Well, you might see why your perfect solution of what the counseling organization was supposed to be up to bears no resemblance to what they in fact were up to.

P.S. You mean they weren't counseling?

F.R. Well, in the sense your perfect solution implies, they weren't.

P.S. Well, if they weren't counseling in my sense, what were they doing? You mean they said they were doing counseling when they weren't? They were perpetuating a big joke.

F.R. Not exactly.

P.S. You mean that they said they were doing counseling when they didn't know quite what they were up to?

F.R. Not exactly.

P.S. Well, what the hell were they up to? Give.

F.R. Well, I don't know exactly. That's what I'm trying to find out.

P.S. Well, in my world managers manage, supervisors supervise, trainers train, and counselors counsel. I don't like any monkey business about that. I don't know what they do in—what did you call it—your phenomenological world.

F.R. Would you like to find out?

P.S. Hell no, I know what they do.

F.R. You mean you know what they are supposed to do.

P.S. Well, how are things in your phenomenological world?

F.R. Ambiguous.

P.S. Well, that's one hell of a note. That's not right. That's what my solution was going to eliminate.

F.R. You mean that's what your solution was going to overlook. You were only eliminating it on paper.

P.S. You mean my solution wasn't eliminating it at the phenomeno-logical level you keep referring to?

F.R. That I do.

P.S. Well, how do you deal with it there?

F.R. We can talk about it there. In your perfect solution you've solved it without any talking-out process.

P.S. What good would that do?

F.R. Well, after reading the next two chapters, let's discuss it some more.

So this is how we finally decided not to offer the perfect solu-tion to the problems that the counseling organization faced. It seemed to us that there were so many people engaged in the process of how business could organize its activities more per-fectly that our services in this direction would be superfluous, and so we could spend our time more profitably in another direction. It looked to us as if those awful green files were getting cluttered up with perfect solutions that no one either knew how to or wished to implement.

It seemed to us, if we were going to suggest any solution at all to the counseling program, that it should be in the direction of some simple next step that they might have taken rather than of any final, complete, definitive perfect solution. This, it seemed to us, was what our role analysis was implying rather than a choice between the way that they had resolved their ambiguity and the perfect solution.

The Problem for the Conclusion

So let us now summarize what we were not interested in doing in these concluding chapters. We were not interested in trying to ex-plain a historical event, that is, why in terms of some simple cause-and-effect analysis the program was discontinued; this was just a dead-end and ennervating question. We did not want to make a case for or against the counseling program; this was too easy. We did not want, as we have said before, to search for villains, fools, heroes, or wisemen; this was too popular. We did not want just to cry over spilt milk and say, "If this hadn't happened, the outcomes might have been otherwise"; this was just being a wiseacre in retrospect. We did not want our conclusions to be something for the birds and for the archives and for those green uncommunicative files; they were already too cluttered up. We did not want to present the perfect solution; there were too many of them already. Nor did we want to try to put "Humpty-Dumpty together again," i.e., make a case for restoring the counseling program; we were no magicians.

So much for what we did not want to do; what did we want to do? After all this talk we feel a bit sheepish now in stating our low level aspirations. All we wanted our conclusions to do was to revive the spirit of inquiry that now lay dormant in those green files. What ideas had created them in the first place which now they could no longer communicate? Had these ideas grown dusty? Were they tired and outworn? Was all their fertility gone? If so, let's shove them back into the files again for the antiquarians to study. But if not, let's brush their dust off and give them wings and let them soar again.

Pardon us. We are speaking grandiloquently; our sentiments are showing; we are not being "objective." Let's state our criteria more matter-of-factly. Having gone to all this bother of analyzing the data we did, we will stick to our guns and see what these analyses (Parts I, II, III, and IV) in toto and not piecemeal add up to? Obviously, we analyzed these data for the purpose of trying to throw light on the questions we were asking. So if we now use them for these purposes, we are not pulling any rabbit out of a hat. We created them for this very purpose, so let's use them for what they were intended.

So in the conclusions we will recast the counseling program in terms of an experiment—an experiment in applying a set of ideas or in testing out the limits of these ideas. We will treat it as an extension of the Hawthorne researches, as a next step in applying what had been learned from them in order to see what had happened to them. We will be looking at the counseling program as an experiment in innovating a new personnel role in the total company structure. In doing so we will be traveling in a reverse direction from the way in which the book was written. Just as in traveling from B to A one sometimes sees some things he has missed in going from A to B, perhaps this too may happen to us now. Moreover, in a certain sense, which we will explain later, this reverse direction will coincide more with the history of the program than the writing of the book did.

So first we will look at what questions, problems and issues Part IV raised. We will look at the counselor's role set problem and the counseling organization's policy of nonintervention as a method of dealing with it and see what ideas they raised for the inquiring mind. We will discuss them but we will not button them up. Rather we will keep looking for the direction in which they point. We will do this in the next chapter—Chapter XVI.

Likewise in the following chapter we will raise and discuss the questions that Part III—the catalytic role of the counselor—and then Part II—the concerns of the employees—(which in a sense the whole hullaballoo was about) conjure up for the inquiring mind. Again our posture will be forward rather than backward looking. We will be just raising new questions for more search behavior.

So from beginning to end this is a book about questions. We began with questions and we will end with questions. But we hope they will be better stated and more answerable ones, that is, empirical questions which, if someone had the inclination to do so, could be researched.

SUMMARY—A HIDDEN AGENDA

This chapter contains a hidden agenda. In it we have been trying to take off the reader's ordinary spectacles and fit him with a new pair which will allow him to read the next two chapters, we hoped, both more profitably and enjoyably, even if no villains, fools, or anything very sexy but only our own ignorance would appear in them.

CHAPTER XVI

The Systemic Problems of Counseling

IN THIS CHAPTER we want to look at the counseling organization's role set problem and examine more closely its policy of non-intervention as a method for dealing with it. How effective was this policy?

THE COUNSELOR'S TASK AND OUTER ROLES

Let us review first the different aspects of the counselor's job that our analysis had differentiated so that now they can be referred to by the shorthand labels we have given them, and thus we will know which aspect of his job we are talking about.

1. We distinguished the original ideas of the program derived from research from the way in which these ideas were implemented by the counseling organization. We called the former the role model and specified its prescriptions in Chapter II; to the latter we gave many different names, such as, for example, the following:
2. We distinguished the counselor's on-the-floor activities from his in-the-interviewing-room activities.
3. In the counselor's on-the-floor activities we distinguished his observer or researcher role, as defined by the role model, from his social role in trying to gain the acceptance of employees and to develop a counseling relationship with all of them.
4. In the counselor's in-the-interviewing-room activities we distinguished his more *active* in-counseling catalytic role, as defined by the role model, from the more *passive* listening role that might also take place there or on the floor. Often we referred to this catalytic role as the counselor's task role, that is, what he was supposed to be doing in the dyadic relationship in the interview.
5. Although it included catharsis (i.e., getting things off your chest), the catalytic role could not be solely reduced to this. So we dis-

tinguished the counselor's catalytic role (which included catharsis) from just his cathartic role, in which this was all that was happening in the relationship.

6. Whenever we referred to how the counselor was structured into the system of role relationships that existed in the Company, we called this his organizational role.

7. Whenever we referred to the counselor's task role in relation to its identification with a professional sanctioning body outside of the Company, we often called it his professional role.

8. Whenever we referred to how the counselor structured his relations to all the other groups with whom he had to relate in order to get his task done, we frequently called these activities his outer roles as distinguished from those activities which defined more specifically his task competence.

9. Whenever we referred to this outer aspect in terms of the counseling organization and not just in terms of the individual counselor, we called this the counselor's role set and we often treated this, instead of the individual counselor, as our unit of analysis, particularly in Part IV. This role set we treated as the organizational environment of the counseling organization with which it had to learn to cope in order to survive.

So although in describing the counselor's job we shifted our labels at different times in order to emphasize this or that aspect of it, in the last analysis a distinction always showed up between those roles which defined his unique special task from those roles he had to conform to or develop in order to perform it, as shown in Table 16.1.

We did not make up these distinctions in order to make matters complex. The complexity to which these distinctions referred resided in the counselor's relationships—not in our thinking about them—and were of the utmost importance. Most of the confusions, misevaluations, and misunderstandings of the counseling program arose because of a failure to make them. Nowhere was this more true than in the problem we now wish to consider, where we will be concentrating upon the counseling organization's outer roles which were concerned with trying to clarify why counseling could not provide the kind of help that different persons and groups were asking of it or of structuring a relationship with them which would allow counseling to render the kind of help they could. This we

TABLE 16.1

THE COUNSELOR'S TASK AND OUTER ROLES

Different Aspects of or Names for the Counselor's Task Roles	*Different Aspects of or Names for the Counselor's Outer Roles*
1. His in-counseling role, or his role in the dyadic relationship in the interviewing room.	1. His social role in seeking coverage and gaining employee acceptance on the floor.
2. His professional counseling role as sanctioned by a reference group outside of the Company.	2. His organizational role as structured by the logics of organization.
3. His catalytic role in the interview.	3. His role relating to trying to develop a counseling relationship with all employees.
4. His observer role on the floor.	4. His structuring role in relation to all the members of his role set in order to gain understanding and acceptance of his task role.

are defining as the counseling organization's role set problem and we are calling their method of coping with it, by developing a counseling relationship with all the members of their role set, their policy of nonintervention.

THE POLICY OF NONINTERVENTION

In Part IV we tried to show how step by step this policy of nonintervention was reached, but throughout the analysis there resided an uneasy feeling that while this policy was solving certain of its problems, on the one hand, it was creating a new set of problems, perhaps even more difficult, on the other. Probably no more basic was the question of what the counseling program was all about. What were in fact its aims and objectives? Could they be achieved by its policy of nonintervention alone or did their achievement require the more active cooperation of all the members of the counseling organization's role set? And around what objectives could such a cooperation be secured?

Probably the clearest thing about the counseling program was that when it was asked for the kind of help it could give, it did an excellent job. This extended to all the members of its role set from employees, to supervisors, to management. If employees wanted to improve the situation in which they found themselves, no matter how tiny the spark in this direction was, then counseling could help. If supervisors wanted to improve their methods of supervision or styles of supervision, then counseling again could help. (See the case of Dick, the young supervisor, in Chapter XI.) If management wanted to consider the effect of their policies upon employee morale, then again counseling could help. In the early days of the counseling program, this was often the way in which it was used by management. The counsel of the counselors was sought about the anticipated effects on employee morale of contemplated organizational or technological changes and what might be done about them in order to minimize their demoralizing effects. During that period it had a place in the inner councils of management, who knew how to employ its services correctly.[1]

But equally clear about the counseling program was that when it was asked for a kind of help it could not give, it did not do as good a job from the point of view of facilitating understanding and communication. It was forced into an ever-increasing justification of its role model to each member of its role set—from the reluctant employee to the doubting supervisor and, as the program continued, to an ever-increasing critical management.[2]

---

[1] This was more true in the early years but held true in a lesser but still significant degree throughout the war years and postwar years. The case of Manager White cited in Chapter XIV was one in which the question asked could not be answered without compromising the counselor's role. Examples of questions which came from the right end up and which were discussed or reported on to management are: "What short and long range consequences might result from a change from four to three levels of supervision in the shop?" "Would an attitude survey conducted by an outside agency be desirable?" "How can we strengthen the vertical relations between supervisory levels?" "How might we best go about integrating minority groups?" "What are the prevailing problems in employee relations which should be brought to management's attention?" "What might be the implications of the adoption of a high potential survey?", etc. W.J.D.

[2] This came about largely because of the extension of the program to plant locations where there was no background of research as there was

Also as part of the process of demonstrating the kind of services they could provide and how it would not interfere with any of the prerogatives of any member of their role set, it was led into developing a counseling relationship with each and every one.

The functionality of this solution for the counselors and the counseling organization in maintaining consistency with their role model was clear. In this way they could maintain their integrity and be consistent with their own self-image. But that this solution also presented an equally consistent image of themselves to all the members of their role set—an assumption that this solution made—was constantly being exposed. To those who had been helped it did. But to those who had not, it sometimes raised the questions: "Who are you and what are you up to? Where does this sanction to develop a counseling relationship to us come from? This is a solution to *your problem;* it's no solution to *our problem.*"

A Perfect Solution?

Here we are getting close to the dilemma of the counseling program. It will be remembered that the method that the counseling organization had chosen to cope with this problem was the only one in their opinion which would work in the industrial setting. Yet our analysis of the counselor's role in Part IV raised some questions about the viability of this solution in the long run. So now we will have to proceed slowly and cautiously because with one slip of the pen we will be back again into the area of controversy instead of inquiry.

Perhaps it might help if we restated the counseling organization's solution so that we can proceed together with a common understanding.

1. Their solution assumed that they could provide their unique services only within the counseling relationship. If they were to be of help they had to operate within this role. The moment they stepped out of this role, they became impotent; only in this role could they

---

at Hawthorne and where there was some resistance to adopting a program developed somewhere else. Also of critical importance was the lack of trained and competent counselors to meet the needs of rapid expansion. W.J.D.

demonstrate their effectiveness and be of help. (So far so good. This assumption checked with many other research findings.)

2. Their solution further assumed that only by staying in this counseling relationship could they keep clean and not interfere with the prerogatives of the other members of their role set who were also concerned with problems of employee morale, although perhaps from other points of view, as shown in Figure 16.1.

Figure 16.1

Related Groups Concerned with Employee Morale

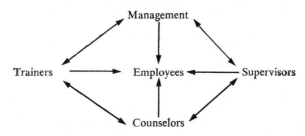

3. So how could they integrate into a consistent self-image these two requirements of their job? How could they *never* get out of role? How could they behave so as *never* to interfere with the prerogatives of the other members of their role set? The perfect solution leaped to the eye. *By developing a counseling relationship with everyone.*

4. No schoolman of the middle ages could have achieved a more logically perfect solution. It seemed watertight, self-contained, and impregnable. Around it developed the mystique of the counseling program which had some persons mesmerized and some persons mystified. How can we proceed so that we do not get into either one of these two boxes?

How to Choose Between Two Perfect Solutions?

Let us step back a moment and take stock. It will be remembered that in the last chapter we were also presented with a perfect solution. It may also be remembered that we annihilated this perfect solution with one stroke of the pen—well, perhaps it took several—on the grounds that it had proceeded from premises quite different from those of the counseling program. This kind of game we did not like to play; by shifting premises in this way only futile controversy resulted. But this was not the problem with which the perfect solution of the counseling organization presented us; they contended that it followed from the premises upon which the counseling program was originally designed; it was their logical outcome when introduced into the industrial arena. This presented us with a much more serious problem which could not be so lightly dismissed.

What made it serious (and also exciting) was that the dissonance introduced in Part IV had also followed from some of the prescriptions of the role model. It had come from its research prescriptions which said, "Don't treat the counseling program as an abstract logical system; instead treat its organizational manifestations as a concrete, open-ended, natural system trying to cope with its organizational environment either *passively as given* or more actively by trying to change it in a direction more favorable to its survival."

When it was looked at in this way, which is what we tried to do in Part IV, the perfect solution no longer seemed so perfect. The phenomena of social organization came tumbling back in and began to raise a number of disquieting questions. For example:

1. Had the counseling organization's solution obliterated the distinction between the counselor's task and outer roles? Had those two sets of roles now become one and the same thing? Was there no longer any distinction between what took place in an interview when a counseling relationship existed in fact and what took place in an interaction between two persons when such a relationship had not been established in fact but was in the process of being developed by the counselor?

2. With this distinction obliterated, was there a danger of assuming that the beneficial results which resulted from the performance of the counselor's task role also would follow from the performance of his outer roles?

3. With this distinction obliterated, was there a danger of assuming that the person with whom the counselor was trying to develop a counseling relationship would perceive the counselor in the same

way as the person who had received help from him in the in-counseling interview because they both had been presented with a consistent self-image by the counselor?

Was There an Alternative?

With these questions in mind, the mute green files became much more cooperative and even communicative, one might say. Many of their materials which previously had seemed disjointed now began to fall into place. For example, the fact that, as the program continued, the reports of the counselors became increasingly concerned with the beneficial effects to employees of the social conversations that they had with them on the floor took on new meaning.[3]

Also the fact that as time when on counselors became less concerned with the conditions under which counseling was effective and more concerned with providing good reasons for how and why the program had to work the way it did seemed to be telling us something.

It almost seemed as if the files were saying, "Dig us for one consistent story and we're not speaking—we'll take the fifth amendment first—but dig us for two interrelated stories and we may open up and reveal our secrets. You can confirm us by citing

---

[3] A more accurate statement is that as time went on there was more reference in the reports to the beneficial effects of counseling to employees who expressed no serious concern. The finding that a person did not need to have a problem to benefit from counseling was for us an exciting new discovery. Many employees, for example, seemed to derive a benefit from discussing their retirement plans or reviewing their careers and the successes they had achieved quite as much as many who were disturbed. This accounts in part for our activity with the 57% of the population who at any one time expressed no serious concern (Figure 4.1). In addition, however, we wanted to make it easy and natural for these people to talk to the counselors in the event they did become concerned (this was the preventive aspect of counseling); we wanted to escape the onus of being labeled a trouble shooter only interested in problem cases: we needed to have some assessment of the attitudes of the total population for our reports and, perhaps most important, counseling was conceived at the time as a way of extending a friendly managerial interest to every employee—not just to those who were in trouble. So for all these reasons there was frequent reference in our reports to the progress we were making in extending and building a counseling relationship with everyone in the counseling territories. W.J.D.

all the cases when we were working very well. You can disconfirm us by citing all those cases when we were not. We can't help obliging you unwillingly either way, but if you really want our active cooperation you'll have to stop assuming that because at times and under certain conditions we were not so good belies in the least the fact that also at other times and under other conditions we were very good and vice versa. Give up that assumption and we'll play ball."

"We'll even give you a clue of how to get us back into the ball game. We didn't quite like the devices you used to disconfirm us— that role analysis in Part IV, for example, where you made us just so many disembodied roles with disembodied role motivations with no concrete personalities and no yearning for villainy or a better life. We thought you were going overboard, sociologically speaking. Nevertheless in spite of this sociological pettifoggery, you were on the right track. Only by such processes of disconfirmation will you be able to get hold of the limits of those ideas which created us in the first place. Only by disconfirming us in this way, elliptically speaking, will you be confirming our power and glory."

THE FIVE IMAGES OF THE COUNSELING PROGRAM

The previously mute files were now chattering away like magpies; we could not get them to stop talking and so like good counselors we listened to their yearnings to get out of the archives where—in a way—so rudely shattering to their egos—they had been deposited. And after they had got these matters off their chests and without offering them the slightest encouragement that they would ever have any better working conditions, we took their cue and started to review the different images of the counseling program which had persisted throughout its twenty years of existence among persons who had not experienced its help. There were five.

Image 1. It was primarily a union-busting activity.
Image 2. It was primarily an evaluative, control, or intelligence activity of management's.
Image 3. It was just concerned with the personal situation of employees; it had little or no relation to their work concerns about

which counseling could do nothing. It was a fringe activity which management could afford.

Image 4. It just provided employees with the opportunity to get things off their chests. This was its major therapeutic effect. It was like a confessional. It was a nonprofessional psychiatric or ministerial service rendered by well-intentioned laymen.

Image 5. It was the prototype of what all good human relationships should be. It was the instrument for all self-change. All human relationships should be turned into counseling relationships. All other forms of influence or intervention were bad.

Image 1 existed more outside than inside of the Company. It existed in certain segments of the academic community and in the minds of certain persons to whom it is self-evident that the motives of management must be always bad. About this image the counseling organization could do little. For those with paranoid tendencies, this image would crop up regardless of anything they could do—even if they strapped their mouths with adhesive tape. So we will discuss this image no more.

Image 2 existed in the minds of some lower levels of supervision (see Chapter XIII) who had not experienced its beneficial effects and who interpreted the reluctance of counseling to provide them with the kind of help (information) which they wanted in only one way. If the information that counseling was obtaining was not coming to them, it must be going topside. Where else could it go? As it was in part to counteract this image that the policy of nonintervention in relation to supervision and management had been developed, the policy itself provided ample testimony to the persistence of this image.

Image 3 developed from the fact that because counseling could not do anything directly with regard to an employee's problems at work, it might be able to do something more directly about his problems outside of work. This image existed at all levels of the organization from employees to top management. It was reinforced by many counseling programs which mushroomed during the war and whose aims were directed more in this direction. It was also in part reinforced by the counseling program itself which tended to cite more successful outcomes in terms of better resolved outside personal situations than inside work situations—a tendency which we tried to counteract in Part III of this book. But we could do this only by making and not obliterating the distinctions we made in Figure 16.1.

Image 4 was by far the most popular and persistent. It was reinforced by many of the simple explanations that counseling itself made to employees in order to gain their acceptance of the beneficial effects of their activities (see Chapter XII). But this oversimplified explanation was also frequently made to supervision and management so that it existed at all levels of the organization.

Together *Images 3 and 4* raised many questions in the minds of topside managers. They both had fringe benefit connotations which raised questions of not only whether the Company could afford them but also whether they should be concerned with them in the first place. Both these images were part of the underlying questions of Parts II and III of this book. How well did they represent the activities of the counseling program? Unless some of the distinctions in Figure 16.1 were made, there was no clear answer.

Image 5 was what many persons heard when the counseling organization waxed eloquently about its services. It communicated (not because the counselors intended to) "we have the key to good human relations; the rest of you don't understand; you are working on a false set of assumptions about human change; we are working on a correct set of assumptions about human change, etc." To many social scientists outside of the Company, this equating of human relations with counseling was a serious error, particularly when the adjectives "good" or "effective" were added to it. An unwarranted assumption was being made. Just how had this leap into the normative from the original Hawthorne researches been made?

It was for this reason that we kept distinguishing the counselor's research role from his therapeutic or communication or helping or catalytic or self-change role in the interview. Once this distinction was obliterated there was little opportunity for self-examination. For many social scientists it was important to distinguish between the way things are and the way they ought to be. For them counseling was teeter-tottering with this distinction; it talked indiscriminantly the language of research and the language of practice. But even among social scientists interested in behavioral changes in the direction of growth, counseling was not the only kind of intervention that could be made. It was one kind but not the only kind. This was a serious error.

As Image 5 raised for the social science community some very fundamental doubts, questions, issues, and problems about the assumptions underlying the counseling program, we will need to examine it more closely. But for this examination we will need to make a fresh start in a new context and so we will postpone it for the next chapter.

THE COUNSELING ORGANIZATION'S DILEMMA: ROLE CONSISTENCY, ORGANIZATIONAL SURVIVAL, OR ORGANIZATIONAL COOPERATION?

For now let us just take stock of what contribution the role analysis of the counselor's job has made to the understanding of the counseling program's organizational problems and what questions and choices it was raising.

1. When counseling was dealing with personal decisions which persons faced at work, it did a good job; when it tried to use the same tool for dealing with its own organizational problems, its effectiveness became more doubtful. While it took care of some problems, it in turn raised others of equal if not of more importance.
2. It looked as if the more counseling tried to explain why counseling was counseling, the more it kept reinforcing why management was management.
3. Was it confusing organizational problems with personal problems and organizational decisions with personal decisions? Was it applying a tool useful for dealing with one kind of problem to another kind of problem where another kind of tool was also needed?
4. For example, was its policy of nonintervention just a personal decision and resolution while its role set problem was an organizational problem requiring an organizational decision and resolution? Had it extended a tool beyond its limits to where it ceased to be useful?
5. By its policy of nonintervention had it succeeded in gaining acceptance only at the cost of being unable to influence the members of its role set in the direction of the behavioral changes it sought on the part of employees?
6. Could the behavioral changes it sought on the part of employees be obtained by counseling alone or did they require the active partic-

ipation of all the members of the counselor's role set? By resolving its problem unilaterally and with no discussion with management, had it set for itself an impossible task and taken on a burden of responsibility that extended way beyond itself?

7. Was counseling the sole unit and instrument of change or was the counselor's role set the unit of change? Could changes be made on the part of one member without any reciprocal changes having to be made on the part of its other members? If so, on what grounds were they cooperating? Was counseling just picking up the pieces that supervision and management dropped?

8. By its policy of nonintervention had it not prevented itself from getting on the table what needed discussion? It could not raise for discussion, for example, why many of the Company's policies and practices were not working in the direction that management thought they were and why as a result they were making for many of the work concerns about which the counselors were counseling employees. By its policy of nonintervention these became taboo topics about which they could now say nothing. Its lines of communication to management were closed.

9. So in the long run how viable was its solution? How could it influence its organizational environment in the direction more favorable to the achievement of its objectives?

However, although on one hand our role analysis was questioning the general applicability of the organizational resolution reached by the counseling program, it was also clarifying on the other hand the conditions under which counseling was useful. It had shown that:

1. Counseling was viable in the realm of personal decision making: in the dyadic helping relationship, where it could provide the kind of help that was being sought.

2. Within this context it had a valuable contribution to make. But this could be done only by differentiating its task from its outer roles. By confusing them or equating them it was only helping to create instead of resolve its organizational problem. Only by differentiating them could a better integration among the different members of its role set be sought.

3. So viewed as an experiment, the counseling program had demonstrated well not only the utility of counseling for certain persons but also its limited utility for securing the organizational changes that were also required to achieve its goals. It had pressed a cer-

tain set of ideas to its limits and, by so doing, learned something, as is said, the hard way.

SUMMARY

But now our role analysis has done the special job for which it was intended. Its purpose—in spite of the way it may have sounded at times—was not sadistic, i.e., to knock the counseling program over the head with a club nor was it aesthetic, i.e., to evoke the feeling, "What a jolly mix of roles the counselor had." Its purpose was utilitarian, i.e., to help us to diagnose better the organizational problems the counseling program faced. Having done its job and served its purpose, let us not ask of it any more or we shall just keep on beating a dead horse. Like counseling, role analysis is also a limited tool; it cannot do the whole job.

So we will stop this narrow line of inquiry and start on a new set of questions in the next chapter which may help to put the counseling program and its problems in a wider and better perspective. The wider question which both the perfect solutions of this and the preceding chapter were raising was, "What were really the aims of the counseling program?" Why could its germinal ideas not be organizationally contained? Why were the counselors always—so to speak—extending their boundaries, seeking a new space, the moon perhaps, in which they could be more comfortable? What made them so restless? What had them so gripped and enthralled that they could not see the handwriting on the wall? In short, what were they really up to? And why could they not tell management this? Were they afraid to or was this a difficult communication to make? Let's consider these questions in the next chapter.

CHAPTER XVII

Worker, Supervisory, and Management Development

IN THIS CHAPTER we want to tie together the data we analyzed in Parts II and III of this book and see what they are telling us about the counseling program and its implications for the future. As these parts relate to the counselor's task roles, the time has come for us to re-examine the assumptions underlying them.

THE IDEAS BEHIND THE COUNSELORS' TASK ROLES

In Chapter II we stated their prescriptions in the terminology of 1936. We have clung to these prescriptions because without them as a point of departure we felt we might become lost in a semantic jungle from which there would be no point of return. But as we realized and commented upon in Chapter II, they did not have all their assumptions spelled out. Although we stated these prescriptions as a set of separate propositions, we realized that they were more a set of interrelated propositions among which we could not separate too clearly the axioms from the theorems and from which many applications besides the counseling program could flow.

However we did differentiate the research prescriptions from what we called the listening-helping-communication ones. They were both components of the counselor's task role. The research prescriptions were concerned with how to think about a certain class of phenomena in order to look for certain uniformities in them, while the listening-helping-communication prescriptions were concerned with how to implement this way of thinking for fruitful practice when engaged with these phenomena. One was a model for investigating interpersonal relations; the other was a model for practicing them. In the beginning of the program it was felt that both these models had to be developed hand in hand; they could or should not be cultivated separately. Theory and practice had to be developed together.

But this is easier said than done because they can become slanted sometimes more in one direction than another. Obviously as the counseling organization expanded and became a service organization, their interest in theorizing about what they were doing and learning lessened and research became practically nonexistent. Nevertheless certain ideas stemming from the original Hawthorne researches lingered on. It is about these ideas that we now want to talk, because they also often influenced why the counseling organization did what it did, the direction the program took, and the images it provoked.

In the counseling program theory and practice tended to converge around three ideas.

(1) The first was around the helping relationship and the processes of natural growth in the individual.

(2) The second was around an ideal helper-helpee cooperative relationship.

(3) The third was around the dislocations that occur between technological, social, and individual development in organizational life.

The Helping Relationship and Natural Individual Development

This first idea was dominant in the early period of the counseling program and in some ways expressed best its aims and aspirations. In the helping relationship they saw the most fruitful coalition between theory and practice. In such a relationship where the person being helped was not treated merely as an object from which research data were to be obtained but also as a subject who needed and could be helped; and where the helper was acting responsibly, they felt they could obtain their best firsthand data from which, in time, knowledge about interpersonal relations in organizational life would emerge.

In this early conception the *unit for investigation* and the *unit for change* was the individual being helped, and the *unit for practice* was the dyadic helping relationship. A (the helper) learned about B (the person being helped) in a relation of involvement to B, and not as a disinterested spectator of B. But also, if A was to improve his relation to B he had to understand not only B but also A, that is, himself. Only by being aware of both how B's behavior was affecting him, as well as how he was affecting B's behavior, could his behavior be modified and could he be helpful to B, as well as correct for the contamination that these two sources might have upon the data he was collecting.

In this conception, diagnosis and treatment went hand in hand but their relation at times was not too clear. Sometimes a person seemed to gain help by the process of listening without too much diagnosis and sometimes a good diagnosis did not seem to provide much help to the person so diagnosed. From this observation, the second insight, which we will talk about later, emerged. But let us first get a picture of how the counselor viewed the worker being helped under the first conception. We have diagrammed it in Figure 17.1

The counselors' model of man-in-organization

In this figure the reader will recognize the major distinctions which have been maintained throughout this book. We felt that these were the major ones that the counselors used in making their diagnoses of an individual or group in the industrial setting, regardless of the varying terminologies which may have been used at different periods of the program to refer to these different dimensions of human behavior. Let us look at them.

1. Under this conception, for example, a distinction needed to be maintained between what the situation was demanding, requiring, or expecting of the person and what he in turn was demanding, needing, and expecting of the situation. By the words "role expectations" (A) and "personal needs and goals" (B) in Figure 17.1 we are referring to these two aspects. At times in the book we used the words "company requirements" and "standards of performance" to refer to A.

2. Second, under this conception a distinction needed to be maintained between a person's individual goals (B) and the goals of the organization (C). These again were different orders of phenomena that could not be reduced one to the other or equated with one another.

FIGURE 17.1

THE COUNSELORS' DIAGNOSTIC MODEL OF MAN-IN-ORGANIZATION

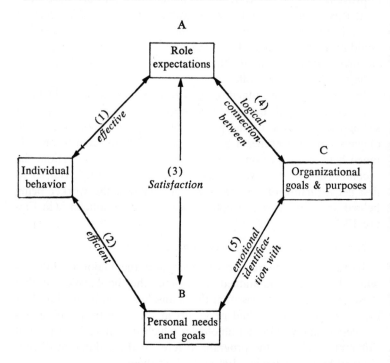

3. Third, under this conception a distinction also needed to be maintained between what a person was expected to do (A) and the goals of the organization (C); that is, between his individual task specialization (A) and its relation to the goals of the organization (C).

In this book we have tried to maintain these distinctions at whatever level of conceptual elegance or sophistication they were made by the counselors, because we felt that they were the ones which helped the counselor to see, for example:

1. There were three different ways of evaluating a person's behavior: (1) in terms of what was expected of him, (2) in terms of his own needs and expectations, and (3) in terms of the relation between his needs and what was expected of him. For these three different

evaluations, as shown in Figure 17.1, we gave separate terms: (1) effective, (2) efficient, and (3) satisfied. To the degree that man was realizing some standard of expectation, his behavior was *effective*. To the degree that his behavior was satisfying his needs, it was *efficient*. To the degree that a person realized his needs by doing what was expected of him in an organizational setting, he was *satisfied*. These were three quite different evaluations. One's behavior could be effective without being efficient and vice versa. Effectiveness was an *external evaluation*. It was an evaluation from the point of view of the organization. Efficiency was an *internal evaluation* from the point of view of the individual and his perceived needs. To the extent that these two evaluations were congruent a person felt *satisfied*.

2. These distinctions also helped the counselor to see two quite different ways in which a person was related to the goals and purposes of the organization. To the degree that he saw some logical connection between what was expected of him (A) and the goals of the organization, the more his sense of rationality was satisfied (see relation 4). To the degree that he could integrate the organization goals (C) into his system of needs (B), the more he could become emotionally identified with them (see relation 5). Again these were quite different evaluations that could not be equated with each other or deduced one from the other.

As we have said, this was the most generalized model of man-in-organization held by the counselors. It was used again and again for purposes of diagnostic appraisal of a total situation of a person or the state of morale of a group. For example, in evaluating a person's total situation, the counselor would have had to say something about all the relations 1, 2, 3, 4, and 5 in Figure 17.1—not just one or two but *all*. He might *not* have stated them in terms of role conflict, need conflict, or role-need conflict. But he would have stated roughly the degree of realization in these different relations, such as, for example, "This worker likes his job (efficient) but the supervisor doesn't think he's meeting standard (effective)," or "This worker doesn't know what is expected of him and this seems to bother him," or "This worker seems to making impossible demands of his job," or "This worker seems to see the reason for what he's doing but still he is apathetic or irresponsible or not too loyal to the interests of the Company," and so on and on.

Let us examine these relations in Figure 17.1 more closely. It can be seen that in the case of any individual or group, if the value for any one of the relations 1, 2, 3, 4, or 5 is zero, then morale is low. For example, if the person or group is *either* (1) not effective *or* (2) not efficient *or* (3) not getting any satisfactions from doing what is expected or required *or* (4) cannot see any logical relation between the requirements of the job and the Company's objectives *or* (5) cannot feel any sense of identification with the Company's goals, then morale is low, no matter how high it may be in any of the other relations.[1]

On the other hand, if the value for any one of the relations 1, 2, 3, 4, or 5 is one, then a very serious confusion would result. All the distinctions between A, B, and C would become obliterated. The person could not distinguish who he was from what the Company was; he could not separate his identity as a person from the identity of the Company as an organization. With the loss of this distinction he would be faced with the dilemma of having to choose between trying either to reduce the Company to himself (i.e., the Company exists solely for the fulfillment of my needs) or to reduce himself to the organization (i.e., I exist only for the fulfillment of the Company's purposes). This would be a serious confusion indeed!

But this possibility exists more as an academic nightmare than as a reality. Underlying the model was the assumption that (1) the purposes of organizations were not in total opposition to the purposes of man, nor (2) were they in complete harmony with them, but instead (3) under certain conditions the relation between them was capable of both deterioration and improvement, and moreover (4) improvement in the relation could only be gained by maintaining the distinctions A, B, and C and by not making false dichotomies of them, and finally (5) by seeing how reasonable levels of realization could be reached in relations 1, 2, 3, 4, and 5 that were more than zero but less than one. Underlying this model, it might be said, was the notion that either (1) "There is no such thing as

[1] See J. W. Getzels and E. C. Guba. "Social Behavior and the Administrative Service" *School Review,* Winter 1957, pp. 423–441, who made this observation and from whose analysis we were greatly helped throughout this section on the model of man-in-organization.

a perfect world" or (2) "This is the best of all possible worlds." We will let the reader choose which one he prefers.

Anyway in terms of this conception the aims of counseling can now be better stated. Looking at Figure 17.1 again, it can be seen that management was doing a much better job in relations 1 and 4 at the top of the diagram than in relations 2, 3, and 5 at the bottom. By many explicitly stated standards the worker knew what was expected of him and, in terms of them, where he stood (i.e., how effective he was). Also in terms of the task structure and flow of work, he was told how his job related to other jobs and the final product or products the Company was producing (i.e., he saw its rationality in terms of technological space).

But what about relations 2, 3, and 5? What functional organizations were looking at them or after them as carefully or as explicitly as relations 1 and 4? What did his job mean in terms of "life space"? Here the picture was not so clear. It looked as if by the overemphasis on one set of relations and the underemphasis on the other, the worker was bifurcated. From his point of view it looked as if he was constantly having to adjust to the requirements of the Company about which he had little or no say except through the union. So as a result only one part of him and his job was being considered by management while another part of him and his job was being considered by the union. When or where could this fragmented worker be conceived as whole again?

Well, we will not keep the reader in suspense. Only in counseling did it look as if this fragmented worker was treated as a whole person with all his dimensions (relations 1, 2, 3, 4, and 5) together. Counseling represented symbolically where all the values underlying these different dimensions were given full recognition. Counseling was not just a piece of organizational machinery; behind it resided an exciting idea that could be implemented by a person with a skill called counseling. Can one see now how the adrenalin in the blood stream of the counselors began flowing, in spite of the fact that they had an ungraded labor grade and did not know where they stood except that they were an expensive expense?

But although this idea was exciting, the reader may still have qualms about its implementation. He may still feel that the underlying idea when implemented might result in a reality that was something quite different from the exciting idea. Granted that the counselor was paying attention to relations 2, 3, and 5, he still could be trying to get the worker just to accede and resign himself to the situation in which he found himself. How were the personal needs and goals of the individual conceived? Did the counselors have a model of man, that is, who he was and what he wanted to be and become apart from what society and the organization expected of him?

The counselors' model of man

Although we did not raise these questions explicitly for discussion in Parts II and III of the book, we were not overlooking them. It will be remembered that in Part II, but with increasing emphasis in Chapter X of Part III, we developed a concept of man in terms of the natural processes of growth and development toward an improved relation to his environment in terms of competence and independence, in order to show the counseling process in relation to them in Chapter XI.

To help us do this we borrowed in part Maslow's concept of a need hierarchy as well as some ideas from Herbert Simon and Carl Rogers. In the case of Carl Rogers we had no qualms about doing this because the counselors read his books and articles avidly and his ideas influenced the second development about which we will talk later. But this was not true of the first two authors. Particularly in Chapter X we talked about the process of personal decision making in a language which many counselors will not recognize. They did not talk that way, that is, they did not use those words. Nevertheless we felt that they would recognize the phenomena to which our new language referred and that it would not distort the underlying conception of man they had but rather confirm it.

In the early days of the program Mayo stressed man's need for an ever increasing complication with the things and persons about him.[2] Man was not satisfied to exist at just the safety level. More-

[2] As stated in Chapter II Elton Mayo's ideas strongly influenced the Hawthorne researches from which the counseling program developed. In the early period of the program all the counselors at Hawthorne not only read his publications; they also knew him personally and had frequent discussions

over in explaining their services the counselors' reports were sprinkled with phrases about "helping people to make up their own minds, to reach their own decisions, to become persons, to strengthen their own egos and to choose their own values, and so forth." They never talked about people as disembodied roles having to learn to live up to the social expectations of others. But on the other hand, learning to live with others was also a prerequisite for future individual development. In man's natural development this stage could not be skipped. So a kind of natural progression from man as a creature of nature to man as a social animal to man as an autonomous person was assumed. This was the tough road to becoming a person and some did not make it.

But also the counselors did not talk the language of psychotherapy. They claimed again and again that they were not engaged in trying to change personalities. They used the language of "natural growth" and not the language of "forced growth" or psychotherapy. So all in all we did not think our new way of talking about the phenomena distorted the underlying idea of the counselors but instead helped to state it more clearly, particularly to a 1966 audience.

The counselors' catalytic role

But it was in Chapter XI, where we tried to conceptualize what happened in the personal encounter between the counselor and the worker in which the counselor made a difference, that we had the greatest difficulty in representing accurately the orientation of the counselor. What happens in this fateful encounter has been expressed in many different languages fraught with nuances of great significance to different schools of thought in counseling and psychotherapy.

One of these nuances is how the counselor intervenes in this encounter and how active or passive is he in these interventions. The counselor at Hawthorne could be easily placed in the middle of two extremes. He was neither a passive doormat upon whom people just spilled their feelings nor an active moralistic interven-

with him. Mayo's best statement about man's relation to his social surroundings is in his small book, *Some Notes on the Psychology of Pierre Janet* (Cambridge, Harvard University Press, 1948).

tionist who told people what to do. His function was not just catharsis or moralizing. He was supposed to help the person clarify
his feelings. But just how far did he go in the process of clarifying
or interpreting feelings? Here again is a continuum fraught with
subtle nuances. Our impression is that, as the program continued,
the counselors went more in the direction of just reflecting feelings
and did less about clarifying or interpreting them.

The counseling organization never did any experimentation with
different forms of intervention nor did they adhere rigidly to any
one school of thought about these matters. As time went on they
were influenced by some of Carl Rogers' ideas but they never became strict Rogerians. Between the two extreme positions mentioned above, the counselor was allowed to develop his or her own
personal style and there was a great deal of individual experimentation.

It will be remembered that we called the role of the counselor in
this fateful encounter catalytic. Now we do not know whether in
chemistry a distinction is made between active and passive catalysts, that is, catalysts whose presence actively or passively make a
difference. But in ordinary language an active catalyst does sound
like a contradiction in terms. And we did describe this role as not
just passive. In Chapter XI we tried to explain this seeming contradiction by saying that by catalytic we meant that the counselor
was not trying to interfere with the phenomena before him, that
he was not trying to make them conform to his preconceived ideas
or wishes, and that he was passive in this sense. Yet on the other
hand by listening he was trying to latch on to these phenomena like
nobody's business and he was active in this sense. And by this
process a favorable change in the counselee would be affected. But
what was being changed? Let us examine the counselor's conception of this because it may help to clarify this unusual role.

The counselors' conception of what was being changed

No word is more laden with emotional meaning than the word
"change." It immediately raises the questions of who or what is being changed by whom and how and for what purposes. What was
the counselor's position on these questions? As we said before, in
the conception of their catalytic role, they were not changing the

personality of the worker. Also in the conception of their outer roles they were not interfering with or changing the company structure, that is, they were not interfering with or trying to change the established roles of the members of their role set. So what were they changing?

In their conception they were trying to change or improve the relations of persons to each other. They were trying to change or improve their interpersonal relations at the point of interaction. So as a result, as we saw in Chapter XI, the counselors concentrated their attention upon those feelings of the worker (of dependence, hostility, distrust, etc.) which would affect the development on his part of more cooperative relations with others, particularly his supervisor. By allowing the worker to express and work through his negative feelings in the interview, he would be ready to express more positive feelings to his supervisor when he next met him, for example. We saw several examples of this in Chapter XI. It was this idea which played an important part in the extension of the program to supervision. By working on both ends of the relationship between supervisor and worker in a counseling fashion, they could improve their relations to each other.

With this conception the counselors were more comfortable and during the middle years of the counseling program it expressed best their aims and aspirations. Let us note, however, the shift of emphasis that now occurred under this conception.

1. In the earlier conception the *unit of investigation* and the *unit of change* was the individual and the *unit of practice* was the dyadic relation between interviewer and interviewee. With this new conception the *unit of investigation* and the *unit of practice* now became one and the same, namely the dyadic counseling relation and the *unit of change* was the changes in relationships between persons that the above could affect. The focus was now more on the properties of *relationships* and less on the properties of the monads being related.

2. The diagnosis of the individual became less important; the diagnosis of the interferences to the development of a more cooperative relation between persons became more important.

3. These interferences could be conceived primarily as feelings or attitudes or misevaluations which prevented more cooperative relations between persons from developing.

4. In many cases the roots of these feelings, attitudes, and misevaluations in the person's total situation did not require any great explorations in depth. They could be corrected in one or two interviews by allowing the worker to express and get some slight control of his negative feelings.

Obviously these two conceptions were not diametrically opposed; they had some overlappings. Although the second conception de-evaluated the need for individual diagnosis, it shared the first conception's values regarding the need for individual growth and development. But in the second conception individual growth and development was not an abstract ideal. Man's needs in this direction had to be caught when they revealed themselves at the point of interaction. It was at the point of interaction that they had to be cultivated, nurtured, and fostered. This was the counselor's catalytic role.

This was, without question, an exciting and challenging idea, but it was a difficult one to practice, communicate, and realize, so let us look at how in fact it did develop.

An Ideal Cooperative Relation and Its Extension

What the counselors saw and felt was that in the catalytic role of the counseling-helping relationship, there seemed to reside the ingredients of an ideal cooperative relationship between two persons. What were some of the properties of such a relationship? We mentioned some in Chapter XII when we considered the viability of the counselor's role.

1. An almost perfect exchange between A and B where neither was profiting at the expense of the other.
2. An almost perfect balance in the values being exchanged so that each was getting what was more valuable to him and less important to the other party. B got the help which he valued more highly than A did (because A did not need it) while A got the satisfaction from being of help by the practice of a skill he valued more highly than B did.
3. An almost perfect congruence of perception of goals so that B was able and willing to accept the kind of help that A was capable of providing.
4. An almost perfect maximization of profits for each in the exchange.

Each party got what he wanted at a minimum cost so that the profit to each was high. B got the help he valued without having to pay the cost of extreme subservience and dependence. A gained a sense of accomplishment without having to pay the cost of exercising power and manipulation.

5. An almost perfect realization of himself for each in the exchange, so that each party could be congruent with himself and his own higher order needs.

It looked as if on almost all scores the properties of this ideal helper-helpee relationship, when realized, seemed to contain the properties of a perfect cooperative relationship between two persons. No siren since Lorelei has sung a sweeter tune than this one. In terms of it the extension and direction of the program can now be better understood and why the perfect solution we considered in Chapter XV was unsatisfactory. The program had higher aims and aspirations than would exist in a conventional program of counseling for workers. Obviously the more this relationship could be developed with more people, the more beneficial results would follow. This in part was behind its notion of coverage, that is, of trying to make its services available to employees by trying to develop a counseling relationship with all of them. It provided the rationale for extending their services to supervision and finally to all the members of its role set. By the extension of this relationship, better cooperation and communication between more persons and groups could be obtained.

But also this idea made sense of and gave meaning to the counselors for the ambiguity of their role around which we spent much time in Part IV. It not only made the ambiguity livable and bearable, it made it exciting and challenging. By living daily their counseling role, they could not only be of help to troubled people but also facilitate improvement in the relations between management and the worker. This would not be accomplished by trying to change the personalities of workers and supervisors or their formal role relationships to each other; it would be accomplished by trying to change their latent role relations which existed in their daily practice with each other at the point of interaction. This could be done by counseling where they could appeal to man's higher order needs for growth and competence. Under this conception the counselors became highly motivated persons; they felt their skills were useful and needed; they were not "zombi roles riddled with ambiguity." In spite of its seemingly ambiguity, their role was both effective and efficient.[3]

Counseling and change agentry

In this conception the counselors had also caught the vision of change agentry, that is, the need to develop a cooperative relationship between the change agent and the client if any improvement of performance in the client system (whether it be a self, group, role, or any larger collectivity) was to be obtained. But with regard to its application it should be noted that: (1) they were practicing it from a position low in the supervisory structure (see Figure 14.3), (2) they were self-appointed but not management-appointed change agents, except for employees, and so (3) it was still not clear and indeed considerably confused as to who their client or clients really were. As a result many of the misunderstandings discussed in the last chapter developed. For example:

1. If under these conditions counseling was not trying to change the organizational environment in any fundamental way, it still looked as if it was addressed mainly to getting employees to adjust to the

---

[3] Before publication the manuscript of the first draft of this book was passed around to many counselors for comment. I was impressed with how many counselors felt that the significance the job had for them did not come through in our account. Many said or implied that this was one of the most rewarding work experiences they had ever had. "Please," they seemed to say, "say something more about this. We were highly motivated not only because it satisfied our needs to be of service but also because we felt we were accomplishing something. We were both effective and efficient." Because as a person I so completely shared their feelings and because their comments made me feel guilty, I would like to say that from the point of view of job design I know of no job at the employee level which so enlisted the cooperation of its doers. From the point of view of securing efficiency it was a natural, and all persons interested in job design should study it carefully for this reason alone, as I shall explain later. But further I believe that when the counseling relationship was achieved in fact, the counselors were also extremely effective. I have no question about that. But this was the paradox—how could something so effective and efficient under certain conditions in the short run also turn out to be not so effective under other conditions and in the long run? This is what I am trying to understand and what in a way this book is all about. F.J.R.

organizational environment in which they lived. The organizational environment was fixed and immutable; to it employees had only to adjust. From this all the images of counseling described in the last chapter could emerge.

2. But moreover under these conditions what did its ideal of human development amount to? It merely amounted to dealing with the constraints that the worker himself brought to the situation which prevented him from developing a better relation to it and what could be done about that. But what about the environmental constraints which prevented him from realizing himself and what could be done about that? Short of doing something about that, counseling looked like a "Band-Aid" operation.

Technological, Social, and Individual Development

The counselors were not unmindful of this question. It kept cropping up again and again and to a sufficient degree to prevent their job from being totally satisfactory. So let us now turn to the analysis of employee concerns we made in Part II and see what light it throws on this question.

When we made this analysis of employee concerns and put it at the beginning of the book, it was to provide a point of departure for showing the contribution that counseling could make to them. But now let us look at these concerns from the point of view of other segments of the organization who also had some say and responsibility for doing and dealing with them. If this were not so, the counseling organization indeed would have been reduced to just ameliorating a hopeless situation. Their work would have been like putting on "Band-Aids" for those who got scratches or perhaps more serious injuries in the scuffle.

If we examine the concerns of employees again from this point of view, it can be seen that they raise the question about the relation between technological, social, and personal development or, to put it another way, the relation between task specialization, social specialization, and person specialization. These different specializations or developments did not seem to be moving together on the same front. In fact at times it looked as if task specialization and person specialization were not only not in harmony but in serious conflict. Stemming from their research role, it was this observation that made the counselors at times despairing of their job.

Two different kinds of specialization

What was the nature of this conflict? It looked as if there were two different principles of specialization operating, leading in two quite different directions.[4]

1. One was in the direction of differentiation of special abilities and skills in the individual which gave him command and influence over his environment and a social function. It was the outcome of a social process arising from his needs to increase mastery over his environment. Such differentiation fulfilled man's needs for competence, achievement, status, and an identity with a socially valued occupation. In this case the processes of differentiation and the person's individual and social needs were reinforcing. Both worked in the direction of greater individual differentiation, development, status, and function. Out of this kind of specialization emerged the trades and the professions.
2. The other was in the direction of specialized tasks that anyone could do, which gave the doer no influence over his environment and little social identity outside of his own immediate work group. It arose from formal organizational processes which moved in the direction of reducing activities to simple, repetitive routines. Such tasks were organizational entities, specialized activities which contained a single program that was here today and gone tomorrow—that had no survival value. Obviously this kind of specialization did not work hand in hand with personal specialization. It produced "output specialists" who were evaluated only in relation to output per unit of time. This kind of specialization reinforced none of man's individual and social needs. To the contrary it tended to deprive work of meaning for the individual. He no longer felt he was engaged in something worthwhile. It provided no opportunity for greater individual differentiation except in terms of increased output. The task provided no opportunity for improved status, function, and social identity.

We have stated these two directions of specialization extremely—not to show, as we have said before, that "east is east and west is west and never the twain shall meet." Both trends exist in modern industry and unless better understood there is bound to be an inevitable conflict. But can they be better understood and how? This

[4] This distinction is developed more fully in Victor A. Thompson, *Modern Organization* (New York, Alfred A. Knopf, 1961).

was the problem of communication the counseling organization faced that they could not spring loose and in which, as we shall see later, they were also enmeshed. Let us examine this.

The bleak scene the counselors surveyed

More in their role as researchers than in their helping role as counselors, the counselors were making an appraisal of worker concerns which went something like this. All the forces in the direction of task specialization, as defined above, produced many of the concerns which the workers had on the job. As we saw in Chapter V, it accentuated their safety needs and concerns about losing and keeping a job. They had no job of their own in the sense of person specialization. They had only an organizational job which could vanish at the drop of a hat. It accentuated their needs to belong and band together in restrictive practices to protect their ephemeral jobs (see Chapter VI). It aroused their sense of injustice when after thirty years of investment in the development of a task specialization one could be put on the same job as a young girl who had been on the job for only a week (see Chapter VII). It accentuated their dependency needs and concerns about authority and being put back in the condition of a dependent child (see Chapter VIII), and finally it made it difficult to develop person specialization, that is, the development of a job that had any personal or social identity (see Chapter IX).

Yet curiously enough, while task specialization was developing more at the bottom level of the organization, at the same time person specialization was developing more in the staff jobs at the middle level of the organization. Many of these staff jobs, moreover, were concerned with worker needs, particularly his basic safety needs. The development of pension plans to provide a margin of safety in old age, of sickness and benefit plans, of safety practices in industry, of unemployment compensation, of thrift plans, of seniority guarantees to assure tenure—all were directed to allaying the worker's safety needs.

However, these developments were peripheral to person specialization for the worker on the job; that is, they did not change in the slightest the unrelatedness of his task to his needs for competence, achievement, self-esteem, or social and individual identity. Most of them were, in this sense, properly designated as fringe benefits —extrinsic but not intrinsic to his job and its development.

So it looked as if, in terms of the opportunity for person specialization, the basic role of the worker had not changed significantly in the past fifty years—in fact ever since the rationalization of industrial processes had begun. Everything else had changed; there had been spectacular advances in science and technology, in standards of living, in educational and aspirational levels, and even in motivational theory, but the role of the worker seemed to be the same today as it had been yesterday.

What were the dominant characteristics of this role? First, it was to service the technology to which he was inexorably bound, so that when the technology changed he had to make new adaptations to it. He did not change the technology; this was the exciting adventure of the engineers. Second, he was told precisely what he should do, how he should do it, and how much he should do. This was all prescribed for him; he could make minor innovations but not unless they were sanctioned. Third, his ties to the specialized task were reinforced by an incentive system which was supposed to reward him for his quantity and quality of work, i.e., for doing what he was told as best he could and which kept activating his safety concerns about keeping his job.

But in addition to this where did the worker stand organizationally and socially? Organizationally, he was a clock number, a payroll number, a bench hand; he appeared neither on the organizational chart nor in the house telephone directory. In terms of social status he was at the bottom of a highly stratified social system; he wore a blue shirt; he punched a clock; he was moved about from job to job; he swung in shifts; he spoke when spoken to; he kept his thoughts to himself and he showed properly deferential behavior.

Had this role changed very much during the history of the counseling program? A little perhaps, but not much. Had the concerns of the worker changed much during this period? In comparing the interviews at the beginning with those at the end, it looked as if the worker was just as much concerned with about the same sort of things today as he was yesterday. His fundamental role in terms of task specialization had not changed very much. It was this observation that allowed us to make the diagnosis of employees' concerns in Part II that we did. There had been no radical shift in them in the twenty years of the program. The fundamental concerns remained the same.

This characterization is likely to arouse protests: we pay him more; we give him more benefits; we treat him more as a human being; he's got a union to protect and, if need be, to protest for him; we give him more information, more vacation and holiday time with pay; etc. But these protests only highlight the point we are making. All these things have come to pass but his basic role is the same and his status relative to others is the same. In short, what we are suggesting is that the worker's concerns are implicit in his role derived from task specialization, that they cannot be alleviated except temporarily without a change in this condition.

So from a research point of view the counselors were surveying a rather bleak scene and, as they appraised their role in it, they were at times not too happy. From this point of view it did look as if they were performing a first-aid operation. The roots for most of the concerns about which they were counseling employees resided in matters about which they could do little and for which there were others who had much more responsibility and authority to do something, if they wished. But many of the other members of the counselors' role set did not perceive the problem of worker development as they did.

The Counseling Program's Unfinished Business

We have examined the ideas underlying the counseling program because in terms of them we can now see more clearly some of the program's unrealized aims and aspirations and alternative ways by which they might have been realized. But also they point to a common company goal around which their role would have been better integrated with the other members of their role set. So in conclusion we want to touch on these matters, warning the reader that from now on we are more definitely in the land of speculation where authors in their concluding chapter are privileged to roam, so long as they do not roam too far afield.

Imbedded in the way counseling was originally conceived was

the notion of self-examination by the Company of its internal operations in relation to worker motivation and satisfaction. Otherwise the perfect solution we discussed in Chapter XV would have been a conceivable alternative. Counseling never conceived of itself in this narrow sense nor was it so conceived by top management when it was first introduced. The notion of self-inquiry derived from the Hawthorne researches was deeply built into it. Once this dimension was gone, counseling could no longer realize fully one of its original aims.[5]

As we have seen, this dimension disappeared as the counseling program expanded and became a full-fledged and accepted personnel activity and was packaged and transplanted to other work locations of the Company. With this development it dropped its research function and with this extinction one important avenue of communication to management was closed. In retrospect it now looks as if this rapid expansion and the dropping of its research function might have been the two most unfortunate things that happened to the counseling program. They had not consolidated their position enough for the former and their life blood ran out with the latter. But these happenings had implications, not only for the program's survival in the long run, but also for the realization of its original aims as commonly shared by both counseling and management. It is the latter aspect we want to concentrate upon.

In the research component of the counselor's role lay the vital link between counseling and management. If the Company was dedicated to the improvement of its internal human operations and if counseling could provide better information by which this could be done, then they shared a common goal around which they could cooperate. Under such a conception, counseling was not just ameliorating the lot of the worker; in its research function it was trying to improve it in the same direction that it was trying to do it on its counseling (practice) side. Both were aimed at the same goal—*worker development*. Moreover this was of a piece with what management wanted. Under this conception management did not want apathetic workers, bench warmers, clock

---

[5] See F. J. Roethlisberger, *Management and Morale* (Cambridge, Harvard University Press, 1941), p. 134.

watchers, etc.; it wanted more highly motivated workers. In counseling, as it was originally conceived, a possible way by which these common goals could be slowly realized was envisaged.

In retrospect it becomes clear that not only in the process of counseling as counseling but also in its research output, i.e., what it was learning through counseling about what really mattered to workers, counseling had an important contribution to make. Around this research output it could have integrated its role with the other members of its role set. For the other members it was not so important to understand the function of counseling as to understand what the workers were concerned about and why.

As our analysis of employee concerns in Part II showed, counseling was not the only service which was involved in or could do something about them. All the personnel functions—placement, employment, and so on—were involved. All the functions involving job design, labor grading, and wage incentive systems were involved. Supervisory training was involved; the lower levels of supervision and the higher levels of management were involved.

To all these staff and line services counseling had an important contribution to make from its research findings but which, as the program expanded, it could only do and try to do in its counseling role. Obviously this communication would not have been easy to make and would have required counseling to extend its activities in new directions that were not strictly counseling. So now one can only speculate upon the difference it might have made if counseling could have fed back for discussion its research findings about employee concerns to small groups of persons interested in, for example, wage incentives, labor grading, job design, and so on. Obviously, if this was to mean much, it could not have been a one shot proposition; it would have required an extension in manpower and a decision by management. But it also would have required a commitment by counseling that this was the direction in which they wanted to go.

But it is not what each of these services could have done separately but what they could have done together in relation to employee concerns that interests us more, and so it is on this note we would like to conclude. Again it seems to us in retrospect that counseling was all around the edges of a problem that it never could quite get on the table for discussion.

WORKER, SUPERVISORY, AND MANAGEMENT DEVELOPMENT

It has always seemed unfortunate that *employee training, supervisory training,* and *management development* came into being historically at different periods under different labels and under different conceptions about what their aims and purposes were. Why were employees and supervisors "trained" and managers "developed"? Was it not because underlying the idea of management development was the concept of person specialization? The generalist or fusionist, as we described him in Chapter X, organized his job according to the phenomena with which he had to deal and not in terms of some abstract job as defined by task specialization. All attempts to define his job in these terms were wooden and static.

By the time management development came into being, the concept of training about matters of human behavior and motivation had changed in a direction far more consistent with the concept counseling had about these matters than trainers had had about them in a historically earlier period. Much of the training for managers today in the human aspects of administration is based upon the realization that much supervisory training, apart from also changing their own orientation to these problems, is superficial.

This aspect of the problem the counseling organization saw clearly and in part explains why they did not join with supervisory training in an adventure together. They saw that without any of the insights of counseling, human relations training for supervisors could easily degenerate into a charm school, an appelation used frequently not only by supervisors but also by counselors, which unfortunately only too often was a fairly accurate evaluation of the actual situation.

Nevertheless, the supervisory training group, as we saw in Chapter XIII, was an important member of the counselor's role set. For counselors and trainers to share common aims and aspirations was of the greatest importance. Around what concept could this have been done? What did they share in common around which they could have become fully integrated? Let's get behind the words and just reconceive counseling as worker development. Was not this what they were up to? Then, just let's think of supervisory training as supervisory development. Did they not share this common aim—the development of a person in a socially useful function? Was the model of man, of motivation and personal development for both groups so different? [6]

Let's extend this idea for managers. Is the model of man, of motivation, and of development different for managers from what it is for supervisors or for workers? Why are these three different activities conducted by three separate functional groups in the organization under such different conceptions of man and his development? Could they not be brought together under a common aim and objective, an employee relations policy of development in the direction of person specialization that makes it possible to find a necessary social function for everyone—for the old and the young, for the short service and the long service, for women and men, for the white and the black, for the grammar school and the college graduate, and finally for the worker, the supervisor, and the manager. Behind all these role designations are concrete persons with strivings to belong, to identify, to become independent and competent.

Under such a common aim and objective, the highly valued differentiated role of counseling could have been integrated with the roles of the other members of its role set. Without it, counseling became a stepchild. This is what we mean when we say that finally counseling faced a role set problem and that the *unit of change* was the role set and not any one of its members alone. Such a change was not an individual decision; it was an organizational decision. Management had not chosen the counselor to be its change agent; the counselor by nonintervention and with all the good intentions in the world could not make the organization its

[6] That counseling and supervisory training did not cooperate together in some such joint adventure is to me one of those missed opportunities that might have made a great difference to the future of the counseling program. F.J.R.

client. For this to happen an organizational decision was required and this was not counseling's *expertise*.

This to us is the exciting idea underlying the counseling program that remained to the end as a piece of unfinished business. That this idea never came to fruition, however, is not so important as that it not remain completely lost.

Counseling started as an innovative role. It was a person and not a task specialization. Its origins sprang from research and not from an organizationally derived task specialization. The counselors had a body of skills which differentiated them from others in terms of which they could help (influence) others. Their skills could not be reduced to a simple programmed activity, as we saw in Chapter XIV, when an attempt to assign a labor grade to their job was made. In fact all of Chapter XIV showed how incongruous from the point of view of task specialization counseling was and why it was ambiguous in this task structure.

In these terms we can understand better counseling's increasing preoccupation with its outer roles. Its survival depended in part upon fitting into the task specialization structure. But its own intrinsic function was a person specialization and not a task specialization in the sense we have defined it. By its policy of nonintervention it tried to reconcile these two forces, and, in our opinion now, unsuccessfully.

Counseling should have remained an innovative role to the very end—a constructive force in the direction of a constant self-examination by the Company of its task structure, payment systems, incentive systems, cost reduction programs, and of its policies, such as, for example, why should employees have to punch clocks? Why are workers hourly rated? Why couldn't they be paid on a salary basis, and so on? This was counseling's original wider mission. It should never have been relinquished and we have no evidence that the Company might not have welcomed the role. But as we now know, this did not come to pass, and—to repeat what we said in Chapter XV—not because there were any villains lurking around but because it was difficult to get those uncommunicative files we referred to in Chapter XV to reveal their secrets. And for this counseling shares a joint responsibility with management.

Counseling was a pioneer effort in worker development. In its program of development it may have started at the wrong end of the hierarchy. But about this we are not so sure. In matters of organizational development it may be better to build from the bottom up. This is the direction of growth and of person specialization.

Let's put counseling in its broader historical perspective. The first industrial revolution was built implicitly on the concept that man could be made to resemble a machine (task specialization) and somehow in the process the greatest good for the greatest number would be achieved. The second industrial revolution is being built under the concept that a machine (the computer) can be made to resemble a man. This is the exciting idea of today. But both ideas are chimeras. Neither can man be reduced to a machine nor can a machine be built to resemble a man. The computer can only answer the questions that the decision rules created by man build into it.

In a curious way, historically speaking, counseling straddled these two worlds. It came into being as an old world was beginning to vanish and as a new world was in the process of being born. This created for us many terminological difficulties. From the point of view of the old world, counseling was "modern" and "progressive"; from the point of view of the new world, counseling was "old hat" and "antiquated." Let's contrast the computer and the counselor and see if we can see the difference.

Not since the Delphic oracles has anything appeared on the scene like the computer to answer man's questions at such a rapid rate. But there is a slight difference. The computer does not answer man's questions in man's own native, natural, and indigenous languages; it answers them only in its own highly specialized tongue—and it is not pidgin English either. So in their quest for certainty, people from all quarters of the globe began studying the language of the computer so that they could get the answer to the kinds of questions it could answer. They wooed it like nothing had ever been wooed before.

What philosophers through the centuries since Plato and even before then had sought in vain, and what the counseling program in its short existence of twenty years by its policy of nonintervention had tried to accomplish, a machine—the computer—had wrought in a period of about nearly half that time. "Please ask me a question I can answer. Please stop talking your gobbledygook; please talk my language. The burden of asking a sensible question is up to you. If you keep asking me unanswerable questions, I'm going to be hard boiled and tell you no go. You search some more. I'm not searching for the questions you ask me; I'm only answering some of them."

It will be remembered that no one had wooed the counselor by trying to understand his language and asking him in his language for the kind of help he could provide. To the contrary, as we saw in Part IV, the counselor was innundated by an avalanche of unanswerable questions, such as "Should I punch my supervisor in the nose?" In the face of such questions all that the counselor could do and all that he was supposed to do, whether he be on the floor, in the interviewing room, or in the manager's office, was to reflect, restate, clarify, pause, wait, and hope that finally in that way a question he could deal with would emerge. But, as it will be remembered, it didn't quite work out that way.

The computer, on the other hand, was about as hard boiled a piece of machinery as man could have devised. It did no *listening*. It did not search out man's hopes and aspirations. Instead it said, "Tell me what you want to minimax and I'll tell you what to do, but if you want to remain vague and uncertain and if you don't know who you are and where you want to go and what you want to be, get out of my computation center. When you've settled all these questions and when you've learned to count (because you're woefully weak and backward in this respect) I'll give you the answer."

So the contrast between the counselor and the computer was clear and sharp. The counselors said, "You talk your gobbledygook and I'll listen and try to understand"; the computer said, "I'll talk my gobbledygook and you listen and understand." And it worked. The computer talked and man listened. A miracle was wrought.

As one can see, the computer is technology's highest achievement to date. It turned things inside out. No idea since the Renaissance has so caught man's creative imagination like this, and with it technological space became king again, and the second industrial revolution was born. All of man's other spaces—man's "cultural spaces," "social spaces," "small group spaces," and "life spaces" had hardly any room left in which to breathe. These spaces of man had to be put in oxygen tents and given psychotherapy—there was no longer any natural growth but only forced growth left.

Nevertheless ideologies to the right and to the left succumbed shamelessly to the computer's blandishments. Be they underdeveloped, overdeveloped, or just "developing," countries from all parts of the globe sought its answers. Before this machine, some power structures and power centers teeter-tottered as they had never done before. They "huffed and they puffed but they couldn't blow the computer's installation centers in."

We mention all these matters not in order to create nightmares but in order to suggest that in spite of all our progress, man's relation to the machine is still an unanswered question. Counseling was smack in the middle of this question and that it failed to provide an answer to it in the very short span of twenty years is insignificant. What is important is that the spirit of inquiry into this question persists. This is counseling's legacy to the future.

Index